EXPERT SYSTEMS TOOLS AND APPLICATIONS

Related titles of interest from John Wiley & Sons

EXPERT SYSTEMS TOOLS AND APPLICATIONS

Paul Harmon
Rex Maus
William Morrissey

JOHN WILEY & SONS, INC.

New York • Chichester • Brisbane • Toronto • Singapore

The figures appearing in this book, unless otherwise noted, originally appeared in the *Expert Systems Strategies* newsletter and are reproduced with the permission of Harmon Associates, San Francisco, CA.

Figures 3.1, 4.1, and 10.2, and Tables 2.5 and 3.1 are modifications of figures and tables that originally appeared in *Expert Systems: Artificial Intelligence in Business*, by Paul Harmon and David King (John Wiley & Sons, 1985).

Publisher: Stephen Kippur
Editor: Therese A. Zak
Managing Editor: Ruth Greif
Editing, Design & Production: G&H SOHO, Ltd.

Library of Congress Cataloging-in-Publication Data

Harmon, Paul.
Expert systems tools and applications /
Paul Harmon, Rex Maus, William Morrissey.
p. cm.
1. Business—Data processing. 2. Expert systems (Computer science) I. Maus, Rex. II. Morrissey, William. III. Title.
HF5548.2.H367 1988
650'.028'5633—dc19 87-17608
CIP

ISBN 0-471-83951-5
ISBN 0-471-83950-7 (pbk.)

Printed in the United States of America

89 10 9 8 7 6 5 4 3

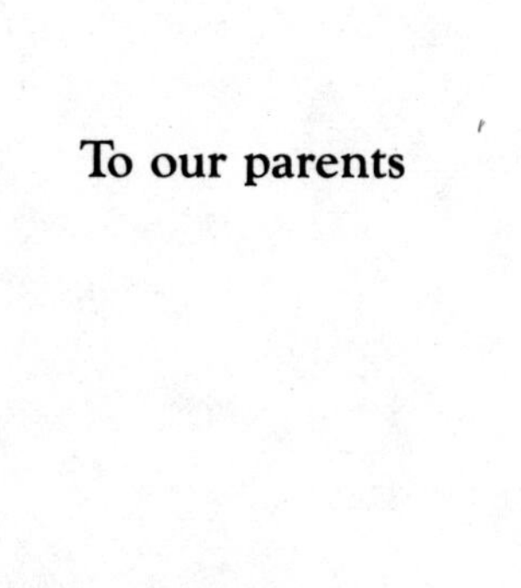

To our parents

Preface

In 1984, David King and I wrote *Expert Systems: Artificial Intelligence in Business*. In the intervening three years the field has grown and changed. Three years ago, expert systems were things to be studied by corporate researchers. Today, most companies that have been involved in expert systems stand ready to move their expert systems efforts out of their research laboratories and into their operational departments. This transition signals the beginning of a new phase in the acceptance of this technology and marks the beginning of an explosive new round of growth and activity.

It is appropriate at this juncture to provide an overview of the expert systems field that will give business people the same perspective *Expert Systems: Artificial Intelligence in Business* provided when it came out.

Expert Systems Tools and Applications is not a revised version of *Expert Systems: Artificial Intelligence in Business*. In that earlier book David and I tried to provide our readers with an understanding of some fundamental AI concepts that led to the then-current interest in expert systems. Thus, we included material on problem solving and a more detailed discussion of some basics of knowledge representation than is included in this book. Readers who are completely new to the field may still find that book a good place to start.

In the intervening years, however, the number of expert system building tools and fielded expert systems applications have multiplied manyfold. This book is addressed to the same audience as the first book: executives, middle managers, and computer systems personnel. We assume, however, that our readers, like ourselves, are now more sophisticated, and that they are concerned with more technical issues. We assume that today's readers are more interested in evaluating specific expert system building tools, learning about applications already fielded, and thinking about how to set up operational expert systems development groups.

This book is divided into four sections. The first section provides an overview of the expert systems market as it stood at the beginning of 1987. The second section provides a detailed discussion of a number of expert system building tools. The tools will keep changing in the years ahead, but these discussions provide insight into the features and capabilities readers will want to think about whenever they approach a purchasing decision. The third section provides an overview of the expert systems development process, and the final section of the book provides a catalog that describes most of the fielded expert systems applications we were able to document at the beginning of 1987. Fielded applications will grow rapidly in the coming years, but this list should provide readers with numerous ideas about how expert systems can be used.

To make this book flow as smoothly as possible, we have avoided footnotes and references. Annotated citations are collected in Appendix B. We have limited our references to commonly available books or magazine articles, consistent with our goal of providing a broad overview for business readers. Readers who want more depth should check the references in Appendix B. Most of the books listed provide citations that will lead the reader into the extensive technical literature.

You can read this book in many ways, depending on your needs. If you want a general introduction to the field, then beginning at the beginning and going through the chapters systematically is your best strategy. On the other hand, if you are especially interested in tools, you may want to start at the beginning of Section Two, read the overview chapter, and then study the chapters that describe the types of tools you are most interested in. If you are considering developing a system, you could begin reading the third section or look through the catalog of applications in Section Four to see what sorts of systems are already being used. If you do skip around, you may encounter terms you don't know. The glossary in Appendix A should help readers who take an unconventional route.

A book that surveys a rapidly changing field is only possible because of the help and cooperation of several different people. At the risk of offending people who are inadvertently omitted, we must try to acknowledge some of the people who have helped make this book possible.

Many of the reviews and the first list of applications originally appeared in our monthly newsletter, *Expert Systems Strategies*. The American publisher, Karen Coburn, and her staff at Cutter Information have been helpful in numerous ways. Our Japanese publisher, Kazuro Fujimoto, Hiro Suzuki, and their staff at Knowledge Engineering Laboratory Corp., have also been very helpful. We circulated our tool and application reviews to the vendors and companies involved, and several people at each company helped by reviewing our drafts and suggesting corrections.

Brian Sawyer taught us a great deal about the particulars of tool design and expert systems programming. In many ways, Brian is an unacknowledged co-author of this book.

Avron Barr also helped with a review of the current mainframe tools and provided many insights into the mainframe market. We are particularly indebted to Avron for helping with Chapter 8.

Many other people have helped us keep up with the field. Each time we interact with one of them, we come away with new insights about what is happening and what is about to happen. An inadequately short list includes Jan Aikins, Gerald Barber, K.C. Branscomb, Ester Dyson, Ed Feigenbaum, Mark Fox, Dick Gabriel, Larry Geisel, Abraham Gutman, Carroll Hall, Steve Hardy, Peter Hart, Carl Hewitt, Alex Jacobson, Bruce Johnson, Greg Kearsley, Tom Kehler, Mark Linesch, Ed Mahler, Claudia Mazzetti, Jim Miller, Makoto Nagao, Harvey Nequest, Penny Nii, Peter O'Farrel, Jeffrey Perione, Bill Peterson, Harry Reinstein, Walley Rhines, Elaine Rich, Herb Schorr, Karl and Henry Seiler, Beau Sheil, Mark Stefik, Harry Tennant, Bill Turpin, Gene Wang, Andrew Whinston, Karl Wiig, Mike Williams, Carl Wolf, and Hirai Yoshimitsu.

In addition to these specific people, many others at various companies have provided considerable help. We can't name them all, but we must mention the help and insight we received from people at AION, Gold Hill Computers, Inference Corp., IntelliCorp, Level Five Research, MBDS, and Texas Instruments.

Other people who are unknown in the expert systems community have worked with us over the past 20 years. They taught us to analyze human performance and communications problems and develop solutions that would work in business settings. Our current work in knowledge engineering draws heavily on the work of these mentors, and we predict that the relevance of Thomas F. Gilbert, Geary Rummler, and Joe Harless, will manifest itself in the next few years.

I also need to thank Nikki Grubb and Willem Smit, who helped with the graphics, and Mike Larrance, who helped get the newsletter started. Finally, of course, I must express my appreciation to my family and office associates and to Therese A. Zak and the other Wiley editors, who all tolerated a lot of neurotic behavior as deadlines came and went.

Paul Harmon
San Francisco

Trademarks

1st-Class is a trademark of Program in Motion, Inc.
ACE and UNIX are trademarks of Bell Telephone Laboratories, Inc.
AION is a trademark of AION Corporation.
Apollo is a trademark of Apollo Computers, Inc.
Apple is a registered trademark of Apple Computer, Inc.
ART is a trademark of Inference Corp.
Can Am Treaty Advisor is a trademark of Raymond, Chabot, and Co.
CATS-1 is a trademark of General Electric Corp.
CBT Analyst is a trademark of Park Row Software, Inc.
Cocomo 1 is a trademark of Level Five Research, Inc.
CV Filter is a trademark of Helix Expert Systems, Ltd.
DASD Advisor is a trademark of Boole and Babbage.
dBASE II and dBASE III are registered trademarks of Ashton-Tate.
Dipmeter Advisor is a trademark of Schlumberger-Doll Research.
Envisage is a trademark of System Designers Software, Inc.
Ex-Tran 7 is a trademark of Intelligent Terminals Ltd.
ExperOPS is a trademark of Expertelligence Inc.
Expert System Environment, OS/360, PC-AT, PC-RT, and YES/MVS are trademarks of International Business Machines, Inc.
Expert-Ease is a copyright product of Intelligent Terminals Ltd.
Expertax is a trademark of Coopers and Lybrand.
Explorer, Personal Consultant, Personal Consultant Plus, and Personal Consultant Easy are trademarks of Texas Instruments, Inc.
Exsys is a trademark of Exsys Corporation.
Genesis is a trademark of IntelliGenetics, Inc.
Golden Common LISP and GOLDWORKS are trademarks of Gold Hill Computers, Inc.
GURU, KnowledgeMan, and MDBS III are trademarks of Micro Data Base Systems, Inc.
IBM is a registered trademark of International Business Machines, Inc.
IDEA is a trademark of Pacific Bell.
Insight 2+ is a trademark of Level Five Research, Inc.
Intel is a trademark of Intel Corporation.
INTELLECT is a trademark of Artificial Intelligence Corporation.
IntelliScope is a trademark of Intellicorp.
INTERLISP, Xerox Star, and Xerox 1100 are registered trademarks of Xerox Corporation.
IQLISP is a trademark of Integral Quality.
KDS is a trademark of KDS Inc.
KEE is a trademark of Intellicorp.
KEEconnection is a trademark of Intellicorp.
KES 2 is a trademark of Software Architecture and Engineering, Inc.
Knowledge Craft is a trademark of Carnegie Group, Inc.
Knowledge Engineering Workbench is a trademark of Silogic, Inc.
Lending Advisor is a trademark of Syntelligence, Inc.
LES is a trademark of Lockheed Corporation.
Letter of Credit Advisor is a trademark of Helix Expert Systems, Ltd.
Lisa, LisaDraw, MacDraw, and MacPaint are trademarks of Apple Computer, Inc.
LISP-ITS is a trademark of Advanced Computer Tutoring, Inc.
Lotus and 1-2-3 are registered trademarks of Lotus Development.
Macintosh is a trademark licensed to Apple Computer, Inc.
Macsyma is a trademark of Symbolics Inc.
Management Advisor is a trademark of Palladian Software, Inc.
MENTOR is a trademark of Honeywell Inc.
Micro Genie is a trademark of Beckman Instruments, Inc.

Contents

SECTION ONE

OPPORTUNITIES

Information processing has become the dominant theme of our age. It is said that one issue of *The New York Times* contains as much information as a sixteenth-century person had to deal with in a *lifetime*. The explosive expansion of information can be viewed either as a threat to the survival of a business or as a tremendous opportunity to advance. One new field, artificial intelligence (AI), is singularly promising in assuring that this wealth of information will present opportunities.

This section presents an overview of the major commercial applications of AI expert systems. You are first introduced to key concepts underlying expert systems and how such systems can use information to improve performance (Chapter 1). You are then presented with some predictions as to who will benefit from these systems and what constitutes the expert systems market (Chapter 2).

1

Using Expert Systems to Improve Performance

INTRODUCTION

This book is about expert systems and how they are changing the business world. The term *expert systems* does not describe a product, but rather a whole set of concepts, procedures, and techniques that enable business people to use computers in a variety of valuable new ways. In fact, expert systems will revolutionize computer use and thus the way you do business.

In the past three years, over 80 percent of the 500 largest companies in the United States have explored using expert systems techniques. Some are still experimenting, but many have already decided that expert systems applications will allow them to improve significantly the way they do business, and are currently introducing expert systems development groups into their operational divisions.

In essence, expert systems techniques enable computers to assist people in analyzing and solving complex problems that can often be stated only in verbal terms. Thus, they extend the power of the computer beyond the usual mathematical and statistical functions and facilitate the creation of computer programs that conduct dialogues with decision makers and use logic to suggest various possible courses of action. By encoding the knowledge and reasoning skills of human experts within expert systems programs, you can create programs to diagnose problems and make recommendations that would previously have required a human expert's attention.

Equally important, some expert systems techniques make it possible for people who lack programming skills to develop powerful programs. Thus, managers or technical experts who know nothing about programming are able to enter their knowledge into a system that will then conduct dialogues and provide recommendations. Other managers or technicians who also lack programming skills can easily examine the knowledge within the system and revise it when necessary.

Many business people realize that computers are powerful aids to business that are likely to permeate every aspect of most business organizations within the next ten years. But most managers are unable to imagine exactly how that will happen, since computer programming currently depends on a very limited, highly skilled group of technicians. The concepts and techniques associated with expert systems are revolutionary precisely because they are the beginning of the second computer revolution, the revolution that will make computer "programming" available to everyone.

This is analogous to the situation faced by an earlier generation of business people who sent messages over telegraph wires. To send messages, they wrote out the message and delivered it to a teletype operator. The operator encoded the message into dots and dashes and sent it over the wires. Another operator at the other end recorded the dots and dashes, decoded the message, and delivered it to its ultimate recipient. It would be hard to convince a manager accustomed to that system that one day managers would have telephones on their desks and think nothing of picking up the phones and calling anyone, anywhere in the world, to exchange information. Like the telephone, expert systems will take some experimentation, but in a reasonably short time computers will become much easier to use, and they will be used to do things that most managers don't yet realize computers can do. Programmers will go the way of the telegraph operator. They will not disappear entirely; engineers and programmers still work for the telephone companies to make the telephone system work. But, increasingly, managers and technical people will feel free to use computers to perform tasks they now think only a programmer can accomplish.

Thus, the current interest in expert systems springs from two sources. Expert systems techniques offer the possibility of developing programs to improve immediately the productivity and profitability of organizations. And they are the beginning of a broader change in the way people think about computers that will soon lead to entirely new ways of conducting business.

This book focuses on the immediate commercial benefits to be derived from the existing generation of expert systems. It provides information managers need *right now* to take advantage of current opportunities. In addition, familiarity with the concepts, techniques, and procedures currently available should prepare forward-looking managers for many changes that will continue to revolutionize business practices throughout the remainder of this century.

WHAT IS ARTIFICIAL INTELLIGENCE? WHAT ARE EXPERT SYSTEMS?

Artificial intelligence, or AI, is an *academic research program* in the same sense that physics is an academic research program. Most computer scientists interested in AI are trying to determine what sorts of things computers can be made to do. Some AI researchers conceptualize their work as an exploration into the nature of human intelligence or cognition, but most are interested in determining how computers can be used to solve specific problems. Some AI researchers are concerned with programming computers to recognize a human voice and with creating programs to enable a computer to translate text from one language to another. Others are interested in developing techniques that will allow robots to identify objects and reason about the consequences of various actions. Still others are concerned with developing computer programs that reason like human experts. Most university-based AI researchers, like most physicists, are not directly concerned with the commercial applications of their work.

Within the last ten years, however, some results of AI research have indicated that many concepts, procedures, and techniques developed in AI laboratories have great commercial value, and a new industry, dedicated to the commercialization of the most promising aspects of AI, has been established. Figure 1.1 shows some commercial offspring of the AI research conducted during the last several years. The five most active areas of commercialization are (1) natural language, (2) robotics, (3) improved human interfaces, (4) exploratory programming, and (5) expert systems. You will be introduced briefly to each area.

Natural language. A natural language is any language that humans speak, e.g., English, French, Japanese. Some AI researchers are trying to develop computer hardware and software that will allow computers to interact with people in a natural language. At the moment, the commercial activity that involves concepts and techiques derived from natural language research is focused on developing natural language interfaces for existing data bases. Thus, with a natural language interface, a manager can ask for information in a data base by typing or speaking a request just as she would ask an assistant for similar information. The natural language program (often called a *frontend* since it stands between the managers and the existing data base program) can convert the manager's typed or spoken request into a set of data base query commands to obtain the information from the data base program.

Robotics. Creating robotic devices is hardly the exclusive concern of AI researchers. AI is concerned only with that subset of robotic devices guided by computer

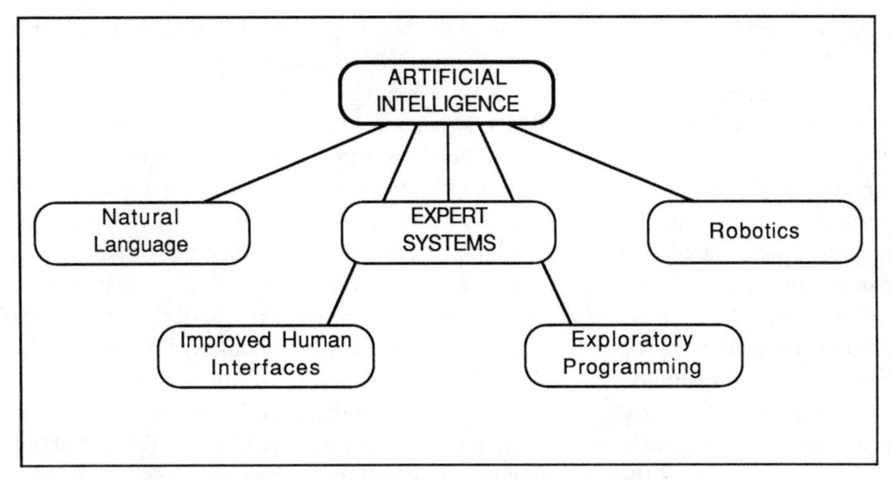

Figure 1.1 *The commercial offspring of artificial intelligence.*

programs that allow the devices to analyze and solve problems they encounter. Such "intelligent robots" use AI techniques to see and manipulate the object they interact with. In essence, the robot can act "intelligent" because it has a model of the world stored in a computer that allows it to identify things and analyze how those things will change in response to the various actions the robot might initiate.

Improved human interfaces. A third area in which AI concepts and techniques are being actively employed to improve existing commercial computer practices involves the design and development of better interfaces. By applying psychological and programming techniques originally developed in AI labs, computers with interfaces like those found on the Macintosh have been developed. The same hardware and software techniques that make a Macintosh easy to use are already on the newer workstations and will soon be available on IBM Personal Computers. Other improved interface techniques will become available as the underlying AI techniques become more widely understood.

Exploratory programming. Exploratory programming refers to the application of AI concepts and techniques to developing large applications. The same techniques that allow AI programmers to quickly develop large applications, including new programming languages and programming environments, modularity, and incremental development, can all be used to increase conventional programmer productivity. The integration of these techniques into conventional programming efforts is currently improving conventional practice, even when no other AI efforts are being contemplated.

Some might include "automatic programming" on the list. Automatic programming uses AI techniques to allow computer programmers to develop computer programs by specifying the goals of the program and leaving it up to an automatic programming system to generate most of the specific code for the application.

Expert systems. Of all the commercial activities resulting from AI research, expert systems have received the most attention. These problem-solving systems were initially called "expert systems" to suggest that they functioned as effectively as human experts at their highly specialized tasks.

An *expert system* is a program that manifests some combination of concepts, procedures, and techniques derived from recent AI research. These techniques allow people to design and develop computer systems that use knowledge and inference techniques to analyze and solve problems. This definition is intentionally broad because the field is very new and developing rapidly. In a few years it will be easier to say what expert systems are and what they are used for, but at the moment, they are more appropriately described in terms of the concepts, procedures, and techniques used to create them.

Many AI and expert systems techniques are powerful generic techniques that will affect many different aspects of how people use computers. When faced with complex and sophisticated problems, expert systems techniques allow programmers to develop larger, more powerful systems than those currently being developed. The idea of large, powerful computer systems that function like human experts has captured the imagination of the media; thus, when most people think of expert systems, they imagine one of the large early systems like MYCIN or XCON.

MYCIN was developed at Stanford University in the early 1980s to prove the power of AI techniques in capturing and reasoning with very sophisticated human knowledge. It was designed to consult with physicians and determine if a patient had bacteremia (infections that involve bacteria in the blood) or meningitis (infections that involve inflammation of the membranes that envelop the brain or spinal cord). These infections can be fatal, in some cases within 24 hours. Thus, the physician must often begin treatment in the absence of complete lab results. Diagnosis and treatment of these diseases are complex enough that an attending physician usually seeks the advice of specialists. In blind-blind tests, MYCIN has proved to be as effective as the medical specialists at the Stanford Medical Center.

XCON was initially developed by Carnegie-Mellon computer scientists to assist Digital Equipment Corporation (DEC) with the configuration of computers. DEC customers request computers with certain characteristics and features, and a configuration expert then determines the exact set of wires and parts necessary to build a computer to satisfy the costumer's request. DEC tried to develop a conventional computer program to help with the configuration task more than once and gave up each time because the parts and specifications for correct assembly kept changing. XCON was developed using incremental procedures and modular techniques developed in AI labs and is now used by DEC to configure its entire line of PDP and VAX computers.

XCON has some 6,000 rules about how parts can be combined to create a computer. To keep XCON up to date, DEC employs 8 full-time programmers at an annual cost of $2 million. It is estimated, however, that XCON saves DEC about $8 million a year. Moreover, if XCON had not been created, DEC would have been forced to eliminate most of the flexibility it offers its customers simply because it couldn't hire or train the highly specialized experts required to configure the vastly increased number of different computers it currently sells. At this point XCON knows more about how to configure DEC computers than any human expert.

As impressive as these large expert systems are, however, the concepts, procedures, and techniques that went into their development are just as important because of some more mundane tasks they allow people to do with computers. These same approaches to computer programming enable nonprogrammers to quickly create their own computer programs. In the long run, allowing managers and technicians who are not programmers to develop and run computer programs *without* having to learn to program will be *the* most profound change to result from the current batch of AI techniques and procedures.

In the last few years, people have developed a wide variety of expert systems. Some are very large and complex and do, indeed, rival the human experts from whom the systems derived their knowledge. Thus, systems like XCON and MYCIN truly deserve to be called expert systems. Other systems, however, use only a small subset of the techniques used in the larger systems. They hardly contain enough knowledge to be called "expert," but they are often very valuable to their developers. AI researchers prefer to call the smaller systems "knowledge systems." This emphasizes that the smaller systems use the knowledge-based techniques developed in AI labs, but avoids suggesting they are designed to function as human experts—a reasonable distinction. Since current practice applies the term *expert system* to both the large and small systems, this book does likewise, but when it uses the term *knowledge system* or *knowledge-based system*, it refers to a smaller system.

THE KEY IDEAS

A number of key concepts and associated techniques that have been developed in the AI research laboratories during the last few years have sparked the current commercial interest in AI. Three of the most important ideas are (1) new ways to represent knowledge, (2) heuristic search, and (3) the separation of knowledge from inference and control. Each idea is important to understanding the technology that is driving the current commercial AI market.

The Representation of Knowledge

Knowledge is more complex than information, and more valuable. Normally the term *knowledge* refers to a body of information about a particular topic that is *organized* to be useful. If you say an individual is very knowledgeable about a subject, you assume the individual not only knows a lot of facts about the subject, but also can use that information to analyze problems and make judgments about related topics.

AI researchers have focused on the verbal and graphic aspects of knowledge rather than the more mathematical aspects of knowledge that conventional software people have studied. Thus, where a conventional programmer might seek to reduce a problem to elements that can be represented in mathematical terms and manipulated by an algorithm, AI programmers are more interested in knowledge expressed in sentences and pictures and manipulated by logical inferences. Most problems confronting companies are of the latter sort. Conventional programming techniques have largely exhausted the problems that can be solved by applying mathematical analysis. If computer use is to continue to expand and provide help to managers facing increasingly complex problems, the computer programs must be able to help managers analyze and solve problems that can be expressed only in linguistic terms.

Encoding linguistic expressions and manipulating those terms with logical procedures leads to a major advance in the types of problems that can be solved by computers. Subsequent chapters will illustrate some of the knowledge representation techniques currently being introduced into commercial computing.

Heuristic Search

Conventional computing depends upon a complete analysis of all the elements and steps in a problem. In effect, this limits the domain of conventional computing to problems that can be exhaustively analyzed. AI researchers, like corporate managers, have routinely concerned themselves with problems that are too large and complex to be understood completely. Humans solve such problems by using heuristics (rules-of-thumb) that allow them to reduce a large problem to a reasonable size. Heuristics, by their very nature, can lead to errors. They do not always guarantee the correct answer; they only increase the likelihood of finding a usable answer.

For example, one afternoon I was tapping randomly trying to locate a stud within the plaster wall of my San Francisco Victorian house. David, a friend who makes his living renovating Victorians, happened to visit while I was engaged in this task. David quickly took a tape measure and extended it first by 12-inch, then by 14-inch, lengths. "As a rule-of-thumb," he said, "the studs in these Victorians were placed either 12 or 14 inches apart." We decided that the people who built my house had placed an upright stud every 14 inches, and then quickly identified the two places near the center of the wall where I could pound a nail into a stud. This illustrates the key features of good heuristics: they depend on knowledge of the specific situation, and they are usually acquired from experience. They do not guarantee success, of course; my house could have been built by some eccentric builder who put uprights every 15 inches. Heuristics represent probable knowledge. They are effective only in some subset of all the cases you will encounter.

Any competent professional has a huge body of heuristics to use when faced with a problem that involves uncertainties. Every manager has rules-of-thumb to use when forced to act with less than a complete analysis of a situation.

By using heuristics, AI programs can suggest actions in situations where conventional programs could not. On the other hand, like human advisors in such situations, the new programs will qualify their recommendations, and they will sometimes be wrong.

Heuristic programming techniques will rapidly expand the variety of tasks computers can do. They will allow programmers to develop larger, more complex programs able to analyze very fuzzy problems and make suggestions. Ultimately, however, heuristics will depend on confidence techniques that allow human experts to qualify their judgments. Typically, heuristic-based programs will not reach *a* correct answer, but will suggest several options and provide some estimate of the likelihood of each.

Separating Knowledge from Inference and Control

In conventional programming, knowledge about a problem and procedures for manipulating that knowledge to solve the problem are mixed together. When nonprogrammers look at the code for a computer application, they cannot begin to figure out what the program knows or assumes about the world. This means the human expert must depend on a programmer to express that knowledge correctly, making it impossible for other experts to look at a program to see what the developer assumed about the problem. It's rather like the situation when people used the telegraph to communicate. Since the sender and receiver of the message could not "read" the dots and dashes, they had to assume the telegraph operators got it correct. This limitation places a great burden on programmers trying to develop large computer applications and makes it impossible for experts to help programmers locate the knowledge "bugs" in their programs.

AI researchers have developed a number of techniques to separate the knowledge in a program from procedures to manipulate that knowledge. In effect, any expert can examine the knowledge in an expert system and determine if the knowledge is correct. Moreover, when knowledge about a problem changes, the expert can point to the exact rules or assumptions to change.

The separation of knowledge from inference and control is probably the most important concept to come out of AI research. On the surface it is a simple concept, and it can be just as easily implemented in conventional languages as in AI languages. The effect of this new approach is to make nonprogrammer programming a reality. As long as the developer of a program needed both to identify the knowledge to be contained in the program and to figure out the exact procedure to manipulate the knowledge, the development of programs was limited to individuals trained in programming (i.e., algorithmic) techniques. Once a programming environment can be created that will "develop its own algorithm" to manipulate a given body of knowledge, anyone who can provide the knowledge can create a program.

The AI techniques that allow a software package to "develop its own algorithm" require more hardware and software resources. In effect, the burden of developing the program has been shifted from a programmer to the hardware and software the developer uses. Ten years ago, these techniques required computer resources that were too expensive to provide. Moreover, the techniques required so much time that no one would be willing to wait while the computer developed its own algorithm. Now, with the reduction in the cost of computer hardware and the huge increase in the power of computers currently in use, it is possible to use these techniques on personal computers. In the recent past it was cheaper to hire programmers than to buy computers powerful enough to allow nonprogrammer programming. Now it is cheaper to buy powerful computers and let nonprogramming managers and technical professionals use expert system building tools to develop their own programs.

As this use of AI techniques becomes better understood, new software will be designed to help people perform many different specialized tasks. The current generation of expert system building tools is only the rough beginning of a whole new way of thinking about the kinds of software that will help managers use computers in their daily work.

WHERE IS AI NOW? WHERE IS AI GOING?

AI and expert systems technologies have just made their commercial appearance during the last three to five years. Initially, university researchers and venture capitalists formed companies to promote the commercial use of expert systems techniques. (See Figure 1.2.) In many cases, the initial proponents of expert systems made assumptions about what would happen in the commercial world that were entirely unjustified. Some assumed that large companies would make sweeping changes in their hardware and software in order to use expert systems techniques in the same way they were used in research labs. Just the opposite has happened, of course: expert systems techniques and procedures have been modified to make them more compatible with existing commercial practices. When you consider the existing corporate investments in hardware, software, and personnel, you realize that companies must necessarily build on their existing base and that change must be evolutionary.

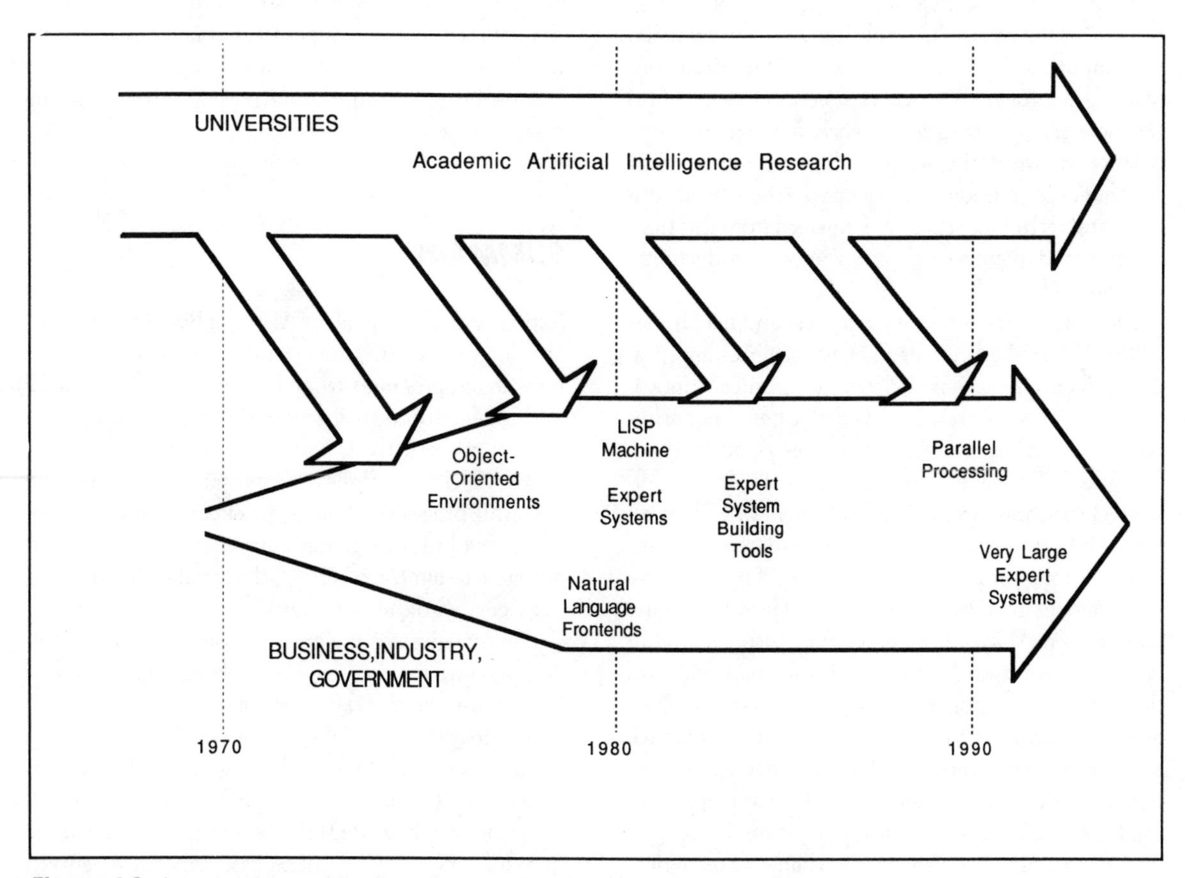

Figure 1.2 *Academic contributions to commercial AI.*

Now, a few years after the initial burst of attention AI received when it emerged from the labs, many companies are beginning to offer expert systems products that seem likely to gain wide acceptance in business, industry, and government. To some academics, AI has been trivialized in the process, but this simply shows that some scholars underestimate the importance of the new concepts and techniques they have created. Business may not be ready to build the huge expert systems that fascinate some researchers, but it *is* ready to use techniques that allow nonprogrammers to program. And it is certainly ready to develop mid-size knowledge systems as frontends to important data bases and existing application programs.

Business and industry have been willing to tolerate many very poorly conceived products and explanations over the last five years simply because they recognized the great value implicit in this new approach to computing. Now, having survived the initial confusion that inevitably occurs when academics and business people struggle to work out a reasonable balance between the ideal and the possible, most companies seem ready and eager to use the refined concepts and techniques that have emerged from this transition period to improve their operations, productivity, and profits.

Ultimately, a network of computers and telephones will emerge as the fundamental basis of all communications. As impressive as the strictly technical innovations will be, however, they will not have much impact unless managers and employees at all levels of business feel confident they can use computers as effectively as they currently use the telephone. This requires friendlier, more intuitive human-computer interfaces than any presently in use. The software technologies to develop those interfaces will come largely from AI labs. Expert systems, with their ability to capture and distribute critical analytical and decision-making knowledge, are just the first step. They are, however, a very important step since they mark a transition between conventional approaches and the next generation of software oriented toward representing knowledge, communicating in natural languages, and reasoning by logical rather than mathematical means.

In one important sense AI and expert systems are just establishing a foothold in the commercial world. Commercial managers are learning about these new techniques and determining which ones can be useful. Once they discover the benefits of some of the techniques, they will be more willing to learn more and see if other AI techniques can be effectively applied. By the same token, several interesting AI techniques are still in the laboratories, not yet ready for commercial application. In some cases they await conceptual breakthroughs to become practical; in other cases they await the introduction of new hardware. What is certain is that AI labs will continue to provide innovations over the next decade or two.

Companies that master the first generation of expert systems technologies will be well positioned to capitalize on the subsequent rounds of software development, while companies that fail to understand the importance of this transition to new uses of the computer will find themselves at an increasing disadvantage.

SUMMARY

Expert systems have taken AI out of R&D laboratories and are permeating the commercial world. You can now create programs to analyze problems and make recommendations that previously required input from human experts. Even more important, some expert systems techniques allow *nonprogrammers* to develop powerful programs. This is, in effect, a second computer revolution, making computer "programming" available to almost everyone, drastically affecting how managers think about computers and business.

The five most active areas of commercialization of AI are (1) natural language, (2) robotics, (3) improved human interfaces, (4) exploratory programming, and (5) expert systems—the focus of this book.

Three key ideas from AI being applied in expert systems are (1) new ways to represent knowledge, (2) heuristic search, and (3) the separation of knowledge from inference and control. A basic difference between conventional software and that developed by AI programmers is that AI focuses on *verbal* and *graphic* aspects of knowledge rather than mathematical aspects. In addition to representing knowledge verbally and graphically, AI programs rely on rules-of-thumb (heuristics) rather than on mathematical certainty; therefore, they allow managers to look at problems even when they have incomplete information, and the recommendations can sometimes be wrong. Finally—and perhaps the most important concept coming out of AI research—techniques have been developed to allow any expert to examine the content in a program *without* knowing how the content is manipulated (programmed). This innovation will make nonprogrammer programming a reality.

2

The Expert Systems Market

INTRODUCTION

The market for AI and expert systems is only in its early stages. The more sophisticated Fortune 500 companies are just beginning to move some of their AI work out of the R&D departments and into operational areas for testing, and the first generic expert systems are now being introduced. Demand for internal development of large expert systems and for purchase of large generic applications is just starting. The market for enhancing conventional PC programs and applications is also in its initial stages. To this point the enhancements have depended on the imagination of the vendors of conventional programs. Expert system building tools will create a large new market among nonprogrammers who want to develop intelligent job aids. In some cases, the users will be people in management information systems departments (MIS) or technical specialists with some programming abilities, but in many cases they will be managers and senior operational people who need to communicate information throughout the organization.

THE CURRENT MARKET FOR EXPERT SYSTEMS

Expert systems come in many shapes and sizes. In some cases expert systems are large application programs designed to solve highly specialized problems. In other cases a few techniques derived from expert systems research are included in an otherwise conventional application. In still others a small expert system is embedded on a microchip and incorporated into a machine. In other words, no single expert systems market exists.

Expert Systems usually refers to a broad collection of concepts and techniques used together or piecemeal to develop or enhance a wide variety of products; any discussion of the market for expert systems is, in fact, a discussion of the various ways expert systems, concepts, and techniques are packaged and sold.

The whole issue is complicated by the fact that *artificial intelligence* refers to a large, complex collection of related academic research programs. Consequently, any definition of the market is, in fact, an attempt to describe how a broad academic research program will fare in the business world and what results that program will deliver over the next several decades.

Some expert systems concepts and techniques are currently practical and are being used commercially. Other concepts and techniques widely associated with expert systems are still in the research laboratory, not yet ready for practical implementation. Still other expert systems techniques exist only in the minds of researchers. Their potential, let alone their practical value, has yet to be demonstrated.

The current expert systems market resembles the agitated waves at the confluence of two rivers. One river is research and the other is commercial application. The researchers mix highly practical results with their current research programs and their desire for future achievements. By the same token, those involved in commercializing expert systems generalize from their early successes to accomplishments yet to be proven. Some expectations of those involved in both research and commercialization will undoubtedly prove of great value, resulting in large expert systems running on very fast computers that process many lines of reasoning simultaneously. Exactly which concepts and techniques will lead to these achievements—and when—however, is uncertain. Hence, business people are faced with sorting out what clearly can be done now, what most likely can be done in the next few years, and what might be done in five or ten years. Many bright, capable people are offering opinions and projections, and they often disagree.

The current accomplishments and near-term prospects have led many businesses to invest in the expert systems market, either as vendors or as customers. This creates an expert systems market and leads to a demand for market projections. But it also means it is difficult to trust the current projections; it's simply too early to be certain about the future direction and successes that will create highly profitable expert systems products.

Not only must analysts estimate the spread of currently successful techniques, but they must also estimate the rate at which new techniques will become available and speculate about the rate at which these subsequent techniques will be adopted. Recent projections of expert systems–related expenditures suggest that by 1990 the U.S. market for expert systems will be somewhere between $350 million and $600 million. The large variation in projections represents both a failure to agree on what should be included in the expert systems market and the uncertainties involved in making such projections.

The market for expert systems is a little over three years old. Prior to 1986, the market had focused primarily on a small group of very specialized sophisticated customers. About 85 percent of the expert systems sales through 1986 were made to universities, the U.S. military, aerospace companies working for the military, and various research groups in the *Fortune 500 companies*. In other words, most expert systems products were sold to scientists to explore the potentials of the technology.

This situation began to change in 1986 as operational

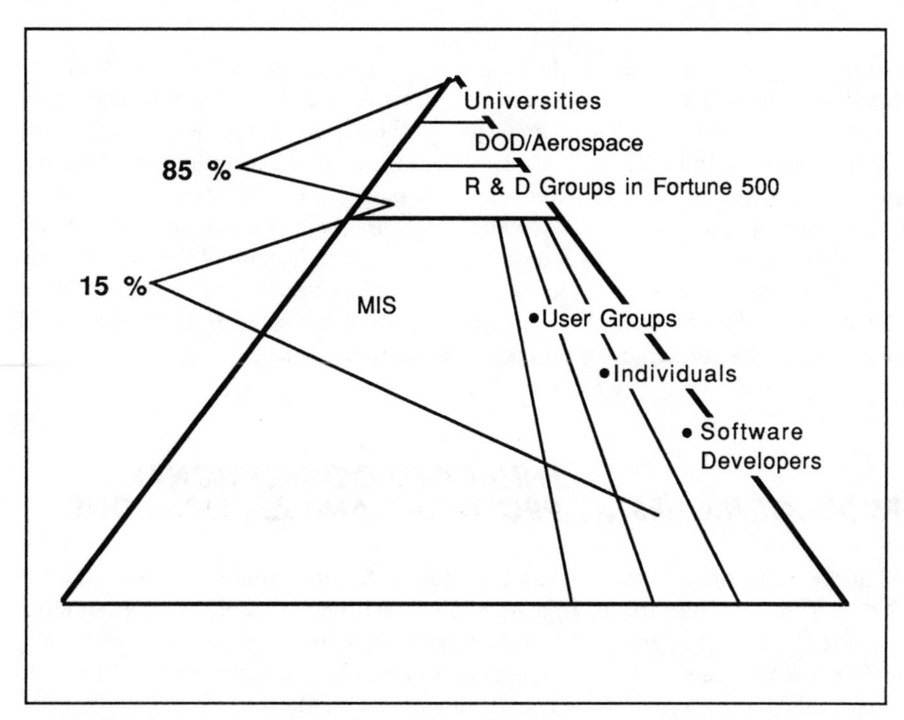

Figure 2.1 *Up to 1986, most products were purchases by R&D, DOD, and universities.*

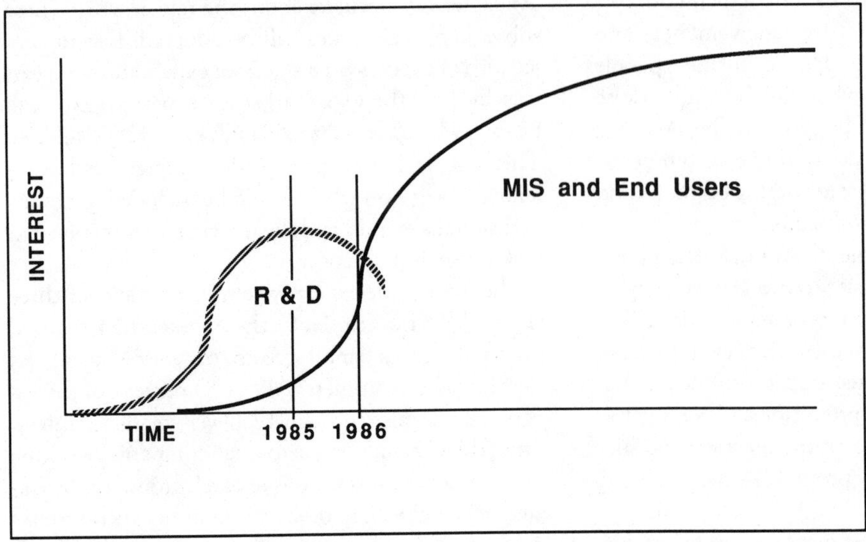

Figure 2.2 *The transition between R&D interest and acceptance by the corporate mainstream.*

groups and traditional management information and data processing groups within Fortune 500 companies became interested in the practical uses of various expert systems technologies. (See Figures 2.1 and 2.2.)

As the market has begun to shift from research groups to MIS and operational groups, the nature of the products has changed to reflect the needs of this new, much larger customer base. This chapter discusses the various product niches that have evolved to date and how each may change and evolve to serve customers in various operational and MIS groups.

EXPERT SYSTEMS PRODUCT NICHES

Figure 2.3 shows four broad market segments used to classify expert systems products. This portion of the chapter focuses on the expert systems marketplace and ignores several other groups of vendors who participate in the overall market, but do not offer products pertinent to these discussions. For example, conventional language vendors are purposely omitted. In fact, many expert systems tools are developed using conventional languages. If there were a box for conventional language vendors, it would connect with the other vendors in the same way the AI language vendors do.

Table 2.1 overviews potential users that vendors will surely target, a rough indication of the potential size of each niche, and when each niche will become most active. The table also lists some early examples of AI products aimed at each niche.

ENHANCED CONVENTIONAL PROGRAMS AND APPLICATIONS

The potential customers of enhanced conventional programs are the current users of large conventional programs and applications; most are located in the MIS departments of business, industry, and government. The potential users for these enhanced applications tend to be vertical operations groups. These customers will not be buying AI or expert systems technologies as such; they will simply purchase programs or applications demonstrably easier or more effective than existing alternatives.

The most successful vendors of products for this particular niche will probably be existing conventional vendors who hire consultants to help improve their existing products. The improvements may be made by using expert system building tools, but may be prototyped using AI languages that are later recoded into the language of the existing application program. These products will be sold by targeted advertising and a field sales force just as large conventional programs are currently sold.

The market for enhanced conventional programs and applications exists now; it simply awaits development of effective products. This will take time, since most conventional program developers are just begin-

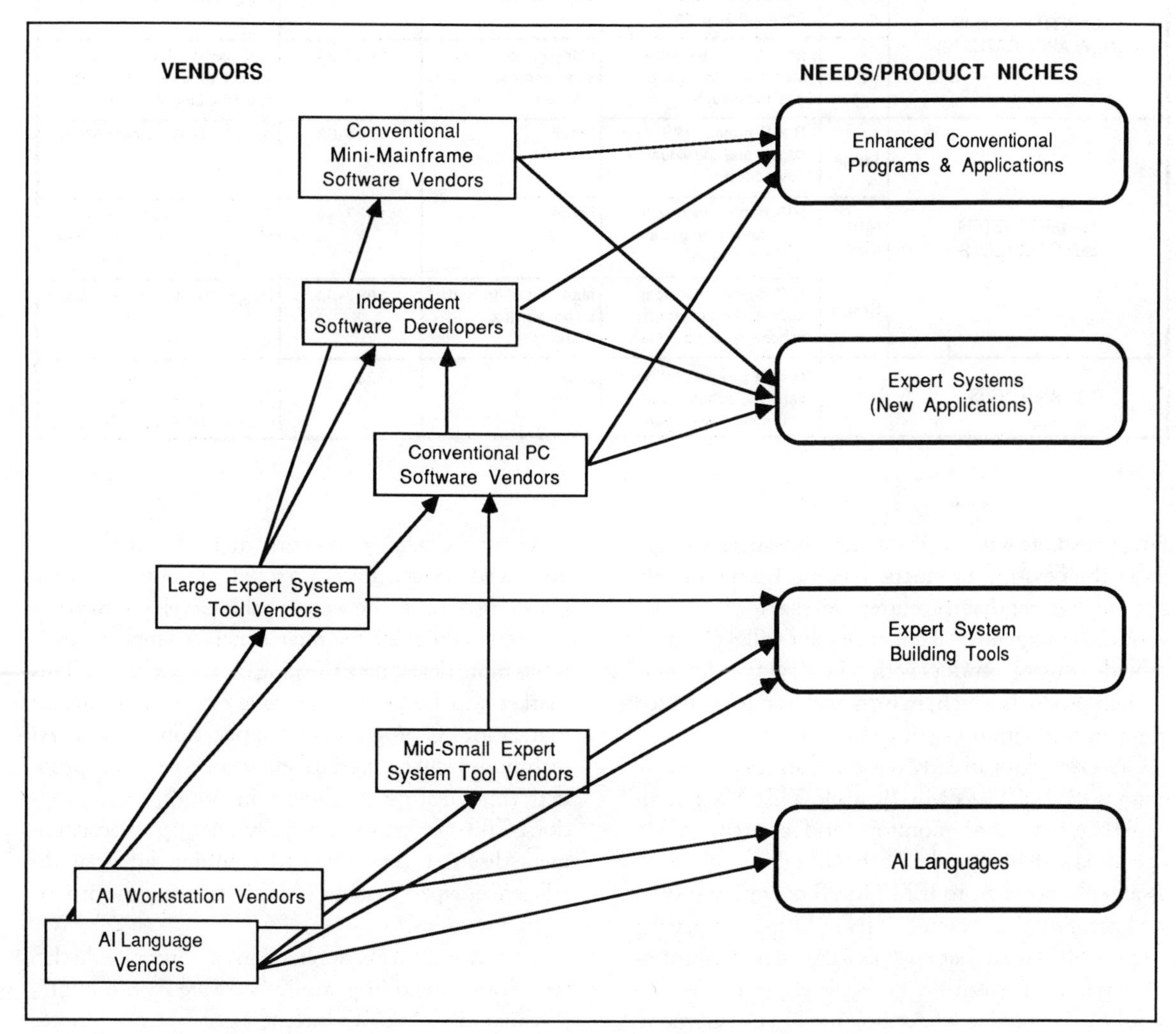

Figure 2.3 *Product niches for AI/expert systems technologies.*

Table 2.1 *Product niches for AI/expert systems technologies.*

Needs/Product Niche		Users to Target	Size of Niche	When Niche Will Be Hot	Good Example of Product for Niche
ENHANCED CONVENTIONAL PROGRAMS AND APPLICATIONS	Large	Current users of large conventional programs and applications	Same as existing market for large software products	1987-90	YES/VMS, INTELLECT
	PC	MIS depts., technical, staff and operational groups, and individuals	Same as existing market for PC software products	1987-89	Q&A, Javelin, GURU, ISS.Three: Computer Capacity Manager
EXPERT SYSTEMS (NEW APPLICATIONS)	Large	Specialized users in management and operational units	Many small to mid-size vertical markets	1988-90	XCON, Financial Advisor, Plan Power, TIMM-Tuner
	PC	MIS depts., technical, staff and user groups and individuals	Many small to mid-size vertical markets	1987-89	COCOMO1, Purdue Grain Market Advisor, WILLARD, 810 Hot Line Advisor
EXPERT SYSTEM BUILDING TOOLS	Large	R & D groups, MIS depts. and individual developers	Small	1986-88	ART, KEE, Knowledge Craft
	Mid-Size	MIS depts., technical staff and user groups, and individuals	Large	1987-90	Personal Consultant Plus, M.1, S.1, AION, KES II, VAX OPS, ES Environment/VM
	Small	MIS depts., technical staff and user groups, schools and individuals	Many small to mid-sized vertical markets	1987-90	Insight 2+, Exsys, 1st-Class
AI LANGUAGES		R & D groups, software vendors, schools and individual developers	Small	1987-90	Arity/Prolog, Golden Common LISP, Lucid Common LISP, TurboPROLOG

ning to explore ways in which AI technologies can improve their existing products. This market is probably not much larger that the current market for large conventional programs. All enhancement will really do is provide existing vendors with new ways to add value to their products which, in turn, will lead to increased competition within existing markets.

One example of an early version of an enhanced program is IBM's YES/VMS. By itself, YES/VMS is an expert system that monitors and controls MVS operating systems. It will probably be offered, however, as an enhancement to IBM's MVS operating system package. Another example is INTELLECT, a natural language frontend that enables users to request information from an existing database with greater ease. INTELLECT, a product of Artifical Intelligence Corporation, is always used in conjunction with existing applications to enhance the user interfaces.

As with the large systems, there is a market for enhanced conventional personal computer (PC) applications. This niche will probably develop somewhat faster than the mini/mainframe market simply because it has more developers working on the programs. This market will be about the same size as the current market for PC programs and application software. AI techniques will be used to add value to existing products, thus creating increased competition among vendors. This market should really heat up as programmers discover new ways to combine artificial intelligence/expert systems (AI/ES) techniques with existing programs.

Already several PC applications incorporate AI/ES techniques, including Javelin Software Corporation's Javelin, mdbs's GURU, International Systems Services Corporation's ISS, and AI Mentor's Performance Mentor. Each package combines some type of conventional software (e.g., word processing, spreadsheet, data base) with some type of knowledge system capability. At the moment, the vendors offering enhanced software are new companies, but eventually the larger PC software vendors probably will become active in this market also or cease to be competitive.

EXPERT SYSTEMS (NEW APPLICATIONS)

The potential customers for products in this niche are corporate and government decision makers who routinely deal with complex problems that in the past have been beyond the scope of their computer programs. Most of these customers are highly paid experts or specialists, for example, managers of complex processing plants, computer configuration experts, bank loan officers, insurance underwriters, and financial planners. Large expert systems being developed to help these individuals will soon be coming into the market. Most will rely on existing data bases and so, in effect, could be called enhancements of existing programs. In fact, however, they so expand the scope and power of existing programs that they constitute a new market for computer software.

The most successful vendors of these products will probably be new companies that combine AI/ES specialists with specialists from a carefully targeted vertical niche or internal development groups. Limited availability of knowledge engineers and the difficulties in developing these large expert systems will surely affect the speed with which this market develops. The first large systems have just become available.

Expert systems, by nature, develop solutions to specific problems. Therefore, most PC-based expert systems have been developed by individuals who thoroughly understand the job to be performed. At the moment, the most active *general* domain is helping managers deal with personnel problems involving complex decisions.

Potential customers for this niche are groups of people who face common problem-solving and decision-making tasks. Auto mechanics, for example, need to troubleshoot a wide variety of new cars each year. Cooks need to review the available food, plan a meal, and then execute several recipes in parallel. These tasks are but a few of the many awaiting good solutions based on small expert systems. The market for these applications will become more active in the next few years, as more people acquire computers and more independent programmers learn to develop small expert systems.

EXPERT SYSTEMS TOOLS

Tools are products sold to customers who want to develop their own applications.

A tool is a constrained programming environment designed to help someone develop expert systems. In practice, the simpler expert system building tools are used much as you use an electronic spreadsheet program (e.g., Lotus 1-2-3). You load the program in your computer, identify the columns and rows, and then insert numbers and formulas to manipulate the numbers (e.g., a formula to add all the numbers in a column and place the total in a box at the bottom of the column). The program does the rest. In a real sense a manager using a spreadsheet program *is* programming; an electronic spreadsheet program is simply a very high-level programming language. By analogy, an expert system building tool is simply a high-level programming language tailored to allow a user to quickly develop expert systems. In the case of an expert system building tool, however, you enter facts and rules rather than numbers and formulas. Like Lotus 1-2-3, an expert system building tool can be used to develop many different expert systems. Using Lotus 1-2-3 you can develop different spreadsheets, calling each as needed. Using a tool, you can develop several different knowledge bases, and then load the appropriate knowledge base for the desired consultation. (See Figure 2.4.)

Well-designed tools save time and effort by providing code to handle interfaces, rule entry, and editing tasks you would normally have to develop from scratch. This is a small but active and expanding niche for AI/ES vendors. These tools are being used primarily by com-

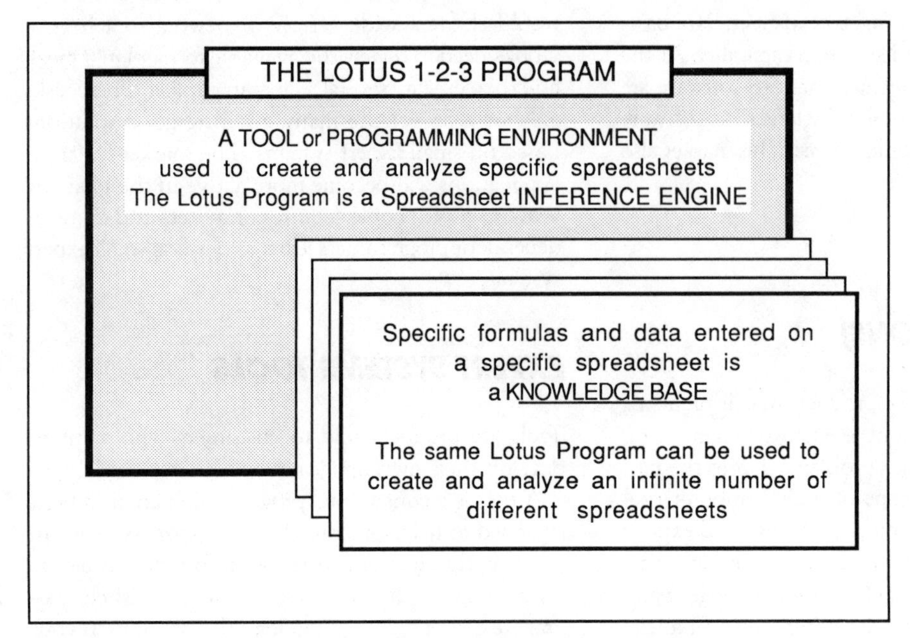

Figure 2.4 *Lotus 1-2-3 as an expert systems tool—an analogy.*

panies to develop knowledge systems for internal use. Examples of large expert system building tools like ART, KEE, and Knowledge Craft will be discussed later in this book.

Some tools will ultimately be targeted at MIS programmers and various user departments. In addition, many managers, professionals, and independent software developers are currently using mid-size tools. While vendors have had little trouble identifying clients for their large tools, they have had more difficulty identifying customers for their mid-size tools. These tools are used to develop many of the same applications developed using small expert system building tools. However, since these tools generally cost more, developers have usually been satisfied to use a small tool and restrict the scope of the system to save money. This market will continue to have problems as long as small system building tools remain popular. Good examples of mid-size tools are Texas Instruments' Personal Consultant Plus and Teknowledge's M.1 and S.1.

Smaller Expert System Building Tools

Small expert system building tools will provide business and industry with the ability to rapidly build small knowledge systems to communicate information about tasks. The potential customers for these tools include people currently using word processing programs, electronic spreadsheets, and PC-based data base programs. The niche for this area barely exists at the moment, but is gaining momentum. Developing this market will be a real task for the vendors, and it is expected they will follow the traditional route for marketing conventional PC software. Examples of these tools include Paperback Software's VP Expert, Level Five Research's Insight 2, Exsys's Exsys, and 1st-Class by Programs in Motion. Each tool allows nonprogrammers to develop programs. Like the electronic spreadsheet programs that initially created the business market for personal computers, improved versions of these smaller tools will allow managers to create their own applications and significantly accelerate the use of computers by non-programming managers and technical personnel.

AI LANGUAGES AND HARDWARE

At the moment, AI languages are being sold primarily to people in research and development departments and to schools. Many people involved in the AI community believe that expert systems development techniques will prove so popular that conventional programmers will increasingly use AI languages to prototype or even develop large systems. It is hard to evaluate this claim, but clearly the investment in existing hardware and software as well as in conventionally trained programmers will make this transition slow.

Learning a new programming language does not occur overnight. If there is to be a significant market for AI languages, it will probably not develop before 1990. Some examples of robust AI languages are Gold Hill Computer's Golden Common LISP, Texas Instruments' Scheme, IBM's Common LISP, Quintus's PROLOG, Arity's Arity/PROLOG, and Borland's TurboPROLOG.

The initial AI market witnessed the establishment of a number of vendors who planned to sell AI hardware, principally LISP machines, to facilitate use of AI software. As the technology has become more commercialized, AI languages have been successfully implemented on conventional hardware, and the current market for AI hardware seems limited to the research environment or to highly specialized large application development efforts. The trend may change with the introduction of LISP chips and subsequent generations of LISP and PROLOG machines, but, at the moment, the future of AI hardware, like the future of AI languages, probably will be confined to research and prototype development environments.

EXPERT SYSTEMS SALES

As noted, about 85 percent of the U.S. sales of AI and expert systems products have been to universities, the military, aerospace companies who primarily do contract work for the military, and research and development departments of the largest U.S. companies.

In other words, most AI products have been sold to those interested in research and experimentation, rather than for solving practical commercial problems. Researchers have different needs than MIS departments and operations managers. They are willing to pay large sums for exotic hardware and to experiment with new programming languages.

The market is changing. Large U.S. companies have convinced themselves that AI, especially expert systems, has the potential to significantly improve effectiveness and productivity. The major targets for the changing expert systems market are DP groups, MIS departments, and operational departments. The transition is just beginning. It will result in much larger sales in the next few years. Companies selling AI products are currently changing their products and their marketing strategies to prepare for sales to mainstream computer users.

The development of the AI market in the United States is being driven by software prices and innovations. As new software is introduced, companies change their hardware plans to accommodate the software. Tables 2.2 and 2.3 illustrate an overview of the types and numbers of expert systems in use in the United States today.

Table 2.2 *Development techniques used to create 115 expert systems in use as of the summer of 1986.*

Developed with Tools	
Inductive tools	6
Simple Rule	34
Structured Rule	35
Large Hybrid	9
Domain Specific	8
TOTAL	**92**
Developed with Language	
LISP	13
PROLOG	5
Conventional	5
TOTAL	**23**

Many companies have fielded systems (systems in actual use) they do not want to talk about, fearing their competitors will learn of efficiencies they have achieved. The actual number of fielded systems in the United States is about three to five times the number shown in Table 2.3, or about 500 to 1,000 expert systems actually used in the United States today. Most fielded systems are used in finance, manufacturing, and equipment maintenance. If they were all production rule systems and could be measured in terms of the number of rules contained in their knowledge bases, then *small systems* would range from 50 to 500 rules, *mid-size systems* would range from 500 to 1,500 rules, and *large systems* would be those exceeding 1,500 rules. Most fielded systems are either small or mid-size systems.

Three years ago, when U.S. companies were just getting into AI and academic researchers were talking about building only large expert systems, it was assumed companies would need LISP machines to develop and field such systems. Small systems were often called *toy systems*. Many early AI companies assumed clients would use a small system to determine how an expert system was built and then move on to large, "real expert systems." That has all changed. Now, most companies are concentrating their efforts on small to mid-size systems. Such systems typically run on personal computers or on workstations (large personal computers configured with a UNIX or VAX operating system). The systems are written in either LISP or C. In other words, most MIS and operations managers are interested in building only expert systems they can field on their *existing* hardware. Expert system building tools allow them to do so.

Rather than being programmed in a language, expert systems can be developed by using tools. An early expert system, MYCIN, was developed in LISP. Later, the rules were removed from MYCIN and the remaining inference, control, and interface code were combined with other rules to develop new expert systems. As a result, most U.S. companies have concentrated on developing expert systems by means of

Table 2.3 *Size and type of expert systems applications fielded as of the summer of 1986.*

	SIZE OF SYSTEM		
APPLICATION	SMALL	MID-SIZE	LARGE
Management, Finance, and Office Automation	11	10	3
Manufacturing (Planning & Scheduling)	3	11	1
Equipment Maintenance (Troubleshooting)	5	14	2
Computer Related	9	12	6
Other	11	17	8
TOTALS	**39**	**64**	**60**

expert system building tools (or shells). At the moment, expert system building tools play the key role in developing the U.S. expert systems market.

Naturally, a need for tools and shells creates a need for marketers of these products. At least 50 such companies sell tools ranging widely both in price and in usefulness. In early 1986, the small, inductive, simple rule tools were selling for about $500 each and were available on personal computers. The better, structured rule tools were priced between $3,000 and $5,000 and were available on personal computers or UNIX workstations. Hybrid tools were selling for around $50,000 and were available only on LISP machines or on workstations configured for LISP. About half the current tools are programmed in conventional languages, with the remainder written in LISP or PROLOG. In the future, we expect the smaller tools to sell for about $100, mid-size tools for about $500–$1,000, and the largest tools for around $5,000–$10,000. Moreover, all should be available for use on personal computers, UNIX workstations, and mainframes.

The preceding reflects the transition from research uses to the practical problems faced by MIS and operations units. Here, developers seek to field expert systems on existing hardware. But not all companies are converting their tools to C or PASCAL. As a result, vendors most concerned with reprogramming their tools are selling primarily to institutions that want to integrate their expert systems with existing data bases, fielding these systems on existing mainframes. On the other side of the coin, companies selling tools to the U.S. military and others involved in research and development of complex systems are more inclined to leave their tools in LISP.

A move away from symbolic languages is likely as expert systems move into the mainstream computing environment, as new hardware becomes available, and as companies begin to undertake harder problems. U.S. companies could return to LISP-based tools in about five years. Most small expert systems are being developed by nonprogrammers, managers, mechanical engineers, and psychologists. In general, these small systems incorporate procedural knowledge. They are being developed to serve in place of documentation manuals, policy guidelines, and materials describing the features and functions of products.

The smallest number of expert systems developed and fielded have been expert systems in the tradition of MYCIN and the other "classic" large expert systems. These systems are the hardest to develop, of course, and more will be developed and fielded eventually. Many academic researchers have been surprised by the way U.S. companies have used the techniques they developed, sometimes speaking as if they are improper systems. In fact, the companies are simply using a subset of available AI techniques to solve urgent problems.

Early advocates of the commercialization of expert systems assumed that a lack of knowledge engineers would create a bottleneck and prevent rapid development of expert systems. This constraint may be real at the upper end of the market, but it is not limiting the overall commercialization of expert systems because most companies are not developing large expert systems. They are developing small and mid-size systems, and existing personnel are quite capable of developing such systems.

Various strategies are being pursued by U.S. companies. Some companies, like Du Pont, are rapidly developing large numbers of small expert systems, encouraging people throughout the company to use small expert system building tools to solve everyday communication problems. Some companies, like GTE, have elected to develop large systems. They have carefully analyzed their problems and selected one or a few problems on which to concentrate. Other companies, like IBM and most major financial institutions, have focused on developing mid-size systems that can be linked to existing data bases and delivered on mainframes. Most companies, including General Motors and Texas Instruments, have elected to use a variety of LISP and UNIX workstations and large personal computers to develop mid-size systems. Most large companies, of course, are pursuing all these strategies simultaneously, but they tend to concentrate on a narrower strategy.

Table 2.4 and Figure 2.5 present data from a Branscomb Associates survey of 500 U.S. companies to project the U.S. market for AI products for the near

Table 2.4 *AI industry forecast through 1990 (in millions of dollars). Hardware includes all LISP-configured machines. Data excludes Personal Computer hardware and software.*

	Hardware	Tools	Expert Systems	Natural Language	Totals
1985	135	26	4	17	182
1986	190	45	12	27	274
1987	240	85	35	39	399
1988	300	125	75	67	567
1989	375	185	175	100	835
1990	465	275	350	130	1220

Data from Branscomb Associates, 1986.

future. These estimates are very conservative, since they exclude personal computer hardware and software and the consulting sevices that vendors use to increase their income. They provide an overall picture of the expected growth. The dark portion of each bar in Figure 2.5 indicates the market that will be concerned with expert systems applications and expert system building tools. Notice that tools keep growing in proportion to all other products. The AI market in the United States is currently being driven by the availability of expert system building *tools*. As companies move expert systems efforts into their mainstream operations, the market will begin to shift toward expert systems *applications*.

HOW WILL BUSINESS USE EXPERT SYSTEMS?

Section Four of this book provides a catalog of some expert systems already in use in business, industry, and government. The picture that emerges from this set of applications is clear. Expert systems will be used wherever people need to analyze and solve problems and wherever they need assistance to make decisions. They will be used wherever people need to communicate information about problems involving analysis and decision making. And they will be used to store and communicate knowledge. In other words, expert systems will be used everywhere computers are used. To get a concrete idea of how expert systems will be used, study the examples in the catalog. This chapter only overviews the types of problems that lead most large and mid-size organizations to explore, develop, and field expert systems.

Many different ways of classifying the corporate need for knowledge engineering have been proposed. Some have suggested that heavy manufacturing industries, those faced with stiff foreign competition and desperate for increased productivity and improved products, will invest heavily in expert systems. Others have argued that expert systems will be deployed more rapidly in the highly competitive service industries, such as banks and insurance companies, that depend on delivering complex advice to their clients.

Expert systems are new and offer so many diverse advantages that many different businesses and industries are trying to determine how to improve their operations via computers. Table 2.5 illustrates the application domains common to all companies and suggests some problems that will yield to knowledge engineering solutions in the next few years.

Expert systems should not be conceptualized as a special type of computer system, but rather as a convenient approach to analyzing and communicating information about problem-solving situations. All businesses face numerous situations requiring decisions that result from problem analysis. Expert systems provide managers throughout organizations with a means of formalizing these decision processes and effectively communicating the results to everyone faced with similar decisions.

SUMMARY

U.S. companies have passed through the initial research and evaluation stage and accepted key AI technologies that they are now implementing. They have discovered the benefits of using knowledge-based approaches to a wide variety of problems and are now alert to the promise offered by AI. They are prepared to commercialize each successive wave of expert systems technology as soon as it is ready to leave the research laboratories. In other words, business has been "sold" on AI and is now ready to reverse the process and "demand" additional techniques.

In the past three years, while most computer sales have slowed, sales of AI and expert systems products have grown rapidly. Businesses are incorporating computers throughout their offices and operations. These

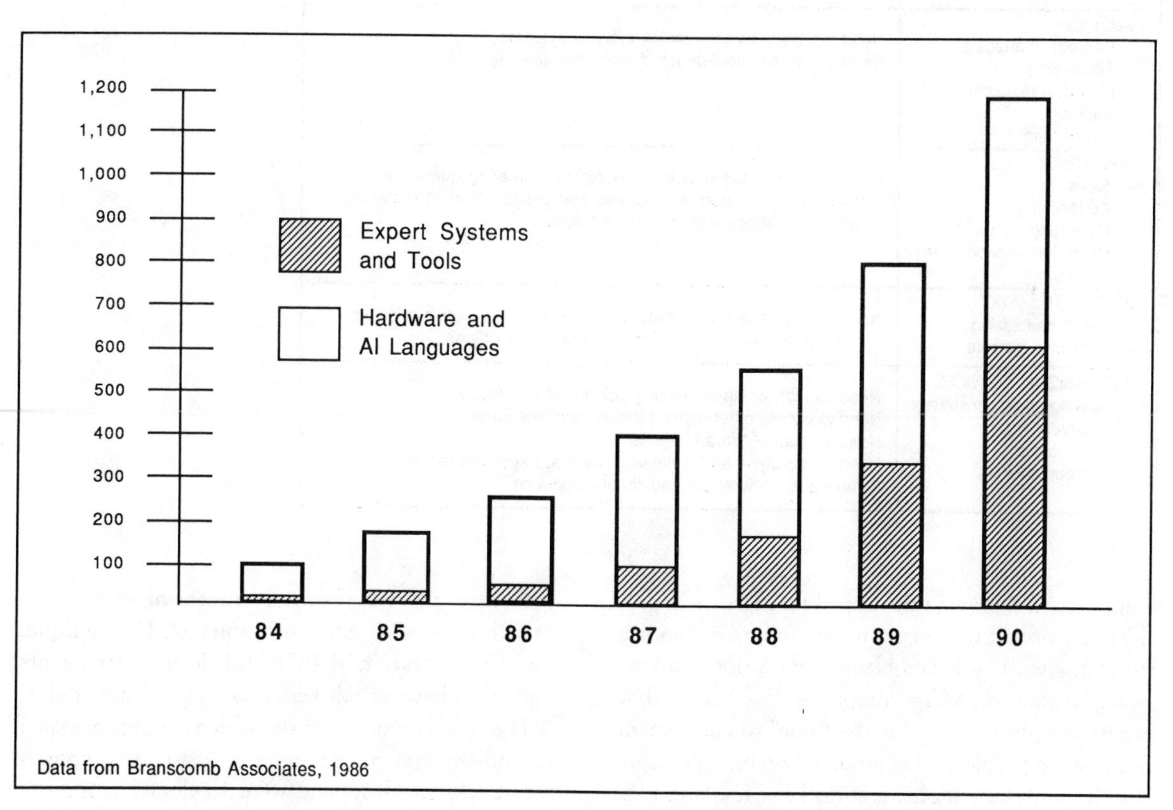

Figure 2.5 *AI industry forecast—the growing role of expert systems and applications.*

Table 2.5 *Overview of knowledge problems common to most companies or professions.*

DOMAIN	PROBLEMS
SENIOR MANAGEMENT: Executive officers Senior managers Strategic planners Senior staff Consultants	Need to reduce organizational complexity Need to monitor an increasing volume of information Need to access experts and consultants for specific advice
OPERATIONS: Manufacturing services, complex equipment operation Energy exploration Quality control Inventory control	Need to improve coordination of organization, scheduling, and management Need for overview of complex systems for rapid decision making Need to monitor/control complex equipment Need to anticipate results of complex, dynamic interactions
SUPPORT SERVICES: Public relations Legal Personnel and training Data processing services Building and maintenance Research and development	Need to train/retrain many people to handle complex jobs Need to communicate new, complex procedures Need to examine/explain policy decisions/options Need to control/reduce costs of computer software development and maintenance
FINANCE: Portfolio managers Accounting Financial managers Auditing Controlling	Need for overview of complex existing systems Need for smart, goal-directed financial planning tools
MARKETING: Sales Advertising Marketing research Customer service Ordering	Need for expert assistance in examining marketing questions Need for sales assistance programs that provide product knowledge and help configure proposals/packages
OFFICE AUTOMATION: Word processing Data management	Need to increase productivity in handling, filing, communicating, retrieving, and distributing information in offices
PROFESSIONAL SERVICES: Management consulting Lawyers Physicians Accountants	Need to monitor an increasing volume of information Need to access other experts and consultants for advice Need to submit "smart reports" Need to prototype and simulate knowledge systems rapidly without having to know about traditional computing

computers will provide the hoped-for increase in productivity only if nonprogrammer employees can use the computers to solve problems that cannot be solved by current means. Many companies now believe that expert systems will provide the "glue" to allow them to integrate people and computer systems into more effective and efficient organizations. The few large U.S. companies that have been experimenting with this approach for several years, companies like Digital Equipment Corporation (DEC) and Texas Instruments, claim they have already begun to realize exciting results.

The majority of currently fielded systems are small to mid-size systems designed to assist in equipment repair. Most such systems were developed by internal technical people who knew the equipment and helped develop small expert systems to answer employee questions that they would otherwise have had to answer themselves. A key insight concerning this market is that small expert systems tools are a new communication medium. At the moment the potential users of small expert systems rely on memos, checklists, procedure manuals, and personal interaction and communication.

So the AI market is just beginning. The commercialization of AI technology is moving fast and is expected to move faster in the next decade. Potential applications are just waiting for this new technology to move in. The introduction of several IBM PC-based expert system building tools is significantly expanding the number of individuals and companies who can begin to experiment with expert systems. As more people learn what these systems can do, demand will accelerate for still more sophisticated expert system building tools. Moreover, the existence of PC-based system building tools will further facilitate the development of smart generic software. This, in turn, will introduce managers at all levels to the possibility of using knowledge-based decision support systems to perform a wide variety of tasks. It will also result in a demand for additional, large-scale expert systems to solve a variety of business problems.

The estimates made in this chapter are conservative. The expansion of the technology in the next five years will be explosive. By 1990, expert systems will be in general use, performing a myriad of applications, in a large number of companies, and, in the early 1990s, most mid-size and large companies will find it necessary to acquire and use knowledge-based systems simply to remain competitive.

SECTION TWO

EXPERT SYSTEMS LANGUAGES AND TOOLS

This section provides an overview of the languages and tools that are being used to develop expert systems. It begins with an introduction to the language and software used in expert systems tools (Chapter 3), as well as an overview of the categories of expert system building tools and how to choose the right tool for a specific problem (Chapter 4). Following this general overview, you are introduced to each category of tool: simple rule-based tools (Chapter 5), inductive tools (Chapter 6), mid-size rule-based tools (Chapter 7), large rule-based tools (Chapter 8), and hybrid tools (Chapter 9).

The systems are reviewed in terms of their power and flexibility, developer interface, user interface, systems interface, runtime speed, and training and support.

3

Language and Software

INTRODUCTION

Chapter 2 discussed several market segments, including the market for AI languages and hardware. If a company decides to explore developing and using expert systems, it should begin by shaping an overall expert systems strategy. Developing such a strategy involves detailed consideration of at least five interacting factors:

- Identifying the overall scope and cost of your company's effort.
- Identifying appropriate areas and problems for expert systems.
- Identifying who will be involved in the effort—both internal and external.
- Identifying the programming languages and/or software tools used to develop and field your expert systems.
- Identifying the computer hardware to use to develop and deliver your expert systems.

We will discuss how you might examine and evaluate these five variables. At this point, however, you are concerned primarily with developing your basic understanding of the underlying concepts and techniques before you try to evaluate what kind of expert systems strategy your company might adopt. This chapter reviews the programming languages and related software issues relevant to developing expert systems.

LEVELS OF SOFTWARE

To begin the discussion of AI software and languages, examine Figure 3.1, which overviews the levels of software between the computer hardware and the human trying to solve a specific problem.

Computers function by manipulating strings of 0's and 1's. The most primitive level of software is machine language, composed of 0's and 1's. The next level up, assembly language, provides higher order symbols that represent various sets of 0's andl's. The lowest level at which human programmers normally operate is the assembly language level. Programmers working in assembly language can develop programs, but it is extremely tedious, and programmers must be very alert not to lose the big picture as they try to get all the details correct.

Most programmers work at the next higher level, referred to as "programming language." Programmers often refer to this level as "higher-level languages." Most programming languages you read about, including BASIC, COBOL, FORTRAN, PASCAL, PL/1, C, and ADA, are higher-level languages. Each language defines a large set of words, standing for large collections of 0's and 1's. By entering a single command in a higher-level language, a programmer can assemble a large set of 0's and 1's to carry out a complex operation. Some high-level languages are better for one thing than another. Thus, FORTRAN is tailored to program scientific procedures while COBOL is tailored to develop programs that will manipulate large financial data bases.

In addition to the higher-level languages mentioned, many other higher-level languages are used for special purposes. The two higher-level languages most commonly used for AI programming are LISP and PROLOG.

At the next level above the higher-level programming languages are programming *environments* designed to help someone accomplish a particular programming task.

In some cases an environment is simply a collection of blocks of code programmers can link together to create a program faster than if they had to write all the code from scratch. FORTRAN, for example, has an environment composed of "libraries of subroutines" that can be chained together to develop specific FORTRAN application programs.

In other cases, environments are highly tailored packages that allow users to develop a very specialized application. These environments are sometimes referred to as "very high-level programming languages." In addition to specialized environments for developing graphics or designing wind tunnel studies, several generic environments help personal computer users develop useful applications. Two examples are Lotus 1-2-3 and dBASE III. Each program is an environment or tool you can use to develop a very special program quickly. You may not think of yourself as a programmer, but when you call up an electronic spreadsheet and enter dates, account numbers, and dollar figures, you are creating a highly specialized program. In effect, Lotus 1-2-3 provides a set of highly specialized commands and an entry format that makes it easy for users to complete and run a spreadsheet program.

Very high-level programming languages tend to be highly specialized, and they can usually be used for only one or a very few functions. Flexibility has been exchanged for ease of programming. A very high-level programming language like Lotus 1-2-3 or dBASE III can be written in assembly language, but most are written in a higher-level language like C or PASCAL.

An electronic spreadsheet program knows how to

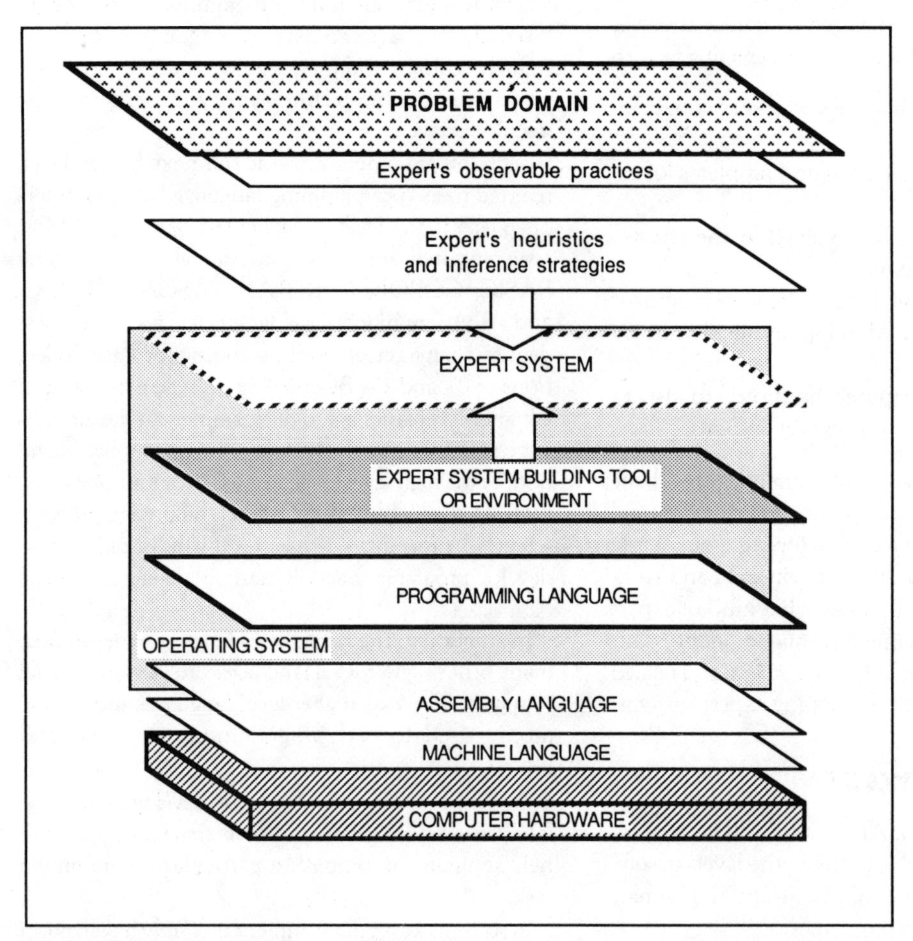

Figure 3.1 *Levels of software between human problems and computer hardware.*

manipulate a spreadsheet, but it is useless until someone provides specific information about the accounts, dates, and amounts to be manipulated. By the same token, expert system building tools are programs for manipulating knowledge about how to solve a particular problem. To develop an expert system, someone must supply information about a particular problem. Thus, an expert system is an application program that includes both information about a problem and information about how to manipulate that information.

You can always use a lower-level programming language to skip an intermediate level and thus, just as a tool can be written in assembly language, an expert system can be written in a higher-level language, like LISP or PROLOG. For speed and convenience, however, most expert systems are developed by entering knowledge into an expert system building tool.

The top three planes in Figure 3.1 illustrate the knowledge that must be put into an expert system to make it useful. Within a specific task domain there are the observable practices of a human expert. Inside the expert's head are facts, rules-of-thumb (heuristics), and various problem-solving strategies the expert uses when faced with a particular problem. To create an expert system you must transfer this knowledge from the human expert to the computer, just as managers must transfer their knowledge of a particular cash flow situation to a spreadsheet.

No matter at what level you operate, certain input and output operations must be performed. Most conventional computers have operating systems that handle all these bookkeeping tasks. When you use an IBM Personal Computer, for example, whether you are dealing with a programming language, an environment, a tool, or an application, the data are taken from the computer keyboard to the software and from that software to the printer or to storage by an operating system called DOS (Disk Operating System). An operating system is not really a level of software but a specialized environment in which other software operates. To a significant degree, languages and tools depend on the operating system in which they operate for their efficiency. Thus, some programming languages operate better in one environment than another; for example, C runs very well in the UNIX operating system.

Until 1986 AI languages ran much better in operating systems written in an AI language. Thus, LISP runs very well on a LISP machine where the operating system is also written in LISP. The Japanese have recently developed PROLOG machines that feature PROLOG operating systems and are especially designed to run PROLOG.

Since the operating system is the medium in which data are passed between various programs, it is much easier to coordinate data-passing operations when both programs run in the same operating system; that is, an expert system running in DOS can obtain data from a data base program running in DOS much easier than an expert system running on a LISP machine can obtain data from a program running on an IBM machine. In the latter case, the data must be passed from one operating system to another, which adds time and difficulty to the process.

Recently, improvements in LISP have made it possible to run LISP almost as well in a conventional operating system as on a LISP machine. This is good news for those who want to use expert systems applications written in LISP on a conventional computer.

AI SOFTWARE VERSUS CONVENTIONAL SOFTWARE

Figure 3.2 provides a general overview of the evolution of computer programming languages. The first computers were programmed in machine language and then in assembly language. In the 1960s the first of the higher-level programming languages were developed, representing a major advance in the speed and effectiveness with which programmers could develop programs.

FORTRAN is the earliest higher-level programming language still in use today. Up until about 1984, if you read a book on programming languages, you read about languages like FORTRAN, COBOL, PL/1, PASCAL and C—all conventional languages primarily designed to allow programmers to develop algorithms for the numerical manipulation of data. As noted, some languages, like COBOL, were designed primarily for manipulating large data bases, and were thus very popular with businesses, while other languages, like FORTRAN and PL/1, were preferred for complex

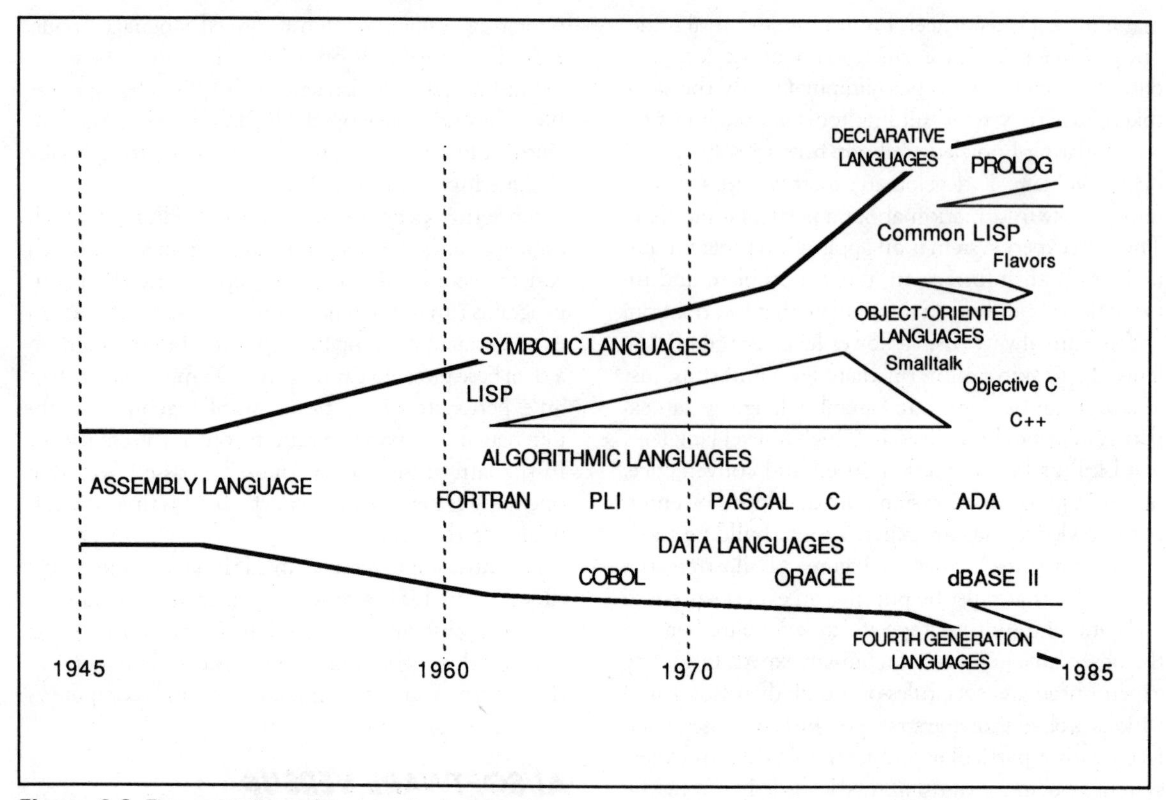

Figure 3.2 *The evolution of computer languages.*

scientific tasks. C was developed by Bell Labs and remains popular with people who develop programs that run on computers integrated into networks of complex communications equipment.

Still, for all their differences, all these conventional languages share two basic assumptions: the programmer will develop an algorithm to solve a problem by taking one step after another, and the data needed by the program will be stored in a data base and called by the algorithm as needed. To develop such a program, whether in C, COBOL, or PASCAL, you initially develop an easy-to-understand algorithm. Then, to get the program to run quickly, the algorithm is improved and in the process becomes so arcane that only a very skilled programmer can figure out what is happening at any point in the program.

At about the same time FORTRAN was developed, John McCarthy, a leading AI researcher, developed a language called LISP (List Processing). Unlike conventional languages designed conceptually to manipulate numbers via mathematical procedures, LISP was designed to manipulate lists via logical procedures. Lists, to a layperson, are like words and sentences rather than numbers. In other words, McCarthy created a programming language that would make it easy to represent something like:

If Socrates is a man,
And all men are mortal,
Then Socrates is mortal.

Numbers are only a small subset of the things called symbols. Languages that can manipulate symbols like words, using logic rather than mathematical operators (i.e., +, −), are called symbolic languages. A very simple way of thinking of the distinction between them is that if you gave a *conventional* language the input (2 + 3), it would always return 5. If you gave a symbolic language the same input (2 + 3), it might return (3 + 2) or (5) or (4 + 1). Symbolic languages are designed to look for and identify similar patterns. This focus is useful if you are trying to solve the syllogism about Socrates and mortality. The problem is resolved by realizing that if you know Socrates is a man and all men are mortal, then, since you have a common term (man/all men), you can assert that Socrates and mortals are also equivalent.

Until recently, symbolic languages were confined to the university research laboratories of computer scientists simply because no one in a commercial setting faced a problem that required such languages. Now, with the advent of commercially valuable expert systems, large numbers of people are interested in learning about symbolic languages. A symbolic language is not "better" than a conventional language, just as COBOL is not "better" than FORTRAN. Languages are better or worse, depending on the problem you face. Moreover, the best language for a particular problem depends, in part, on the hardware and the operating system the language will be run on. The question facing managers considering developing an expert system is whether they want to use a symbolic language or a tool written in a symbolic language, or whether they should stick with a conventional language they already know. This complex question will be considered in several different contexts throughout this book.

Table 3.1 summarizes the differences between the two types of languages. Words and sentences tend to be more complex than data as commonly used in computing. Data typically refer to individual bits of information, like "6" or "54634." The number "54634" may represent an employee named "Jones," but that relationship is unknown to the computer. A sentence, on the other hand, is like a "fact" in logic. It relates two pieces of information, like Socrates and man. Since symbolic languages store facts together, the "data unit" most symbolic languages manipulate is referred to as *knowledge*. Knowledge implies a relationship instead of a simple number. It is knowledge that allows a person to make a decision, not specific pieces of data. Thus, symbolic languages are good for programming logical problems because they allow the programmer to manipulate knowledge more easily.

Table 3.1 *The differences between conventional and symbolic programming.*

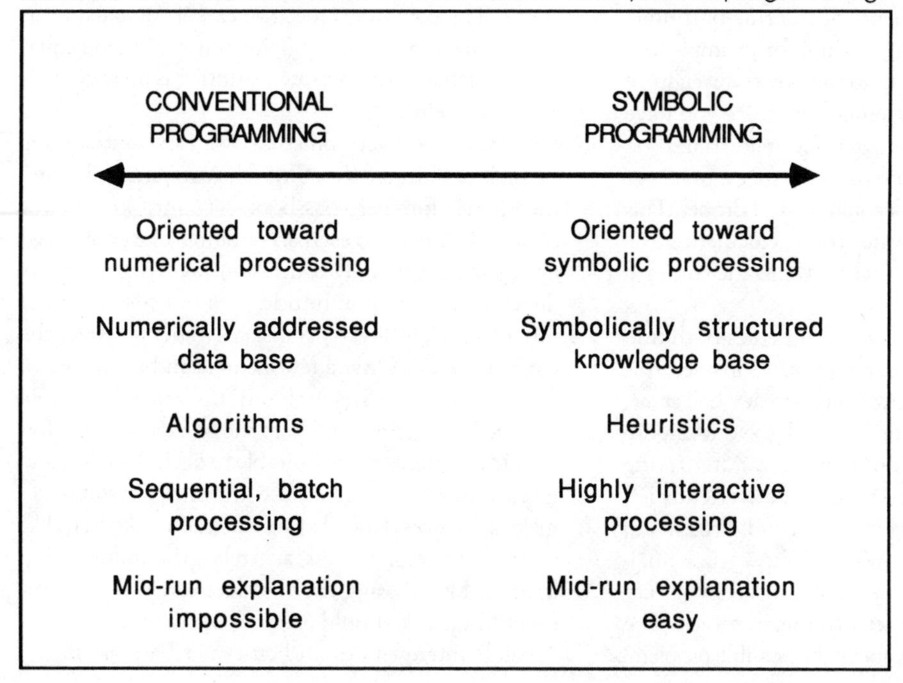

CONVENTIONAL PROGRAMMING	SYMBOLIC PROGRAMMING
Oriented toward numerical processing	Oriented toward symbolic processing
Numerically addressed data base	Symbolically structured knowledge base
Algorithms	Heuristics
Sequential, batch processing	Highly interactive processing
Mid-run explanation impossible	Mid-run explanation easy

To illustrate, imagine you are a supervisor of cashiers in a bank and at the end of the business day you find a particular teller's cash drawer is out of balance by $1,500. The "$1,500" is data, an individual bit of information with little meaning by itself. In fact, it has meaning only when related to other data, for example, that "$1,500 is an imbalance" and an imbalance will have several consequences. You know the teller must balance out before the bank closes, so you have to find where the teller's error might have occurred. Now the insignificant data of $1,500 becomes related to other data—what the correct balance should be. You question the teller and help determine where the $1,500 error may have happened. Finally the teller finds the mistake: a check has been misplaced under a stack of papers. The insignificant $1,500 has been related to the real world of paper shuffling. You can now infer new knowledge by simply combining a few facts and procedures. In a matter of seconds you instruct the teller to add the $1,500 check to the previous out-of-balance total, and the teller's cash drawer balances.

A second difference between conventional languages and symbolic languages is that conventional languages depend on algorithms, while symbolic languages rely on both algorithms and heuristics. An algorithm is basically an equation. A heuristic is a rule-of-thumb, a paradigm. In a general algorithm, for example, the price of steak per pound, multiplied by the weight of the steak you want to buy, equals the price you have to pay for your dinner. No matter how many times you shop for a steak, the routine never changes: price per pound times weight of steak equals cost of dinner. This is how conventional software works, calculating the price, with no mistakes, several thousand times a second.

Heuristics, in contrast, depend on rules-of-thumb people develop through experience. Consider this problem. You've spent a rainy afternoon at a ball game, and after leaving the stadium you walk to your car, only to find the engine will not turn over. After trying for several minutes, you discover you inadvertently left the lights on and the car's battery is dead. Frustrated, you phone for a tow truck. When the tow truck finally arrives, the driver pulls up to the front of your car and hops out carrying a set of jumper cables. The driver hasn't spoken to you about the possible problem, but is already prepared to jump-start your car. The conclusion was reached based on *heuristic* knowledge. The driver has been out to the stadium on other rainy days and knows people often forget to turn off their lights, thus running down their batteries. Of course, there may be serious problems with your car other than a dead battery. From the personal experience of the driver, however, a jump-start is the place to begin. There is little need to perform elaborate engine analysis before such a simple measure is taken first.

This is how symbolic languages work. Although they do use algorithms when available, making knowledge more precise, they also use heuristics in cases where the knowledge is not precise or certain.

A third distinction is that conventional programming tends to rely on repetitive processes; symbolic programming depends on logical or inferential processes.

Conventional software is generally very reliable and accurate in repeating the same routine. If, for example, you need to figure interest earned for $10,000 passbook saving accounts at a rate of 5 percent per account, you would apply a precise algorithm repeatedly. The computer uses conventional software, applying the same algorithm to every passbook saving account. The computer does not care if the balance in an account is $2 or $20,000; it applies the same equation to each account repeatedly until it is finished with all the accounts.

Inferences are very different. We can use the same example to illustrate this. Since the computer calculates the interest for every passbook account, the amount of interest applied to each account must be established first. This is generally a decision made by the bank directors. Based upon hundreds, if not thousands, of other factors, it directly translates to the revenues the bank will earn. Only a few factors can be reduced to neat equations. In such an instance, a simple knowledge system could help the bank's directors formulate an interest rate equitable to both the bank and its customers. This is because knowledge systems can make inferences. Knowledge systems can take facts, like a planned rate of interest, and relate that information in many logical ways, thus producing new facts—how much the bank should earn off the deposits from its "liberal" interest rates and customer base. To help a bank's directors arrive at an interest rate, the knowledge system is constructed from software that can carry out symbolic reasoning. It is symbolic because both facts and the way facts are related are put into a computer, not as numbers, but rather in words manipulated according to strict rules of logic, that is, reasoning by drawing inferences or conclusions from facts.

SYMBOLIC LANGUAGES

If you intend to develop an expert system and to write all the code in a high-level language, you are well advised to use LISP, PROLOG, or some other symbolic language. These languages offer the support and flexibility an expert systems developer wants, just as COBOL offers support to someone developing business applications.

Most expert systems are not being developed in high-level languages, however, they are being developed in *tools*. In this case, developers must choose between a tool written in a conventional language or in a symbolic language—not a simple choice, because it depends on a number of things tied to the specific application. As a broad generalization, the larger, more powerful expert system building tools are written in LISP. This allows programmers who face difficult problems to get into the underlying language to add specific procedural code or to modify the tools when necessary. Most expert systems are not so large, however, and with smaller systems it is harder to say whether a tool in a symbolic or conventional language is preferable.

The most popular symbolic languages are LISP, PROLOG, and several object-oriented languages.

LISP

All the large early expert systems were developed in LISP or a tool written in LISP. LISP deals with symbols. A symbol can be any combination of characters on a keyboard; however, LISP deals primarily with alphanumeric strings that look like words (atoms) or sentences (lists).

In an article written in 1978, John McCarthy, inventor of LISP, described the key ideas in LISP as follows:

1. Computing with symbolic expressions rather than numbers; that is, bit patterns in a computer's memory and registers can stand for arbitrary symbols, not just those of arithmetic.
2. List processing; that is, representing data as linked-list structures in the machine and as multilevel lists on paper.
3. Control structure based on the composition of functions to form more complex functions.
4. Recursion as a way to describe processes and problems.
5. Representation of LISP programs internally as linked lists and externally as multilevel lists, that is, in the same form as all data are represented.
6. The function EVAL, written in LISP itself, serves as an interpreter for LISP and as a formal definition of the language.

In essence, LISP makes no distinction between data and programs, so LISP programs can use other LISP programs as data. You can easily see how this alone would speed up the programming process. LISP is a highly interactive, flexible, and recursive language. The major advantage of LISP is its unique "nesting" nature. This lends powerful capabilities to many problem-solving techniques like searching. With recursion, LISP can break problems into smaller problems where the program calls itself with simplified arguments. However, LISP's recursion capabilities must have a termination point—it cannot recur forever. These properties of LISP don't always make for easily read syntax, but they allow for elegant solutions to complex problems that are very difficult to solve in the various conventional programming languages.

A major reason LISP is so popular is that a LISP program can be naturally represented in LISP data structures. Since programs and data have the same form, they can be interchanged at will, allowing developers to write programs that can, themselves, run and modify other LISP programs. This process lets an expert systems program modify lines of its own code while the program runs. Another attribute of LISP is that memory management is completely automatic, and data typing and storage allocation take place at program runtime. LISP relies on dynamic allocation of space for data storage, so the developer does not have to worry about assigning program space. This makes LISP very modular as property lists need not be adjacent in memory since everything in LISP is done with pointers to select and identify needed data. As a result, LISP manages storage space very efficiently, freeing the developer to create more complex flexible programs.

LISP has only a few basic functions. All other LISP functions are defined in terms of these. Thus, you can easily create a LISP operating system and then work up to whatever higher level you desire. Because of this flexibility, until recently LISP was not standardized in the way FORTRAN and BASIC were, and people often had trouble moving between one dialect of LISP and another. By 1985, however, a standardized version of LISP, Common LISP, had replaced all the other dialects in the commercial marketplace. Thus, when you speak of LISP now, you assume it is Common LISP.

Other specialized features of LISP include its powerful debugging facilities, the availability of both a compiler and interpreter for program development, its automatic runtime checking, and its macro facility that allows for easy extensions of the language.

PROLOG

PROLOG, another popular AI language in wide use today, was developed around 1970 by Alain Colmerauer and his associates at the University of Marseilles. PROLOG (PROgramming in LOGic) implements a simplified version of predicate calculus. Thus, when you write a PROLOG program you are programming in logic.

The basis of PROLOG is true logic programming where computation uses controlled, logical inferences. This makes PROLOG ideal for applications that require simulation of intelligence, including expert systems development, deductive data bases, language processing, robotic control, planning systems, and design applications. PROLOG does away with familiar programming concepts like "goto," and "do-for" and instead incorporates features required by intelligent programs such as advanced pattern matching, generalized record structuring, list manipulation, assertional data bases (PROLOG is very effective with relational data bases since they both can be represented as logical formalisms), and depth-first search capabilities based on back-chaining.

PROLOG is a declarative language that uses the code and data to describe what is true about a particular problem domain. As a result, it is useful at list processing. Also, PROLOG is an interpreted language that responds to queries by attempting to return an answer immediately.

Two steps are essential in developing a PROLOG program:

1. You specify some facts about objects and relationships.
2. You ask questions about objects and relationships (you make an assertion and ask if it is true). PROLOG "answers" by saying yes or no.

PROLOG specifies known facts and relationships about a particular problem domain using the language's symbolic representations of objects and the relationships between objects, thus creating clauses. *Clauses* are implications, and they make up the program with conclusions being stated first. Programming with PROLOG is very different from using a conventional language. For example, instead of asking "What is the equation that will solve my problem?" the developer simply asks, "What formal facts and relationships occur in the problem?" and "What rules are associated with these facts and relationships?" PROLOG expresses facts, rules, and relations in a more natural form which, in turn, produces clear, concise programs. Since programming languages cannot be strictly logical (input and output operations necessarily entail some extralogical procedures), PROLOG incorporates some basic code to control the procedural aspects of its operation. These procedural aspects are kept to a minimum, but one cannot classify PROLOG as a totally logical system.

PROLOG has two programming styles: a declarative style and a procedural style. *Declarative programming* focuses on telling the system what it should know and relies on the system to handle the procedures. *Procedural programming* considers the specific problem-solving behavior the computer will exhibit. Most knowledge engineers building expert systems concentrate on procedural details of PROLOG. Users don't have to concern themselves with this aspect and are free to simply provide facts and ask questions of the system. Naturally, this declarative style has made PROLOG very popular as an AI programming tool.

PROLOG is designed to automate searches through a tree-structured domain by performing depth-first searches by backward chaining. The real power of PROLOG lies in its ability to infer facts from other facts; a user can input non-numeric information, and the system deduces additional non-numeric information. Conversely, PROLOG demands an awkward mix of procedural and nonprocedural styles. PROLOG is not able to express any negative conclusions or embedded conditionals, nor is it able to express any definitions containing more than one "if" statement. PROLOG's true flexibility is its ability to infer facts from other facts.

PROLOG has enjoyed great international popularity. The Hungarian government has encouraged extensive industrial use of the language, and the Japanese, in their much-publicized Fifth-Generation project, have adopted PROLOG as the fundamental language for the supercomputers they hope to develop.

PROLOG is readily available on both large IBM systems and a wide variety of personal computers. It also seems to be an ideal candidate for use in developing parallel processing systems. PROLOG has several dialects, all judged against the standard version of PROLOG described in a text written by Clocksin and Mellish.

Object-Oriented Languages

Object-oriented languages are a bit more complex. You can view object-oriented languages as either a unique category of programming languages or as a subset of symbolic languages. Either way, they are more conceptual than LISP or PROLOG.

The original object-oriented language was Smalltalk, developed at Xerox Palo Alto Research Centers, a major center of AI research. Written in assembly language, Smalltalk has been used to develop expert systems, but its primary use has been to develop user-friendly programming environments. Xerox developed the interface for the Xerox Star computer using Smalltalk, and later Apple developed the interface for the Macintosh using a derivative of Smalltalk.

The basic concepts underlying object-oriented programming have been incorporated into LISP in a variety of ways. One LISP version of an object-oriented language, for example, is Flavors. When LISP programmers want to develop windows for a computer screen, they can use Flavors to develop the code to manage the windows. When LISP programmers develop object-oriented environments, they tend to refer to objects as *frames*. Several of the larger expert system building tools incorporate object-oriented techniques.

Object-oriented concepts can also be implemented in conventional languages. Bell Labs has developed a superset of the C programming language called C++, which turns C into an object-oriented programming environment. Productivity Products International has developed a language called Objective C, which allows for object-oriented programming in an environment very similar to C.

Two key concepts underline object-oriented programming:

- *Encapsulation* of procedures and data into self-contained entities called objects.
- *Inheritance* of code from *parent objects* to *offspring*.

In effect, each object is a small world unto itself. The object contains programs and data, and it interacts with other objects by sending messages. Unlike the commands of a conventional programming language that contain specific instructions about how to carry out the command, a message simply tells an object what should be done and leaves it to the object to figure out how to do it. This means that different objects can respond to the same command in different ways. (It also means that there is no operating system, in the conventional sense, since there are no common standards for handling input and output of information. This, in turn, has made it very difficult for Apple to develop interfaces between the Macintosh and computers using conventional operating systems.)

Figure 3.3 overviews how an object-oriented system works. You create an object by taking a copy of a preexisting object (the parent) and then telling that object how it is to behave differently than the parent. In Figure 3.3, Object 1.1 is an offspring of Object 1. The process of creating new objects is often referred to as *instantiation* in the sense that the new objects are new

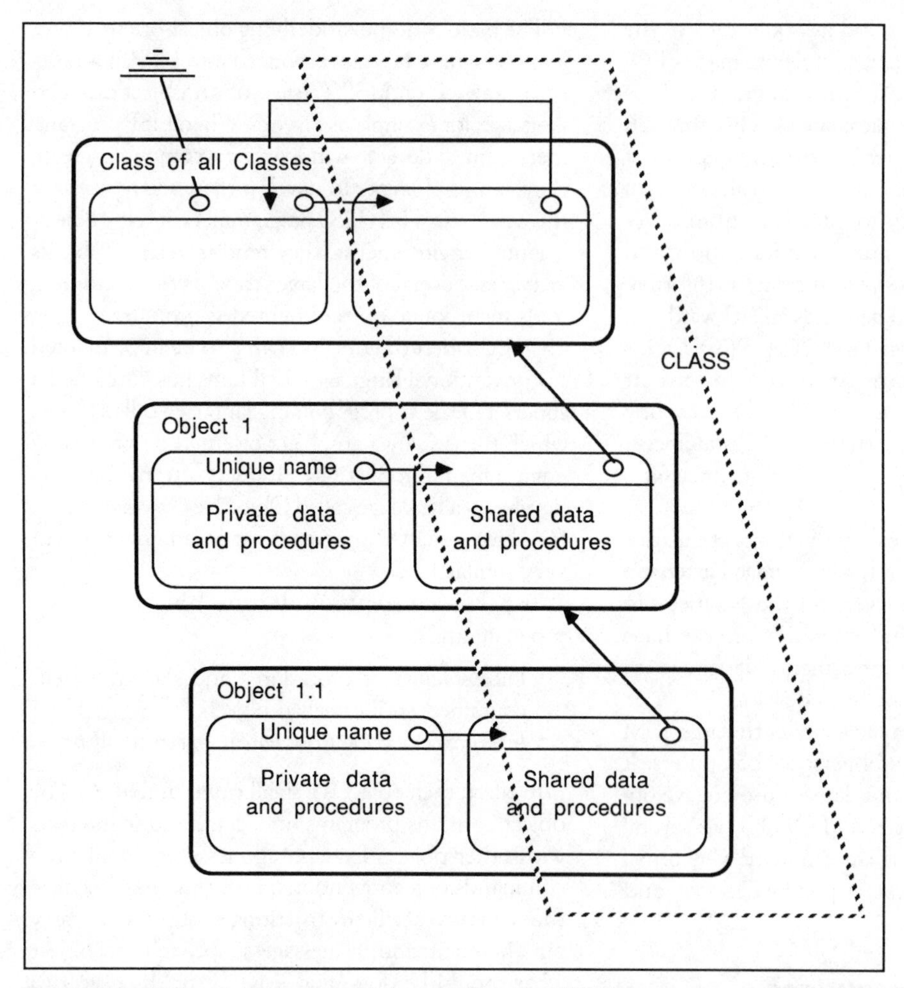

Figure 3.3 *Object Inheritance. Object 1.1 inherits all its data and procedures from Object 1, except for its name and whatever private data and procedures it has. Likewise, except for its name and some private data and procedures, Object 1 inherits all its data and procedures from the ultimate source of data and procedures about objects—the class of all classes (the only object that does not have a private part). Everything held in common between a set of objects is the class of the objects.*

instances of the older objects. When a new object is created, a space is set aside that contains the new object's unique name and any information unique to that object. The rest of the object consists of a pointer that points to the parent object. Thus, when you send a message to Object 1.1, it checks its private data and procedures to see how to handle the message. If it finds an appropriate procedure, it uses it; otherwise, it moves to its parent and checks for a procedure there that it can use. It first checks its parent's private procedures and then moves to the parent's parent, and so on. In a system like Macintosh, thousands of objects exist at many hierarchical levels. Ultimately, the whole system is grounded in an object called the "Class of All Classes" which is, in effect, the minimal definition of the data and procedures that comprise an object. The

Class of All Classes is the only object whose private data are, in fact, public. The information an object inherits from the other objects in the stream that flows from the Class of All Classes to that particular object is referred to as a *Class*.

Consider Figure 3.4, which reproduces a screen from a Lisa computer. (The Lisa was an early version of the Macintosh, and its interface makes the following discussion a little easier to follow than it would be on a Macintosh, although the underlying concepts are exactly the same.) Notice the icon (a small graphic picture) of a pad of LisaDraw "paper" in the upper right corner. LisaDraw is a graphics program. In fact, it is an object that contains all the procedures you need to create instances of graphics. (All the graphics for this book, for example, were created in MacDraw.)

By moving the mouse (a hand-held device you can slide about on the desktop to move the arrow on the screen), you locate the arrow on the LisaDraw icon and press the button on the mouse. This results in the LisaDraw window that is below and to the left of the LisaDraw icon. In effect, you have torn a sheet of drawing paper off the drawing pad. Each time you do this, you create another window, a window that is an instantiation of the LisaDraw object.

If you give the windows names and create graphics within them, then you create unique offspring of the LisaDraw object. The screen in Figure 3.4 illustrates

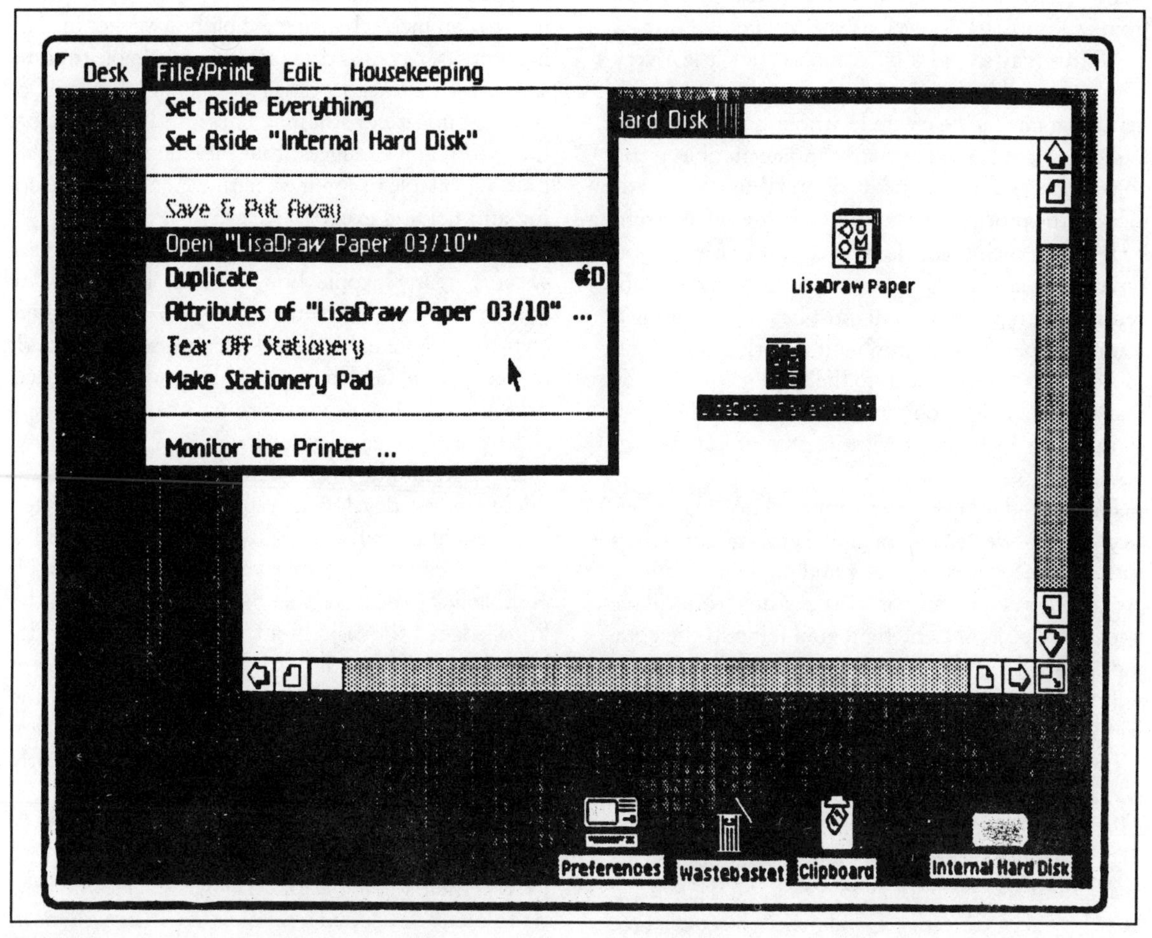

Figure 3.4 *Lisa screen showing objects.*

such an offspring. You could then duplicate the offspring, name it Offspring 1, and then modify your "Copy of Offspring 1" to create another design.

If you "sent a message" to "Copy of Offspring 1" that told it to print itself, "Copy" would check the code encapsulated in memory and associated with the name "Copy" and find some unique data, namely the box with its hatching. It would not find procedural information about how to print itself, however, so it would follow a pointer to "Offspring 1." There additional unique data would be found, namely the two circles, but there would still be no procedural information about how to pass data to the printer, so the task would be passed to the LisaDraw object. There printing procedures would be found and passed back down so that when "Copy" was printed it would include the circles from "Offspring 1" as well as the square.

All this may sound a bit complex, but it is a very powerful breakthrough in programming since it means new programs can be created without having to write lots of new code. When you instantiate an object, the object inherits all its parent's code and thus comes with most of the procedures you want. By the same token, by isolating each object from every other object, you can create a large program one object at a time. In conventional programming you must begin by creating a common operating environment and then assure all subsequent code conforms to the specifications set by that environment. In object-oriented programming you can provide each object with its own unique way of doing things.

Thus, in addition to providing superior user interfaces, object-oriented programming provides developers with unprecedented flexibility and modularity during program development. For these reasons, you will see a lot more object-oriented programming in the coming years. Object-oriented environments already provide the best desktop publishing environments on the various UNIX workstations and on the Macintosh. Moreover, when the next generation of IBM PCs become available, object-oriented environments like Microsoft's Windows will make object-oriented techniques available for DOS users. Additionally, the availability of conventional object-oriented languages like C++ and Objective C will make object-oriented programming more common with applications programmers who work on mainframes.

The Future of Symbolic Languages

When you think of AI you naturally think of programming languages associated with AI: LISP, PROLOG, and object-oriented languages like Smalltalk. Whenever a group of AI researchers gather, expect to hear a discussion of the merits of the various languages.

The commercial world, however, is concerned with such pragmatic issues as compatibility between existing languages and equipment and AI languages. Moreover, they face many practical problems including retraining programmers, changing established ways of managing projects, recoding data, achieving desirable runtime speeds without overloading existing hardware, and, of course, budget constraints. These and other factors have led many to suggest that AI languages will play only a small role in commercializing AI and in developing and fielding expert systems.

In the initial wave of enthusiasm for AI and expert systems, many people bought LISP, PROLOG, or Smalltalk and experimented with constructing their own expert system. It's a good learning experience and, indeed, several fielded expert systems were developed from scratch. If you are working on a large expert system or in a large AI group in an aerospace company, then programming in an AI language is probably productive. Most developers, especially those interested in developing small to mid-size systems, have decided it is much easier to use an expert system building tool. A tool allows the developer to focus on capturing the knowledge of the task. In addition, the tool provides several features like editors, utilities for allowing users to ask "How" or "Why" and various other formatting or natural language components difficult to develop from scratch that prove very useful during the early stages of prototyping.

Dr. Herb Schorr, the vice president who heads IBM's AI efforts, recently stated that IBM was going to wait to see if there was a role for AI languages. He said IBM had already developed a number of expert systems in its expert system building tool: E.S. Environment/VM (written in PASCAL) and that, so far, it seemed that all that was needed was the tool. Likewise, Teknowledge has rewritten both of its tools, S.1 and M.1, in C, arguing that the tools were really independent of the language they were written in and that their clients demanded a conventional language to facilitate fielding their expert systems. Software A & E has recoded its tool, KES II, in C for exactly the same reasons. AION initially wrote their tool, ADS, in PASCAL for the same reasons Dr. Schorr suggested.

You could argue that E.S. Environment/VM, S.1, M.1, KES II, and ADS are all relatively straightforward rule-based tools, and that the large, hybrid tool vendors have so far resisted recoding ART, KEE, and Knowledge Craft into conventional languages. ART, however, is now available in C, and one way or another the various large hybrid tools will probably become available in conventional languages.

The argument for writing a tool in an AI language or for programming in an AI language is that you gain greater flexibility. An AI language is designed for symbolic programming and for the type of rapid prototyping associated with expert systems development efforts. If you have a tool that fits your problem, you need not be concerned about the language in which it is written. When you encounter complex problems that do not fit the tool, however, problems arise. If the problems involve obtaining data from a conventional data base or including code that handles a well-defined procedure, then having a tool written in a conventional language is a great help. On the other hand, if the problem involves representing knowledge in some complex manner, handling a complex search problem, or quickly modifying a tool to incorporate active values or some of the more sophisticated reasoning techniques, then you would probably prefer the tool to be coded in an AI language.

Most expert systems now being developed involve access to data bases and use of conventional procedural code; hence the emphasis has been on writing or recoding tools into conventional languages. As time passes and organizations begin to tackle more complex problems, the emphasis will change.

The argument between those who prefer PROLOG and those who favor LISP, both in the United States and abroad, seems to be settling down. PROLOG has found a niche, primarily with applications that involve interfacing with relational data bases, but increasingly, even those who initially preferred PROLOG seem to be coming to prefer LISP or one of the object-oriented languages. It appears that interest in LISP is increasing in both Europe and Japan while the initial interest in PROLOG in the United States is slacking off rather than growing. The success of the Common LISP movement has certainly helped make LISP more accessible, but one major piece of unfinished business for LISP people is to incorporate an object-oriented standard for Common LISP. (Flavors or Common Loops are both candidates.)

PROLOG, of course, is still very popular. Borland's recent release and promotion of TurboPROLOG may result in a subsequent generation of PC programmers who feel very comfortable with PROLOG. Borland's decision to promote PROLOG rather than LISP was wise. PROLOG is simpler to learn and involves much less code than an implementation of Common LISP. In essence, because PROLOG allows you to enter lots of facts and relations quickly and comes with automatic backward chaining, PROLOG, in its most elementary form, is closer to an expert system building tool than LISP. It is much easier to teach a student to create a small knowledge system in PROLOG than LISP, and Borland has clearly opted to provide its clients with the easiest possible entry to AI programming.

One way to think of the current AI language market is in terms of a "LISP Gap," a period of time between the current concerns of those involved in commercializing expert systems, technological innovations, and changes, and a set of concerns that will emerge in the next few years (see Figure 3.5). On the left side of the field you see the trends driving people to abandon or avoid AI languages: an immediate need to field expert systems to demonstrate their value, coupled with existing problems with getting AI languages to run fast or to obtain or pass information to conventional programs or data bases. Other "down arrows" include a lack of trained LISP programmers, an organizational prejudice or inertia that favors COBOL or FOR-

TRAN, and the high cost of specialized LISP hardware.

Trends that may reverse the current trend away from AI languages include new versions of AI languages that are faster and that compile in a manner that facilitates their interaction with conventional languages (e.g., Gold Hill Computer's new "runtime" version of LISP). You can also expect to see much better versions of LISP becoming available on mainframes. In addition, new hardware should significantly lower the cost of dedicated LISP machines. Texas Instruments' LISP chip became available in early 1987. LISP co-processor boards that you could put into a PC-AT to let you use it as a powerful LISP machine will undoubtedly become available. At the same time, non-LISP machine hardware will continue to improve. LISP will get significantly better on UNIX workstations and on machines like IBM's new PC-RT. You can also expect to see high-quality LISPs running on 386-based machines as they become available in the coming years. Other trends that will promote AI languages include the tendency of companies to tackle harder problems and the desire to include natural language components in systems. In addition, as time passes, more AI programmers will become available, since most computer science programs are now teaching LISP and PROLOG.

Programmers operating on PCs or workstations will want to use LISP and PROLOG before programmers working in mainframe environments. In fact, the next generation of PC/workstation programmers probably will be dedicated AI programmers, while those whose mainframes will continue to use tools and conventional languages for a long time.

Eventually, however, computing will tackle more and more tasks that involve symbolic knowledge and fewer that involve simple number crunching. Therefore, the long-term trend will be in the direction of one of the current AI languages or toward some new language that supports the features expected from LISP, PROLOG, and Smalltalk.

CONVENTIONAL LANGUAGES

You have already learned of the currently popular practice of writing expert system building tools in a conventional language. By far the most popular conven-

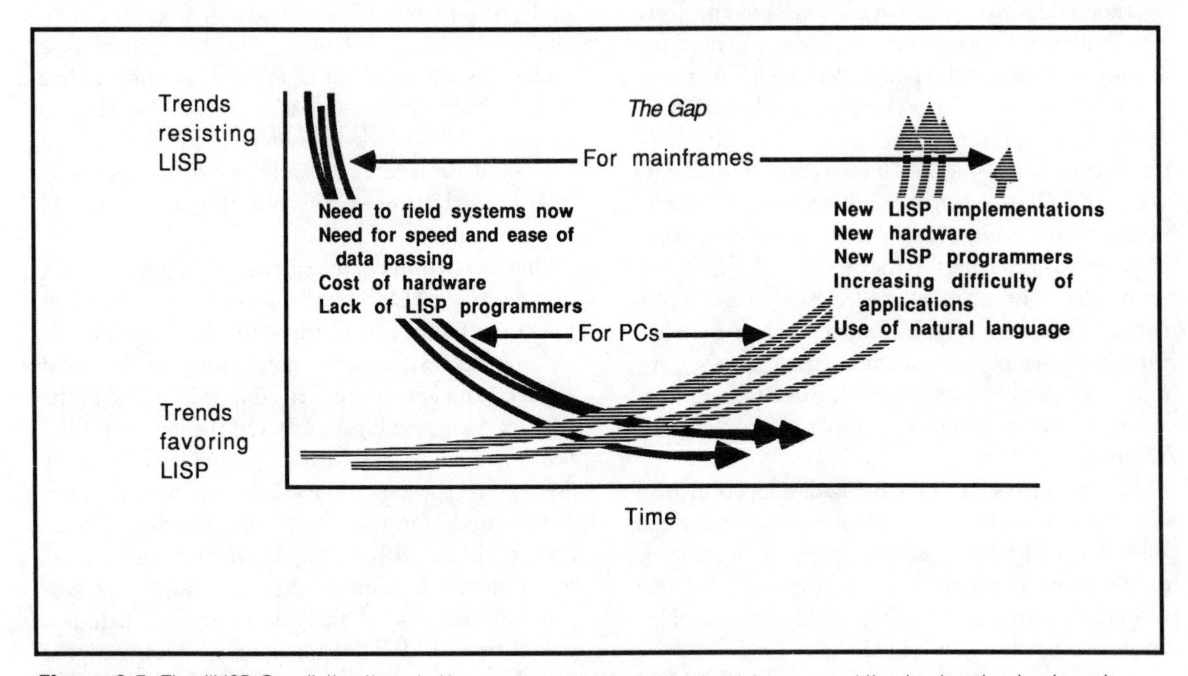

Figure 3.5 *The "LISP Gap": the time between the problems that exist now and the technological and social changes that will make LISP a viable commercial language.*

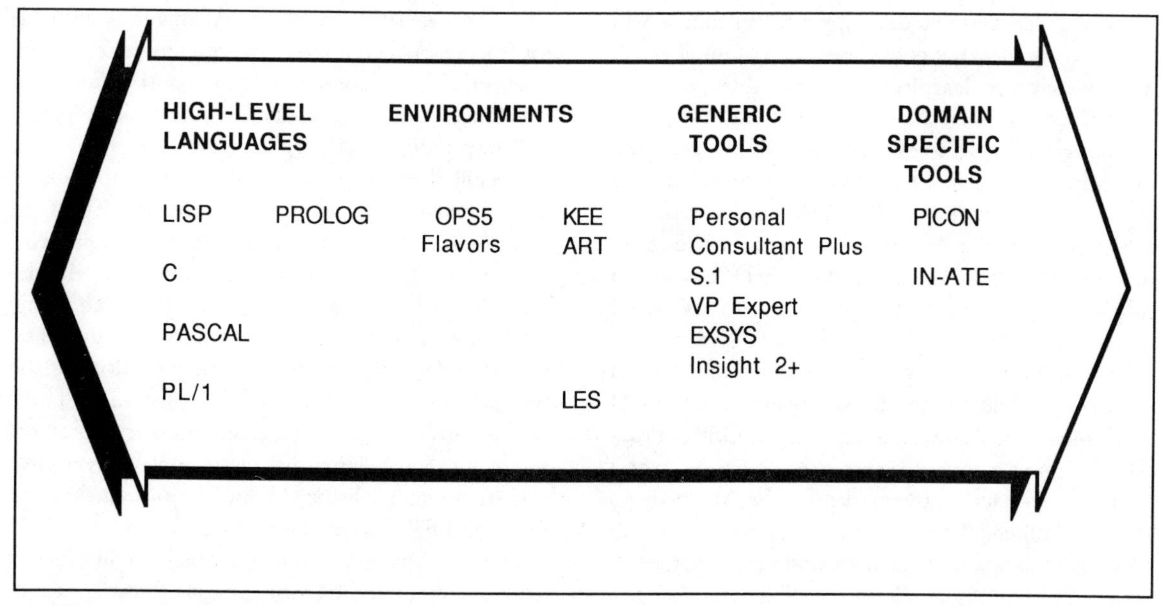

Figure 3.6 *The language-tool continuum.*

tional language for this purpose is C, followed by PASCAL. Some more sophisticated tools are being written in PL/1 and ADA.

THE LANGUAGE-TOOL CONTINUUM

The language-tool continuum (see Figure 3.6) is a simple way to classify the various AI languages and tools and their interrelated uses. As stated earlier, languages are more flexible than tools, but languages are more time-intensive to use to build an expert system. Only well-trained developers are able to build knowledge systems from scratch using AI languages like LISP or PROLOG.

On the other hand, a tool can be used only when the intended application matches the tool's capabilities. If the application matches, however, use of a tool means an application can be developed relatively quickly. Even nonprogrammers can use many of the tools to build small but useful expert systems.

Environments stand midway between languages and tools in terms of both flexibility and ease of use.

Figure 3.6 illustrates the language-tool continuum; including some better known software packages and languages. Flavors is an object-oriented environment written in LISP. PROLOG can be used as a language, but it has a number of features that make it particularly suited for developing expert systems applications. (Several versions of LISP contain a version of PROLOG, written in LISP, that is used for backward chaining inference problems.) OPS5 is a rule-based programming environment written in LISP. (OPS5 has also been written in other languages.) Environments are more specialized than languages, but they are more flexible than tools like Insight 2+, M.1, or Personal Consultant. Some of the larger tools, like KEE, ART, and Lockheed's LES, offer more flexibility than most other tools. Some would call these packages environments, but this text describes them as large hybrid tools. While it is true that they are very flexible, they also contain editing and user interface facilities for developing expert systems normally associated with tools rather than environments.

SUMMARY

At the moment, AI languages are being sold primarily to people in research and development departments and to colleges and universities. Many people in AI believe expert systems development techniques will prove so popular that conventional programmers will increasingly start learning and using AI languages to prototype or even develop knowledge systems. Although it is hard to evaluate this claim, clearly the investment in existing hardware and software (as well as conventionally trained programmers) will make the overall transition a slow process. Moreover, the adoption of ADA by the U.S. Department of Defense is also likely to stem any quick transition to using AI languages.

A transition, if it is to occur, will ultimately depend on the availability of new technologies to integrate AI and conventional languages and to make LISP or PROLOG a viable competitor with existing hardware and software. As a result, the market for the AI languages is very limited. They will continue to be used to develop tools and for limited application development. Then the resulting applications will be recoded in a conventional language like C. If there is a significant market for AI languages used by programmers to develop large applications for mini or mainframe computers, in all likelihood it will not occur until the early 1990s. In the meantime, AI languages will be sold to R&D groups, schools, and vendors who are prototyping tools and making enhancements to existing expert systems.

AI languages that operate on personal computers may actually develop faster than their larger counterparts because PC programmers have more flexibility. On the other hand, the current AI languages available for the personal computer environment lack the rich environment of programming aids and editors that have made AI languages popular with developers working on prototypes of large programs.

Overall, the commercial world continues to focus on such pragmatic issues as the compatibility of AI languages with existing languages and equipment. Moreover, this uphill battle faces many practical problems including retraining programmers, changing established ways of managing projects, recoding data, achieving desirable run speeds without overloading the hardware, and, as always, budget constraints. These and other factors have led many industry observers to suggest that AI languages may not play a very large role in commercializing AI and the overall development and fielding of expert systems.

The following six chapters discuss several types of expert system building tools, and, as you will see, different companies have adapted different marketing strategies when offering these tools. Some tools are written in conventional languages to run on standard computers, others are written in AI languages to run on AI specific hardware like LISP machines. Likewise, some tools are narrowly focused; others are designed to enable the user to develop systems appropriate to several different consultation paradigms. The knowledge engineering field is new and evolving very rapidly. The only safe prediction is that a wide variety of languages and tools will be used in the coming years.

4

An Overview of Expert System Building Tools

INTRODUCTION

The preceding chapter discussed programming languages and the language-tool continuum that describes the various programming approaches for developing expert systems. It also described how symbolic and object-oriented languages differ from conventional programming languages. This chapter introduces software programs called *expert system building tools*, or just *tools*. (They are also commonly called *shells*, especially in Europe.) The following discussion uses these terms interchangeably.

Most expert system building tools make a sharp distinction between the knowledge base and the inference engine. Moreover, you expect the inference engine to incorporate a number of utilities or interfaces that make developing an expert system much easier than it would be if you were to develop it in a programming language (see Figure 4.1).

As discussed, a language like PROLOG or an environment like OPS5 makes it relatively easy to develop an expert system. This is not to say they are tools. Tools make it easier still by providing various interface utilities. Thus, the discussion of tools does *not* include a discussion of environments like OPS5 or PROLOG. It does, on the other hand, include hybrid tools, which some call environments. Hybrid tools force the user to assemble a desired set of knowledge representation, inference, and control techniques from among several available within the tool. Unlike the true environments, however, the hybrid tools provide powerful editing and interface development facilities and thus are classified as tools. The continuum in Figure 4.2 indicates where we draw the line between tools and environments.

CATEGORIES OF EXPERT SYSTEMS TOOLS

Expert system building tools are classified in a number of different ways. If you focus on the overall knowledge representation techniques available in a tool, then you can divide the current crop of commercially available tools into five general types:

- Inductive tools.
- Simple rule-based tools.
- Structured rule-based tools.
- Hybrid tools.
- Domain specific tools.

Previous tool classifications included a category for logic-based tools. At that time several tools had been written in PROLOG and were closer to a logic programming environment than to a rule-based tool. Now, however, most logic-based tools have been improved to the point where the developer is not aware of the logic underlying the tool and is free simply to focus on developing rules. Hence, logic-based tools are incorporated under the preceding categories.

The tools are listed in an order and use names like "simple" and "structured." This should not suggest that

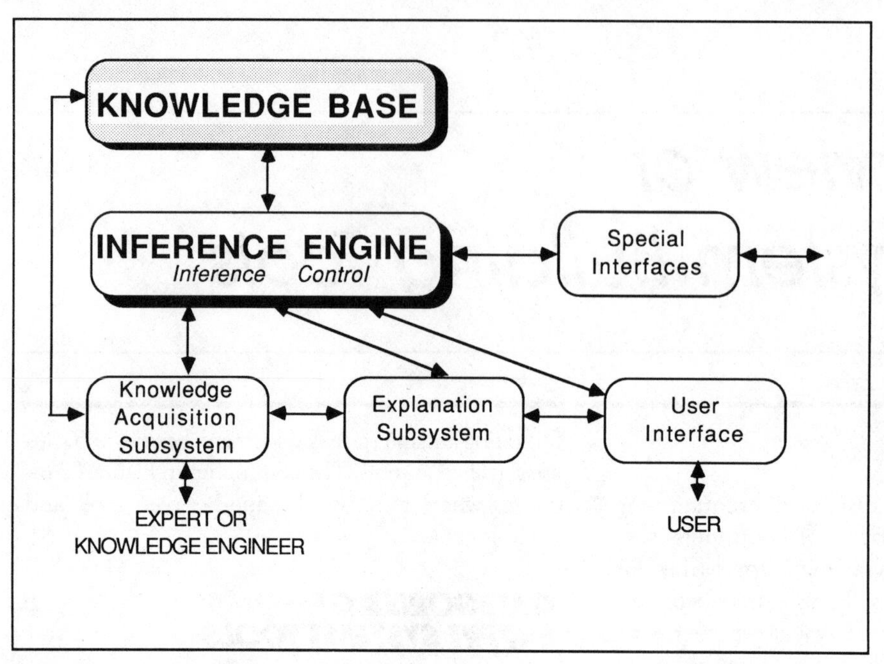

Figure 4.1 *The architecture of an expert system.*

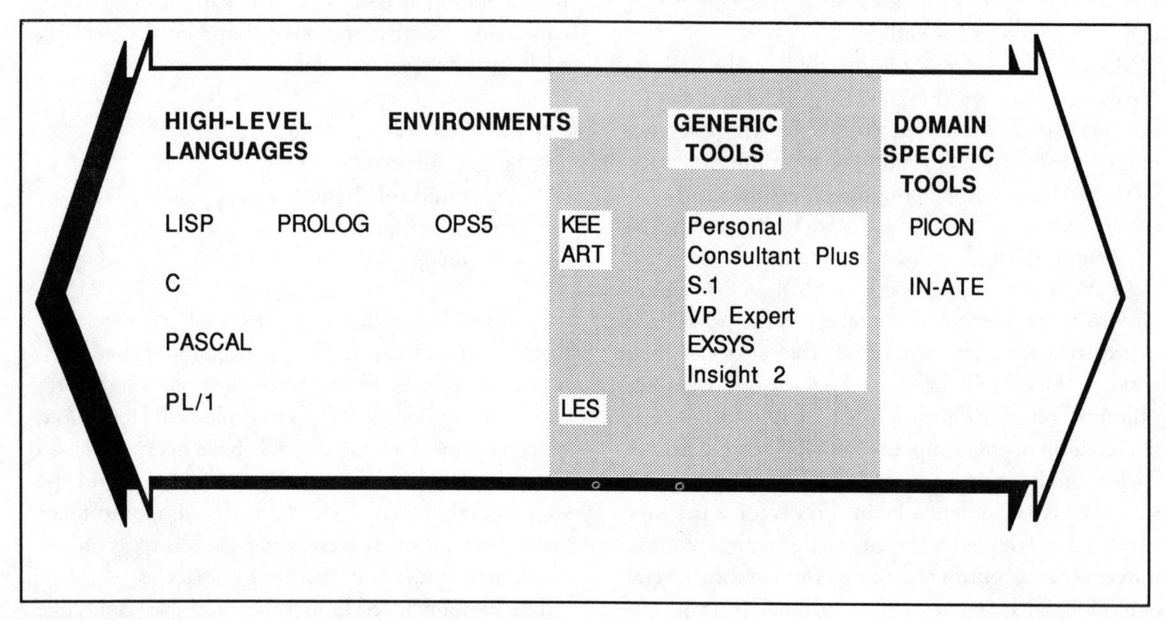

Figure 4.2 *The language-tool continuum. The following chapters will focus on tools that fall in the shaded section of the continuum.*

tools in any one group are better than those in another. Ultimately a tool should be judged by whether it helps you solve your problem, not by the techniques included in the tool. Some problems demand inductive tools, while others require structured rule-based tools. Still other problems require hybrid tools. It is frustrating to attempt a complex problem with a weak, inflexible tool, but it is equally foolish to attempt to master the complexities of a large tool to solve a problem you can quickly solve using a small one.

This chapter overviews the basic types of tools and some knowledge representation and interface issues you should consider in selecting a tool. The chapters that follow present a more comprehensive discussion of each type of tool.

Inductive Tools

Inductive tools generate rules from examples. These weak but friendly matrix-based tools come in two sizes: *large* inductive tools, which run on mainframes and PCs, and *small* inductive tools, which run only on personal computers. These tools are derived from experiments conducted in machine learning. They operate on minicomputers and personal computers. With these tools, a developer enters a large number of examples for the machine's information base. To make a recommendation, the tool uses an algorithm to convert the examples into a rule and to determine the order the system will follow when questioning the user. These tools, of which Expert-Ease, and TIMM (microcomputer version) are examples, are useful for simple tasks that rely on examples, but cannot be used to develop complex knowledge representations.

Simple Rule-Based Tools

Simple rule-based tools use if–then rules to represent knowledge. These tools can be run on personal computers and are most effective if you want to develop expert systems containing fewer than 500 rules. They are "simple" in contrast to "structured" rule systems. Simple rule-based tools lack context trees as well as some other editing features commonly available in structured rule-based tools. However, when the problems the system will work on are very unstructured, small rule systems can be quite equal to more sophisticated, expensive, structured tools.

Structured Rule-Based Tools

Structured rule-based tools tend to offer context trees, multiple instantiation, EMYCIN-like confidence factors, and more powerful editors. The larger rule-based tools tend to run on mainframes, VAX's, LISP machines, or UNIX workstations. Mid-size structured rule tools also tend to offer context trees, but they run on personal computers. These tools use if–then rules arranged into sets. These "rule sets" are like separate knowledge bases. One set of rules can inherit information acquired when other rule sets are examined. These systems are more desirable in cases where a large number of rules are involved, if the rules can be subdivided into sets.

Hybrid Tools

Hybrid tools represent the most complex expert systems development environments currently available. Until recently these tools were available only in LISP and ran only on LISP machines, VAX's, and UNIX workstations configured for LISP. Mid-size hybrid tools is a new category of tools that provide a number of knowledge representation paradigms and run on personal computers. Mid-size hybrid tools will expand rapidly as PC hardware improves and people find they can build and run large, multi-paradigm systems on PCs. These tools use object-oriented programming techniques to represent elements of each problem the system will work on as objects. An object, in turn, can contain facts, if–then rules, or pointers to other objects. These tools are much more complex to use, and they typically require a thorough understanding of LISP as well as a larger computer on which to run.

Hybrid tools are designed to build systems that contain 500 to several thousand rules and can include the features of several different paradigms. They usually facilitate the development of complex, graphically oriented user interfaces. They are very powerful; however, they are justified only when the target problems are complex enough to be worth the cost and effort of development.

Large hybrid tools lack the narrow focus of the tools previously mentioned. In other words, their designers have not created these tools to build a specific type of knowledge system. Instead, these tools have been developed to build other tools that, in turn, build a knowledge system. Presently most of these large hybrid tools should be considered research tools rather than practical tools to rapidly prototype an expert system. They are not ideally suited for a company initiating its first expert system. On the other hand, these tools are unquestionably the tools of the future. As companies learn more about knowledge engineering and gain experience in developing their own knowledge systems, these tools will offer the necessary capabilities needed to efficiently design and implement complex expert systems.

Domain Specific Tools

Domain specific tools are specifically designed to be used only to develop expert systems for a particular domain. A domain specific tool could incorporate any of the techniques listed above and, thus, could be classified among the previous categories. These tools, however, provide special development and user interfaces that make it possible to develop an expert system in a particular domain considerably faster than the tools listed above; therefore they have a special category. You can expect to see this category expand rapidly in coming years.

STRUCTURED RULE TOOLS VERSUS OBJECT-ORIENTED TOOLS

It would be much easier if all existing tools could be neatly placed in one or another category. In fact, classifying some of the more interesting tools is not that easy. Vendors are constantly adding new features and giving them new names. One confusing distinction is that between tools with significant object-oriented capabilities and those that are essentially structured rule-based systems.

A little history may help. The original EMYCIN tool represented facts as context–parameter–value triplets. When you created a knowledge base, you began by creating one or more contexts and then placed individual rules within one of the contexts. The contexts were related together to form a context tree. In general, context trees were like hierarchical organization charts, with each context related to one specific parent context, all ultimately related to a root context. Figure 4.3 shows a generic version of the context tree used in EMYCIN.

Teknowledge originally developed a tool that was a very slight modification of EMYCIN (i.e., KS300) and used the EMYCIN terminology. Later, when they modified their original tool to create S.1, they changed their vocabulary and referred to facts as object–attribute–value triplets and started calling context trees object trees. It was an unfortunate move since it confused the meaning of "object," as derived from context, with the use of object in frame or object-oriented systems like KEE.

When Texas Instruments first developed their EMYCIN clone (the original Personal Consultant), they used the context–parameter–value terminology of EMYCIN. In their subsequent version, Personal Consultant Plus, however, they started referring to facts as frame–parameter–value triplets and introduced frame trees in place of context trees.

The basic ideas behind the frame systems employed by KEE and Knowledge Craft are derived from *semantic nets*. The fundamental concept is that a number of objects can be related in any of a wide variety of ways. In other words, semantic nets are not necessarily hierarchical, while EMYCIN's context trees are. Mathematically speaking, context trees are "tree structures," while object-oriented systems are "lattice structures." Like context trees, object-oriented systems derive (instantiate) more complex (or specific) objects from root objects (usually called classes). But object-oriented systems usually result in a complex network of objects, each related to other objects in a wide variety of ways. More important, unlike EMYCIN's con-

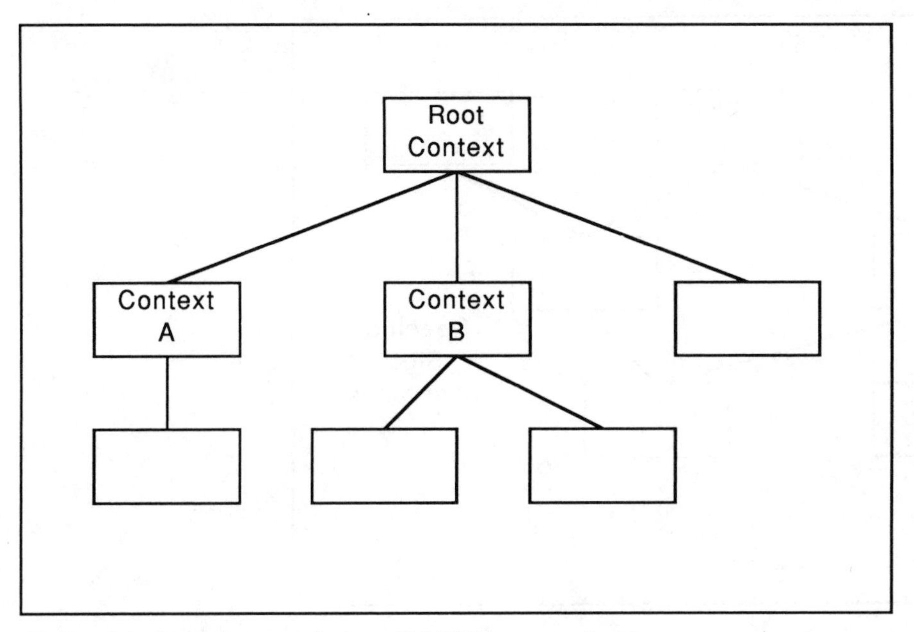

Figure 4.3 *Generic model of an EMYCIN-type context tree.*

texts, objects or frames are made up of slots that can contain facts, pointers to other objects, or rules. In object-oriented systems, slots can usually inherit information from other objects or other slots in a wide variety of ways. In other words, the inheritance relationships in object-oriented systems are usually much more complex (see Figure 4.4).

Considered from a different perspective, when you build a rule-based system, you focus on the rules an expert uses to solve problems. In other words, you focus on procedures. When you develop an expert system in a structured rule system, you think about the contexts into which you will group the rules, but your focus is still primarily rules and how sets of rules will be used.

When you build an object-oriented system in a tool like KEE, you focus on describing the objects in the expert's world, the components that make up those objects, and the relationships that exist among the various objects and their components. Rules are often a very secondary consideration. You initially focus on describing objects and their relationships, not rules and procedures.

As noted, a structured rule tool is neither better nor worse than an object-oriented tool. They are designed to help developers accomplish different tasks. A developer uses a structured rule tool to develop a system in which the expert's knowledge can be captured in rules and can be subdivided into subsets of rules (contexts). An object-oriented tool is used to capture expert knowledge that is primarily descriptive rather than rule based.

If the world were simply divided between structured rule-based tools like EMYCIN and object-oriented tools like Knowledge Craft and KEE, it would all be simple. In fact, of course, as vendors have added features to their tools, they have blurred this simple distinction.

Some tools are clearly structured rule tools. AION and E.S. Environment/VM are good examples. And some tools, like GOLDWORKS, KEE, and Knowledge Craft, are clearly based on an object-oriented approach.

A third group of tools began life as either simple rule tools or structured rule tools and have added some object-oriented features. Good examples are KS300,

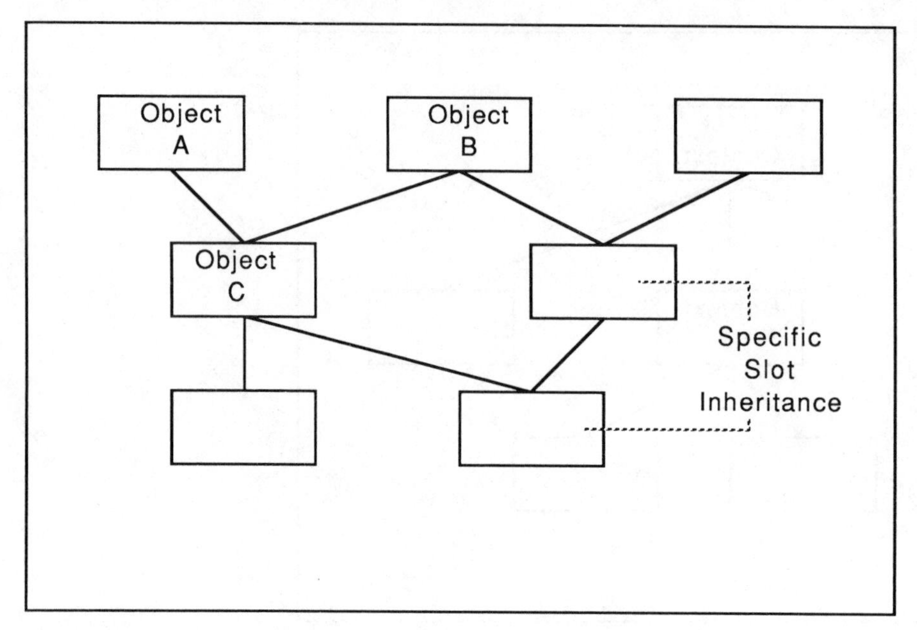

Figure 4.4 *An object network.*

Personal Consultant, and KES. These tools have context trees with some additional modifications, like being able to put facts into contexts or incorporate demons (a forward-chaining rule that fires during any consulation in which its If-clause is validated). In general, when you use one of these tools, you begin by thinking in terms of rules. Moreover, though you can get some additional flexibility, the contexts or "objects," "frames," or "classes" provided by these tools tend to be related hierarchically. It is difficult or even impossible to arrange for facts included in the contexts of these tools to inherit information from other facts included in other contexts.

For the present, continue to think of the larger, more sophisticated rule-based tools as structured rule tools and ignore the fact that their vendors talk as if they were actually object-oriented tools. They can be used to do a kind of object-oriented programming (in the hands of a sufficiently skilled programmer, any LISP-based tool can be made to do all manner of strange and wonderful things), but it's more confusing to emphasize this fact than to de-emphasize it. See Figure 4.5 for an illustration of how rules, context trees, and object-oriented systems relate.

SMALL, MID-SIZE, AND LARGE RULE-BASED TOOLS

When you focus on the expert systems tool marketplace, rather than on the techniques incorporated in particular tools, a slightly different picture emerges. Some tools run on personal computers, provide limited support, and sell for between $95 and $500. Most are simple rule-based tools.

Other rule-based tools run on either large personal computers (ATs with lots of memory) or on workstations, provide more elaborate support, and sell for from $2,000 to $6,000. Some are simple rule-based tools, but most are structured rule tools.

Still other rule-based tools run on workstations, LISP

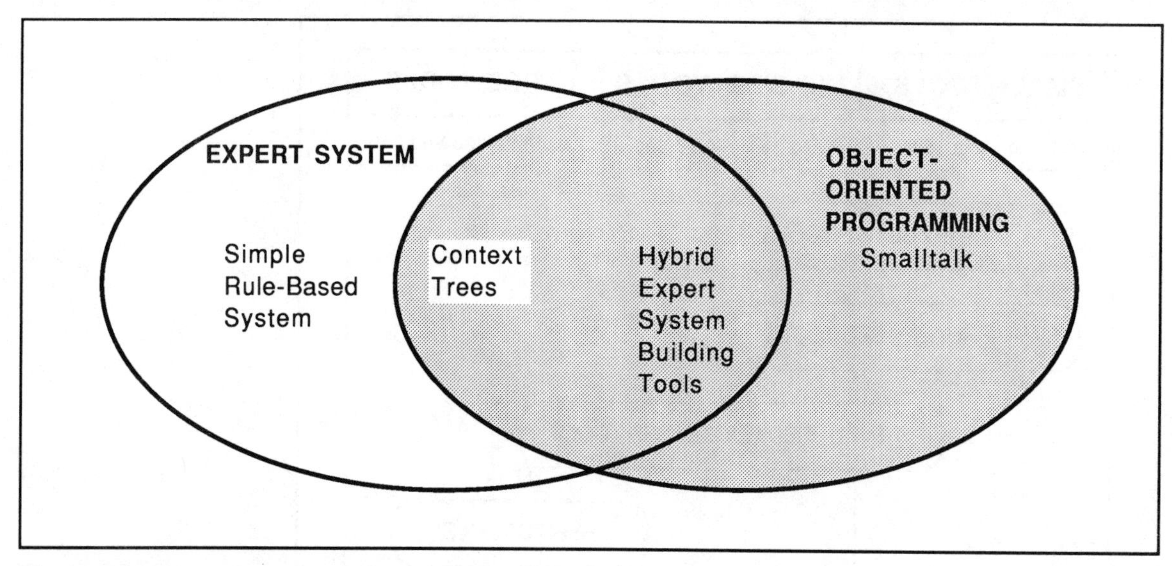

Figure 4.5 *Rules, context trees, and object-oriented systems.*

machines, or mainframes, provide elaborate support, and sell for from $7,000 to $60,000. These tools are called large rule-based tools. (See Figure 4.6.) In the chapters that follow, tools are divided according to their market positioning rather than the techniques they incorporate.

CHOOSING THE RIGHT TOOL FOR THE JOB

Human experts use many different approaches to solve problems, and the knowledge they use can be represented in many different ways. Likewise, there are different approaches to reasoning. Cognitive psychologists, AI researchers, and knowledge engineers have barely started to identify and formalize the problem-solving strategies and methods people routinely use in everyday activities. Table 4.1 lists some better-known problem-solving strategies human experts commonly use.

Briefly, the major types of human knowledge represented by the current generation of expert system building tools include:

- *Procedures.* Conventional programs are very effective at handling procedures. Many small knowledge systems have been developed to automate procedural processes simply because the people who developed the system were not programmers and could use the expert systems tool to develop an application they needed.
- *Diagnostic.* Diagnostic systems analyze data and recommend some action. To develop such a system, you must know (or have an expert who knows) what recommendations are possible. You must also identify the observations that would allow your system to choose between one recommendation and another. Most existing expert systems are diagnostic systems.
- *Monitoring.* Several small diagnostic systems have been developed and used to monitor some activity. For example, several systems are used to monitor hospital patients. These systems operate by doing

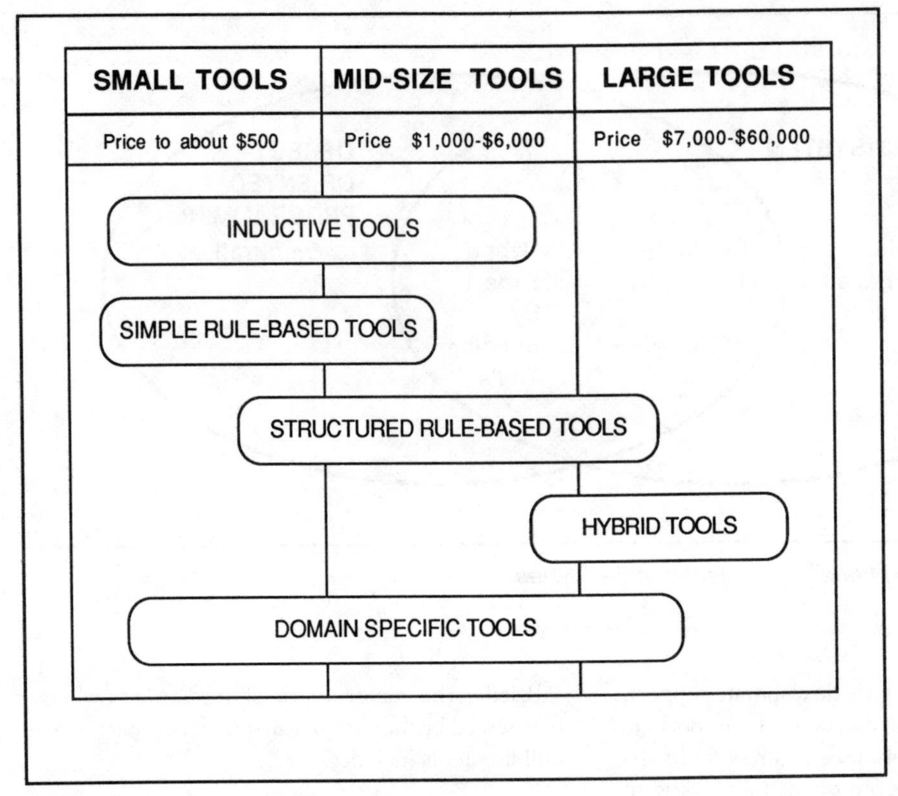

Figure 4.6 *Tool size versus tool technology.*

a diagnosis, determining the patient is normal, and then immediately beginning another diagnosis. In effect, the system cycles until it runs a diagnosis that indicates something is wrong, then it sounds an alarm.

- *Configuration/Design.* Configuration systems use initial data to identify an acceptable way to fit some set of components together. The primary data stored in such systems are the constraints regarding components that cannot go together and dependencies about components that must always occur together.
- *Scheduling.* Scheduling systems determine the path some product must pass through to reach some goal. In factory operations, scheduling systems quickly rearrange sequences of operations to accommodate changes in the availability of resources, machines, and so on.
- *Planning.* Planning systems are concerned with designing and scheduling the development of some product or process. A planning system must know about legal combinations and constraints on what can be done.

Generally, diagnostic systems are easy to build, design systems are of intermediate difficulty, and planning and scheduling systems are difficult. As you move from simpler to harder problems, specific rules become less important, and descriptive information about structures and relationships between objects become more important.

To capture human expertise in computerized form, the underlying reasoning strategy must be identified. The reasoning strategies described above are fairly well understood, but many other common forms of human reasoning (e.g., reasoning from analogies) are not well understood. At the moment, the best commercial strategy is to focus on problems that involve reasoning processes already well understood.

It should also be emphasized that software techniques and the associated problems do not match one-to-one; one programmer might approach a diagnostic problem using a tool based on backward chaining while another knowledge engineer, faced with the same problem, might choose a tool that uses forward chaining. As you move from the simpler problems to the more difficult problems, however, most knowledge engineers move from rule-based tools to the more powerful object-oriented tools that allow more flexibility in designing both the knowledge base and the inference strategy their system will use.

When you choose a tool, be sure the specific tool is truly appropriate for the problem. This can be difficult because most knowledge engineers don't understand how to handle most problems human experts routinely solve. In addition, many types of expert behavior cannot be easily encoded and captured using existing tools. As a result, managers and executives wishing to utilize knowledge engineering techniques have a choice—they can focus on well-understood problems and ignore those for which no tools are currently available, or they can develop a knowledge engineering team and try to build a system by creating a unique set of knowledge representation, inference, and control techniques in some general-purpose AI language or environment such as PROLOG or OPS5. Most companies facing the choice have decided to focus on solving problems where tools are already established. Given the large number of existing problems and opportunities, this is certainly a sound management strategy. Companies that *have* decided to start from scratch have usually organized the problem-solving team to attack an already familiar, well-understood problem.

EVALUATING A TOOL

The key to successful use of today's available expert systems tools is to use the tools only for appropriate

Table 4.1 *Generic types of problem solving knowledge.*

Well Definied (Algorithmic) ↑	Type	Knowledge Representation Schema	Tool Size
easily could be done in conventional language	PROCEDURES	Rules	Small
	DIAGNOSTIC	Rules	Small/Mid-size
	MONITORING	Rules	Small/Mid-size
structure most important	CONFIGURATION/ DESIGN	Rules/Hybrid	Mid-size/large
	SCHEDULING	Hybrid	Large
relationship most important	PLANNING	Hybrid	Large
↓ Vague (Heuristic)			

problems, those narrowly defined tasks that involve problem diagnosis and problem resolution. Some specific problem characteristics suitable for various tools are fully described in the following pages.

When evaluating a tool, consider the following general types of features and characteristics:

1. Knowledge representation, inference, and control, or power and flexibility (which is really a description of the type of problem [knowledge] the tool can handle).
2. Developer interface.
3. User interface.

Tool: ______________________ Version: __________ Contact: ______________________ Date: __________	
Power and Flexibility of Knowledge Representation and Inference and Control Techniques.	
Developer Interface: Ease of use and power of editing utilities.	
User Interface: Ease and flexibility of user interface development utilities.	
System Interface: Ability of tool to send and obtain data from other programs and data bases. Hardware the tool runs on.	
Training and Support: Documentation, courses, consulting availability, and vendor experience with particular domains and hardware.	
Runtime speed.	
Cost: Initial, multiple copies, runtime copies, training, support, and updates.	

Figure 4.7 *Checklist for evaluating an expert system building tool.*

4. System interface (including runtime speed).
5. Training and support.
6. Cost.

The worksheet reproduced in Figure 4.7 is helpful for looking at a new tool. Consider each characteristic in turn.

Knowledge Representation, Inference, and Control

The first classification presented above divided tools according to the type of knowledge representation they facilitated. Once you examine a problem and determine that the expert or the task involves a particular type of knowledge, be sure you use a tool that easily allows you to encode such knowledge. Hence, in evaluating a tool, be sure you understand exactly what types of knowledge are best represented in the tool.

An overview of knowledge representation. Figure 4.1 (on page 46) pictures the knowledge base as one box and the inference engine as a separate box with a number of interfaces attached to it. Figure 4.8 represents the inference engine as a shaded box and

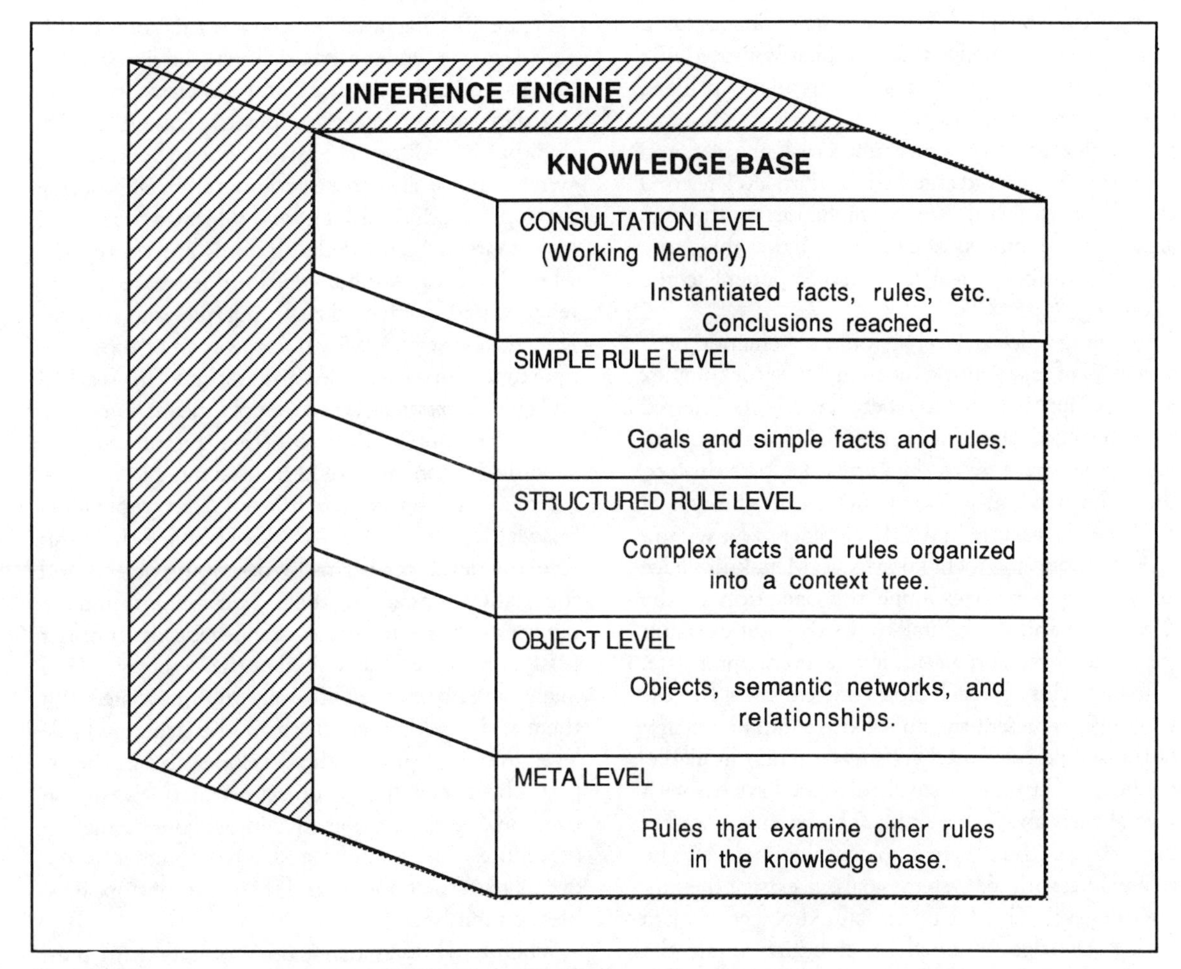

Figure 4.8 *An inference engine and a knowledge base showing all the types of knowledge that might be present in a knowledge base during a consultation.*

the knowledge base in front of it. Ideally, the inference and control techniques exist independent of the knowledge in the knowledge base and simply manipulate the knowledge during development or during a consultation according to criteria established by the tool.

The knowledge base can be thought of as a multilayered space, each level representing a particular type of knowledge.

The top level represents knowledge created and used during a consultation. In other words, the consultation level is, in effect, working memory.

Simple facts (attribute–value) and rules are represented on the second level, referred to as the simple rule level. Simple rule-based systems are best used to represent knowledge that is primarily procedural. The expert thinks in terms of if–then rules which are, in effect, procedural steps.

Complex facts (context–attribute–value), rules, and context trees are represented on the third level, referred to as the structure rule level to emphasize that the rules are structured into sets or contexts and that these context trees introduce a descriptive component to the knowledge base.

At the next lower level are objects, semantic nets, and ways of representing the many different complex relationships that can exist between objects, referred to as the object level. Like contexts, objects introduce descriptive structure to the knowledge base. In fact, they introduce a significant increase in the role of descriptive structure in the development of a system.

At the bottom is meta-knowledge. Meta-knowledge allows a system to examine the operation of the descriptive and procedural knowledge that exists on the higher levels and modify it whenever appropriate.

To make this approach more concrete, consider how you might represent the knowledge contained in any of the simple rule-based systems currently available. Figure 4.9 illustrates a small rule-based system with several rules about some task. The system is not being used and, thus, there is no consultation level. The rules, along with the system's goals, all exist at the simple rule level. There is no structured object or meta level knowledge. When the user begins to use the system, the consultation level (or working memory) is created, and all the facts developed during the consultation are stored at that level. If the tool were a backward chaining system, the inference and control portion of the tool would employ *modus ponens* (an elementary logical principle) and backward chaining to locate rules that could satisfy the goals stored in the knowledge base. Some rules would lead to other rules, but eventually questions (which might also be stored in the knowledge base) would be asked, and facts would be established. As appropriate, the questions and facts would be instantiated at the consultation level. The facts would remain at the consultation level, stored in working memory (cached) as long as the consultation was in progress.

Figure 4.10 diagrams a structured rule tool. In this case, facts are represented as context–attribute–value triplets and then the facts and associated rules are stored in various contexts (or subsets). This type of subdivision introduces efficiencies into the resulting systems, but it also creates additional hassles during development, since each fact and rule must be assigned to a context. Structured rule tools are worthwhile when a lot of easily subdivided knowledge is to be represented in the system. Structuring rules into contexts also creates the possibility that rules can be used multiple times during a single consultation. This is called *multiple instantiation*, which simply means some rule in a higher context determines that the rules in some subordinate context should be used more than once.

Now consider a hybrid tool that represents knowledge in terms of objects. (See Figure 4.11.) In this case, the developer begins by describing objects and the relationships among them. These objects and the network of relationships so established exist at object level. Some objects described at the descriptive level might have object–attribute–value rules associated with them and would, in effect, create the structured rule level. Initially, however, the developer and/or the expert who is creating an object-oriented system can focus on describing a domain without considering any procedures. Rules can be added to objects after the overall pattern of objects and their relationships have been established.

When a hybrid system is used, objects defined on the descriptive level are instantiated on the consulta-

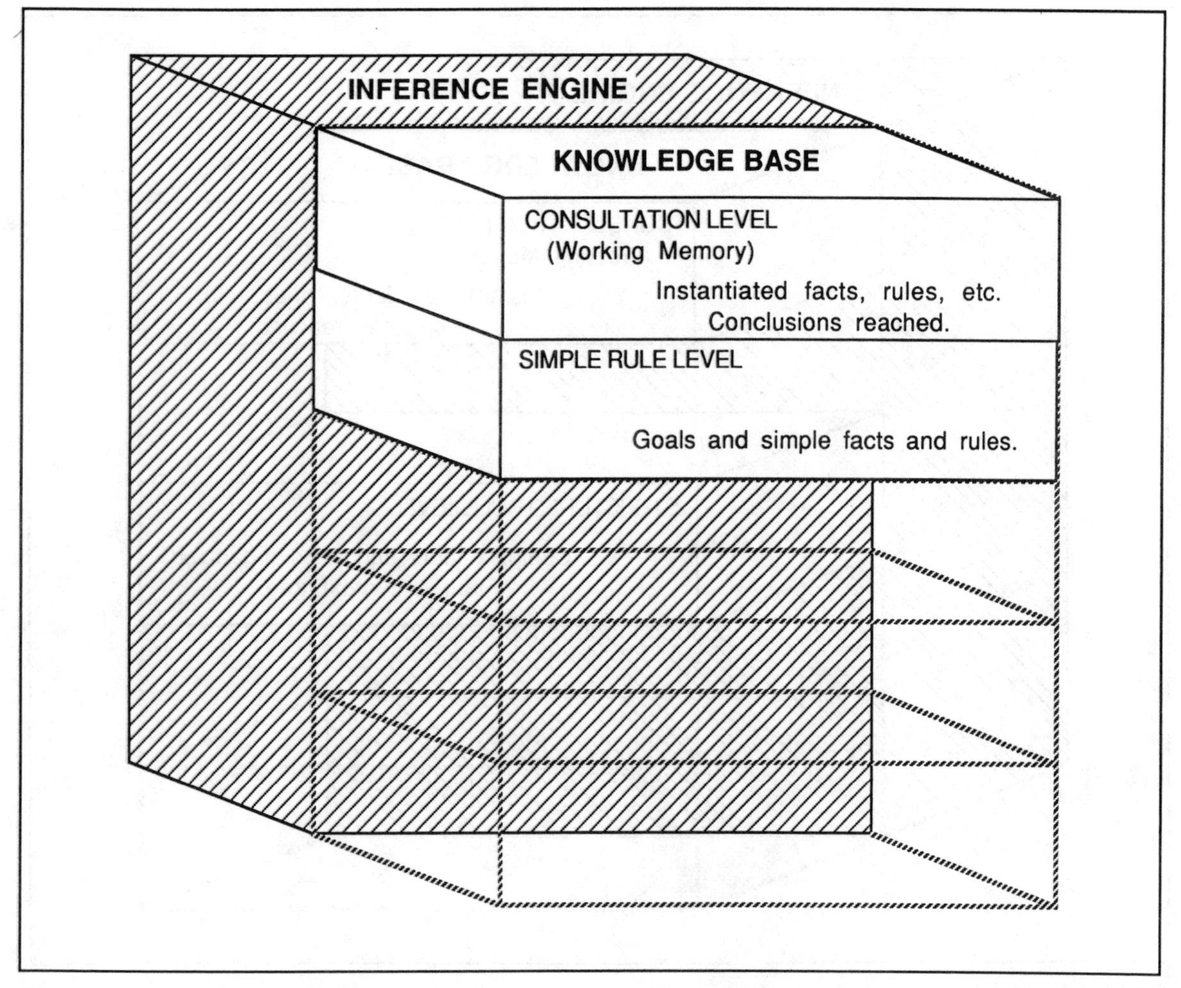

Figure 4.9 *An inference engine and a knowledge base showing the types of knowledge included in a simple rule system during a consultation.*

tion level (e.g., copies of "static objects" are created in working memory at the consultation level which contain the specific data collected during the consultation). As each instance of an object is created, information about that object is stored within the object. That information, combined with information the object can inherit from parent objects and the rules contained within those objects, will be activated to infer additional information. A very important feature of such an approach is that the same static object can be instantiated over and over on the consultation level, each time data about a new instance of the object are encountered (i.e., multiple instantiation). This allows you to "reuse" facts and rules to consider alternative versions of the same object.

Semantic nets can also be represented on the object level, being, essentially, just a more fine-grained, flexible form of an object/relationship network.

In a strong sense, contexts are like objects. Conceptually, to develop a structured rule system you begin by determining the contexts in the domain. Most structured rule systems have from 2 to 20 contexts.

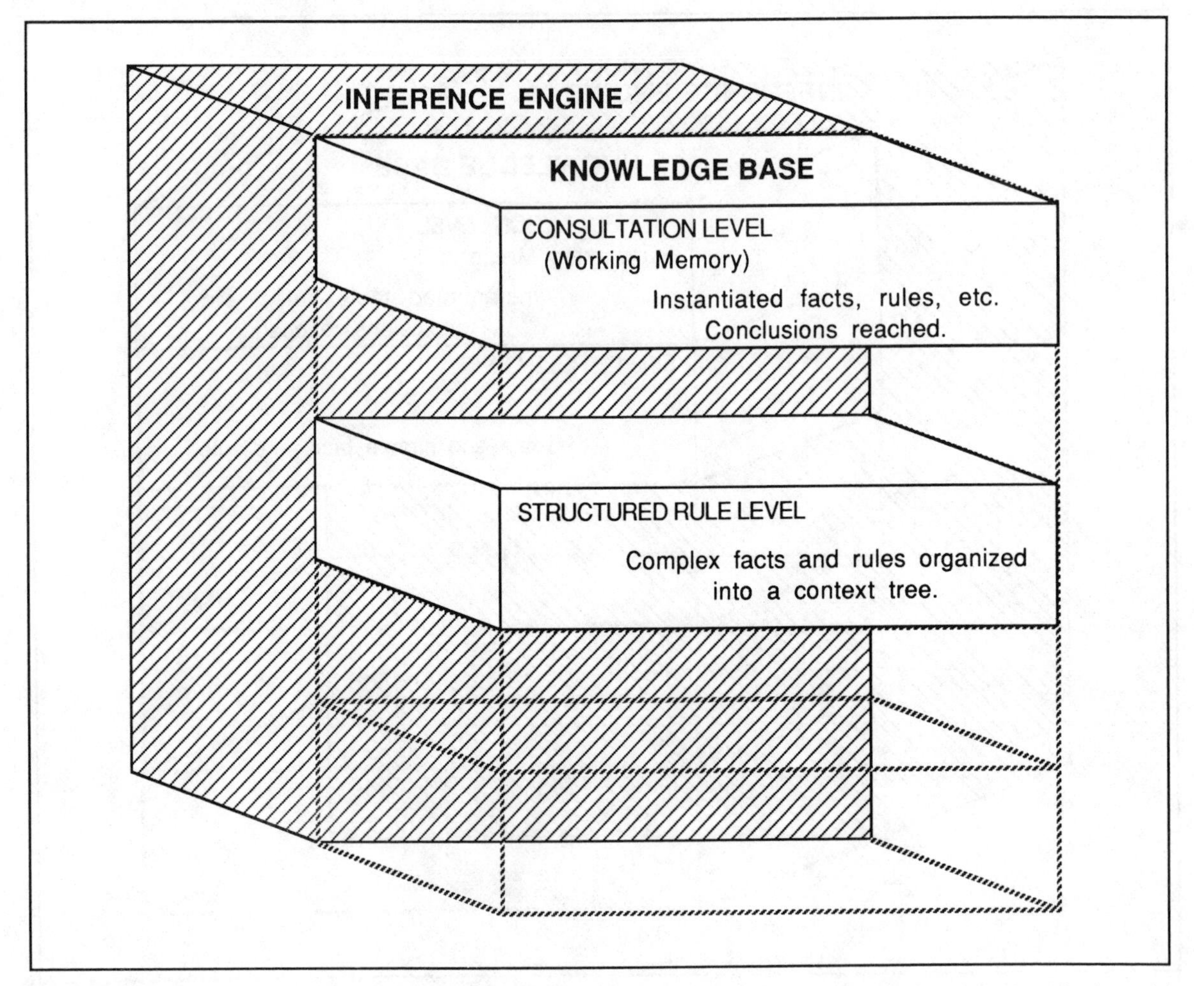

Figure 4.10 *An inference engine and a knowledge base showing all the types of knowledge that would be included in a structured rule system during a consultation.*

Thus, although contexts are important, they are really just preparation for focusing on rules. When using a true object-oriented system, you can easily have hundreds of objects and many complex relationships. Thus, while context trees are a step in the direction of object-oriented programming, they nonetheless seem closer to a procedural approach than a descriptive approach (see Figure 4.5 on page 51).

Another concept encountered in hybrid tools is multiple worlds or viewpoints. A *viewpoint* is a multiple instantiation of all or part of a context tree or a set of objects and their relationships. You use multiple worlds to consider two or more possibilities simultaneously. That is, you reach a junction, and rather than choosing between alternatives, you answer the question in two or more ways. The information collected to that point is kept in common for two or more alternative sets of subsequent objects, each instantiated independently. In other words, you say both yes and no and then duplicate the subsequent objects so you can explore the consequences of the two alternative answers. This is just what human experts do when they can't decide between two possibilities and proceed to explore both alternatives equally (they reserve judgment). Multiple worlds or viewpoints exist at the consultation level, as instantiations of portions of a context tree or set of objects in the same sense that facts are instantiated from rules during a consultation (see Figure 4.12).

The lowest level of the model provides for meta-objects and rules, things that look at the activities on the higher levels and then modify the knowledge base itself. Some structured rule tools and all hybrid tools provide some kind of meta-knowledge representation.

This model of knowledge representation has limitations but it makes it easier to understand the relationship between networks of objects and relationships and multiple worlds. It also focuses attention on the important difference between tools, no matter what specific features they claim, that essentially focus the efforts of the expert and the developer on rules and other procedural information and those that free the developer to focus on the objects and relationships that define the expert's domain.

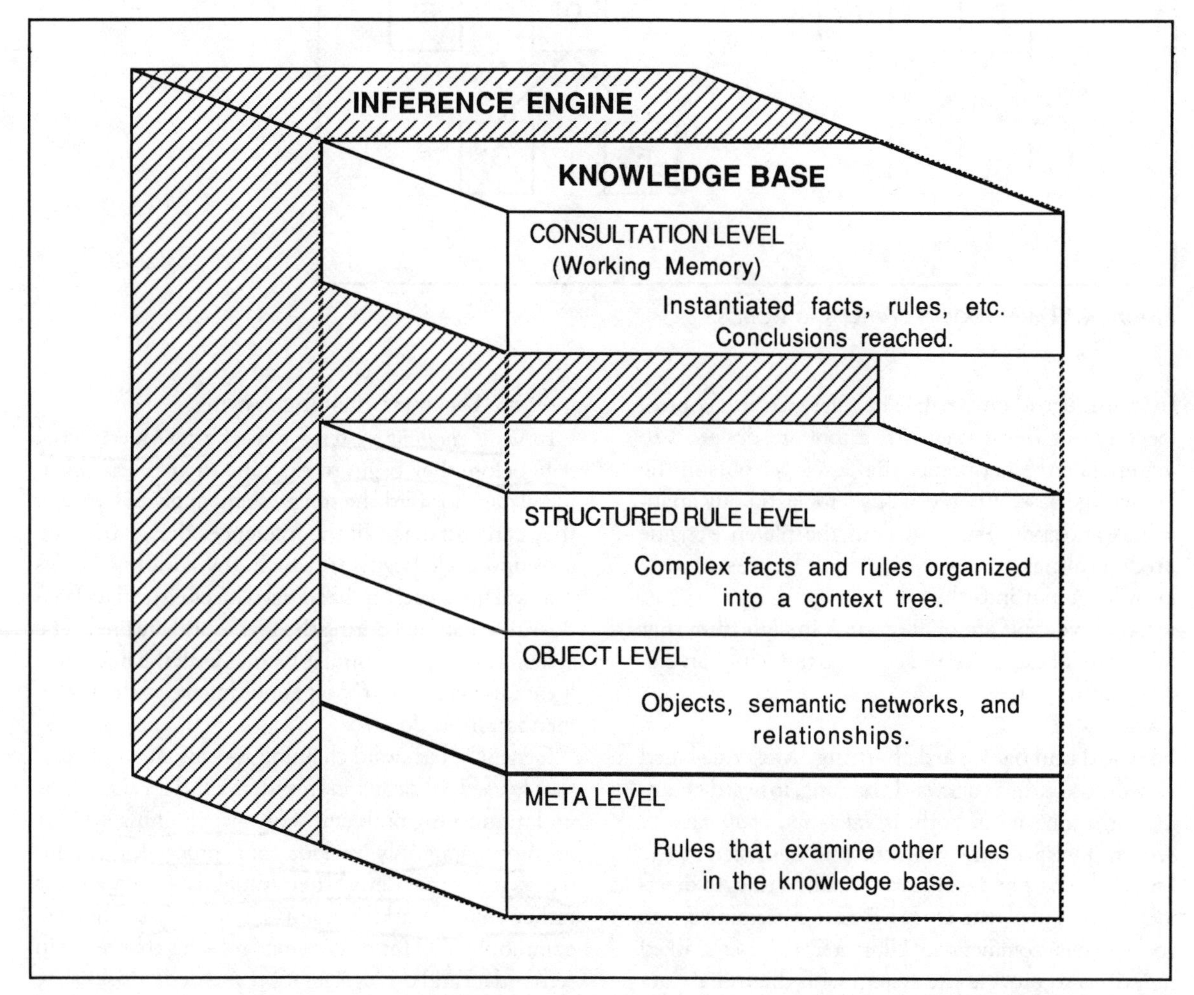

Figure 4.11 *An inference engine and a knowledge base showing all the types of knowledge that would be present in a hybrid system during a consultation.*

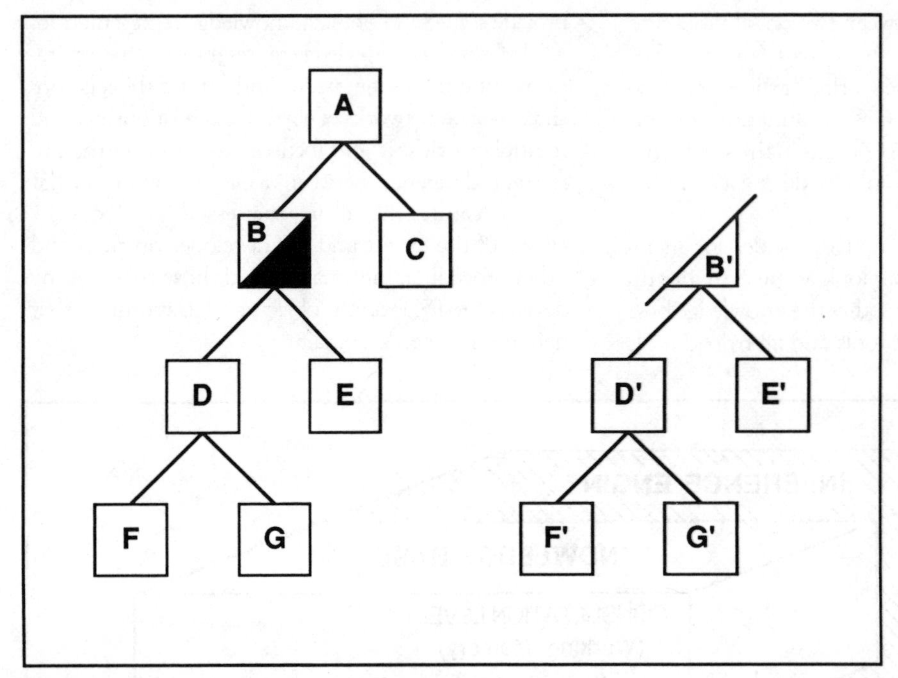

Figure 4.12 Viewpoints or multiple worlds.

Inference and control. The inference and control mechanisms that come with a tool are designed to manipulate the knowledge the developer puts in the knowledge base. When you buy a tool, you buy an inference and control strategy. Thus, the inference engine predetermines the way you must represent any knowledge put into the system.

Inductive tools are built around an algorithm that takes a set of examples and converts them into an efficient decision tree.

Forward and backward chaining. Most rule-based systems use either backward chaining, forward chaining, or a mixture of both. In *backward chaining*, the system starts with the goals the user has listed in the knowledge base and works backward via rules to determine what initial data are required to determine if that goal can be recommended. Ultimately the user is asked questions to provide the system with the initial data it needs to qualify or disqualify a particular recommendation. Most small and mid-size expert system building tools are backward chaining systems.

Forward chaining systems must be provided initial data before they begin to examine their rules. Given initial data, forward chaining systems apply all the rules they can and make all the inferences they can. Then a second cycle begins in which any additional rules that will fire based on the initial data plus the data from the rules that fired during the first round are fired. The system keeps cycling until it has made all the inferences it can. If it can infer that it should make some recommendation, it does so.

Generally, backward chaining systems are most commonly used in consultation systems and for diagnostic and monitoring problems. Forward chaining systems are most commonly used for signal processing systems (i.e., systems that derive their initial data from sensors rather than by asking questions to users). They are commonly used for diagnosing problems that result in sensor data and on configuration and design tasks. The hybrid tools are used for most planning and scheduling problems. All provide the developer with the option of using either forward or backward chaining or mixing the two strategies together. When building small to mid-size expert systems, inference and controls can be accepted as a given—you choose your tool and you take the strategy you get. As you build larger systems, however, a number of complex control issues arise that affect the efficiency and ultimately the processing speed of the system.

Certainty factors. Certainty factors are "probability-like" numbers attached to facts and rules that indicate either the certainty the expert has in a rule or the user has in a fact. A system that uses certainty factors can make several recommendations and indicate its unique confidence in each recommendation. In some cases the system may indicate evidence both for and against a decision and then add weights to the conflicting recommendations. Not all problems require "probabilistic" knowledge, but many do. Sometimes algorithms must be used in the system to accumulate all the evidence for and against each fact or rule and then attach a final confidence to each recommendation offered.

Inheritance. If you think of chaining as the inference strategy that allows a system to determine new facts from the initial data, then inheritance is the inference strategy used by object-oriented systems. A child object inherits facts from its parent object(s). New facts about an object are established by determining the relationship between that object and other objects, and inheriting any usable facts. There are many different approaches to inheritance to accommodate different needs (See Figure 4.13).

Developer Interface

The *developer interface* refers to the capabilities the tool provides for the initial development and subsequent modification of the knowledge base. Development facilities are crucial to the successful development and implementation of any expert system. Important development facilities include the following.

Knowledge base creation. All types of tools provide some capabilities for creating and storing knowledge bases. Some tools provide internal utilities for writing and editing a knowledge base. Many tools even allow a developer to create a knowledge base using a conventional word processor and then simply load this word processor file into the tool when the knowledge base is required. In a case like this, however, the developer must have access to a word processing program. But it also means the developer is already familiar with the editing commands and, in turn, can create and edit large sets of rules rapidly.

Explanations (used in developing a system). Most tools allow a developer to include information that can be obtained by the user if the user asks for a more elaborate explanation. For example, if a user is queried by the system to state whether a client is "nonexempt," and the user doesn't understand the term, it is easy for the user to query the system for an explanation of the term in question. Most tools facilitate explanation expansion, and many problems require this feature if they are to be effectively used. In these cases, everything else being equal, developers will want to use a tool that makes it quick and easy to attach explanations to facts and rules.

How and why explanations. If a system developer or end user is running a system and is asked a question, the developer or user might want to ask "why" the question was asked. On most systems this can be done simply by pressing a pre-assigned function key. The system then presents the question that generated the rule. The more sophisticated systems allow users to ask why over and over until they have traced the system's entire line of reasoning. Similarly, a "how" probe asks the system how it reached a particular conclusion. For example, you might encounter a question you didn't expect and ask why the system asked you that question. In turn, the system might say it was using a rule that said:

```
If     pressure = normal
and    humidity = rising
Then   weather change = possible.
```

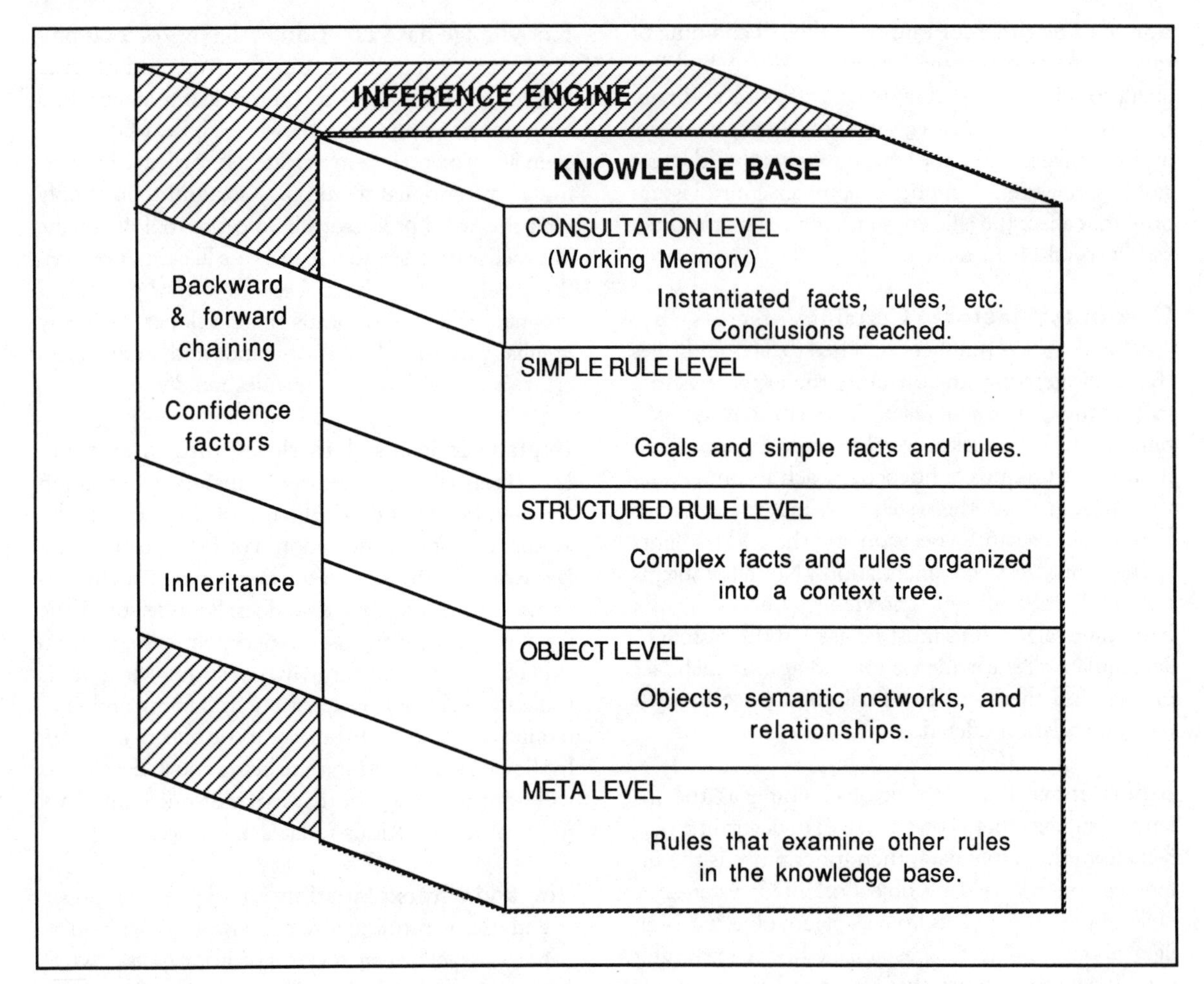

Figure 4.13 *Inference strategies associated with different types of knowledge.*

As soon as you see the rule, you understand why the system asked you about humidity, but since you never told the system the pressure was normal, you wonder how it inferred that from other data you gave it, so you now ask "how" it determined that pressure is normal. Such explanation capabilities can be very useful to users. They are especially useful, however, to system developers when they are trying to debug a large knowledge base.

Inference tracing. *Inference tracing* refers to a detailed list of the inferences a system has provided during a consultation. Developers frequently use this capability when creating knowledge bases. This can be a very important attribute to a system from the developer's point of view.

Locating specific attributes. Imagine you have developed a small knowledge system containing information about auto parts, and now one part is to be replaced by another. You need to find every fact and rule in the knowledge base that refers to the former part and replace the outdated part information with the name and characteristics of the new part. A

Specific Attribute Editor lets you identify every reference to any particular attribute (e.g., the old part) contained in the knowledge base. Obviously, if you have the knowledge base stored using a conventional word processing program, you can perform this task by simply using the SEARCH/REPLACE command. Some of the more sophisticated programs even allow you to perform these functions on-line.

On-line knowledge base editor. A knowledge base editor allows a developer to quickly examine and change items contained in the knowledge base. Some tools provide for this even when the knowledge base was created via an external word processing system. Others that use compiled knowledge bases do not allow this type of on-line editing, and the developer is usually forced to return to the word processor program to change a particular knowledge base entry.

Cases saved. The primary technique used in evaluating and improving most expert systems is simply to run well-known cases until the system can consistently and correctly solve them. Thus, time is saved if the developer can store a library of cases and automatically re-enter these cases after making modifications in the knowledge base. Some tools provide the utilities for storing and quickly re-entering cases.

Screen format utilities. To different degrees, just about all tools enable a developer to create a screen the end user will interact with. Some tools also make it easy for developers to create good interfaces and to provide methods for displaying titles or copyright information.

User Interface

When considering the nature of a problem to be solved by an expert system, you should also consider how the end user will need to interact with the resulting system. Today's tools provide different types of user interfaces, including features outlined in the following paragraphs.

Line/menu screen. Some tools are designed to interact with users via menus, others prompt the user for line entries. While line entry can be used in some cases, the increased friendliness and speed of menu-oriented tools make them desirable in cases where the system will be built or used by individuals who are not very familiar with either computers or with the subject of the problem.

Initial pruning. *Initial pruning* refers to techniques that enable end users to quickly indicate with which aspects of a problem they wish assistance. For example, if an auto technician starts to consult a particular system designed for automobile problems, already knowing the problem is electrical rather than mechanical, the technician would like to be able to begin the consultation by pruning the system so it considers only electrical problems. If a tool lacks this feature, and if the problem situation frequently requires the user to answer questions that may be known to be irrelevant, the expert system will not be well received and probably will not be fully utilized.

Accepting multiple and uncertain answers. The ability of a system to accept multiple answers is closely associated with the ability of the system to handle expressions of user confidence in the information provided by the system. Imagine a situation in which a system asks end users if they would prefer a solution that uses technique A or technique B. In this case the user might not be prepared to express a clear preference or might want to reserve judgment until later. A tool that allows multiple or uncertain answers allows the user to answer "Technique A, 40%, Technique B, 60%." Or the user can simply answer "unknown." If the problem is tightly structured and involves analyzing documents that are always complete, multiple answers and "unknown" might not be necessary. Most problems involving judgment, however, benefit from this capability.

Graphics. No existing tools provide for developing graphics within the tool itself. Some tools provide hooks to graphics packages, and others have graphics packages bundled in with a larger package that includes the tool. One vendor has announced a tool that has hooks to video presentations. Good graphics can be very important to developing effective user interfaces, and tools that allow developers to use graphics are very desirable.

The Systems Interface

The systems interface refers to the attributes of expert systems tools that enable developers and users to access and use information or programming languages contained in data files separate from the knowledge base. These functions are described in the following paragraphs.

Fast/slow interaction. This somewhat subjective evaluation depends on exactly what a particular expert system is designed to do. In general, tools written in conventional languages run very fast and are quite adequate in most job environments. However, tools written in LISP, which cannot as yet be compiled, often run too slowly for most practical purposes or applications. (There is no LISP for a personal computer that can be compiled, though a compiler has been promised for some time by at least two vendors.) The rest of the tools fall in the middle and may or may not be sufficiently fast, again depending on the specific application for which the tool is intended.

Hooks to data bases. Some expert systems tools can be programmed to automatically access information stored in other data bases by using the programming language that underlies the particular tool being used. Some tools are already programmed to allow use of a specific external data base program (e.g., dBASE II). Others simply cannot provide such interface hooks. The nature of the tool's application will indicate if it is important to draw data from conventional data bases. In some cases data base hooks prove very valuable.

Hooks to other languages. Just as some tools let developers exit the system to obtain information in external data bases, others allow the use of external languages. If you are considering an expert system as a frontend to an already developed system, this could be a very important consideration when qualifying commercially available tools.

Other system-related issues. Still other considerations should be introduced before the complete picture of what an expert systems tool can do becomes clear. They include both software and hardware issues.

Software

The software, as well as the programming language used to develop it, is also a very important consideration in evaluating an expert systems tool. Software considerations when choosing a tool include several factors.

Language of the tool. Tools are written in various programming languages, as described in Chapter 3. In some tools, the developer can gain access to the language the particular tool is written in. However, to take advantage of this access, the developer must be able to program in that particular language.

Can the system be compiled? Not all systems can be compiled, especially smaller systems like a personal computer. As a rule, those that can be compiled run much faster. On the other hand, compiling tends to limit on-line editing during system development.

Other languages required for tool use. Some tools require a separate language to be running on the computer before they will properly function or work at all. Still other tools are complete packages and do not require any underlying languages to be available.

Operating system required for the tool. The operating system required for tool usage varies from tool to tool. The disk operating system (DOS) is used primarily with personal computers; however, minicomputers and mainframe computers generally have operating systems of UNIX, LISP, VS, or VMS.

Is the tool locked? Most current tools on the market are locked so they may not be tampered with or the code altered. This provides some protection for the vendor while causing some difficulties for the actual users and developers. With some tools, protection is an asset because it enables a business to develop a system using the tool and then to be confident the end users will not modify the system once it is in daily use.

Hardware

Expert systems tools also have different hardware requirements because of the many different types of computers available. Overall, hardware is divided into four general categories:

- Mini and mainframe computers.
- Conventional workstations (mostly UNIX-based systems such as Sun, Apollo; MicroVax, and IBM's new PC-RT).
- LISP machines (workstations that are especially designed to run LISP).
- Personal computers (including DOS machines such as the IBM PC, IBM PC-AT, and the Macintosh).

Hardware issues will be considered when you consider specific tools.

Training/Support

The issues of training, documentation, and support are often what separate good tools from bad. Many current tools lack good training, documentation, and support programs simply because their developers have spent all their time developing the product and have not taken the time to explain how to use it. If you are willing to thrash around in the documentation, you can eventually figure out how to operate the smaller tools, but the larger tools require good documentation and training. This will increasingly distinguish between the better tool vendors who are in the business for the long run and those who lack the resources for the long haul.

Training. The great promise of most tool vendors is complete training support for their products. The larger tool vendors generally provide more training support than smaller vendors. The quality of on-line support varies considerably.

Documentation. Tools usually come with a manual that tells how to use the tool. Since the majority of tools are relatively friendly, especially compared with other types of software, the manuals perform an adequate job in a very narrow sense. The real trick to getting a lot of value out of the tools lies in selecting appropriate problems and analyzing those problems effectively. Here the manuals typically fall short. Some vendors provide extensive documentation, including step-by-step examples and knowledge bases for study. This is a great help, but more often hands-on training via workshops is the best way to go.

Consulting. Do the vendors have experience consulting with their clients and helping them resolve the types of problems you are considering? Some vendors have considerable experience in particular areas that can prove very valuable to other clients facing similar problems.

Cost Considerations

Just as types of tools vary, so do the costs of such tools. The variety of expert system building tools keeps increasing, prices continue to drop, and new features keep getting added to the established tools. Figure 4.14 illustrates this rapidly evolving software market.

The horizontal axis plots the costs (note the breaks where the scale is changed to keep the chart to a manageable size). The cost indicated refers to the price of a single tool. Several tools have a range of prices, depending on the hardware on which it is used. In those cases the tool is priced near the bottom of the range. Thus, if a tool runs on both a PC and a mainframe, the price shown is the price for a PC version of the tool.

The vertical axis indicates some features you can expect in the various tools. In general, there is a progression in the ability of tools to represent knowledge. Inductive tools are the most limited, rule-based tools are next, and object-oriented or hybrid tools are the most sophisticated. The right tool should be chosen by considering the problem you intend to use it on. Some problems are ideal for inductive tools. In such a case, to acquire a more sophisticated tool would be like killing ants with a sledgehammer.

The small size of Figure 4.14, and the fact that it emphasizes certain features and not others, means you cannot use this chart for fine-grained comparisons. Assume that tools lying close together are essentially similar. For example, the position of ART, KEE, and Knowledge Craft, or of Insight 2 and Exsys, does not provide an evaluation of the relative merits of those closely related tools.

The horizontal lines drawn between the various types of tools indicate the knowledge representation, inference, and control techniques, and the developer, user, and system interface utilities you should expect to get with each class of tool. This analysis reflects a preference for tools that are easy to use and that provide user and developer interfaces that facilitate clear communication about the knowledge contained in the system. You can do about the same things using an EMYCIN-type context tree or variable rules (in either the form provided by M.1 or in the newer versions, like GURU, that allow you to write a rule that instantiates itself several times by obtaining variables from

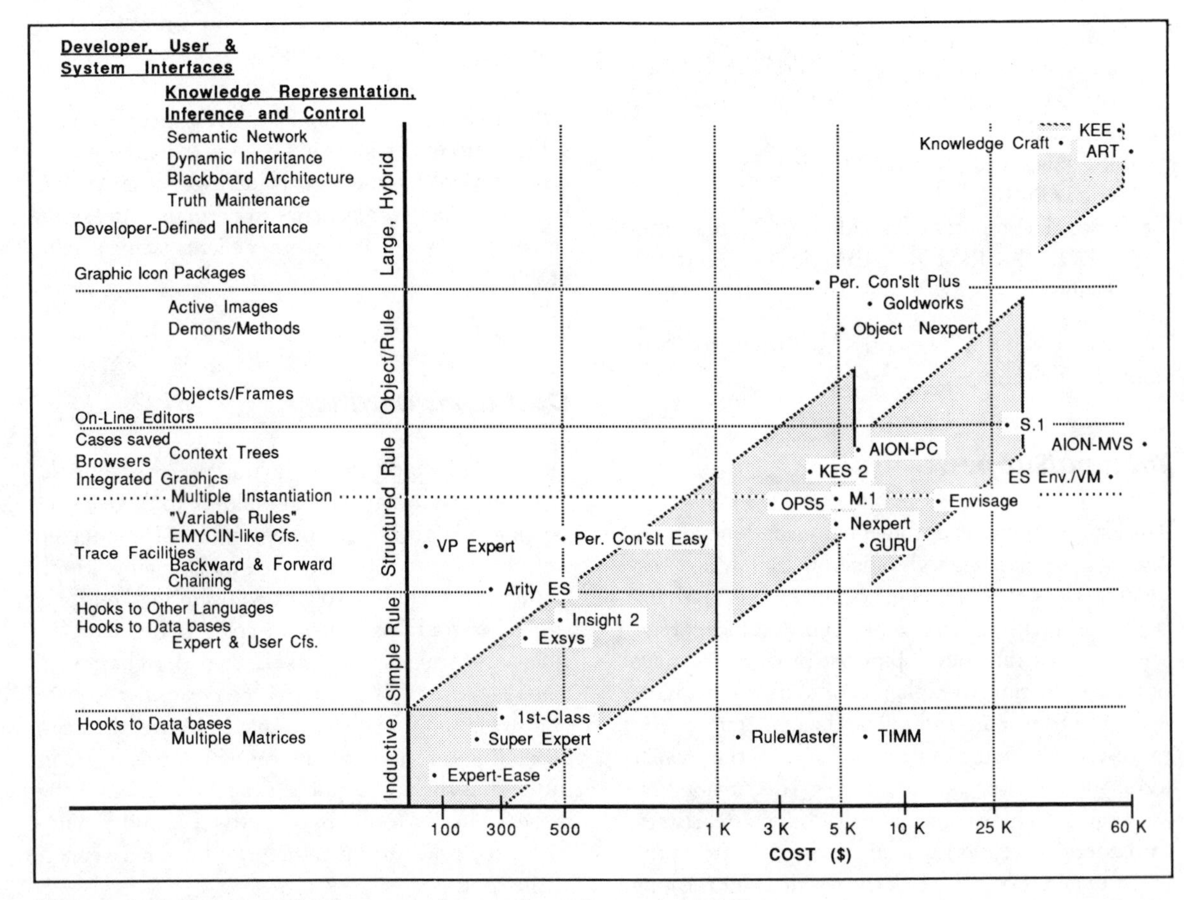

Figure 4.14 The cost-effectiveness of a number of popular tools.

a data base). A context tree, however, provides both the developer and the expert with a much clearer idea of how the knowledge is organized, while variable rules make sense only to the programmer.

A generic OPS5 is located in about the middle of Figure 4.14. Many versions of OPS5 sell at various prices. As noted at the beginning of this chapter, most versions of OPS5 lack developer and user interfaces. Moreover, OPS5 is hard to use, and it is better thought of as a programming environment than a tool. Because so many people have used OPS5 to develop good expert systems, however, it is located on Figure 4.14, just to provide a reference point. Its exact placement would depend on the particular version of OPS5 considered (e.g., some versions of OPS5 sell for under $100 while others sell for thousands).

Numerous factors are not adequately represented in Figure 4.14. For example, it does not provide a convenient way to indicate that IBM's tool, while generally an EMYCIN clone, runs on a mainframe and provides for multiple simultaneous users. Likewise, even though GURU is priced at $6,000, it's hard to rely too much on price in GURU's case since you get so much additional software in the package (e.g,. a relational data base, a word processor, a spreadsheet program, etc.). Similarly, this chart does not clearly indicate that VP Expert is unique among the rule-based tools because it includes an inductive system that can be used to create rules. It also excludes questions about the hardware the tools run on or how they work with other languages or programs. Thus, Figure 4.14 does not indicate that KES 2 can be completely embedded in a C program, etc.

Even though Figure 4.14 fails to consider many things, it still provides a reasonably good perspective on the current tool market. The broad band that slants from the lower left to the upper right indicates the price range most vendors have positioned themselves in. Tools that fall below the band (in the right corner) are generally less cost-effective, and those that rise above the band are generally more cost-effective than the average.

SUMMARY

Many companies are involved in developing and marketing expert system building tools. Many vendors are very business-oriented and have provided commercially designed packages that include support, training, and documentation. Other vendors, while positioning themselves for commercial sales, haven't really packaged or supported their tools adequately. Some vendors go to extreme lengths to explain the tasks for which their tools are appropriate, while others claim their tools can handle almost any conceivable application. Prudent business people investigating the expert system building tool market must ask questions, see how the different vendors respond, and examine each product, including its training and support services, before deciding on a particular tool package.

The market for AI tools is very new, so be advised: the decision to purchase any particular tool should be made only after you've done a lot of research and matched the tool to your particular application.

It's important to get started as soon as possible. The potential for improving employee effectiveness and efficiency is huge. From the smallest tool to the largest, all have the potential to make your business more productive in a relatively short time. However, remember that a sizable amount of up-front work must take place before even the most sophisticated tool can be of any assistance.

The availability of cost-effective tools is really only part of the complete picture. More critical to the success of using any tool is your ability to identify the proper problems within your company where an expert system would be most valuable. You must learn to analyze expertise and convert this knowledge into a form that the tools can use. In other words, the tools themselves are not as important as the overall analysis and design that ultimately leads to building a system with a tool.

5

Simple Rule-Based Tools

INTRODUCTION

This chapter focuses on the smaller rule-based tools. You will examine four of the more popular tools: Insight 2, Exsys, Personal Consultant Easy, and VP Expert. These small rule-based tools are rapidly enabling more people to become familiar with the operation and use of expert systems.

These tools are called *simple* because they place all their knowledge in a single knowledge base. This does not imply they are less useful than larger, structured rule tools. In many ways they are more important. They are contributing a great deal to the development of the expert systems market by acquainting large numbers of people with expert systems techniques. They are also responsible for a large portion of the successful expert systems fielded to date, and, most important, they hold the promise of spawning a whole generation of tools that nonprogrammers can use as computers spread throughout the workplace.

The year 1984 saw the development of rule-based expert systems capable of operating on personal computers. As a result, the expert systems market split into two major segments, one focusing on the need for large expert systems, the other concentrating on the potential applications for small systems operating in a PC environment.

Small expert systems do not try to capture true expertise. Instead, they offer users specific advice regarding how to deal with small but still difficult problems. These small systems rely on AI techniques, but the techniques are not as sophisticated as those in larger systems. The main advantage of small systems is that users can learn to develop the system much more quickly than when using larger systems. And this expertise can be learned with minimal upfront knowledge about computer operations.

Small tools are designed to run primarily on IBM Personal Computers and compatible machines. Some are quite trivial, whereas others are very powerful. Most small tools can be employed by users willing to spend a great deal of time learning about the processes of knowledge engineering. In many cases, it is recommended that a knowledge engineer familiar with these systems be available to assist during development and implementation of the systems. Powerful personal computer-based tools are becoming more widely available, at a cost similar to other types of software (e.g., word processing, spreadsheet, data base).

SMALL TOOL BASICS

Small expert systems tools typically represent knowledge in the form of rules and use backward chaining to process the rules. They usually run in a DOS environment and require at least 256K of random access memory to operate efficiently. Many are reasonably priced and provide users with a sophisticated capability to design expert systems containing 150 to 500 rules. They are often used in business environments in which a customer waits while the system is used to help solve a problem. Many are actually capable of processing thousands of rules; however, they often lack advanced editing capabilities of larger system tools, making them inefficient for large system development efforts. In addition, many of the small tools are produced by small companies staffed by people eager to help their customers learn to use the tools and maximize their productivity when using the tool.

Small tools are sophisticated programs that facilitate design of small expert systems. They operate much like electronic spreadsheets, but require the developer to input facts and rules, usually in an almost-English syntax rather than in numbers. Even among these small tools, an important distinction can be made between tools designed to be more open and flexible and those that totally constrain the developer to a single paradigm. For example, some small tools enable a user to enter the programming language underlying the tool to create special subroutines or to create program connections to an external data base. Naturally, this procedure requires a thorough familiarity with the programming language used to develop the tool.

Other small system tools are designed to prevent the developer from accessing the underlying language. Those users possessing programming experience may prefer the small expert tools that are more open or environmentlike in structure, while others may be perfectly content simply to use the surface utilities provided by the tool. The key characteristic of these small system tools is that they can be used by nonprogrammers.

In addition to tools, small system developers could use programming languages like LISP and PASCAL. An experienced programmer might enjoy developing a small expert system using LISP, PROLOG, or Smalltalk; these languages have recently become available for PCs and undoubtedly will be further used to develop more small system tools. However, most small system designers will probably prefer the benefits and capabilities provided by one of the small tools.

The current market for these tools is very confused and will likely require some time to settle. When this occurs, there will likely be more cost-effective options than there are now. This next generation of small tools will probably offer inductionlike frontends to help developers generate initial sets of rules more rapidly. Moreover, in the near future, object-oriented hybrid tools will also be available for the small system tool market.

WHAT ARE SMALL TOOLS GOOD FOR?

Small tools can be used to develop small to mid-size expert systems. Since they lack powerful editing facilities, they work best when the knowledge being encoded is primarily procedural and not heuristic. The best of the small tools allow nonprogrammers to develop programs. Most applications developed with the small tools assist people in performing small analysis and decision-making tasks.

Small expert systems are sometimes referred to as knowledge systems, technician systems, or intelligent job aids. The concept of a job aid is already well established in the area of training professionals. A *job aid* is a device used to obtain assistance when performing a task. Small expert systems fit this definition perfectly. Job aids have become increasingly popular because they can reduce training time while simultaneously increasing the quality and amount of the work performed. They minimize memorization and maximize accurate responses. In fact, in many instances, job aids allow less-trained users to accomplish tasks that previously required more highly trained, and hence more expensive, individuals.

Job aids have generally consisted of checklists, step-by-step procedures, cookbooks, and other paper devices. To a great extent PCs have become important job aids in the office environment. For example, the bank teller who uses a small terminal to determine a customer's balance is relying on a job aid, as is the executive who uses a PC-based spreadsheet program to prepare financial forecasts. In fact, even the on-screen menus and help screens are examples of job aids available within conventional computer programs.

Until recently job aids couldn't be designed to effectively help individuals perform complex tasks. These complex tasks usually required a person to take into account a large number of different facts and then apply this information to determine a correct response, much as a loan officer does when evaluating a loan application. In the past, a job aid that assisted an individual in performing a complex task was so complicated that it was useless. Conventional wisdom held that you were better off simply hiring a specialist already familiar with the tasks or problems at hand.

Today, however, all this is rapidly changing. Small expert systems (intelligent job aids) are enabling skilled individuals to record their knowledge in knowledge bases and then provide that knowledge to a large number of individuals. Consider the problem of helping clerks process insurance applications. The knowledge required to accomplish this task wouldn't normally be compared with the expertise possessed by a highly specialized physician; however, the clerk must possess a lot of knowledge to prevent costly mistakes. In a typical insurance company, knowledge of application processing is usually possessed by one or more senior application examiners. To spread this knowledge, new trainees often receive only a week or two of training and a procedures manual. It becomes a "learn as you do" environment. Once trainees actually start working at the tasks, they gradually acquire additional knowledge and heuristics from their own experiences and by relying on the knowledge base provided by the senior examiners—this by asking questions when problems occur or unusual cases arise.

By using a small expert system building tool, a senior examiner can quickly develop an intelligent job aid to help trainees learn the tasks of reviewing applications. The new clerks can turn to this small expert system instead of consulting the manual or senior clerk.

Unquestionably, the senior clerk might not get the system right on the first try, but this is one virtue of small knowledge systems; they are highly modularized and can be quickly revised and updated. For example, every time the system fails to help a clerk and the clerk must consult the senior clerk or manual, the system can be easily updated with this new required knowledge. This makes small expert systems much like their larger counterparts. They do not have to be completely finished to begin being used productively. They are simply used, updated, used, updated, and so on. Like human experts, they continue to add to their knowledge base. In the aforementioned example, the Application Advisor System would most likely become the responsibility of a senior clerk to input information and maintain the system. After the initial information is complete, the system soon begins to save all the clerks time, thus increasing efficiency and reducing costs.

Obviously, an effort such as developing an Application Advisor System could not happen if the senior clerk first had to learn a sophisticated AI programming language and then also learn to operate a mainframe computer. In fact, a task such as this could not be accomplished if the senior clerk had to rely on the resources of a dedicated data processing department to design and implement such a system. This could take years simply to become marginally functional and in the process very, very expensive. But now small expert systems tools have come to assist people in many everyday jobs.

The success of these small systems depends on user-friendly small expert system building tools that are at least as easy to use and operate as some of the popular PC software packages (e.g, spreadsheet programs). Moreover, these new aids must operate on personal computers.

FOUR SMALL EXPERT SYSTEM BUILDING TOOLS

Of all the small tools, Level Five Research's Insight 2 and Exsys Inc.'s Exsys are among the most popular, each having a large installed base. These tools provide very sophisticated capabilities that can make you more efficient and productive. Personal Consultant Easy is a new, simplified version of Personal Consultant, a tool Texas Instruments introduced two years ago and has now modified to create two tools, Easy, for the low end of the market, and Personal Consultant Plus, for the more sophisticated user. A fourth tool recently released, VP Expert, offers new capabilities at a reduced price and will help define the low end of the market in the next few years.

If you have been considering developing a small expert system, these tools can help you:

- To access information stored in dBASE II and Lotus 1-2-3.

- To make frequent use of confidence factors associated with user input or confidence derived from other rules.
- To provide an index or table of contents that will enable users to start by pinpointing the part of the problem that needs immediate attention.
- To quickly create screens of information that can be displayed throughout a consultation.
- To use the abilities of PASCAL or C to build subroutines.
- To start with an inexpensive scaled-down version of a tool to develop one or more proof-of concept or prototype systems before investing more money.
- To interface with external programs.
- To create simulations.
- To use complex algebraic expressions including trig, log, exponent, and square root functions.

No one tool can perform all the aforementioned tasks; however, each possesses some of the attributes.

INSIGHT 2 AND EXSYS: A COMPARISON

Both Insight 2 and Exsys represent knowledge as rules and use backward chaining to process these rules. They are each reasonably priced, and either would be a good tool to develop a small expert system. They are ideal for applications where customers wait while you help them solve a problem.

The first and probably best known rule-based tool developed was EMYCIN, the interface engine that derived from the MYCIN system developed at Stanford University during the mid-1970s. Insight 2, Exsys, and just about all other small expert system building tools currently being marketed are limited versions of EMYCIN.

To provide further detail, the two systems are contrasted and compared according to the following criteria:

1. Overall power and flexibility.
2. Knowledge engineering interface.
3. User (runtime) interface.
4. Runtime speed.
5. Training and support.

To objectively evaluate the two tools, a small knowledge base (KB) system was developed to test their basic power and flexibility. For this test the KB is called Alpha, illustrated in Figure 5.1. Letters are used instead of attributes to make the "knowledge" easier to enter and change. All rules entered into Alpha are kept to a minimum (10 rules), but they still address all the obvious variations. After Alpha was created two other KBs were developed to capture Alpha's knowledge, one for Insight 2 and one for Exsys. Each KB failed to capture some knowledge. However, equally important, when the KBs were being created, the tutorials and manuals had to be studied repeatedly. In spite of this recurring reference, each KB still had to be modified several more times. The resultant exercise provided valuable insight for using each tool. Results of the comparison are included in the following paragraphs.

Power and Flexibility of the Tools

When analyzing power and flexibility, several questions need to be addressed.

How are facts represented? In both Insight 2 and Exsys, facts are represented as *attribute–value* pairs. For example, *color* (attribute) is *red* (value). The documentation for Exsys refers to object–attribute–value triplets (or O–A–V), which is very confusing. In more sophisticated rule-based systems, such as EMYCIN or Personal Consultant, facts are represented as triplets, for example, "Object 1's color is red." Use of the third term (the object) lets the user create a structured rule system that can inherit information and instantiate multiple versions of a situation. In this case, neither Insight 2 nor Exsys is a structured rule system and cannot perform as a structured system might. This is of small consequence if your use of these two tools is limited to building a small KB. Still, it is a bit bothersome that Insight 2 refers to "triplets" and presents unnecessary confusion.

Both tools let you represent facts as true/false, as a

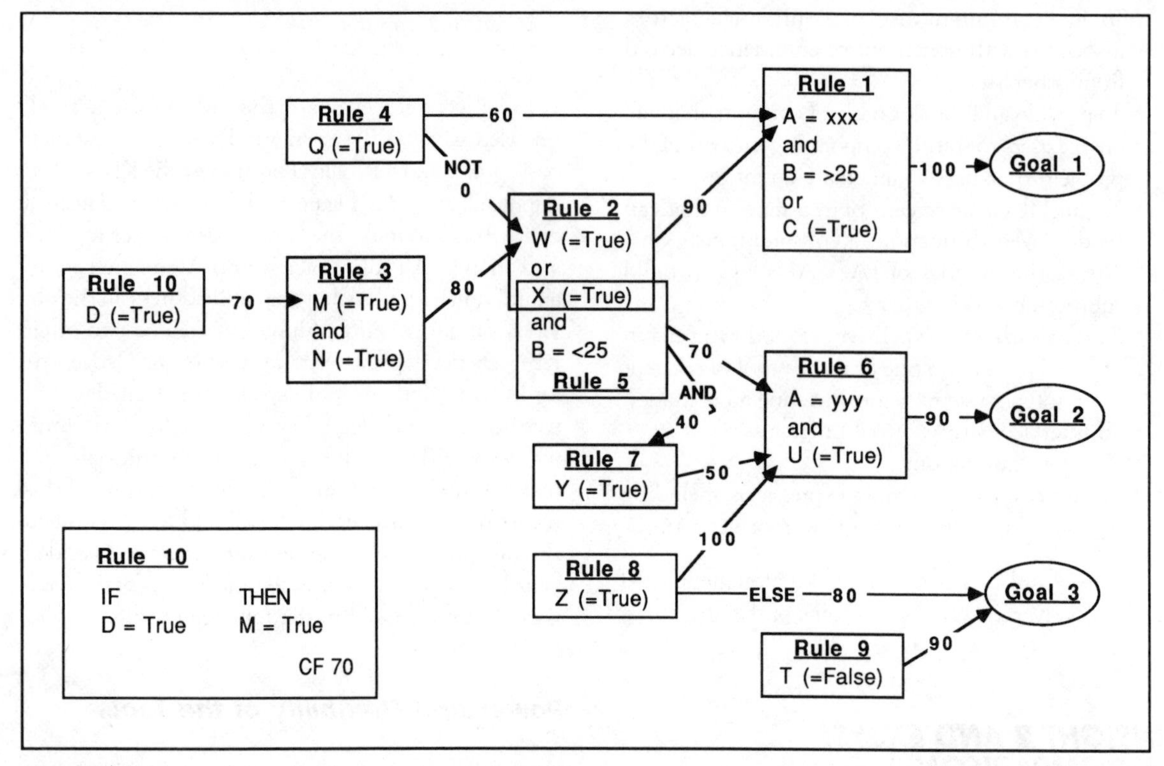

Figure 5.1 *Alpha. A small system designed to test the power and flexibility of a small expert system building tool.*

set of literals (e.g., red, green, blue), or as various mathematical relations (e.g., =, <, >). In addition, each tool lets you develop rules that incorporate higher mathematical functions and use numeric variables. Insight 2 cannot handle trigonometry functions directly, but allows you to call in other programs, developed using Turbo PASCAL, to perform these advanced mathematical operations. Neither tool lets you create rules with symbolic variables, and in turn, neither tool supports the abstract pattern-matching techniques (unification) of other tools like ExperOPS and M.1.

How are relationships between facts represented? Both tools use if–then rules to represent relationships between facts. Insight 2's provision for rules with OR clauses make it somewhat easier to capture some of Alpha's rules; however, you can obviously break a rule with OR into two simpler rules, which is what was done when the testing occurred.

INSIGHT RULE		EXSYS RULE	
IF		IF	
	AND		AND
	NOT		NOT
	OR		
THEN		THEN	
	ELSE		ELSE

Both tools enable you to write special rules to handle arithmetic operations and to go outside the tool, if needed, to create special subroutines. Insight 2 makes it very easy to develop and manipulate dBASE II files and allows you to use Turbo PASCAL to write any subroutines you need. You cannot, however, call in any external programs while running an Insight 2 KB. Exsys, on the other hand, enables you to call in external programs and write subroutines in any other programming language.

How are inference and control handled? Both tools rely on backward chaining as their main method search strategy. Thus, both tools begin to process a consultation by examining the goals in the knowledge base and then working backward from rule to rule to determine if there is sufficient data to conclude that one or more of the goals is true. Insight 2 explicitly allows you to create forward chaining rules, and a similar effect can be achieved indirectly when using Exsys. Both tools let you create systems in which more than one goal can be recommended.

Both tools also rely on depth-first search to determine the order in which rules occur in the KB and the order in which clauses occur in the rules. Therefore, when Insight 2 runs the Alpha data base (see Table 5.1), it begins at the top of the list of rules and works down looking for the first rule that concludes the goal (1. Recommendation). Rule 01 concludes "THEN Recommendation IS Goal 1 CONFIDENCE 100." Therefore, the system backs up and starts at the top and searches for a rule that concludes about the value of A (the first clause in Rule 01). It finds Rule 02, which concludes about A and then begins again, looking for the value of W, and so on. If Rule

Table 5.1 *The Insight 2 knowledge base for Alpha.*

```
!       ALPHA.prl
!        This small system is designed to test the
!         power and flexibility of a small expert
!        system building tool.
!
TITLE  ALPHA KB TEST SYSTEM
!
THRESHOLD  = 40
!
CONFIDENCE ON
!
MULTI  Recommendation
AND  A
AND  M
!
        1. Recommendation
!
RULE 01
IF  A  IS  xxx
AND B >25
OR C
THEN Recommendation IS Goal 1  CONFIDENCE 100
!
RULE 02
IF W
OR X
THEN A IS xxx  CONFIDENCE 90
!
RULE 03
IF M
AND N
THEN W  CONFIDENCE 80
!
RULE 04
IF Q
THEN A IS xxx  CONFIDENCE 60
AND NOT W  CONFIDENCE 30
!
RULE 05
IF X
AND B <25
THEN A IS yyy  CONFIDENCE 70
AND Y CONFIDENCE 40
!
RULE 06
IF  A  IS  yyy
AND U
THEN Recommendation IS Goal 2  CONFIDENCE 90
!
RULE 07
IF Y
THEN U  CONFIDENCE 50
!
RULE 08
IF Z
THEN U  CONFIDENCE 100
ELSE Recommendation IS Goal 3  CONFIDENCE 80
!
RULE 09
IF NOT T
THEN Recommendation IS Goal 3  CONFIDENCE 90
!
RULE 10
IF D
THEN M  CONFIDENCE 70
!
END
```

08 were moved to the top of the list, Insight 2 would start looking for the value of Z instead of A. Likewise, if Rule 01 is altered to read:

```
IF B > 25
AND A IS xxx
OR C
THEN Recommendation is Goal 1
                CONFIDENCE 100
```

then the system would start looking for B before it seeks A. Altering the order of the rules and the clauses of the rules is one way a developer can force a consultation to proceed in a particular order.

Two types of "confidence" are associated with expert systems. *Expert confidence* refers to the confidence the expert associates with a particular rule. In the rule above, the expert is 100 percent confident that if A and B or C, then Goal 1 should be recommended. *User*

Table 5.2 *Printout of Exsys Alpha knowledge base rules.*

```
RULE NUMBER: 1
IF:
    A  is  xxx
 and   B is >25
THEN:
    Goal  1  -  Probability=100/100
----------------------------------------
RULE NUMBER: 2
IF:
    W  is  T
THEN:
    A  is  xxx
----------------------------------------
RULE NUMBER: 3
IF:
    Q  is  T
THEN:
    W  is  F
----------------------------------------
RULE NUMBER: 4
IF:
    M  is  T
 and   N is T
THEN:
    W  is  T
----------------------------------------
RULE NUMBER: 5
IF:
    X  is  T
 and   B is <25
THEN:
    A  is  yyy
----------------------------------------
RULE NUMBER: 6
IF:
    A  is  yyy
 and   U is T
THEN:
    Goal  2  -  Probability=90/100

RULE NUMBER: 7
IF:
    Z  is  T
THEN:
    U  is  T
ELSE:
    Goal  2  -  Probability=90/100
----------------------------------------
RULE NUMBER: 8
IF:
    T  is  F
THEN:
    Goal  3  -  Probability=90/100
----------------------------------------
RULE NUMBER: 9
IF:
    D  is  T
THEN:
    M  is  T
----------------------------------------
RULE NUMBER: 10
IF:
    A  is  xxx
 and   C is T
THEN:
          Goal 1 - Probability=100/100
----------------------------------------
RULE NUMBER: 11
IF:
    Y  is  T
THEN:
    U  is  T
----------------------------------------
```

confidence refers to the confidence a user has in a particular answer. Therefore, if the system asks users if A is xxx or yyy, the users may wish to say they are 80 percent certain it is xxx.

Insight 2 allows you to associate expert confidence with each rule. Exsys allows you to attach confidence only to rules that conclude about goals. In the Alpha KB for Exsys illustrated in Table 5.2, notice the conclusion in RULE NUMBER:1 is asserted with Probability = 100/100. Exsys enables you to express probabilities in three different ways. Exsys doesn't associate confidence with other rules, however, and loses some of the flavor of the original Alpha by knowledge being lost. You can associate confidence with each rule in Exsys by attaching numerical variables to each rule. Using such an approach, RULE NUMBER:1 in the Alpha KB will take the following form:

```
IF

A IS xxx
and [A X CONF] > O
and [B] >/= 25
and [B CONF] > O

THEN

[GOAL 1 CONF] IS GIVEN THE VALUE
100-((100-[GOAL 1 CONF])*(1-([A
X CONF]*[B CONF]/100)/100))
```

This example demonstrates that both Insight 2 and Exsys enable developers to get around almost anything if they are willing to do (or learn) some programming.

Both tools handle complex confidence calculations rather poorly. They each conceptualize confidence in terms of probability, an inadequate approach. Consider this example in the original Alpha knowledge base. An expert indicates that if Q is true, then he is 60 percent sure A is true. In addition, the expert indicates that if W or X is true then he is 90 percent sure of A. Now, assume these two tests are totally unrelated to one another. If you find X is true, then you are 90 percent certain A is true. Finding that an independent test (Q) shows A is true 60 percent should not lower the confidence that A is at least 90 percent true. Traditional approaches to probability assume that Q and X are related and multiply the two confidences, thus reducing the confidence well below 90 percent.

Insight 2 has much better built-in features for handling expert confidence than does Exsys. Both, however, still leave a lot to be desired. Most small expert systems can't handle complex confidence considerations. Some experienced knowledge engineers prefer to avoid rule confidence altogether, feeling this simply confuses experts who do not think in terms of probability in the first place. If, however, you know you face a tricky problem involving a lot of rules that accumulate evidence for and against a specific fact, you should probably avoid both these tools.

One related flexibility issue involves the ability to port KBs developed using these two tools. Insight 2 enables you to port a KB developed using Insight 1.2, its smaller tool, to Insight 2. Exsys can be ported to a NEC9801 (a computer sold exclusively in Japan), and both tools are available for the VAX.

The Knowledge Engineering Interface

To enter Insight 2, you type "I2" and are presented with a menu screen like the one illustrated in Figure 5.2. From this screen you can move to Insight's text editor, its compiler, or the runtime system. Likewise, you can enter programs to create, compile, and run auxiliary data base programs. A function key lets you return to the main menu from any of these other programs. Moreover, once you begin to work with a particular KB, Insight 2 always assumes you want to use that particular KB unless you tell it otherwise. Therefore, it is easy to move from the text editor to the compiler to the runtime system in Insight 2. Compiling a large KB can take some time, particularly if it must be performed frequently.

To create a KB using Insight 2, the knowledge engineer enters rules using any word processing program (e.g., WordStar, MultiMate). This lets you create nondocument files (some of the newer paragraph-oriented word processors will not work). Or you can use the text editor of Insight 2 (it works like WordStar). In either case, you can move the cursor about and change the KB until it suits you. The control com-

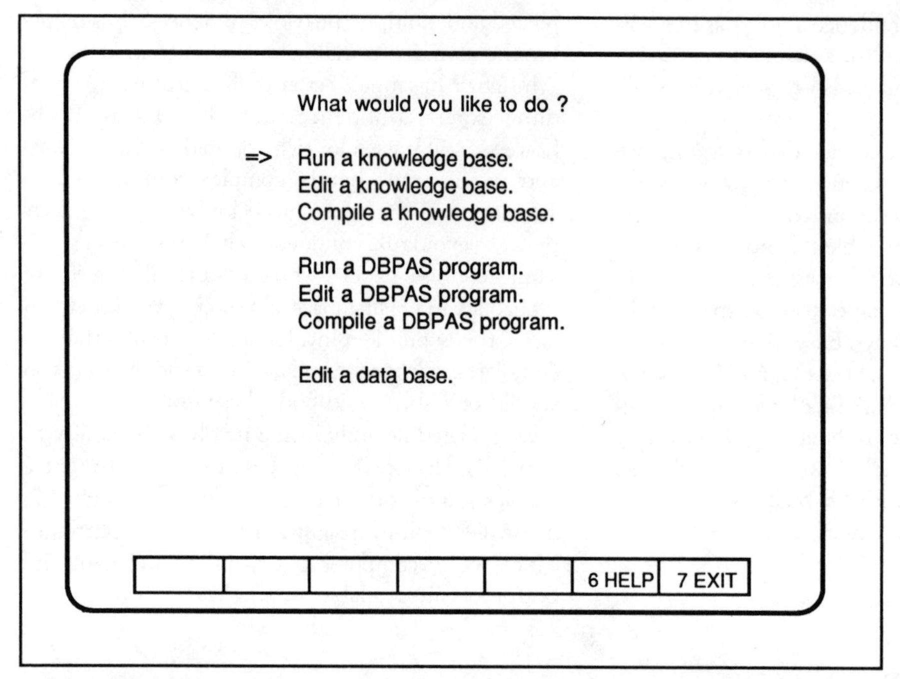

Figure 5.2 *The main menu screen of Insight 2. By using the cursor arrows you can locate a choice and then select it with return. Different uses of the function keys appear as different screens are selected. Note that you can use DBPAS to create and manipulate dBASE II files.*

mands that control confidence, the display of the goal hierarchy, and so on are all entered into the system this way. The advantage of this approach is that you can always get a printout so you can inspect everything contained in the KB. For example, only a glance will tell you the confidence assigned to a rule. Using "!" at the beginning of a line tells the computer to ignore that particular line. This lets you insert notes or comments anywhere in the KB for future reference, a good way to document your KBs.

Exsys has two main programs: a system development program for creating, editing, running, and testing expert systems called Editxs, and a separate runtime program, Exsys, intended to be distributed with completed expert systems applications. To start Exsys you type EDITXS, which can be followed by a filename and a wide range of commands for controlling the program default settings. The editor is not a true word processor but a special editor used to enter rules. All input to the system is performed by menu selection or by typing the text of an attribute or an algebraic expression. When a new attribute is entered, the developer is asked to provide a list of values to be associated with it. You then select the items from the displayed list to build statements in the rule.

Whenever this particular attribute list is needed later, it is easy to recall without having to rekey it. The associated values are presented, and you can select the ones to be associated with the attribute in the new instance. With a little practice this method proves to be much faster than typing text and, more important, it prevents typing errors. If an algebraic expression is needed, you simply press "M" and enter the desired expression. Exsys checks all algebraic expressions for new variables and, if one is found, requests information on the prompt to use when asking for information, initialization, and acceptable range limits.

The Editxs work screen, shown in Figure 5.3, is divided into three panels. The panel to the right is where most work is actually performed. The panel on the left displays the rule as it is built, and the lower portion of the panel displays the actual command options. You can enter a note or reference with each rule entered. A variety of methods allows you to rapidly edit, delete, move, or scroll through rules. As each rule is entered, it is immediately compiled. This presents two advantages: (1) the program can check new rules against existing rules to search for any possible conflicts which may create logic errors, and (2) the rules can be instantly run by simply pressing "R" to test them (you automatically drop back into the edit mode after a run if you press the ESC key). This allows fast switching between edit and run modes.

Each tool lets you obtain a report regarding the consultation. Knowledge engineers use this documentation so they can determine exactly how a KB is processed by the system. Both Insight 2 and Exsys provide adequate reports, but neither gives good reports; in both instances, you may find yourself referring to rule-based listings to make sure exactly what has occurred when running the KB.

When knowledge engineers create a system, they generally begin by simply inputting lots of rules to capture the basic knowledge about a specific domain. Next, after the knowledge engineers are satisfied that the basic descriptive knowledge is correct, the rules are rearranged, clauses changed for order, and so on to create a smoother-flowing consultation. Finally, questions are recorded, displays added, and other information inserted to make the KB easier to use and understand. Because you can always examine all rules contained in a text file, Insight 2 facilitates this iterative process. It lets you create skeletal KBs and run them until you are satisfied the knowledge is present. Then you can reorder clauses and rules, add goal hierarchies, and adjust confidence levels, all making the KB pro-

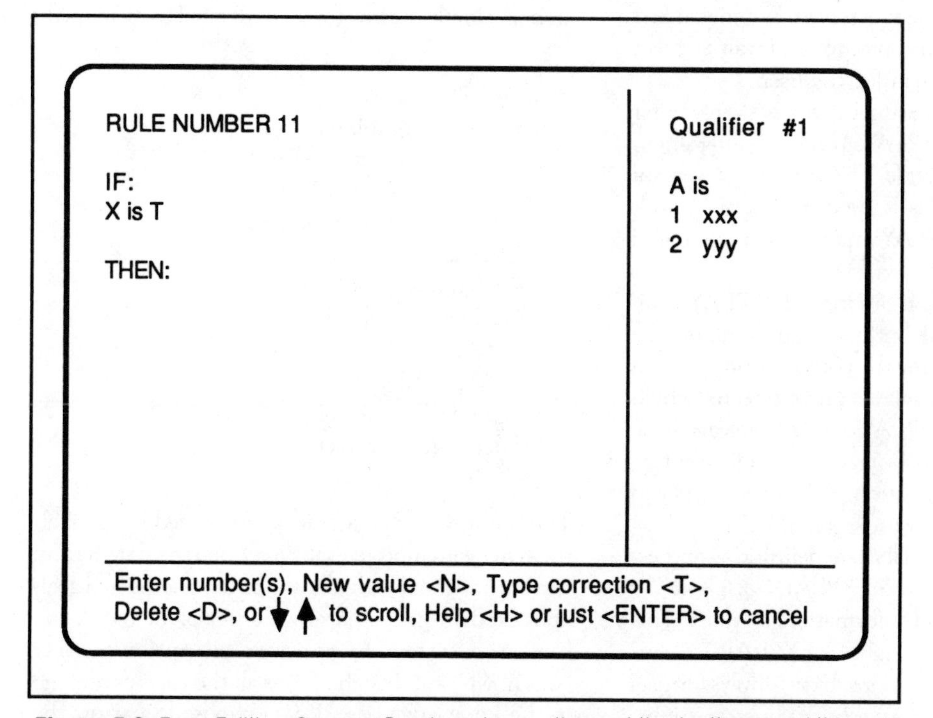

Figure 5.3 *Exsys Editing Screen. By choosing options at the bottom and then on the right side, you create a rule in the top left panel. In this example, the IF portion of the rule is complete. In the example above, the user has selected a previous qualifier (or attribute)—A—and will complete the rule by typing 1 and pressing return. Exsys will then enter "A is xxx" under THEN on the right side.*

ceed as you desire. Finally, knowledge engineers can add DISPLAY, EXPLAIN, and TEXT information to tailor the final user interface. The ability to perform these tasks using successive iterations and obtaining printouts of each successive KB is a powerful learning tool. Since Exsys forces you to edit one rule at a time and encourages you to specify all values for an attribute, the tool seems to "pressure" you to create too much of the KB too early.

The User Interface

Once you have developed a prototype KB that works, you want to refine it for the user. This process typically begins with a title screen that informs the user of the name of the advisor, its author, and so on. In Exsys you are prompted to insert whatever information you want to appear on the title screen. When you first create your KB, ignore this prompt and wait to use it when preparing the system for the user.

To create a title screen using Insight 2, simply enter the command word DISPLAY in the KB after entering the short form of the title. Then type whatever you wish. When Insight 2 runs, it displays whatever it finds between the word DISPLAY and the next command word.

In a similar manner, you can insert DISPLAY commands throughout the KB, thus creating full display screens at any point during the consultation. You can also create EXPLAIN displays. These screens, which you create just like DISPLAY screens, are available whenever you press a function key. They allow you to create a two-track consultation. Advanced users can move quickly while newer users can move more slowly and refer to the more elaborate definitions and explanations contained in the EXPLAIN displays.

Exsys lets you append information to rules. This feature can function like Insight 2's EXPLAIN screens to create two-track consultations. Exsys always formats in the same way as the screen asks the user questions. The user is presented with a question and then prompted either to indicate the number that identifies the correct response or to enter a numerical value. This can force you into some awkward situations, but it does let you work through a large number of questions by simply alternating between tracks 1 and 2. If you need more elaborate screen formatting, use an external program called by any Exsys rule which starts with RUN (filename).

Insight 2 presents the exact words or phrases you use when writing the rule and highlights the top one. You can highlight by using the cursor arrows and then pressing the RETURN key when you have highlighted the right answer. Alternately, you can also enter a mnemonic in the rule and then add the command word TEXT together with the exact phrase or sentence you wish the system to display whenever that particular mnemonic is encountered. In short, Insight 2 lets you have complete control over the screen and thereby lets you create much more elaborate and friendly user interfaces.

Insight 2 also enables you to create a goal outline and present it to users at the beginning of a consultation. A simple outline for an auto repair system might be:

1. Drive train problems
   - 1.1 Axle problems
   - 1.2 Driveshaft problems
   - 1.3 Transmission problems
2. Electrical problems
   - 2.1 Ignition problems
   - 2.2 Light problems
     - 2.2.1 Headlight problems
     - 2.2.2. Taillight problems
     - 2.2.3. Turn signal problems
3. Fuel system problems

The outline is a hierarchically organized set of goals the system attempts to evaluate. When the system runs, you are presented with all the one-digit numbered goals and asked if you can narrow the area of interest. If you want the system to consider all options, select "unknown" and Insight 2 uses all the rules contained in the knowledge base. If you choose to narrow the search by selecting "2. Electrical problems," then Insight 2 presents the two-digit goals and once again asks you to narrow the field. In short, if you specify the subproblem you want help with, this frontend lets you avoid answering irrelevant questions, thus reducing the corresponding consulting time.

Insight 2 also supports user confidence. If desired, you can allow users to indicate how confident they are in their answers. If you instruct Insight 2 to check for user confidence (i.e., you enter "CONFIDENCE ON" in the KB as in the first KB illustrated earlier), Insight 2 first asks you a question and then presents a screen with a solid bar and lets you shorten or extend the displayed bar to indicate the percentage of confidence you have in the answer. The bar idea is probably good for special issues, but it is rather tedious to use. It is preferable simply to type in a number or choose one of the five options (e.g., completely confident in answer, very confident, moderately confident). Still, in some problems it is very useful to determine just how confident the user really is when furnishing answers to displayed prompts.

Exsys has a helpful feature that lets you ask for a list of all your answers once the initial consultation is complete. You can then change any answer and rerun the KB. In an instant, Exsys reruns the consultation and furnishes new recommendations. In this manner you can use the system to perform simulations. It is easy to imagine developing a program, running a standard case, and then presenting only the outcome of the case, letting you make changes so you can examine the other possible alternatives. Using this same feature you can further test the significance of an answer based on the system's final recommendations. Exsys retains the previous values and then displays the old and new values in a side-by-side display format that facilitates easy comparison between values.

Both tools let you use graphics developed using external graphics programs. In the case of Insight 2, the external graphics editor has to be accessed using Turbo PASCAL (e.g., Halo Graphics). Both Exsys and Insight 2 allow color displays.

The Systems Interface

Both Insight 2 and Exsys can run a 300-rule KB faster than most users could ever consider the questions and indicate their answers. Both tools run so fast that either would perform equally well in any practical field applications. Exsys has a utility called FASTER that rearranges rules so they run at maximum speed. This is useful when using very large KBs with no special need to ascertain particular questions in a set order.

Training and Support

The tools also both have manuals. Overall, the Insight 2 manual is much better organized. Both provide adequate instruction for users just learning to develop a small system, but neither provides the kind of detailed support needed to use the full power of the tools. Exsys provides an effective tutorial disk that walks users through the process of creating a KB, giving new users an effective introduction to the tool.

Since both companies are relatively small operations, you can call them and get any information you might need. Any shortcomings in the software or documentation is compensated for by the telephone support their respective employees offer.

Two Additional Tools

Two newer small tools will undoubtedly redefine the low end of the tool market in the next few years: Personal Consultant Easy, a new tool from Texas Instruments, and VP Expert, from Paperback Software.

PERSONAL CONSULTANT EASY

Texas Instruments introduced Personal Consultant Easy at the American Association of Artificial Intelligence meeting in August 1986. The original version of Personal Consultant was introduced at the 1984 AAAI convention in Austin, Texas. A comparison of the two tools provides an overview of how far commercial expert systems tools have come.

The original Personal Consultant was a nearly complete copy of EMYCIN. Like EMYCIN, Personal Consultant was a structured rule tool. It represented facts as context–parameter–value triplets and allowed the developer to divide the rules into contexts (or subsets). The context mechanism allowed for multiple instantiation. Personal Consultant used the confidence factor system developed for EMYCIN. The system was a backward chainer that allowed for limited forward chaining. Personal Consultant incorporated EMYCIN's natural language components and thus allowed the developer to control the interaction with the user by entering words and phrases and relying on the tool to develop good sentences to ask for information and to handle How and Why explanations. Moreover, Personal Consultant incorporated EMYCIN's powerful interface and editing utilities. In this one area, Texas Instruments improved on the original EMYCIN by introducing menu screens to facilitate development and user interaction with the system.

Personal Consultant was written in IQ LISP, which could not be compiled; thus, it ran slowly. In addition, the context structure was both a blessing and a curse. If you faced a problem that required subdividing the rules and/or using multiple instantiation to reuse the same rules multiple times, then Personal Consultant had the power you needed, and although it was slow, nothing else on the personal computer offered the same combination of power plus a good knowledge engineering interface. Personal Consultant sold for $3,000, a good buy when it first appeared.

Since the introduction of the original Personal Consultant, the market for PC-based tools has changed dramatically. Tools have been introduced in conventional languages. The price of the simple rule-based tools now ranges from $49 to $500, and the interface features of all the tools have improved considerably.

At this point, the main division among the PC-based tools is between those tools written in conventional languages that can thus be embedded into other conventional programs and/or fielded via mainframes, and tools used to develop applications fielded on a personal computer. The conventional language tools are incorporating more and more conventional code and are becoming harder for an expert, an end user, or a nonprogrammer to use. The LISP and PROLOG-based tools continue to offer high-quality knowledge engineering environments that allow the developer and user to read a knowledge base without worrying about strange programming calls and procedural code.

Texas Instruments has responded to the changing market by replacing the original Personal Consultant with two new tools, Personal Consultant Plus, a much more powerful version of the original (see Chapter 6), and now Personal Consultant Easy, a tool positioned and priced to compete with the simple rule tools.

Power and Flexibility

Personal Consultant Easy (EASY) represents facts as attribute–value pairs. Facts are combined into rules. EASY does not support context trees and, thus, as with Exsys, Insight 2, and VP Expert, all rules are stored in a single knowledge base and can be used only once. (In fact, with each tool you can write rules that call on data in dBASE II and get the effect of limited multiple instantiation, at the expense of the readability of the knowledge base.)

EASY is upwardly compatible with Personal Consultant Plus, however, so you can create an expert system in EASY and then decide that you need the additional power of a context tree and move up to Personal Consultant Plus. (When you do this, your EASY rule base becomes a single context, or frame in the language of Personal Consultant Plus.) In fact, a knowledge base written in EASY can be moved to Personal Consultant Plus/Explorer, the Common LISP version of Personal Consultant Plus. That means you can begin developing an expert system on EASY, then move it to a LISP machine, or in the near future to a LISP chip. No other low-end tool offers anything like this range of development and delivery options.

Developer Interface

Texas Instruments has done an effective job of refining the original Personal Consultant interfaces. All the editing, trace, and explanation facilities remain, but new pop-up menus make it much easier to move about and develop or examine a system.

By removing the context tree structure, EASY has become simple to use. You no longer have to enter information about a context when all you want to do is enter five rules. Moreover, the addition of several defaults makes entering facts and rules a cinch. You can probably enter five rules in EASY in one-third the time it formerly took in Personal Consultant.

EASY is written in Texas Instruments' Scheme (a subset of Common LISP). Unlike Personal Consultant Plus, the developer is unable to enter and program directly in Scheme. This is a considerable advantage for nonprogrammers and end users who are only confused when they find themselves in the language underlying a tool. Since the serious developer has the option of migrating to Personal Consultant Plus and gaining access to Scheme and the ability to write and incorporate LISP code into an application, it seems to offer the best of both worlds.

Scheme is incrementally compiled, so a developer can quickly access a rule, make a change, and rerun a consultation with hardly any delay. EASY's menus and internal editors make it simple to locate a fact or rule you need to change.

In the manner of EMYCIN, EASY lets you specify that the user is to be asked for a value as soon as the consultation begins; thus EASY, like most other simple rule tools, allows the developer to implement a limited form of forward chaining.

EASY supports access to DOS files that can be controlled by a single command. It supports very sophisticated interactions with dBase, providing a number of commands to control the use of data stored in a dBase file. In addition, EASY makes it possible to insert externally developed graphics into a consultation. From the beginning, Personal Consultant has supported the best color graphics of any small or mid-size tool, and EASY becomes the first simple rule tool to provide developers with high-quality graphic capabilities. (Ideally the graphics development environment would be inside the tool, but that can wait awhile, especially given the price.)

EASY supports the EMYCIN confidence factor approach. It is clearly superior to systems based on standard probabilities. Some simple rule tools offer the option of creating their own confidence factor mechanism and incorporating it into each rule they write. This approach may be appropriate for the mid- to large-size tools, but it makes no sense for nonprogrammers or for most small applications. EASY offers the best general approach to both user and expert confidence and incorporates it in such a way that it is very easy to use, edit, or turn off.

See Figures 5.4 and 5.5 for examples of two EASY screens.

User Interface

The menu screens and automatic generation of English sentences guarantee a reasonable user interface. EASY is set up to generate a menu of options when the user must choose among several possible literal values. If the developer wants graphics as well, EASY can generate the best user interface on any tool selling for under $5,000. (Other tools allow for equally impressive interfaces, but they require the developer to develop each interface individually while EASY does most of the work for you.)

Systems Interface

EASY runs in DOS on a personal computer. DOS files can be called from EASY, and data can be moved back and forth between dBASE and Easy. Scheme is incrementally compiled, and while still not as fast as a tool running in C or PASCAL, it is much faster than any earlier LISP or PROLOG-based tools. For most applications, EASY should run at an adequate speed. If you were using it in a sales situation where a customer was waiting for an answer, it would probably be too slow, but for equipment troubleshooting it would probably be fine.

AUTOMOTIVE MECHANIC

Is there a strong smell of gasoline?

YES

Why:

Whether there is a strong smell of gasoline is needed to determine my diagnosis of the problem with the car

RULE013

If 1) the problem is Engine won't start, and
2) the cranking action of the engine is NORMAL, and
3) the fuel gauge is not empty, and
4) there is a strong smell of gasoline,

Then it is definite (100%) that my diagnosis of the problem with the car is The carburetor may be flooded. Take a break and let some of the gas in the carburetor evaporate. Try again in a few minutes..

** End - RETURN/ENTER to continue

2. Press RETURN/ENTER to continue.

Figure 5.4 *Screen showing a Personal Consultant Easy application.*

Select the axis of error if the robot is considered to be in a cylindrical coordinate system with center in the Synchronize position

X-AXIS
Y-AXIS
Z-AXIS
UNKNOWN

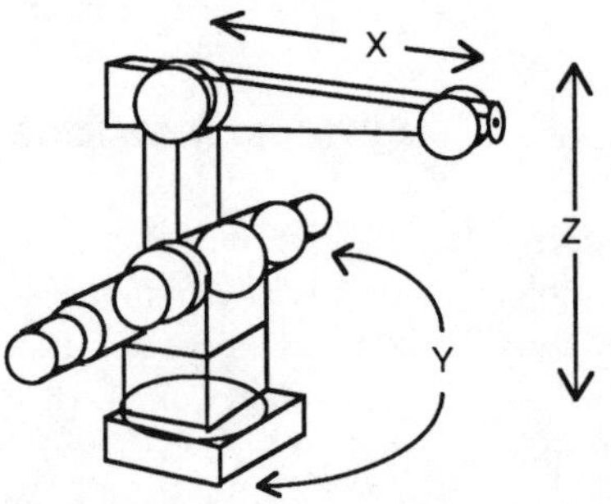

1. Use the arrow keys or first letter of item to position the cursor.
2. Press RETURN/ENTER to continue.

Figure 5.5 *Screen showing Personal Consultant Easy's use of graphics.*

Training and Support

EASY comes with the best documentation accompanying any tool for under $500. The manuals are well written, easy to use, and provide not only the technical description of the program but also a comprehensive introduction to the expert systems development process.

Texas Instruments has probably developed as many applications in Personal Consultant, both internally and in consultation with knowledge engineering clients, as have been developed in any PC-based tool. They have encouraged staff people in all their divisions to use Personal Consultant to solve manufacturing, troubleshooting, and configuration problems and have created some very useful systems.

If you decide to move up, the TI knowledge engineering group has the experience to help you develop systems in Scheme and Personal Consultant Plus and/or develop or field systems in Common LISP on the Explorer. Predictably, they will also be the first knowledge engineering consultants to help clients field systems on LISP chips incorporated within sophisticated equipment or instruments or run as coprocessors inside conventional computer hardware. If you want to play with EASY before making up your mind, Texas Instruments sells a demo disk version of EASY for $25 that allows you to develop and save a 10 rule system.

Summary

Many individuals who have started small companies and developed interesting small tools have been innovative entrepreneurs in the best sense of the word. Personal Consultant Easy reminds us, however, that when a large, well-capitalized corporation decides to create and support a superior product, it can usually dominate the market. Personal Consultant Easy is just such a tool, and it is clearly positioned to capture the below-$500 market. The other vendors in that market are going to have to specialize or work very hard to compete with the price and the benefits offered by Texas Instruments' Personal Consultant Easy.

At the moment, you can divide the tools at the bottom end of the market between those written in conventional languages and those written in symbolic languages. Personal Consultant Easy is clearly the best buy among the symbolically coded tools, and it offers a very strong alternative to most conventionally coded tools, except in cases where users want to integrate a tool with conventional code or pass lots of data from a conventional program. In the latter case, Insight 2, Exsys, and VP Expert are strong alternatives.

If you want a tool a nonprogrammer can use, EASY is superior to anything else at the low end of the market, especially when you consider the support Texas Instruments provides, both directly and by making it possible to systematically scale up to Personal Consultant Plus.

VP EXPERT

VP Expert is a high-quality tool that combines some powerful new features with a variety of features currently found only in mid-size tools costing from $995 to $5,000. And, it's priced at $99!

Like Personal Consultant Easy, VP Expert was introduced at AAAI in the summer of 1986. The program, promoted by Adam Osborne's Paperback Software, is a rule-based system with an inductive frontend. Several current inductive tools (discussed in the next chapter) claim to combine rules and induction, but, in fact, they simply allow you to create matrices that contain a single "example" (which functions as a rule). However, since these tools still apply an inductive algorithm to the matrices, you end up without the power of a rule-based system. VP Expert is a rule-based tool that provides the developer with the option of entering a set of cases or examples that the system converts into rules (eliminating unnecessary rules or clauses in the process). In essence, VP Expert is a rule-based tool with all the power and flexibility you might expect from a rule-based tool.

VP Expert is written in C and it is fast. It can read or write directly to dBASE II and III, Lotus 1-2-3, VP-INFO, and VP-PLANNER. A developer, through a single command, can create a system to search multiple records or whole ranges of cells. Most tools (like GURU) either limit you to accessing a single cell or record, or they force you to resort to a serious programming effort to do more complex searches. Moreover, calls to external programs are accomplished very quickly.

VP Expert represents facts as attribute–value pairs. VP Expert supports multivalued attributes that enable a developer to insert variables in rules via subscribed attributes (e.g., TIME[1], TIME[2] . . .). This feature is especially useful for processing multiple spreadsheet cells or multiple data base records.

VP Expert allows the developer to create special *data base rules*, generalized rules that can replace several similar rules. VP Expert allows these rules to be derived from data base records. Data base rules are inherently multiple instantiated since they are applied to every record in a data base.

Most small and mid-sized rule-based tools either lack confidence factors or implement them using standard probabilities, which makes them more undesirable if you are serious about using confidence factors. VP Expert provides the full implementation of the confidence factor schema otherwise found only in the expensive mid-size tools. VP Expert supports floating-point math expressions in the premises or conclusions of rules. It can also support a variety of trigonometric functions.

Backward chaining is the primary control strategy in VP Expert; however, commands in rule conclusions can be given to force limited forward chaining.

To create a knowledge base in VP Expert, you use an internal text editor. If you want, you can also use other text editors like WordStar to create or edit a knowledge-based file. The developer writes rules and adds text or questions by associating them with attributes and adding them to the end of the knowledge base. Many prefer this method of entry as it is the most elegant and efficient syntax to use to quickly develop a small to mid-size knowledge base.

VP Expert uses menus and color to provide one of the best interfaces available on a PC-based tool. Windows can be opened during a consultation to let the user see what rules are being tried and what conclusions have been reached. VP Expert also provides "intelligent help," by loading and running a knowledge base that consults with users when they have trouble

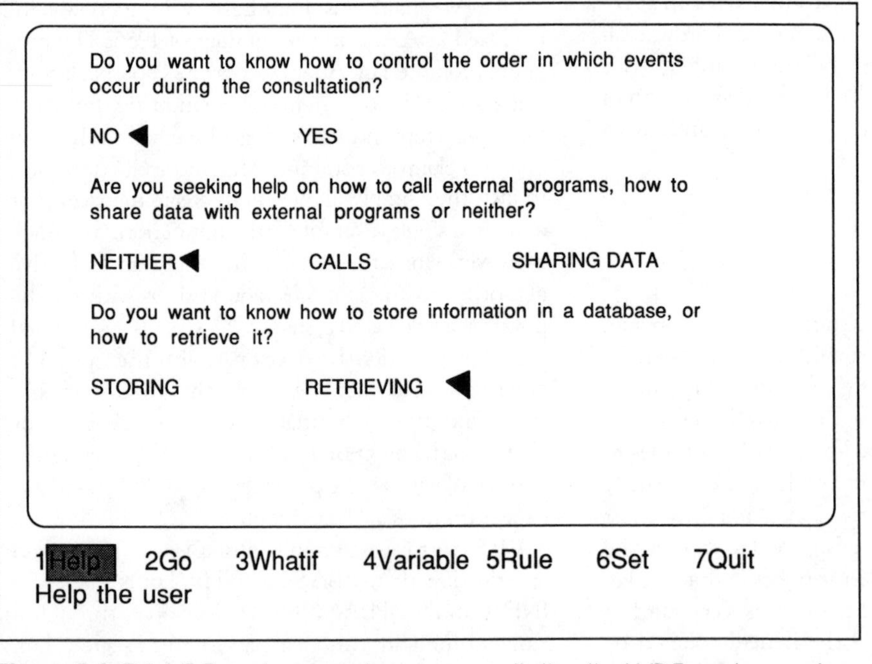

Figure 5.6 *This VP Expert screen shows a consultation that VP Expert runs when a user requests help with a problem.*

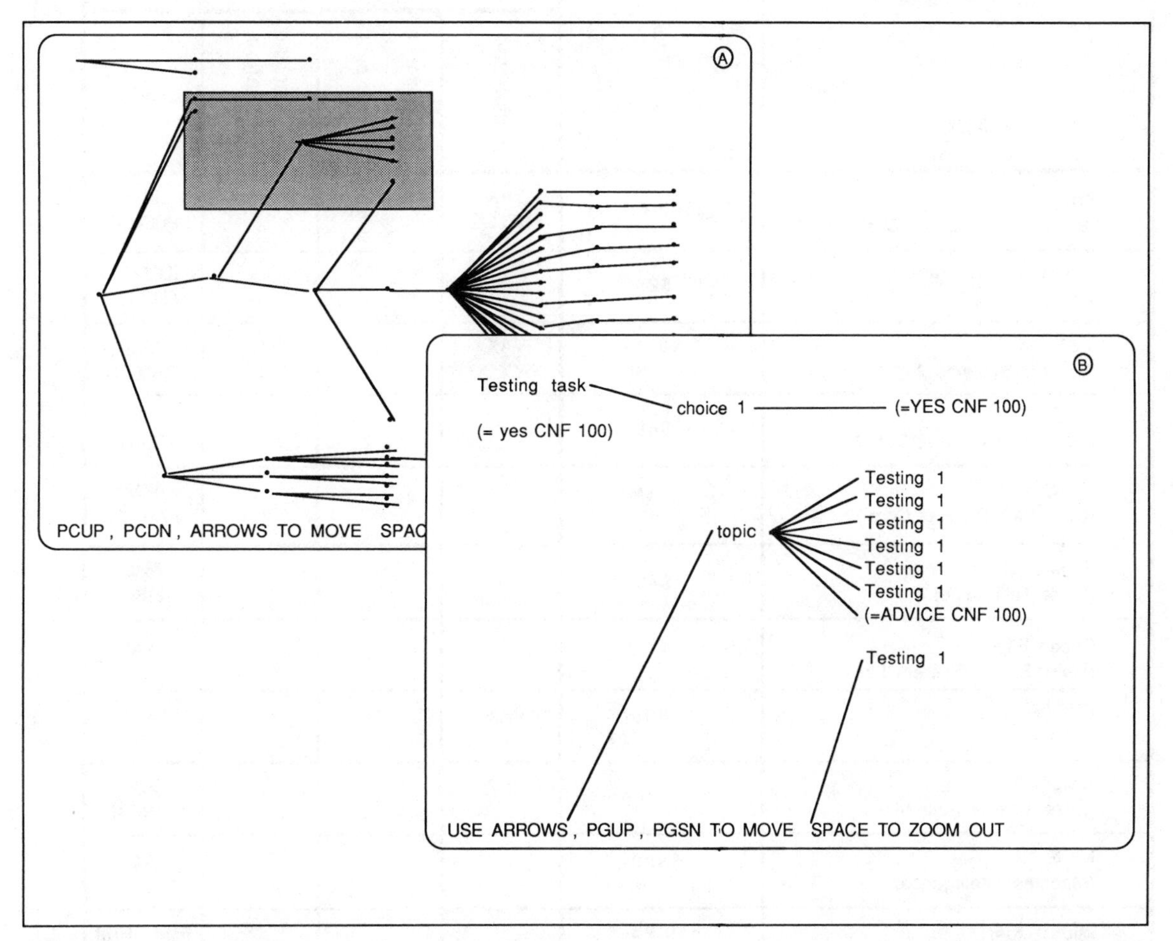

Figure 5.7 *Two VP Expert screens showing a graphic trace of a consultation. (A) shows how the screen appears. (B) is an enlargement of the shaded area.*

using the tool (see Figure 5.6). Full trace facilities are also provided. In addition, VP Expert provides a color graphic depiction of how rules relate to each other (see Figure 5.7). VP Expert supports explanations and lets users ask What–If questions after a consultation. This allows users to see how the results would have changed if different responses had been given. In effect, it is a simulator.

VP Expert is one of the best tools available for the PC. And for its price, it is clearly the most cost-effective PC tool currently available. When you stop to consider that VP Expert is being promoted by a marketing-organization like Paperback Software, you realize the expert system building tools market is about to enter a new phase, a phase in which these tools will be mass-marketed to corporate MIS departments. VP Expert's existence guarantees that current vendors who want to continue to compete in the expanding small to mid-size tool market must offer more power and functionality and better user interfaces for less money if they hope to remain competitive.

OTHER SMALL TOOLS

Several other small tools perform admirably for various applications. Table 5.3 lists most of the other small tools and provides an overview of their capabilities and characteristics.

Table 5.3 *Small expert system building tools.*

TOOL (Vendor)	Price of Tool	Hardware			
		Mini/ Mainframe	Workstation (UNIX, RISC, VMS, etc.)	LISP Machine Workstation	PC
Apes (Programming Logic Systems)	$395-6K	VAX PROLOG			IBM PROLOG
Arity E.S. Dev. Package (Arity Corp.)	$295				IBM-AT PROLOG
ESP Advisor (Expert Systems Int'l.)	$895-3K	VAX PROLOG			IBM PROLOG
EST (Mind Path Product Corp.)	$495				IBM TI PC
ES Starter (Mind Path Product Corp.)	$49				IBM PASCAL
ExperOPS+ (ExperTelligence)	$495				Mac LISP
Expert Edge (Helix Expert System Ltd.)	$795				IBM C
EXSYS (Exsys Inc.)	$395-5K	VAX C	• C		IBM C
Insight 2+ (Level Five Research)	$485				IBM PASCAL
MICE (Machine Intelligence)	$300-9K		• C		IBM C
MicroExpert (McGraw-Hill)	$49.95-59.95				IBM,CP/M PASCAL
TOPSI (Dynamic Master Systems)	$125-375				IBM,CP/M C
VP Expert (Paperback Software)	$99				IBM C
Wisdom XS (Software Intelligence Laboratory)	$750-20K		Apollo C		IBM C
Xi User (Expertech)	$275				IBM PROLOG
XPER (Abacus Software)	$39.95				Commodore C

• = Wide variety of hardware

SUMMARY

The small system tool market is growing. These tools are designed to run on personal computers and can be used to develop knowledge systems of up to about 500 rules. Some of the tools are quite trivial, but others are very powerful—some as powerful as the original EMYCIN tool that underlies MYCIN. Most small tools can be used by individuals who are willing to spend it is helpful to have a knowledge engineer assist your experts.

Although the pricing of these tools is confusing—some less powerful products are priced high, while some of the less expensive tools are very credible—this, however, is certain: powerful, personal computer-based tools will soon be sold for about the price of other more sophisticated software. And their value as a job aid is high. They can make your office more productive and efficient when applied to situations that are not enormously complex.

6

Inductive Tools

INTRODUCTION

When the various types of tools were introduced in Chapter 4, inductive tools were cited as very user-friendly, but also relatively weak and inflexible. This does not mean they are poor tools; it simply means you must exercise care to be sure they are used for purposes for which they are most effective. Inductive tools are ideal in situations where the client has numerous examples of a correct analysis and decision-making process. An inductive tool allows such a client to quickly develop a good system to guide future decisions. Moreover, the development process is so straightforward that the developer can skip most of the knowledge acquisition effort associated with developing other expert systems.

Inductive tools were derived from experiments in machine learning. Their developers were interested in how to generalize rules from examples. The original algorithm for induction, called CLS, was developed in 1962 by Earl Hunt. It has been improved by Ross Quinlan, who developed an early inductive tool called ID3. The initial research and development by these two individuals has since been improved upon and made available to business and educational markets through the efforts of Dr. Donald Michie and his co-workers at the University of Edinburgh, the Turing Institute, and by Dr. Michie's company, Intelligent Terminals, Ltd.

Inductive tools use an algorithm that constructs a simple decision tree from a number of initial examples entered by the developer (see Figure 6.1). To make a recommendation, the tool uses an algorithm to convert the examples into a decision tree and in the process prioritizes the order of questions asked the user. The best of these tools are well designed, easy to use, and quite fast. While they minimize the knowledge engineering task, they do not eliminate it; they require the developer to analyze the examples and specify each attribute in each example.

Inductive tools can operate on a wide range of hardware; some operate on personal computers, while others run on mini or mainframe computers.

AN EXAMPLE OF INDUCTION

Consider the following example. You want to choose an instructional medium to present information to a group of trainees. The basic theory that will guide your choice of medium assumes the medium you use in a particular unit of instruction should simulate, as closely as possible, the real-life environment in which trainees will work after completing the training. Thus, if trainees will be asked to evaluate applications using a computer once they complete a course on Application Evaluation, the training program should present applications and expect responses via a computer.

Assume you have developed a number of instructional programs and have saved the data from each. As you review the previous choices, you see that previous media decisions were based on similar considerations: the nature of the task the trainees would undertake after completing the training program, the nature of the responses the trainees would make on the job, the cost of the medium, and so on.

If you were using 1st-Class to develop your Media Advisor, you would begin by creating a file called "Media." 1st-Class would then prompt you through

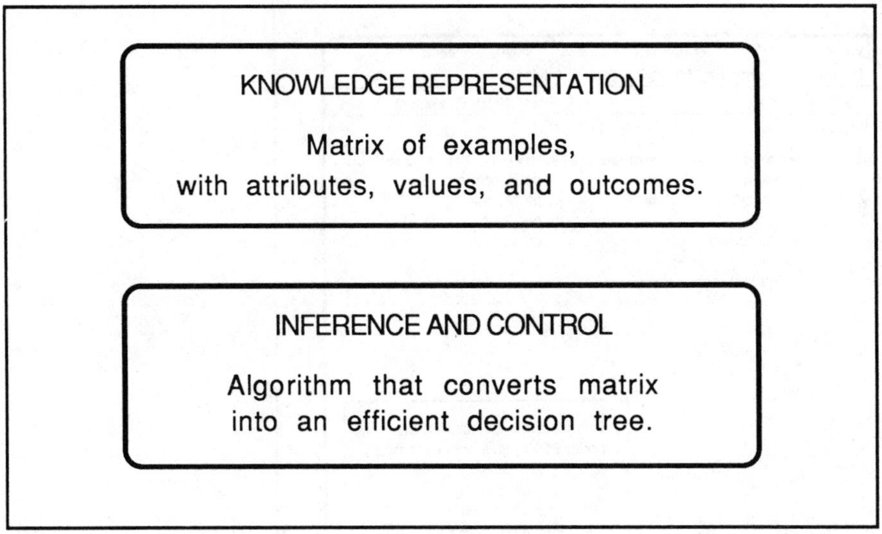

Figure 6.1 *Architecture of an inductive tool.*

developing a knowledge base. You would begin on a menu screen called "Definitions." On this menu you would define the attributes needed to analyze a media problem and then provide a list of values each attribute could take. Figure 6.2 provides an example of the 1st-Class menu with the attributes and values for a sample Media Advisor.

Notice the six attributes of media selection listed:

- **situation** Situation: What trainees will face when they return to the job.
- **stimDuratn** Stimulus duration: How long trainees will have to interact with whatever situation they face when they return to the job.
- **appr_respon** Appropriate response: The type of responses trainees will normally make on the job.
- **immFeedback** Immediate feedback: Instructors must specify if they want to provide trainees with feedback after each response during the training program.
- **review_int** Review interval: The point at which the instructor wants to provide trainees with a review of their progress in the training program.
- **budget** Budget: The amount of money available to develop and present the training program.

Having identified these six attributes as appropriate to use in analyzing previous instructional design efforts, next list the possible values each attribute can take. For example, notice in Figure 6.2 that the situation trainees must respond to can be either environmental, pictorial, symbolic, or verbal.

Notice at the bottom of the screen in Figure 6.2 the beginning of a sentence: "When the student completes the training program and returns to the job." When you define attributes and values in 1st-Class, you can also "page down" and enter a sentence that defines the attribute or value. That sentence will later be used in the dialogue the system conducts with a user.

Once you have listed the attributes of the problem, move on to the "Examples" menu. 1st-Class lists the attributes you defined at the top of a matrix and expects you to enter as many examples as you want, using the values previously defined. (It's easy to go back and add values, so you are not really limited.) Figure 6.3 shows four screens created to capture 38 examples. Since you could not enter all the information for one example on one screen (notice the "weights → " prompt that appears on the right side of the first

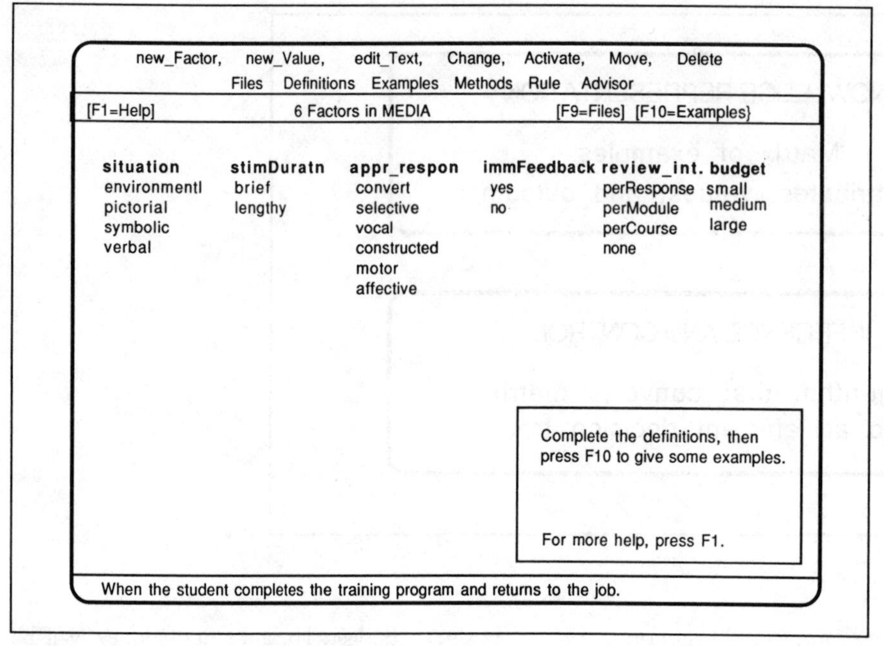

Figure 6.2 *1st-Class media definitions screen.*

screen), simply move the cursor right until you are on the second screen where you complete your entry of each example.

On the right side is a column for "Result" and a final column for "weight" (a type of confidence factor). The result column is where you enter the medium selected in each particular case. In Figure 6.3 all weights have been set at "1.00."

For the purposes of the example, assume you had 38 examples of medium selections done by a media consultant. You are trying to capture the consultant's analysis skills in the advisor. Thus, you enter each media decision made by your expert, starting with the six values that describe the particular case and then the resulting media selection. Note that some cases are exactly like others. In the same circumstances, your expert chooses the same medium.

Once you have entered all the case data, move on to the next menu, "Methods," and tell the system to generate a rule (or decision tree) that describes the most efficient way to approach the media selection problem.

When 1st-Class is done, move to the "Rule" screen to review 1st-Class's analysis of the problem. The rule that 1st-Class developed is shown in Figure 6.4. (The decision tree takes up two screens accessed by "Page Down" and "Page Up.") Notice that 1st-Class has rearranged the order of the attributes to ask the user questions in the most efficient way. By asking about the "Review Interval" first, 1st-Class isolates two results: "Human Tutor" and "Workbooks" and can then discriminate between them by asking about the stimulus duration, and so on.

Figure 6.5 illustrates a series of screens that make up a typical consultation. In each case, the cursor is used to position a highlighted bar over the correct option. The text the developer associated with each attribute and value and typed at the bottom of the "Definitions" screen generates the questions and options. Assume the developer entered all the cases or "problems" the media consultant had previously solved. Now a user wants similar advice on some new problem. The user provides the system with a description of the problem

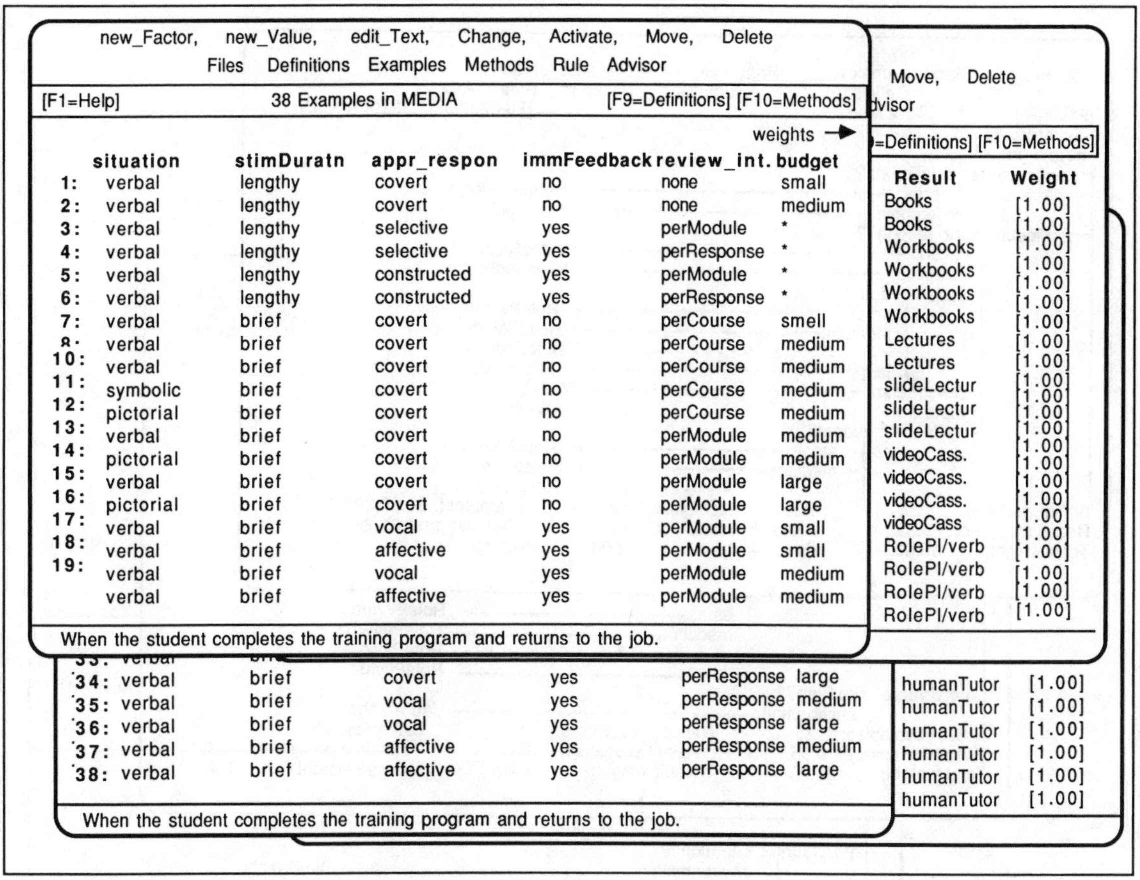

new_Factor, new_Value, edit_Text, Change, Activate, Move, Delete
Files Definitions Examples Methods Rule Advisor

[F1=Help] 38 Examples in MEDIA [F9=Definitions] [F10=Methods]

weights →

	situation	stimDuratn	appr_respon	immFeedback	review_int.	budget	Result	Weight
1:	verbal	lengthy	covert	no	none	small	Books	[1.00]
2:	verbal	lengthy	covert	no	none	medium	Books	[1.00]
3:	verbal	lengthy	selective	yes	perModule	*	Workbooks	[1.00]
4:	verbal	lengthy	selective	yes	perResponse	*	Workbooks	[1.00]
5:	verbal	lengthy	constructed	yes	perModule	*	Workbooks	[1.00]
6:	verbal	lengthy	constructed	yes	perResponse	*	Workbooks	[1.00]
7:	verbal	brief	covert	no	perCourse	smell	Lectures	[1.00]
8:	verbal	brief	covert	no	perCourse	medium	Lectures	[1.00]
10:	verbal	brief	covert	no	perCourse	medium	slideLectur	[1.00]
11:	symbolic	brief	covert	no	perCourse	medium	slideLectur	[1.00]
12:	pictorial	brief	covert	no	perCourse	medium	slideLectur	[1.00]
13:	verbal	brief	covert	no	perModule	medium	videoCass.	[1.00]
14:	pictorial	brief	covert	no	perModule	medium	videoCass.	[1.00]
15:	verbal	brief	covert	no	perModule	large	videoCass.	[1.00]
16:	pictorial	brief	covert	no	perModule	large	videoCass	[1.00]
17:	verbal	brief	vocal	yes	perModule	small	RolePl/verb	[1.00]
18:	verbal	brief	affective	yes	perModule	small	RolePl/verb	[1.00]
19:	verbal	brief	vocal	yes	perModule	medium	RolePl/verb	[1.00]
	verbal	brief	affective	yes	perModule	medium	RolePl/verb	[1.00]

When the student completes the training program and returns to the job.

	situation	stimDuratn	appr_respon	immFeedback	review_int.	budget	Result	Weight
33:	verbal	brief					humanTutor	[1.00]
34:	verbal	brief	covert	yes	perResponse	large	humanTutor	[1.00]
35:	verbal	brief	vocal	yes	perResponse	medium	humanTutor	[1.00]
36:	verbal	brief	vocal	yes	perResponse	large	humanTutor	[1.00]
37:	verbal	brief	affective	yes	perResponse	medium	humanTutor	[1.00]
38:	verbal	brief	affective	yes	perResponse	large	humanTutor	[1.00]

When the student completes the training program and returns to the job.

Figure 6.3 *1st-Class screens with examples of media.*

by answering the questions asked by the Media Advisor program. The system provides advice on the last screen—the user should consider a workbook.

The developer does not have to create rules or worry about the order of the questions. The developer *does* have to identify the appropriate attributes (and values) that describe the problem, enter cases or examples, and provide textual descriptions of each attribute and value. The inductive system does the rest.

Similar Advice Via a Rule-Based System

Notice you could just as well represent the knowledge involved in this decision-making process in a rule format. Table 6.1 provides a summary of the expert's decision-making process. Table 6.2 shows the five rules you would need to capture that information.

When you examine the knowledge contained in the matrix in Table 6.1, think of each column as an example. It's as if you consulted a human expert and were told there were five things to consider in selecting an instruction medium. So you write the five considerations across the top of the matrix and then ask for an example to illustrate the particular approach. The human expert continues, "If the on-the-job stimulus is to be verbal, and the stimulus is to be persistent, and . . ., then I recommend a book as the most appropriate instructional medium."

By continuing in this manner, you might develop

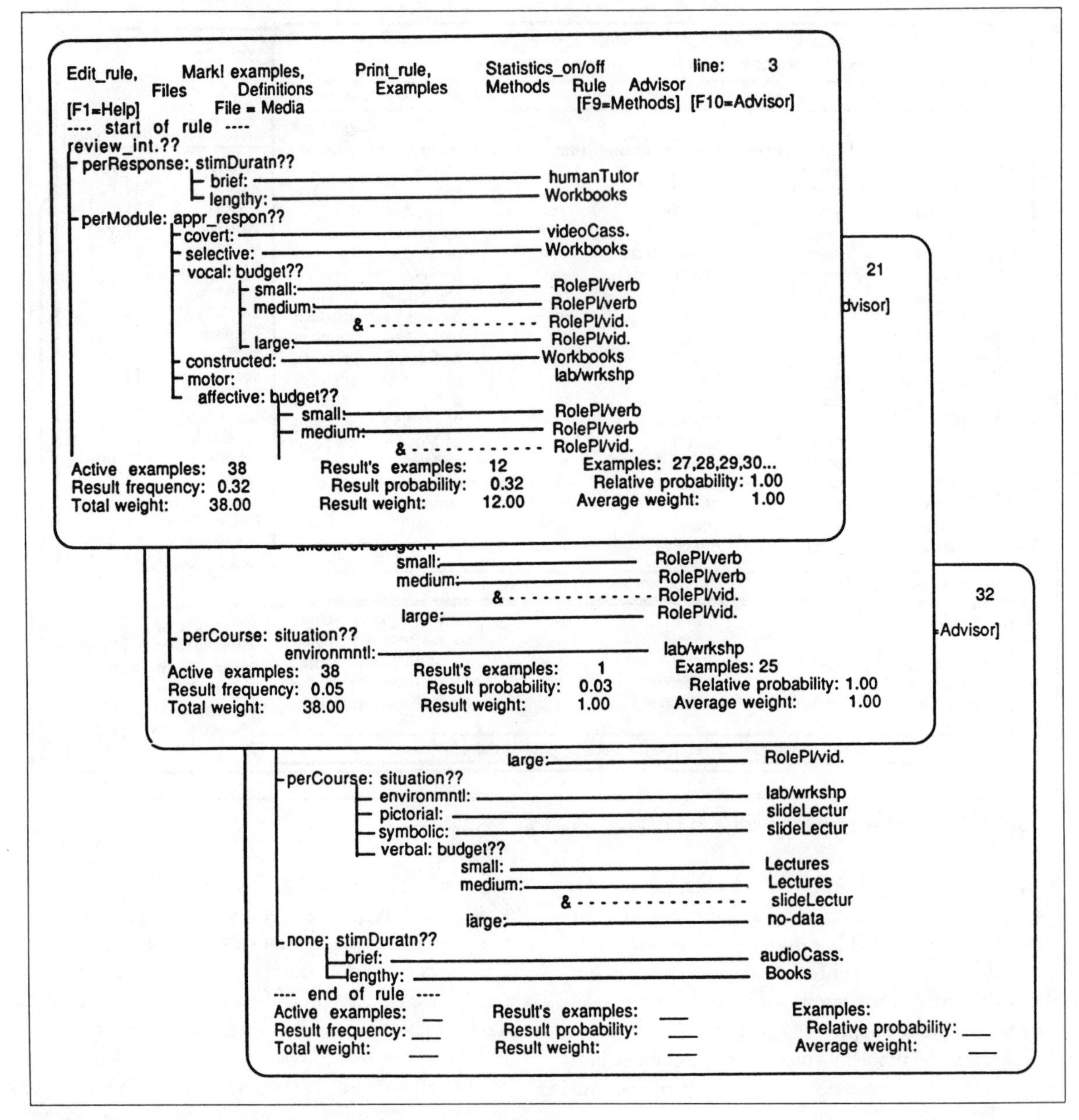

Figure 6.4 *Media "Rule" (Decision Tree).*

a matrix similar to that pictured in Table 6.1. Note, however, that neither the matrix in Table 6.1 nor the 38 examples listed in 1st-Class begin to include all the combinations actually possible. You also might consider, for example, creating a new possibility by working across the matrix and selecting a new combination such as the following:

(Rule 6)

If stimulus situation is ENVIRONMENTAL

and stimulus duration is PERSISTENT
and appropriate response is AFFECTIVE
and instructional feedback is NO
and presentation modification is NONE
and training budget is >\$100

Then medium to consider is . . .

By considering an alternative set of combinations, you create a new rule. The human expert might review this rule and decide that in this case the best recommendation would be a lecture. Thus, from the six categories placed at the top of the matrix, it is possible to generate a very large set of rules, each covering a different set of combinations.

An inductive-based tool such as TIMM, for example, has a mode in which it reviews a matrix (called a *knowledge base*) before proposing a combination of attributes and values that have not yet been associated

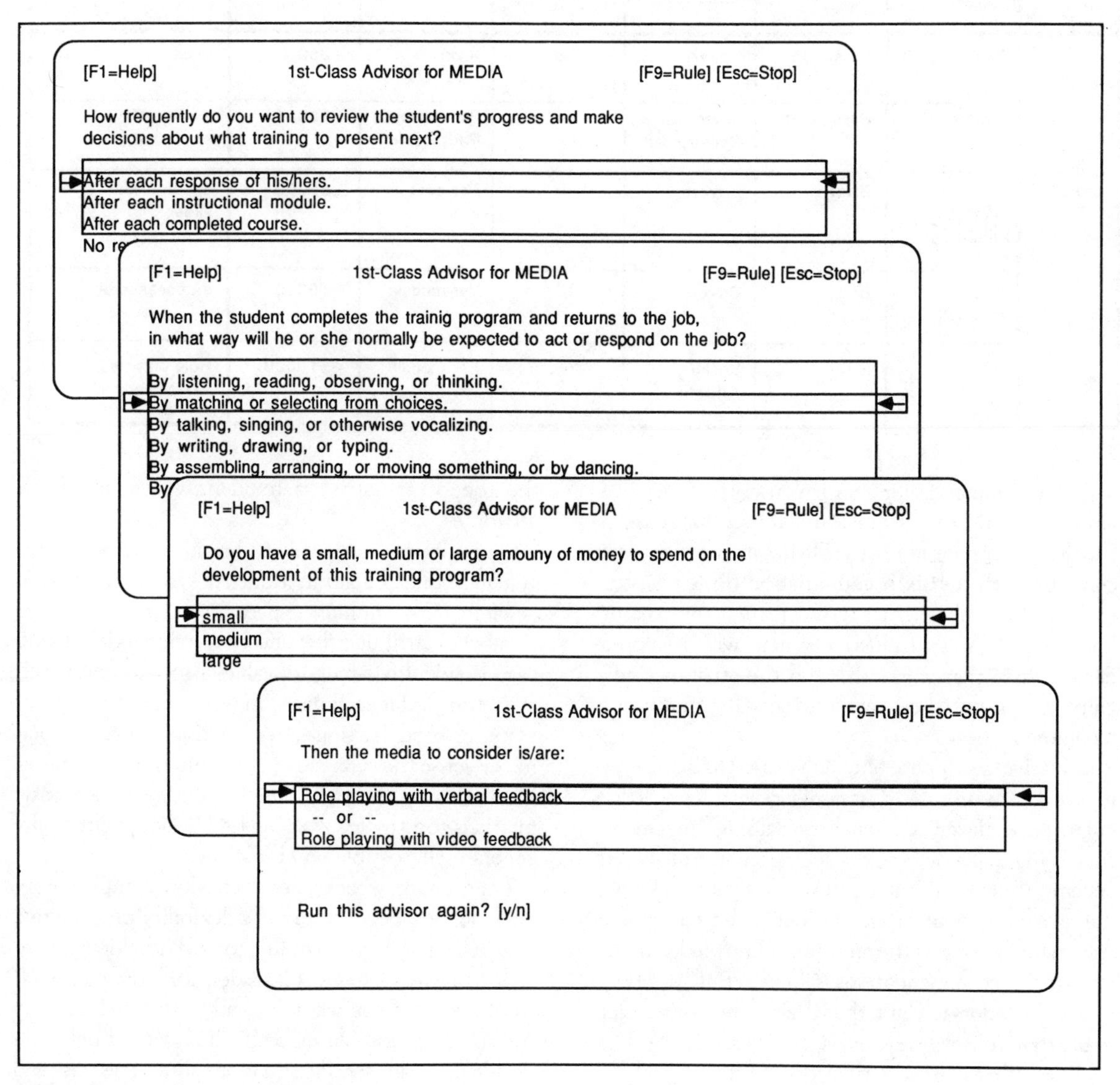

Figure 6.5 *Media consultation.*

Table 6.1 *Instructional media selection decision matrix.*

	IF						THEN
Attribute	Stimulus Situation	Stimulus Duration	Appropriate Response	Instructional Feedback	Presentation Modification	Training Budget	Media to Consider
Values of Attribute	Environmental Pictorial Symbolic Verbal	Brief - Persistent	Covert Selective Constructed Vocal Motor Affective	Yes No	Per response Per module Per course None	$	(Recommendation)
Examples or Rules	Verbal	Persistent	Covert	No	None	$500	Book
	Verbal	Persistent	Selective Constructed	Yes	Per response Per module	$500	Self-study workbook
	Verbal Symbolic Pictorial	Brief	Covert	No	Per course	$2000	Lecture with slides
	Verbal Pictorial	Brief	Covert	No	Per module	$5000	Videocassette
	Verbal	Brief	Vocal Affective	Yes	Per module	$10000	Role-play with Video Feedback

with a recommendation. So if you entered the five aforementioned rules (shown in Table 6.2) and asked TIMM to propose another, TIMM might very well come up with the sixth combination (Rule 6) listed earlier. Remember, once you create a matrix or knowledge base, an inductive system will develop a decision tree that works through the attributes efficiently, asking questions and finally making a recommendation.

Inductive systems are often advertised as being easy to use by those totally unfamiliar with knowledge engineering. Taken one way, this claim is the same as that being made by vendors selling small, rule-based systems: "Individuals can create systems without knowing anything about programming!" It's a reasonable statement, as long as the amount of knowledge needed to make recommendations is limited. But for inductive tool vendors to claim that their systems are easier to use than rule-based systems is simply confusing. The trick, whether you write rules or list attributes along the top of a matrix, is to identify the important attributes.

Certain types of problems are ideal for inductive systems. For example, an inductive system can be very efficient if the human expert first identifies a large number of attributes that affect a recommendation and can also identify a range of values associated with each attribute, and if each decision is the ultimate result of working through a single, basic, decision pattern (much in the sense that choosing a medium is only a matter of identifying the right "media rule"). Once a basic matrix is constructed, you can let TIMM systematically generate all possible combinations.

There are drawbacks, however. More complex problems quickly begin to tax the flexibility of inductive systems, a major shortcoming toward developing complex knowledge bases. Consider, for example, what would occur if you wanted to add two more rules (to the six previously developed) which would help you decide if certain specific situations should be classified

Table 6.2 *Five rules about instructional media selection.*

Rule 1:

IF stimulus situation is verbal
AND stimulus duration is persistent
AND appropriate response is covert
AND instructional feedback is no
AND training budget is > $500
THEN media to consider is book

RULE 2:

IF stimulus situation is verbal
AND stimulus duration is persistent
AND appropriate response is selective or constructed
AND instructional feedback is yes
AND presentation modification is per-response or per-module
AND training budget is > $500
THEN media to consider is self-study workbook

Rule 3:

IF stimulus situation is verbal or symbolic or pictorial
AND stimulus duration is brief
AND appropriate response is covert
AND instructional feedback is no
AND presentation modification is per-course
AND training budget is > $2000
THEN media to consider is lecture with slides

Rule 4:

IF stimulus is verbal or pictorial
AND stimulus duration is brief
AND appropriate response is covert
AND instructional feedback is no
AND presentation modification is per-module
AND training budget is > $5000
THEN media to consider is videocassette

Rule 5:

IF stimulus situation is verbal
AND stimulus duration is brief
AND appropriate response is vocal or effective
AND instructional feedback is yes
AND presentation modification is per-module
AND training budget is > $10000
THEN media to consider is role-play video with feedback

as verbal or symbolic. The resulting rules might look something like the following:

(Rule 7)
If situation is graphics or schematics or numbers or formulas or symbols
Then stimulus situation is symbolic

(Rule 8)
If situation is listening or conversation or dialogue or reading or textual materials or verbal
Then stimulus situation is verbal

In effect, you want to add rules to determine the value of an attribute defined in your initial matrix. In a backward chaining rule-based system, you would simply add the two new rules. Then the user is asked about the SITUATION when the system attempts to determine the value of STIMULUS SITUATION. This procedure is not possible using inductive tools. In an inductive system you would have to create another matrix to accommodate the new rules.

MORE ABOUT 1ST-CLASS

The first expert system building tool available on a personal computer was Expert-Ease, an inductive tool developed by Dr. Michie of Edinburgh, Scotland. The first version of Expert-Ease ran in UCSD PASCAL and cost $2,000. William Hapgood saw Expert-Ease demonstrated at the Boston Computer Society in the fall of 1984 and resolved to develop a better version of an inductive tool.

William Hapgood, formerly principal engineer and manager of Raytheon's Computer Systems Department, New Products Center, founded Programs in Motion Inc. to sell his new tool. The first version of 1st-Class was introduced in the summer of 1985. The current version, (3.0) considerably improved, was introduced at AAAI in August of 1986.

1st-Class is written in Microsoft PASCAL and assembler and runs in DOS on an IBM Personal Computer with at least 256K of memory.

Power and Flexibility

Hapgood employed the same algorithm used to develop Expert-Ease. ID3, developed by Ross Quinlan, creates a compact decision tree from a number of examples. In the process, it eliminates unnecessary factors and arranges questions in an optimized order that minimizes the number of questions required to get to a recommendation.

In addition, 1st-Class provides facilities that allow users either to construct decision trees or to design data base searches. In addition, Hapgood incorporated several additional features, rewrote the algorithm in Microsoft PASCAL so it will run in DOS, and developed an effective interface.

If you think of knowledge in terms of a matrix, think of each row as an example and each column as a set of values for any attribute. It's as if your media expert said there were six things she always considered when asked to recommend an instructional media. As she speaks, you write down each consideration and ask her to tell you what values each attribute could take.

When you use 1st-Class, you begin by naming a knowledge base, say "Media," then creating a matrix, starting with all possible outcomes (results), and then including all attributes (factors), and all possible values each attribute could take.

If you had entered this knowledge base as a set of 38 rules, it would have taken longer in most rule-based systems than it took in 1st-Class, although you could have entered the rules just as fast in a tool like Exsys that has a very efficient editor.

In Figure 6.3, each example is different. If appropriate, you could have entered the same examples more than once, perhaps modifying the overall weight in the process.

If your examples were drawn from actual data samples, you would expect to have several duplicate examples.

Once you enter all the examples you want (you can come back later and enter more), press F10 and move to a screen called Methods, which offers four options.

Optimized. If you select this option, 1st-Class automatically creates a rule or decision tree from the examples entered. Unnecessary factors are eliminated, and the remaining factors are rearranged to assure that the questions will be asked in an order that guarantees the minimal number of questions asked to get a particular result.

Left-right. This asks questions based on the order you entered the factors when you defined the matrix. Actually, since it asks the questions from left to right, it asks for factors in the reverse of the order you entered the factors. Still, since it is easy to rearrange the order of the factors whenever you want, with a little planning you can use this approach to control the exact sequence of questions asked to the user.

Customize. This lets you build your own rule using the decision tree diagram. If you use this facility to create rules similar to the rules you might enter in an ordinary rule-based tool, it is very tedious compared to any simple rule system.

In fact, you do not create a simple rule like you would in a rule-based system; you create a rule that incorporates all the simple rules concerning a common set of attributes and outcomes. Thus, the rule that recommends a media, as shown in Figure 6.4, is equivalent to 32 simple rules. If you know what you are doing, it's possible to use this mechanism, but it would be much harder for a beginner than writing simple rules for tools like Insight and Exsys.

On the other hand, if the developer wants to design a decision tree rather than a set of rules, this is a very powerful, user-friendly way to create decision trees. When you consider that many nonprogrammers are using small expert system building tools to allow them to program checklists and troubleshooting charts, you realize how useful this option can be.

Match. This option avoids compiling the examples into a decision tree and simply works through the factors, one at a time, trying to find an example that matches the answers the user provides. This option allows you to run systems that are too complex to compile into a decision tree, at some expense in speed. It is also used when the user responds "unknown" to a question. Since "unknown" eliminates the possibility of the system following the decision tree, the system automatically resorts to match.

In commenting on the uses of 1st-Class, Bill Hapgood says:

> The four methods in 1st-Class are used approximately equally by my customers, so I can no longer represent 1st-Class as an induction tool. It is a combination tool: a combination of induction, direct decision tree construction, and a data-base look-up technique of admittedly less power but easier access than dBASE III has.
>
> The point I am making is that often users have problems for which you and I might realize that an expert system is overkill. "Why," I asked a radiologist who was using the Match method exclusively, "not do this in dBASE II?" to which he responded that 1st-Class was a quicker way to build the menus and package his data.

To continue to develop the inductive example, assume your user wants to convert the examples entered into a rule. Figure 6.4 shows the rule or decision tree that 1st-Class generated for Media. Notice that 1st-Class modified the order of the factors to create a decision tree that asks the minimum number of questions necessary to reach a decision.

In discussing the use of rule or decision tree generation, Bill Hapgood remarked:

> I find a great deal of interest from customers in the rule screen, since it shows them both another view of their data (but one that is 100% correlated to it) and an exact map of how the consultation session will run. This visual feedback is crucial to inexperienced users, and it is probably the single most important reason for the success of 1st-Class. I have often heard users complain of bad experiences with rule-based systems, because after two dozen rules they can no longer see what is happening.

By pressing F10 again, you can run a Media consultation (see Figure 6.5). The text you created when you first entered the factors and values is now used to create questions. You choose an answer by moving a highlighted bar to the answer you wish and pressing return. Users are not allowed to answer with less than full certainty, though they can use "unknown" if the developer has activated that option. 1st-Class normally provides users with all possible results, but it can be made to provide only the result with the highest weight.

If you want to create a knowledge base like the one just demonstrated, 1st-Class is a viable tool. If you decided to create a knowledge base where you had a rule that decided about the value of a factor in another knowledge base, you face a very different challenge. For example, consider what would happen if you wanted to enter a rule that specified that:

If	the worker is required to go from one site to another in the course of the job = true
and	the condition of the individual site affects the appropriate response = true
Then	Situation = environmental

This rule could not be placed on the Media matrix shown in Figure 6.3 since it has factors that decide on the value of another factor already in that matrix. You would need to create another matrix or rule and then link the two matrices together. 1st-Class provides for chaining matrices and allows the developer to specify the order in which the system should examine the matrices (forward or backward chaining), but it's not nearly as easy to do as it is to create a single matrix.

If you select Optimized, then inference and control is handled by the algorithm that generates the rule or decision tree. The weights are handled by a statistical program, but you can exercise considerable control over it.

1st-Class uses standard probabilities to analyze confidence and has trouble passing confidence factors from one matrix to another. You would not want to use 1st-Class if you had a problem that required tight control over confidence calculations. It would be impossible to create the Alpha knowledge base previously used to test several small rule systems in 1st-Class.

The Developer Interface

Building a simple knowledge base like the media example is simple. Moreover, since 1st-Class can handle a matrix that contains 32 factors, 32 different results (recommendations), and 255 examples, large problems can be quickly entered and analyzed. The trick, however, is not in entering the factors and values, but in determining the factors and values in the first place. If you are considering a problem like Media, where an expert has already worked out a theory and can tell you exactly what factors and values to consider, system development goes very fast. Moreover, in the nature of the decision tree algorithm, if unnecessary factors or values are entered, they will be ignored. The problem occurs when you encounter a large problem that is not well understood and you omit a factor.

As with all expert systems development efforts, of course, you can ask the expert to review case studies and suggest improvements when the system fails to provide the correct answers. Still, induction is not magic, and the suggestion that using an induction system is simpler than using a simple rule system can hardly be justified, except if the knowledge base is already well understood. Inductive systems are obviously easier to use whenever you already have a lot of data organized according to factors and values. You can easily add factors and values as you enter examples, so your initial analysis need not be exhaustive. However, the more you add, the more you have to worry about what you may still have omitted, and you run into increasingly complex weighting problems.

1st-Class provides a number of helpful editing and trace facilities. You can switch back and forth during a consultation to see where you are in the decision tree, save copies of consultations, and ask "what if" questions to see how the consultation would have gone otherwise. You can print out copies of the knowledge base. You can also exit to DOS in the middle of a session and then return. All in all, the developer interface is well designed and easy to use, as long as you simply want to develop systems by entering examples and optimizing rules.

Writing rules in 1st-Class by developing your own decision trees would be very tedious. (You can't use weights for individual rules.) Linking matrices together is hard to figure out. It can be done, but no editing facilities help you keep track of what you are doing.

The User Interface

If you want to produce a simple dialogue-based consultation like the one shown in Figure 6.5, then 1st-Class works about as smoothly as any small tool examined so far.

With a little additional work you can create title screens and tailor the questions that appear on the screen. It is also easy to select the colors you want to use, if appropriate.

The developer controls whether users can answer "unknown" and also provides text explanations of any questions, if desired.

If you want to create special screens with graphics, however, you will probably want to avoid 1st-Class since it doesn't make it easy to use graphics, though a programmer could probably work some graphics into a program.

Systems Interface

1st-Class allows a programmer to develop connections between 1st-Class and external programs. You can look up an answer in a data base file or get data from instrumentation, write a report to a special format, automatically control a video disk player or speech synthesizer, or calculate a result using a statistical program, all by passing files via MS-DOS. 1st-Class has a file interface to Lotus 1-2-3 and can call procedures written in BASIC, PASCAL, and other languages.

1st-Class can be used as a logic engine that can be called by external programs. This would work well if the external program needed an analysis of a set of well-defined factors, but would get very complex if the problem involved multiple matrices or complex confidence considerations.

1st-Class comes with a runtime system. Once you create a knowledge base, you can combine it with the runtime system and make copies to distribute.

Training and Support

1st-Class comes with an 8- by 9-inch three-ring binder. As long as you are content to use 1st-Class to develop a single matrix knowledge base, the documentation is adequate. If you decide to chain together two matrices, however, the documentation becomes nearly useless, and you are in for a lot of painful trial and error experiments.

Programs in Motion is a small company whose people are eager to help others develop systems with 1st-Class, so you can get a lot of help via the phone.

One Success Story

One successful expert system built with 1st-Class provides an example of how useful inductive tools can be when you face a problem that lends itself to this approach. NORCOM, a software company located in Juneau, Alaska, sells a software product called SCREENIO. NORCOM has over 500 corporate customers who use SCREENIO to design IBM PC screens for their Realia COBOL programs. NORCOM found that most of its customer support problems resulted from difficulties in using "editmasks" (patterns used in SCREENIO to specify output). Incorrect use of the "masks" could result from any of several errors, and customers often had to call several times before the problem was identified.

NORCOM used 1st-Class to develop an expert system to help customer service people handle the calls. Since they had nine months of data on typical problems and recommended fixes, they could simply enter the examples of their calls. The examples could be represented by nine factors, and the resulting rule or decision tree was composed of 30 lines. The system took one day to develop.

Now, when customers call, the customer support person simply asks each question asked by 1st-Class and then offers the customer the suggested fix. According to NORCOM general partner John Anderson, the system has "made a major improvement in our customer support responsiveness and efficiency. Since the customer support person doesn't have to understand anything about the problem, we can now use entry level people instead of senior technicians. And we can get an answer in under three minutes, compared to up to a week before. Since we're Lotus 1-2-3 spreadsheet users, 1st-Class is intuitively obvious to use. We were able to work with it immediately right out of the box, before even reading the manual."

Summary

1st-Class is one of the most popular inductive tools available today, and it is certainly one of the easiest to use.

If you think of the tools market segmenting, the lower end of the market is focused on providing tools for individuals who do not program, but who want to capture and distribute knowledge via a computer. Several market surveys have suggested that Lotus 1-2-3 has been responsible for the sale of more personal computers to managers than all other computer software programs combined. Lotus 1-2-3 is a tool or programming environment, not an application. Managers use it to develop their own spreadsheet programs. The potential of expert systems technology at the low end of the market is to provide many other tools that managers can use to develop useful applications.

Inductive tools like 1st-Class provide an ideal way for a manager who is not a programmer to develop a small application that can be used by employees to quickly analyze simple problems and determine the appropriate answers.

With its additional features, including its decision tree generation facility and its ability to serve as an easy-to-use data base, 1st-Class is one of the most popular tools among those who want to put expert systems into the hands of nonprogrammers.

The inductive approach has limitations, but it also has power when used on an appropriate problem. If you are managing an expert systems support group, you would probably want copies of 1st-Class around for managers and technicians to use with problems that 1st-Class is good at—problems for which the user has abundant data (examples) and can analyze the factors involved in choosing between one recommendation and another.

USING TIMM TO REPRESENT THE ALPHA KNOWLEDGE BASE

TIMM, the Intelligent Machine Model, is an inductive expert system building tool marketed by General Research Corporation. TIMM is written in FORTRAN and is focused entirely on induction. It contains a well-thought-out prompt interface that makes it easy to develop a rule base. You can enter individual rules indirectly by creating a knowledge base with only one rule (as discussed earlier).

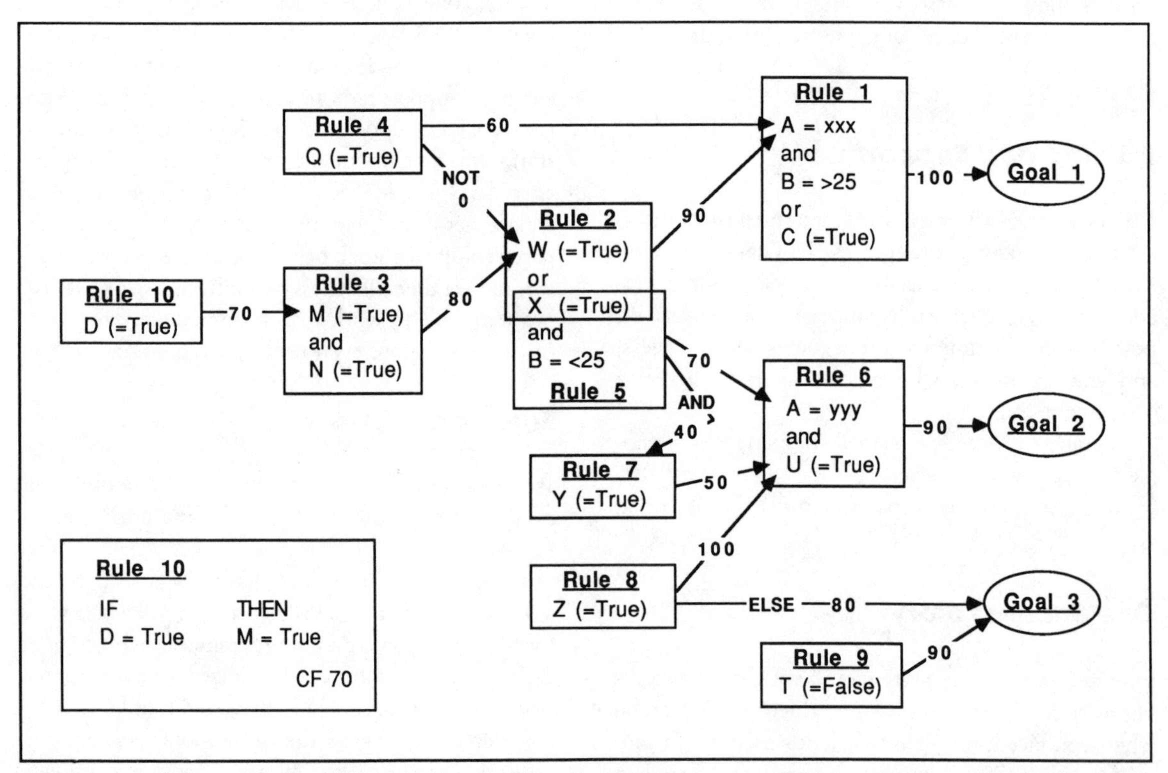

Figure 6.6 *Alpha. A small system designed to test the power and flexibility of a small expert system building tool.*

TIMM has a unique feature that lets it identify the rule that is the closest match to existing rules within a particular KB. Therefore, TIMM is very well suited for users who have knowledge that either involves several similar rules with many possible outcomes, or situations in which the human expert can identify a large number of variables that will affect a variety of outcomes. It does, however, lack the ability to identify specific rules. TIMM can provide assistance in developing rules implicit in a knowledge base matrix.

TIMM is sold to both business and government. It is available in a PC-AT version, and time-sharing capabilities are also supported. Several mid-size military applications have already been developed using TIMM. In addition, General Research has developed a generic application, TIMM-Tuner, an expert system that can assist a system manager in optimizing the performance of a VAX/VMS system.

If you consider the problems in creating the Alpha knowledge base used to test Insight 2 and Exsys in TIMM, you can see some of the problems encountered in using inductive systems for more complex problems. For simplicity, Alpha consists of only letters (see Figure 6.6). Alpha has four levels of rules, a variety of logical operators, and also passes information about confidence from one rule to the next. To represent Alpha using TIMM would require six different matrices as illustrated in Figure 6.7 (Dennis Cooper of General Research prepared this example).

Just by glancing at the Insight and Exsys knowledge bases in Chapter 5, you can see how easily Alpha can be represented using a rule-based system. Stop to consider why it looks so much more complex in TIMM.

To begin with, you can represent a simple rule in TIMM, but you must first create a knowledge base (a matrix) to contain it (i.e., knowledge base 1). Then, however, since TIMM uses a conventional approach to probability, it can't accept a rule that asserts that "if D is true, then M is true with a confidence of 70%." Traditional probability theory, and TIMM, hold that if you're 70 percent confident M is true if D is true, then you must be 30 percent confident M is false if

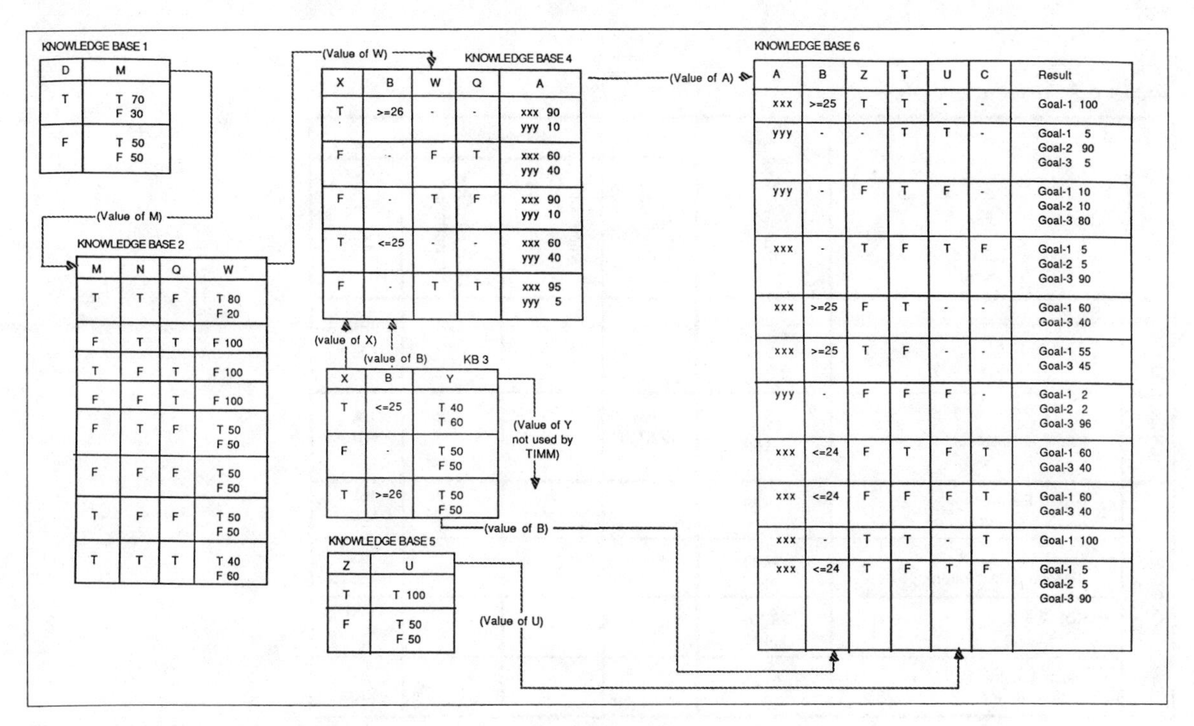

Figure 6.7 *The Alpha knowledge base represented in TIMM.*

D is false. Most human experts deny this type of inference, claiming that simply because they have a certain confidence in a relationship in one situation, they are not necessarily confident of the reverse. This objection led the creators of MYCIN to avoid traditional probability considerations and develop the confidence factors approach as an alternative.

On the other hand, because TIMM uses traditional probability theory, it is in a position to identify the existing rule that best matches a new example. So, for example, if you present EMYCIN with the following rules:

If a = 8, Then b = True
If a = 2, Then b = False

and then, when you are asked the value of a, you respond with a "3," EMYCIN will tell you it can't conclude anything about b. TIMM, on the other hand, will tell you that b is false, with some associated reliability factor. The reliability factor represents the degree to which the answer is closer to a = 2 than it is to a = 8. For certain problems this can be very useful, but in other situations it could be totally misleading.

Returning to TIMM's representation of Alpha, notice that the value of Y is unnecessary to TIMM. In the original version of Alpha, if Z was true, then U was true with a confidence of 100 percent. If Y was true, then U was true with a confidence of 50 percent. To satisfy TIMM's need for completeness, you have to tell it that if Z was false, then U was true with a confidence of 50 percent, and false with a confidence of 50 percent. Therefore, in essence, Y does not even affect the outcome, since U is always 50 percent true—which is something never intended to be said when the Alpha knowledge base was created.

In effect, when Ex-Tran 7 and RuleMaster (see opposite) claim to be handling individual rules, they are actually simply creating small matrices just as TIMM does. However, TIMM is a little more explicit about it, if only because TIMM's use of probabilities makes it more important that you create at least two rules to cover the possibility the rule is falsified.

Table 6.3 *Inductive tools.*

	TOOL (Vendor)	Price of Tool	Hardware: Mini/ Mainframe	Workstation (UNIX, RISC, VMS, etc.)	LISP Machine Workstation	PC
LARGE INDUCTIVE TOOLS	RuleMaster (Radian Corp.)	$1-17K	VAX C	• C		IBM C
	TIMM (General Research)	$1.9-19K	IBM FORTRAN			IBM FORTRAN
SMALL INDUCTIVE TOOLS	Expert-Ease (Softsync, Inc.)	$95				IBM PASCAL
	1st-Class (Programs in Motion)	$495				IBM PASCAL
	KDS 2 & 3 (KDS Corp)	$970-1,495				IBM Assembly
	Super Expert (Softsync, Inc.)	$199				IBM PASCAL

• = Wide variety of hardware.

OTHER INDUCTIVE TOOLS

Several inductive tools are available at the moment. Table 6.3 provides an overview of seven such tools. Three are available on both personal computers and mainframes or VAX systems, while the other four are available only on PCs.

Ex-Tran 7

Ex-Tran 7 is really a combination inductive and rule-based tool, but it is included as an inductive tool because that is its primary attribute. It was developed by Intelligent Terminals Ltd. in Scotland. Dr. Donald Michie was involved in its design and development. With Ex-Tran 7, rules can either be inferred from examples (using the tool's inductive capability) or entered into the system directly (as in traditional rule-based systems).

Ex-Tran 7 can automatically generate FORTRAN 77 code and enables the system developer to link the system with external FORTRAN subroutines to capture data or to run external programs or routines. Versions of Ex-Tran 7 are commercially available for IBM mainframe computers and Digital VAX machines.

This tool mixes induction and rules. However, since it was developed from an inductive perspective, the tool is limited in both power and flexibility. It is not nearly as flexible as any second-generation tools, but it can still be very useful if you are familiar with knowledge engineering and want to encode knowledge that can be formalized as examples or rules, and if you do not desire much sophistication with regard to inheritance and multiple instantiation factors.

Ex-Tran 7 is distributed in the United States by Jeffery Perrone & Associates, Inc.; however, it must be installed and supported by Scotland-based technicians employed by Intelligent Terminals Ltd. Because of this, an international company might want to consider this tool if it has research operations in Europe. It should also be considered by companies who possess a strong desire to develop an expert system using FORTRAN programming routines; this would allow the system to run on a personal computer, an IBM mini or mainframe system, or Digital machines.

RuleMaster

RuleMaster has its roots in Dr. Michie's conceptual approach to expert systems tool design. It is marketed by Radian Corporation. Like Ex-Tran 7, it is a combination inductive and rule-based tool. It is written in C language; therefore, it will operate in just about all UNIX environments. Although you can enter rules into the system directly, this tool is definitely oriented toward inductive. RuleMaster has the feel of a conventional programming language rather than that of a user-friendly rule-based tool like EMYCIN. A PC-AT version of the tool is available, as is a version that supports intelligent workstations.

Radian, using this tool itself, has developed several small- to medium-size applications, including TOGA (Transformer Oil Gas Analysis); WILLARD, a system that forecasts severe storm simulations based on information received from the National Weather Service; TITAN, a system developed to aid field technicians to diagnose faults in Texas Instruments' 990 microcomputers; and TURBOMAC, which diagnoses faults in large utility company turbines. In addition to its experience, the Radian AI group offers training and consulting services.

Expert One (Formerly Expert-Ease) and Super Expert

Expert-Ease and Super Expert were both designed by Dr. Michie and are both now sold by Softsync, Inc. Expert-Ease, the first PC-based expert system building tool sold in the United States, first sold in 1983 for $2,000. Later it was sold by Human Edge, Inc., for $695. When it was acquired by Softsync, Inc., it was renamed Expert One. Softsync sells Expert One for $95 and positions it as an inexpensive way to get started.

The price of Super Expert varies depending on the

size matrix you want to build. The largest version of Super Expert allows you to enter up to 1,000 examples, each with up to 50 attributes. It allows you to string matrices together; you can string together eight matrices for backward chaining execution, and up to 20 matrices for forward chaining execution. In addition, Super Expert can be linked with Reports Plus, which, in turn, allows you to retrieve data from dBASE II or III or Lotus 1-2-3. You can also take data from a dBASE II or III or Lotus 1-2-3 program and then induce rules from that data. Although the user interface of Super Expert is inferior to that of 1st-Class, this new inductive tool offers power and flexibility.

SUMMARY

Inductive system building tools, like 1st-Class, Super Expert, TIMM, and RuleMaster, are all well designed and easy to use. They provide a knowledge acquisition methodology that can aid in diagnosing complex situations. They work best, however, in situations when considerable case data (or examples) are already available and if an expert is available to analyze the problem-solving process in terms of a limited number of independent factors (attributes) that jointly determine which one of a set of recommendations to make—in other words, a problem whose knowledge can be represented by rules, each with the same attributes and each concluding one possible outcome. A large number of problems which business people must address daily possess these characteristics. Inductive systems can certainly be used to help solve such problems.

7

Mid-Size Rule-Based Tools

INTRODUCTION

The upper end of the expert system building tool market is dominated by large hybrid tools and a few large structured rule-based tools. The lower end features inductive tools and the simple rule-based tools. In the middle are a number of mid-size tools that run on personal computers and UNIX workstations. Most mid-size tools are structured rule tools. They tend to cost several thousands rather than hundreds of dollars and to be supported by larger companies that not only sell tools but provide training programs and consulting services. Most mid-size tools enable a developer to create and field very sophisticated systems. Indeed, these tools are probably responsible for most expert systems fielded as of the end of 1986. This chapter discusses five mid-size tools in some detail.

Structured rule tools differ from the simple rule tools by providing some mechanism to allow the developer to divide rules into hierarchically arranged sets. The simplest of these tools accomplish this by allowing the developer to write variable rules or rules that call on information in a data base, while the more sophisticated tools allow the developer to design a context tree and assign rules to a specific context. In context-based systems, one set of rules can inherit information acquired from rules in another context. These tools allow the developer to rely on multiple instantiation and are very desirable whenever you are building a system that contains a large number of rules or whenever the problem naturally lends itself to structured subdivision.

To describe a tool as structured rule-based doesn't necessarily imply it is better than a small tool. As noted, many small tools have practical uses and might be more important in the spread of knowledge-based systems than mid-size tools. Structured rule-based tools run the risk of trying to do too much, using limited hardware, or being overly complex for everyday practical use by those who are not knowledge engineers. Further, if these tools become overly sophisticated, they start competing with the larger tool market where their limitations become very pronounced.

Ideally, a true structured rule-based tool lets a serious knowledge engineer develop a structured rule-based expert system using the powerful attributes of a personal computer and the developer's knowledge of computer programming, as opposed to a small expert systems tool with which a person can develop a small system using a PC, but without having to know any programming language.

Why such a difference? Because programmers generally want to develop expert systems that draw their information from external data bases, other external programs, or subroutines, or allow for the incorporation of procedural code within a program. Moreover, since many of today's structured rule-based tool programs use signal data, these tools enable the developer (programmer) to program hooks to external sensors; a very valuable attribute.

MID-SIZE TOOL BASICS

Mid-size tools typically allow you to partition the rule base and take advantage of multiple instantiation and simple inheritance.

They also provide confidence factors or Bayesian probabilities or allow the developer to easily encode a method of handling uncertainty. A system that uses ordinary probabilities is generally not sophisticated enough for many of the uses characteristic of a structured rule-based tool.

A good structured rule-based tool should make it easy to create any user interface display desired. And with a little programming, a developer could use graphic displays whenever necessary, making the user interface friendlier.

Finally, a structured rule-based tool should be supported by documentation that explains, clearly and effectively, how to use the tool to accomplish each of the aforementioned tasks. Vendors offering these tools should also offer or provide an effective training program on how to use the tool to do elementary knowledge engineering. In addition, vendors should offer consulting for anyone wishing experienced help in their first development efforts.

No existing tool offers all the features mentioned. Some of the better known candidates for a mid-size structured rule-based tool are M.1, Nexpert, Personal Consultant Plus, KES 2, and GURU.

FIVE MID-SIZE TOOLS

The year 1985 witnessed the emergence of a number of powerful PC-based expert system building tools. In part, this new class of tools evolved from the enhancement of existing PC tools and, in part, resulted from the release of even newer, more powerful tools. Not all these tools are structured rule-based tools. Some fall into the mid-size tool category based on their price, their editing capabilities, and the support that accompanies them. These tools make it possible for programmers to develop and field very sophisticated expert systems while using the affordability and power of a personal computer.

M.1, NEXPERT, AND PERSONAL CONSULTANT PLUS

To become acquainted with the tools and test their performance, consider the knowledge base "Beta," designed to use a number of features that might be found in a mid-size tool application. The process of designing Beta was itself revealing. In some areas the tools were so different it was hard to find common knowledge representation problems to test them. This chapter evaluates the common features of the tools and provides a discussion of each tool's unique features. Ultimately, the decision to buy one of these tools rests on an analysis of your specific needs and your personal preferences and resources.

The Beta knowledge base, shown in Figure 7.1, has rules to propagate various certainties. In addition, assume that file data are derived from a spreadsheet and that conclusions cause graphic displays developed in external graphic programs to be displayed. Also included is a demon as well as a generic rule that can be handled by either multiple instantiation in a frame, by structured-rule system, or by M.1's variable rules approach. This Beta knowledge base represents a common body of knowledge. Using it, you can see what kind of problems you encounter when trying to capture this knowledge in a small expert system developed in each of three mid-size tools.

The description and evaluation of each tool is limited to features clearly supported by the tool and explained in the documentation accompanying it. All three tools allow you to program your way around various limitations. Thus, each vendor has suggested that its tool could be used to do things often overlooked. However, a tool should not be credited with a feature if only a skilled programmer can create it with considerable difficulty. The essence of a tool is that you get a set of well-documented, easy, ready-to-use features.

The Three Tools

M.1 (Version 2) is a tool for the IBM PC produced by Teknowledge, Inc. M.1, first released in the summer of 1984, was originally written in PROLOG and has since been rereleased in C. Conceptually, M.1 is a cross between EMYCIN and PROLOG. It is unique among the mid-size tools for use of an external editor to create the knowledge base and for variable rules that permit a single rule with variables to be instantiated as a number of particular rules. Of the three tools under review, M.1 is most clearly targeted at programmers who want to develop expert systems that can be easily integrated into a conventional computer environment. Teknowledge also offers a version of M.1 for IBM mainframes.

Nexpert (Version 0.96) is a rule-based tool from Neuron Data designed to run on a 512K Macintosh. Nexpert is well adapted to the Mac's highly graphic and interactive window environment. At first glance, it bears a resemblance to a high-end tool running on a LISP workstation. Nexpert introduces a powerful new inference strategy that allows you to write rules without specifying forward or backward chaining. During a consultation the system can use either strategy, as appropriate. Originally developed in LISP, Nexpert has been converted into a mixture of C, PASCAL, and assembly language. Nexpert was premiered at the International Joint Conference on Artificial Intelligence (IJCAI) in August 1985 and is primarily targeted at the research community.

Texas Instruments' Personal Consultant Plus is a significantly enhanced version of Personal Consultant, an expert system building tool for TI and IBM PCs of the XT and AT class. Personal Consultant Plus runs under PC Scheme (a subset of Common LISP). Personal Consultant, a nearly perfect clone of EMYCIN released in the summer of 1984, has expanded beyond the EMYCIN model by including a number of new features, including frames and demons. Of the three tools, Personal Consultant Plus is targeted at the widest audience. Being written in LISP, the tool is popular among researchers and educators. Individuals interested in embedding applications into hardware are also interested in the Personal Consultant Plus, which allows developers to write a program on this tool and then transfer it to the "LISP Chip." Finally, Texas Instruments has established a strong lead in helping clients develop small, practical, standalone applications, and thus Personal Consultant Plus is popular with those who are interested in developing intelligent job aids.

You can compare and contrast the three tools accord-

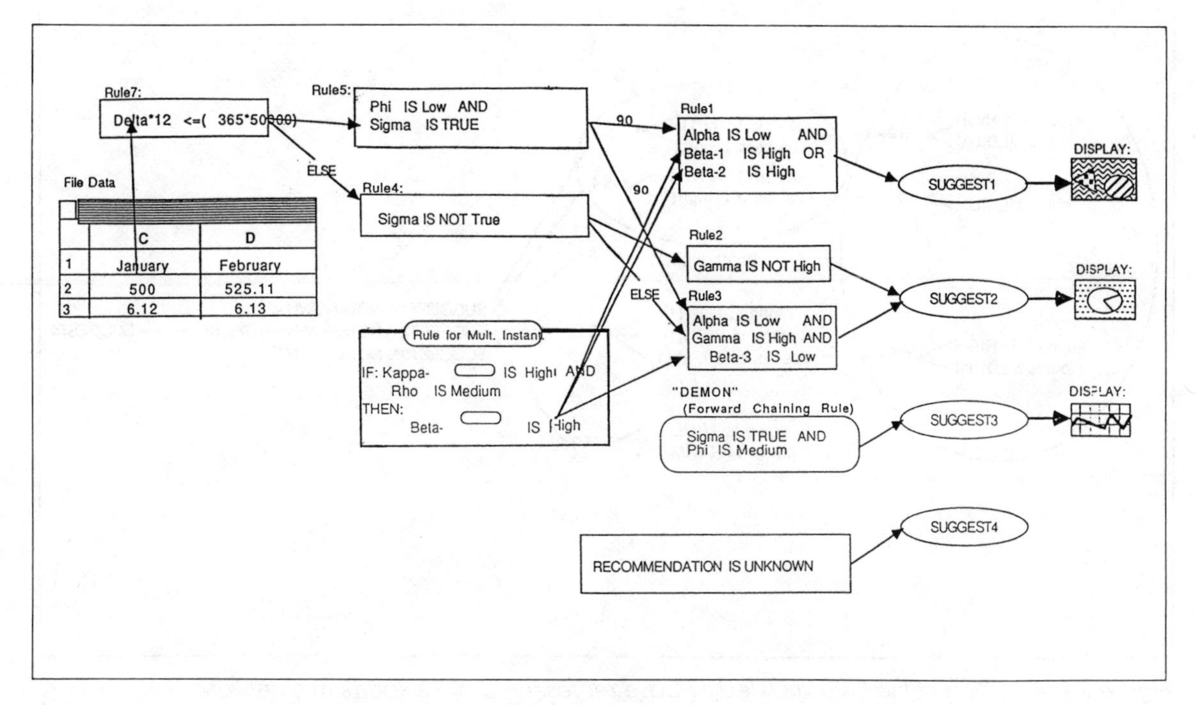

Figure 7.1 *Beta knowledge base. A small system for testing a mid-size expert system building tool.*

ing to five broad sets of criteria: (1) overall power and flexibility, (2) the knowledge engineering interface, (3) the user (or runtime) interface, (4) runtime speed, and (5) training and support.

Power and Flexibility

Under "power and flexibility" consider the various ways knowledge can be represented in each tool.

How facts are represented. In Nexpert, facts are represented as simple attribute–value pairs. For example, the fact "the temperature is high" would be expressed as TEMPERATURE = HIGH (attribute = value).

Personal Consultant Plus is designed to represent all its knowledge as object–attribute–value triplets. Using triplets, the fact "The temperature in Dallas is high" would be represented as DALLAS-TEMPERATURE-HIGH (object–attribute–value).

M.1 can represent facts as attribute–value pairs, but can also use variable rules to effectively represent facts with any number of levels of description. Consider, for example, a fact in the form episode–object–attribute–value. "Episode" is a fourth level of description added to the triplet to qualify the data with the timeframe for which it is relevant.

How relationships are represented. All three tools use if–then rules to define relationships between facts. The conditions of the IF part of the rule ("the premise") are connected with Boolean operators AND and NOT. M.1 and Personal Consultant Plus also have rules with OR operators. Nexpert does not allow rules with OR, thus, in Nexpert complex rules must be split into simpler rules. For example, the two rules marked B in Figure 7.2 are combined to form Rule 1 in the M.1 knowledge base.

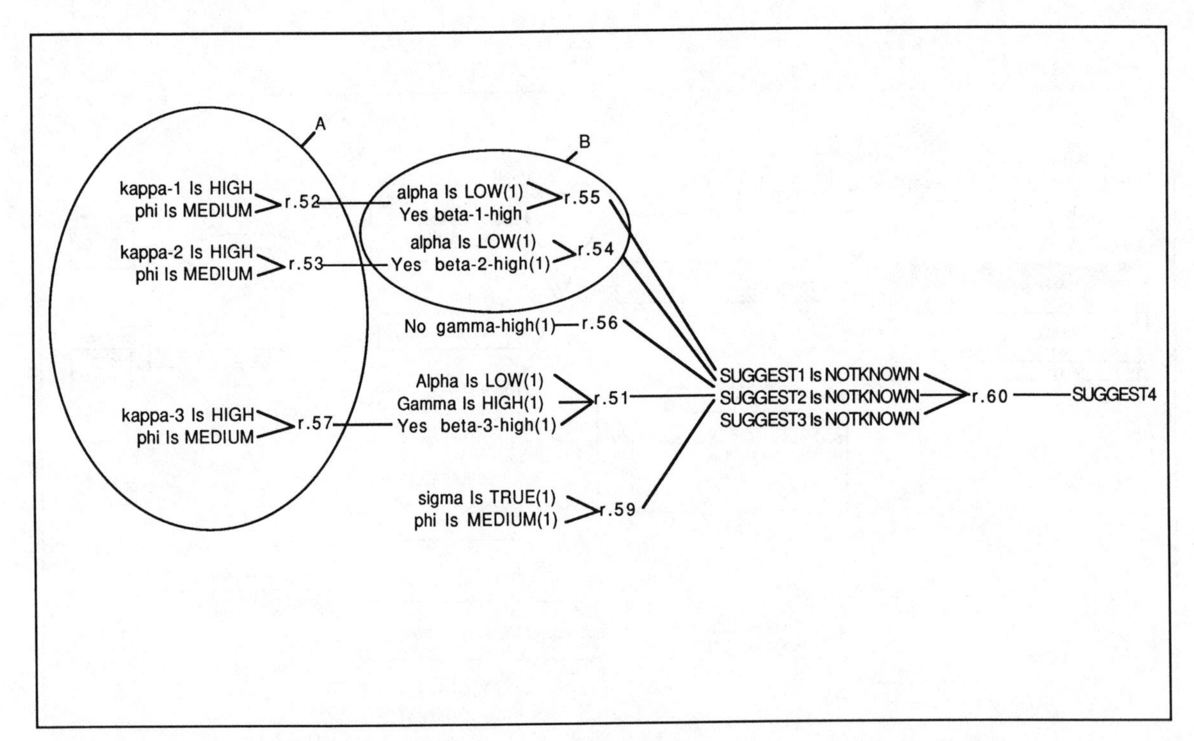

Figure 7.2 A portion of the Beta knowledge base represented by Nexpert's rule network.

A portion of the Beta knowledge base, as represented in M.1, is shown in Table 7.1. Notice that Rule 1 has beta-1 and beta-2, to take advantage of M.1's variable rule convention. Rule 10 is a variable rule using the general expression "kappa-X." This rule is used by the system three times: once to find a value for beta-1, once to find a value for beta-2, and once to find a value for beta-3. A portion of the same knowledge base, represented as a network produced upon command in Nexpert, is shown in Figure 7.2. In Nexpert, the three rules circled and marked A in Figure 7.2 represent the single variable rule used in M.1. The same portion of the Beta knowledge base, represented in a hypothetical diagram intended to indicate Personal Consultant Plus frames, is pictured in Figure 7.3.

Table 7.1 *Partial printout of M.1 Beta knowledge base rules.*

```
goal=recommend.

rule1: if
      alpha = low and
       beta-1 = high or
       beta-2 = high
then recommend = suggest1.

rule2: if
      gamma = not high
then recommend = suggest2.

rule3: if
      alpha = low and
      gamma = low and
       beta-3 = high
then recommend = suggest2.

rule5: if
      phi = low and
      sigma = true
then alpha = low cf 90.

rule10: if
      kappa-X = high and
       rho = medium
then beta-X = high.


legalvals(alpha)=[low,medium,high).
```

All three tools can use floating-point math expressions in the rules, although none provide built-in trigonometric functions. In both M.1 and Nexpert, arithmetic operators can appear on only one side of an equation, so the burden is on the developer to convert the equation into proper form.

How knowledge is structured. Both M.1 and Nexpert are simple rule systems; all their rules are kept together in one set. In M.1, this means that each "normal" rule can be used by the system only one time during the consultation. M.1's "variable rules" can be tried more than once, making M.1 more like a structured rule system. Nexpert's forward chaining mode may use the same rule more than once, but it is unable to instantiate the same rule for different objects.

Personal Consultant Plus uses *frames* to structure rules into discrete sets. Each frame contains facts and rules that address a piece of the overall problem. They are related to one another by a frame tree that describes their hierarchical structure.

When a certain part of the problem needs to be solved, a frame for it is created. This is called frame "instantiation." During a consultation, parts of the problem that are not considered are never instantiated as frames. This prevents waste of both memory and time.

Multiple instantiation is a useful feature for systems that must solve many instances of the same kind of problem. For example, consider an expert system to write a will. Part of the system involves setting up a trust for each dependent. The choice of a trust is based on rules about the dependent's age, income, and other information. These same rules apply for every dependent, but the values will be different. Rather than creating a set of rules for each dependent, a single frame can be made with one set of general rules about choosing a trust. This frame can then be instantiated once for each dependent. The same rules will be used for a number of different objects.

Figure 7.4 shows how the general rule from the Beta KB can be instantiated three times during a consulta-

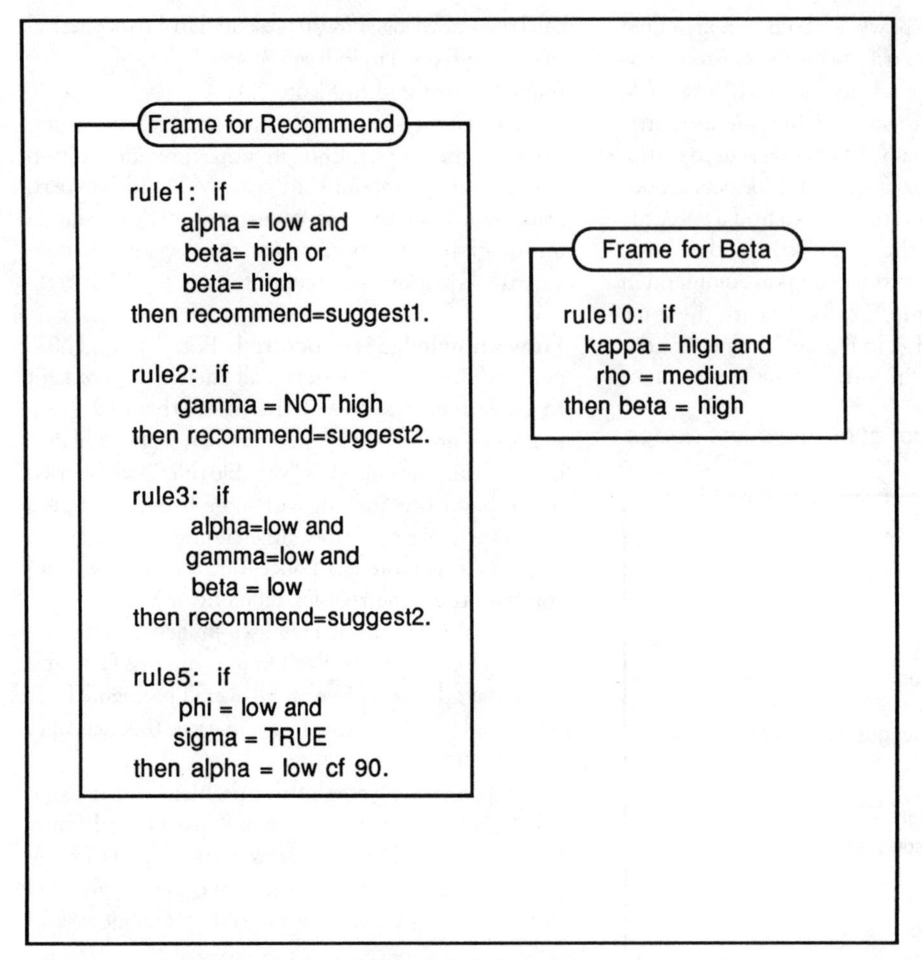

Figure 7.3 *Partial printout of PC-Plus's Beta knowledge base rules.*

tion. To accomplish this in Nexpert you would have to write three separate rules. These rules are circled and marked A in Figure 7.2.

In M.1, *variables* can occur in facts, meta-facts, and rules. They allow rules with a repetitive pattern to be collapsed into a single, generalized rule.

This is more than just a convenient way to abbreviate rules. Variable rules give M.1 the same kind of power as Personal Consultant Plus's multiple frame instantiation. Instead of writing rules for every instance of a common problem, you can write general rules to apply to many instances of the problem.

One variable rule for a trust problem might look like this:

rule:

```
if      age-X > 21 OR
        income-X > 20000
then    trust-X=none.
```

Somewhere in the knowledge base you would need to include a lookup table with all the sets of values that could be substituted into this rule. When a consultation is run, the system instantiates the variable X with each dependent's name. In addition to using a lookup table, M.1 can also manipulate structured data such as lists and symbolic expressions.

Both variable rules and frames permit you to write rules that support inheritance. *Inheritance* refers to the

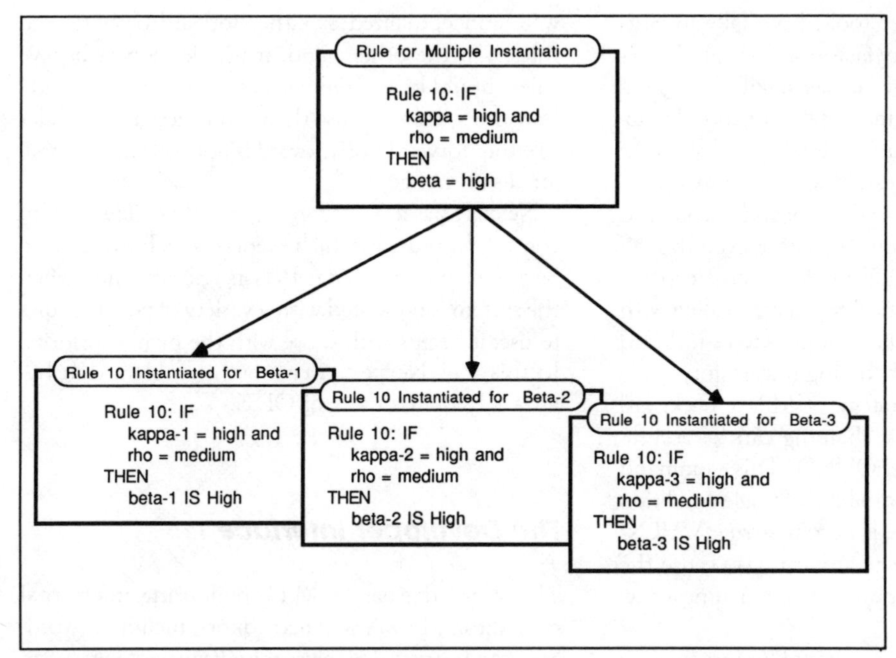

Figure 7.4 *Example of multiple instantiation.*

ability of an object to inherit the characteristics of a more general class to which it belongs. For example, you could create a class or frame called "mammals" and enter in that frame the fact that all mammals are warm blooded. You could then create another frame called "antelope" and indicate it was a "type of mammal" frame. You would not have to tell the system that an antelope had warm blood. The system would know an antelope was a mammal, and since mammals have warm blood, it would automatically assume antelopes have warm blood. In other words, the object or frame "antelope" would inherit any information possessed by its "parent" object, "mammal."

While it is theoretically possible to do about the same thing with variable rules that you can do with a frame system, in fact, it is conceptually much more difficult. The practical effect of variable rules is to allow the developer to avoid writing lots of similar rules by substituting one generic rule and a lookup table. Frames, on the other hand, encourage the developer to think of the knowledge domain in a much more systematic and hierarchically organized way. A frame system encourages the developer to explore dependencies and build inheritance throughout the knowledge base. More important, frames allow nonprogramming experts to think about their knowledge in a much more concrete manner.

Inference and control uncertainty. Both M.1 and Personal Consultant Plus support built-in *confidence levels* in both rule statements (expert confidence) and in user's responses (user's confidence). In both cases, the tools use the confidence factor approach developed in EMYCIN, not the ordinary, highly unsatisfactory approach to probability used in most smaller PC-based tools. Confidence factors in both M.1 and Personal Consultant Plus range from 100 (TRUE) to −100 (FALSE).

Nexpert lacks a built-in means of handling uncertain information. All knowledge is either true or false. This omission will alienate two audiences: (1) novice developers who may want to experiment with reasoning under uncertainty, and (2) developers who find certainty factors suitable for their problems.

Opinions vary on the usefulness and integrity of confidence factors or certainty factors used by

EMYCIN and many other tools. Especially in large problems, built-in certainty factors are not always appropriate. Moreover, as noted earlier, a skilled programmer can program ways around most of the tools' limitations. Thus, you can program certainty calculations into Nexpert's rules. This text, however, focuses on only the facilities designed into the tool and encouraged by the tool's documentation. Moreover, even though you can insert confidence calculations into Nexpert's rules, this is not very practical if you are dealing with a large system, since it requires a formula to be included as a clause in every rule handling uncertainty.

The primary *control* strategy of M.1 is backward chaining. Limited forward chaining can be accomplished by using WHENFOUND. This command allows the developer to write a kind of single-condition rule that triggers any time it becomes true. WHENFOUND can conclude facts and can also cause the system to undertake an action such as pursuing a new goal.

Every rule in Personal Consultant Plus is defined as a forward or backward chaining rule at the time it is created. In addition, Personal Consultant Plus includes "Access Methods" (active values and method properties) that enable developers to trigger actions based on access to certain parameters as well as through rules. This capability gives developers a powerful alternative way to accomplish forward chaining. In addition, Personal Consultant Plus can prescan a rule to determine if any clause will disqualify it before pursuing the first "if-clause," and it allows the developer to use meta-rules and/or a "utility property" to specify the optimal ordering of the rules.

The control strategy used by Nexpert can be (1) backward chaining, in which rules are enlisted to solve a goal or subgoal, (2) forward chaining, in which rules wait in the background to be triggered whenever their conditions are fulfilled, or (3) both forward and backward chaining. Operating in the third mode, it is assumed that all rules are candidates for either forward or backward chaining. This important new feature, not previously found in PC-based tools, allows the system to make greater use of the same amount of knowledge. In some cases it allows the system to find information it would have to ask the user for, if its rules were conceptualized as either forward or backward rules. On the other hand, many developers believe rules should be written with an awareness of exactly how the system will use them; thus designating rules as either forward or backward is not considered a major disadvantage.

Nexpert has a "Category Editor" that allows you to control the order in which events occur. Each rule can be given a number that reflects its priority. Thus, when the system is presented with a variety of possible rules to use, it begins with those with the highest priority. In this way, Nexpert overcomes a problem that has always bothered users of OPS5.

The Developer Interface

The knowledge base in M.1 is built using an external text editor. Most ASCII text editors, including WordStar, can be used. This gives the advantage of a familiar, powerful environment for writing rules, but also poses a problem. Since the knowledge base cannot be modified within M.1, making a change is not easy. It requires you to exit M.1, enter the editor, make the changes, and then return to M.1. This is most irritating during the debugging phase of development when many small changes need to be made and tested. (Developers using M.1 often use Sidekick as an editor.)

The editing facilities of Nexpert and Personal Consultant Plus are an integrated part of the tools; rules and other knowledge are entered and edited without ever leaving the program. Adding a rule is like completing a form, the developer fills in the blank clauses of an if–then rule. Both Personal Consultant Plus and Nexpert allow responses to be typed from the keyboard or selected from pull-down menus. These menus display a list of the attributes already defined and the user can copy an attribute name into the rule. Attributes are selected using the arrow key in Personal Consultant Plus or using the mouse in Nexpert. This feature saves time and also minimizes the chance of typos.

Some problems require that a consistent set of questions be asked every time a consultation is run. "Input forms" can be designed in Nexpert to automatically appear on the screen at the beginning of every consultation. Both M.1 and Personal Consultant Plus accomplish a similar function with the INITIALDATA command, which specifies a list of values to seek at the start of a consultation, but this command does not have any effect on the screen formatting.

Nexpert's *rule network* uses graphics to show the links between the rules in the knowledge base. This is more than an aesthetic feature. It enhances the speed and ease of developing a knowledge base, and it addresses the common problem of not knowing how the addition of a new rule will affect a complex system. The rule network is like a road map rather than an isolated street sign — it gives a much higher perspective on information.

Both M.1 and Personal Consultant Plus produce a text *trace*, a report detailing the events of the consultation, telling which rules were tried, what conclusions were reached, and so on.

Both M.1 and Nexpert have windows that show the activity of the system as it happens. One window shows which rules are being tried; another shows what conclusions have been reached.

The ability to integrate *graphics* into a consultation is an important step toward making an expert system more accessible to the end user unfamiliar with its subject. Graphics can be useful in two ways: (1) they can show information about a question posed by the system, or (2) they can illustrate a conclusion the system has reached. In Nexpert it is easy for the developer to add graphics. A single command can be written in a rule to display a picture created in MacPaint or digitized by Thunderscan. Being a Macintosh program, Nexpert's diagrams can be very detailed, but they are necessarily black and white.

Personal Consultant Plus can display color graphics and pictures created in an external graphics editor like PC Paint or Dr. Halo. All three tools allow you to combine graphics and forward chaining to create graphics with dials and then change the dials and watch the graphic adjust. The process of integrating them into the consultation requires more effort than is required for Nexpert, but considerably less than required by M.1.

Displaying graphics is hardest in M.1. An external procedure has to be written in C to create the display and also to remove it before continuing with the consultation.

File communication and external program control is another important feature of the mid-size tool. It enhances the potential of the expert system by letting it communicate with the I/O ports, files, and external applications. These abilities permit applications to be developed which read sensors, search data bases, criticize spreadsheets, and much more.

Personal Consultant Plus's environment gives the developer full access to the underlying LISP language, allowing LISP procedures to be compiled and called directly from rules.

For procedures that cannot be programmed within the tool, both Personal Consultant Plus and Nexpert can make calls to the operating system to execute another program. The system remains dormant until the external program finishes, and then the consultation continues from where it left off.

The Macintosh's "Desk Accessories" environment allows Nexpert to lie dormant in the background until executed by another program. At execution, arguments can be passed to Nexpert specifying data and hypotheses to consider. An even closer level of integration can be achieved in M.1, which actually provides the object code to link a runtime expert system directly into another C program, producing a single executable file.

All three tools can exchange information with other applications through the stack. Likewise, all three tools allow information to be exchanged with an application via data files.

The User Interface

Starting a consultation in either Personal Consultant Plus or M.1 is very straightforward. Since the goals of the system are specified in the knowledge base, all the user need do to start a consultation is tell the system to load the rules and begin.

To begin a consultation with Nexpert, the user either

provides facts (to start forward chaining) or suggests that a specific hypothesis should be considered (to initiate backward chaining). To conduct a Nexpert dialogue, the user must sometimes suggest every potential outcome as a possibility for the system to explore. This task of identifying all potential outcomes is laborious and confusing since the user might be unfamiliar with the system and thus be at a loss to know which hypothesis to suggest. This imposes a burden on the end user to learn the rules or on the developer to write additional rules that automatically suggest hypotheses. In some cases, however, this can be an advantage rather than a limitation. If the user knows the subject matter and has already narrowed down the possible causes of a problem, this can be a very efficient way to begin a consultation.

Initiating the consultation is illustrated in Figure 7.5 for M.1, Figure 7.6 for Nexpert, and Figure 7.7 for Personal Consultant Plus.

The consultation unfolds in a similar way for all three tools:

1. The system queries the user for any initial information.
2. The user answers questions posed by the system.
3. The system displays its conclusions.

The user answers the system's questions either by typing a response on the keyboard or making a selection from a list of possible responses generated by the system. Both Nexpert and Personal Consultant Plus make it easy for the developer to present multiple-choice questions, thus informing users of their choices. The new version of M.1 will also generate multiple-choice questions, but, in general, M.1 does not provide much help to the developer trying to create a good user interface.

In M.1 and Personal Consultant Plus, users can give

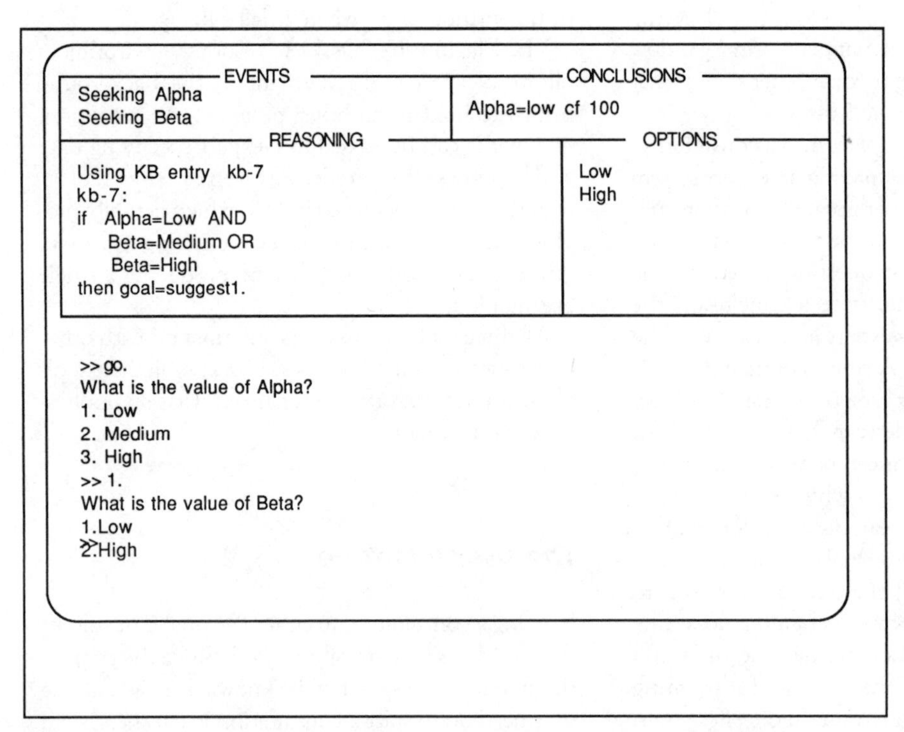

Figure 7.5 *A consultation screen from M.1's development phase.*

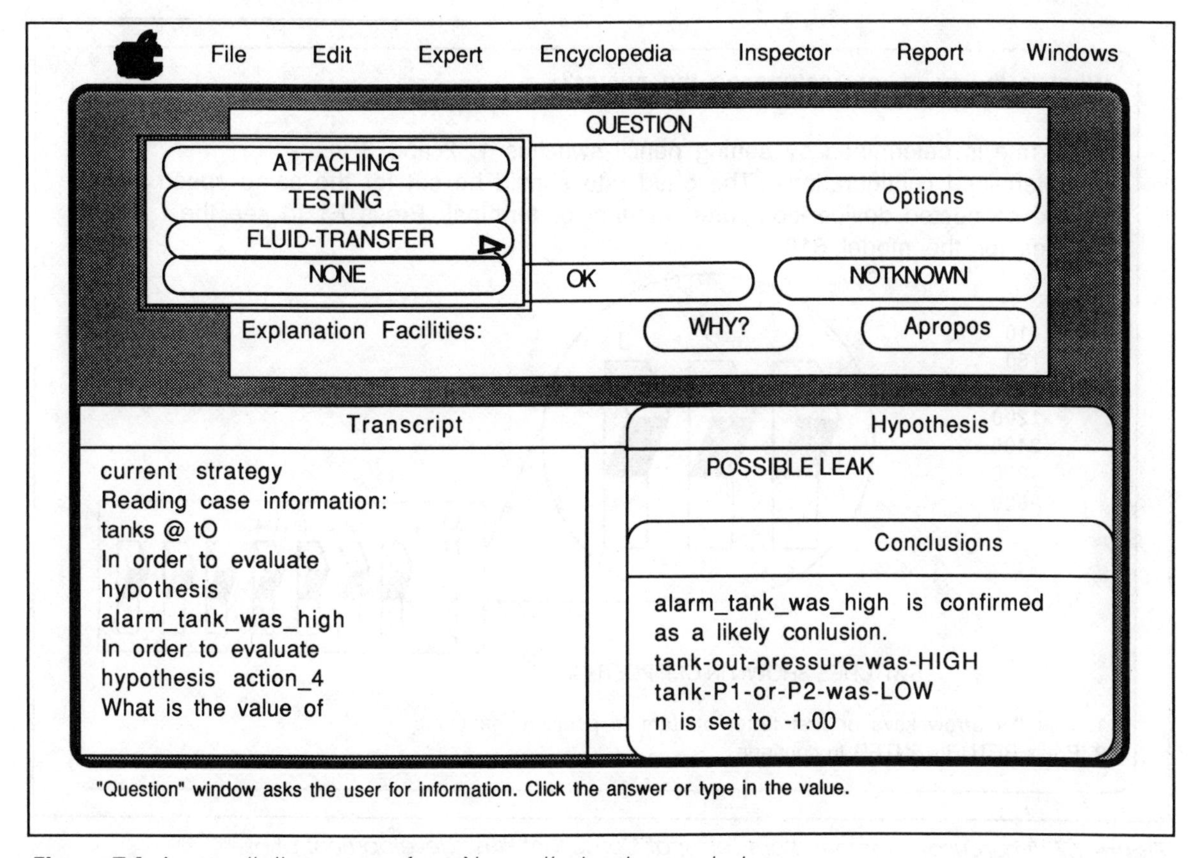

Figure 7.6 *A consultation screen from Nexpert's development phase.*

a certainty factor along with a response to a question from the system. In M.1, users simply type a number from 0 to 100 beside the input. If the number is omitted, a certainty of 100 is assumed. Personal Consultant Plus has a more elegant way of choosing certainty. The arrow keys can be used to enlarge or shrink an icon whose size reflects the certainty factor. Nexpert does not support user certainty.

All three tools allow users to interrupt the consultation to ask the system to explain its reasoning. Users can ask the system "How" a conclusion was reached or "Why" a question is being asked. In Nexpert and Personal Consultant Plus, users can also ask to see text that provides a detailed description of a piece of knowledge.

Runtime Speed

M.1 is written in C and is very fast. Nexpert is written in a mix of C, PASCAL, and assembler and is reasonably fast. Personal Consultant Plus runs significantly more slowly than the other two tools.

Training and Support

With the more sophisticated mid-size tools, training becomes a very important issue. Assuming you intend to have several people within your company learn to use these tools, you need to have each person ade-

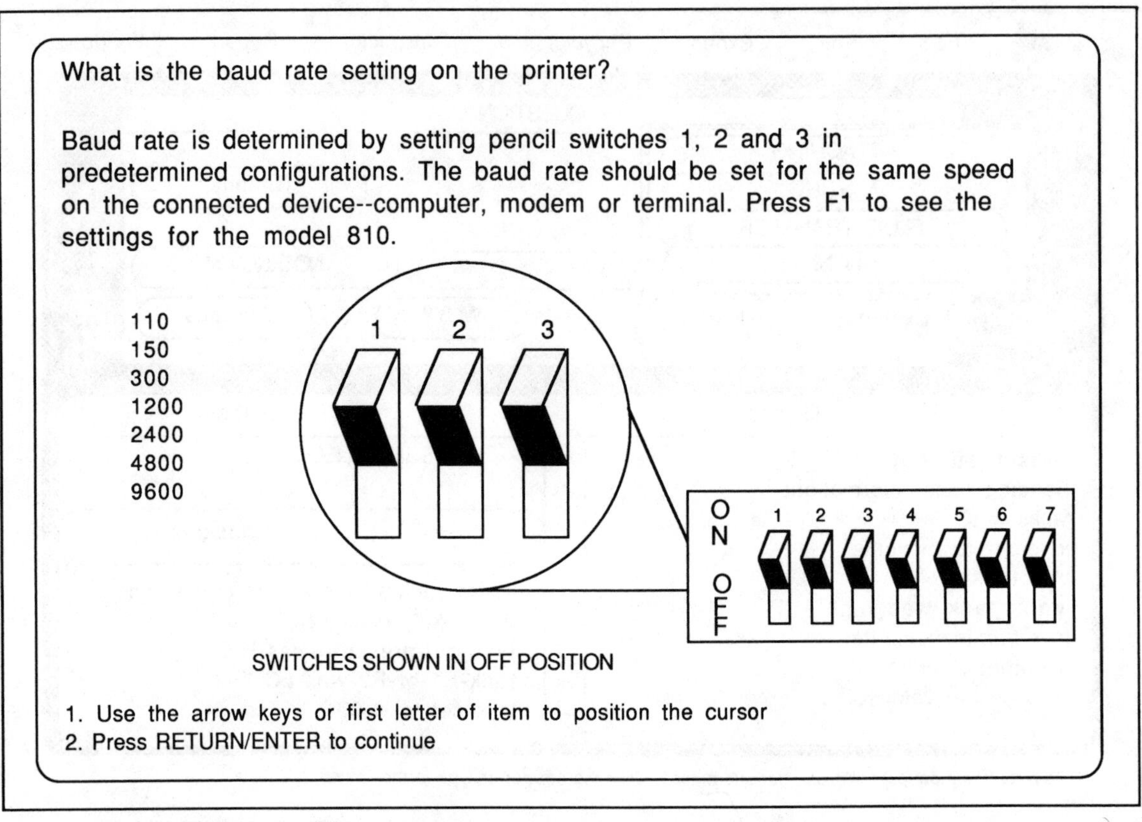

Figure 7.7 *A consultation screen from Personal Consultant Plus's development phase.*

quately trained. In addition, you want to be assured you can get support if you encounter bugs or difficulties connecting a system you develop to some other program or a data base. Moreover, as you proceed to build larger systems, you want to know you can call on consulting support from someone experienced in using the tool.

M.1 is sold by Teknowledge, Inc., a company of some 100 people with sales offices in the largest cities in the country. Teknowledge offers a one-week basic training course in using M.1 and advanced courses in knowledge engineering. Teknowledge's training programs are effective, and the product is supported by good documentation. In addition, Teknowledge earns a significant portion of its revenue from providing consulting and is strongly associated with some of the best-known names in academic AI research.

Nexpert is sold by Neuron Data, Inc., a small start-up company. Neuron Data does not offer training and provides poor documentation for their product, but they are in the process of working out distribution arrangements that should significantly improve the training and documentation accompanying Nexpert.

Personal Consultant Plus is sold by Texas Instruments, Inc., a major corporation with sales and service offices throughout the world. TI offers a number of courses to teach users about AI, the use of Personal Consultant Plus and Scheme, and various advanced aspects of knowledge engineering. The documentation for Personal Consultant Plus is excellent. In addition, TI has a staff of knowledge engineers available to consult with clients developing expert systems. Where Teknowledge has a reputation in consulting on the development of large prototypes of expert systems, TI has rapidly built a reputation for helping clients develop and field mid-size expert systems.

Since this comparison was written, all three tools described here have been modified. The changes in M.1 have been minor, but the new version of Nexpert, called Nexpert Object, and the additions to Personal Consultant Plus have, in effect, moved each of those tools much closer to hybrid tools. Nexpert Object, for example, has incorporated an object-oriented representation and now runs on both a VAX and a PC AT.

In addition to many small improvements, TI has introduced several modules that can enhance both Personal Consultant Plus and EASY. PC ONLINE is a utility that facilitates the development of a system to take electronic data from some process you wish to monitor. PC IMAGES provides a set of active image icons to enhance graphics applications. Further, each of the basic tools can now deliver expert systems in any of four ways: on a PC running in Scheme, on a PC running in C, on a VAX (running in C under VMS), and on an Explorer (running in Common LISP). (See Figure 7.8.)

To round out our discussion of mid-size tools, we will now consider two other tools, KES 2.2 and GURU.

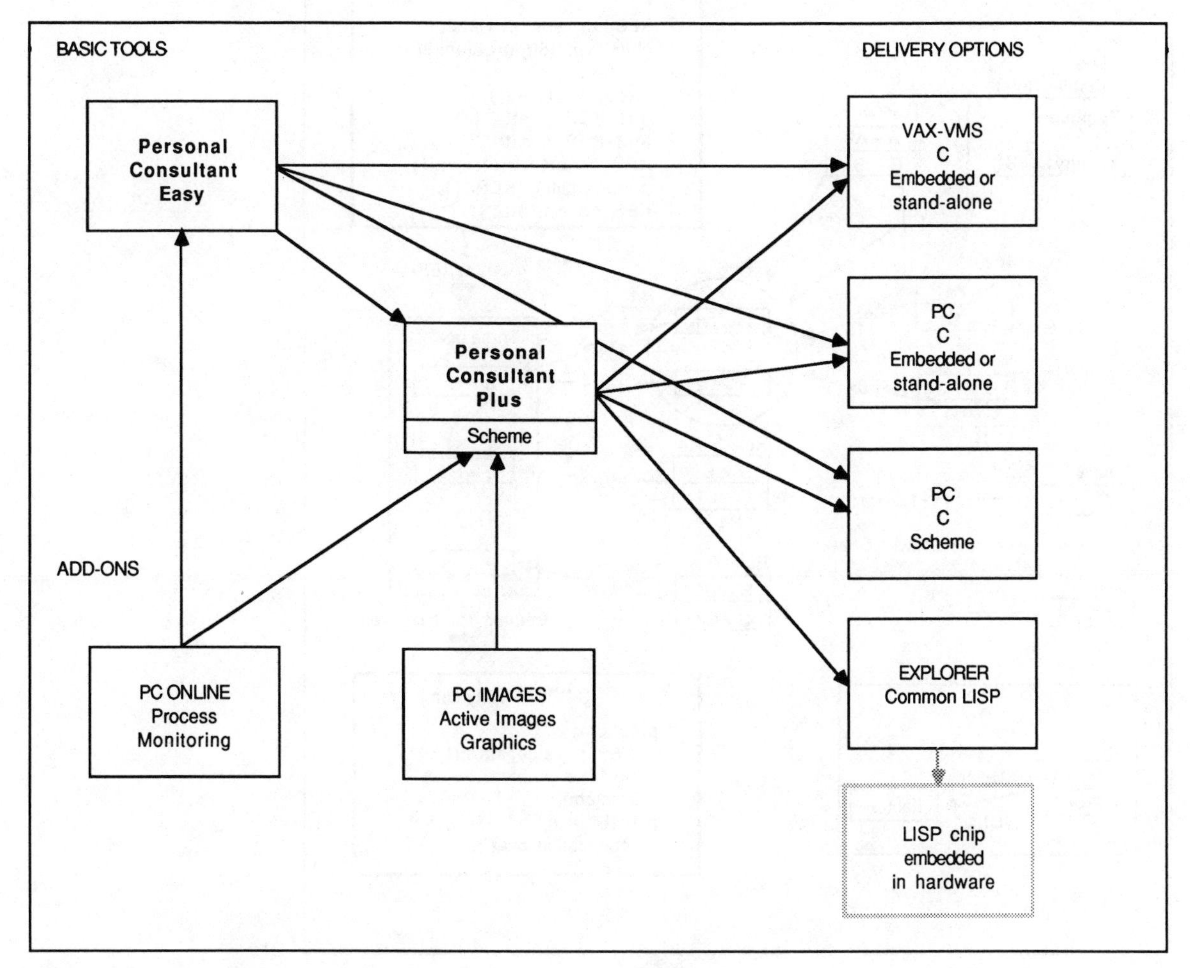

Figure 7.8 *TI's Personal Consultant family of tools.*

KES 2.2

KES 2, the Knowledge Engineering System (Release 2.2), is an expert system building tool produced and sold by Software Architecture and Engineering (Software A&E).

Software A&E was founded in 1978. The founders, former government and IBM Federal Systems Division people, set up a consulting company to offer services to government agencies. Their initial contracts were for software engineering efforts. In 1981 the company shifted its focus to specialize in AI contracts, and in 1982 they begin to sell KES. KES is based on KMS, a tool James Reggia developed while completing a Ph.D. at the University of Maryland.

The original LISP version of KES had three sub-

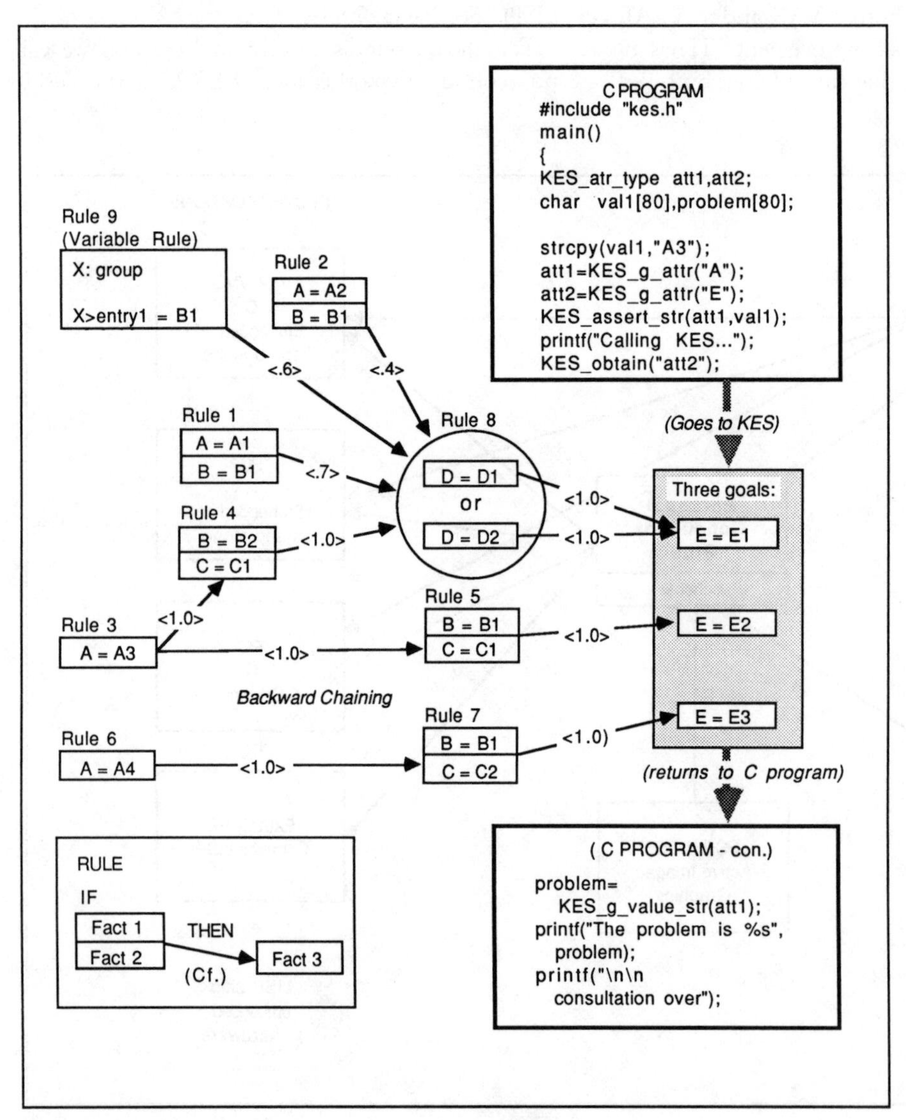

Figure 7.9 *Sample KES 2 knowledge base embedded in C.*

systems: KES.PR, a production-rule module; KES.HT, a hypothesis and test module; and KES.BAYES, a statistical pattern classification subsystem. The LISP version of KES is being incrementally ported from LISP to C. Thus, KES 2.1 was the C version of the former KES.PR. The C version of KES.HT and the KES.BAYES subsystem have also been released. Before releasing the second subsystem, however, Software A&E modified its original KES.PS subsystem to incorporate contexts, called *classes*, and thus they changed their original simple rule-based system (KES Release 2.1) into the much more interesting structured rule-based system (KES Release 2.2).

The PC version of KES 2.2 comes on three disks and includes a manual in a three-ring binder. KES is delivered with a one-year maintenance agreement.

See the sample knowledge base in Figure 7.9 and code to form that knowledge base in Table 7.2 for an example of how KES 2 works.

KES 2 is clearly positioned to compete with other mid-size tools like Personal Consultant Plus, M.1, S.1, and GURU. In evaluating KES 2, again consider (1) power and flexibility, (2) the developer interface, (3) the user interface, (4) the systems interface, and (5) training and support.

Power and Flexibility

In general, KES 2.2 is a structured rule tool. The new enhanced version, KES 2.2, allows the developer to write general rules about entire classes of attributes. These rules can then be instantiated for each member of the class that arises during a consultation.

Facts can be declared as single valued or multi-valued when they are defined at the beginning of the knowledge base. Other options present in definitions include a default value for the attribute or a formula to find a value for the attribute.

KES represents rules in the form:

```
RULENAME

IF
        Premise
THEN
        Conclusion
endif
ATTACHMENTS.
```

Conditions in the premise can be connected with AND or OR. As shown in Rule 2 of the sample knowledge base, redundant OR conditions can be listed in the syntax:

```
D=D1 : D2
```

rather than the less convenient:

```
D=D1 or
D=D2
```

ATTACHMENTS are optional lines of English text that provide an explanation of the rule for end users.

KES 2.2's addition of classes gives the user the same power as M.1's variable rules or Personal Consultant Plus's frames. KES's way of indicating classes is a little easier to understand and use than the variable rules in M.1 and GURU, but hardly as straightforward as AION, Personal Consultant Plus, or any other system that implements the standard EMYCIN context tree mechanism. A special classes section in the knowledge base defines the attributes in each class. An example of this can be found in the knowledge base shown in Table 7.2.

```
classes:
    group:
        attributes:
        entry1: mlt (B1,B2,B3)
        entry2: mlt (B1,B2,B3)
    %
```

This defines a class named "group." Every element of "group" has two attributes: "entry1" and "entry2." You would refer to a particular element of an instance X of the class "group" as "Xentry1."

Once the structure of the class is defined, the knowledge base can contain a rule to apply to all its members. This repeated execution of the same rule for many members of a class is an example of multiple instantiation.

Table 7.2 *The code for the KES sample knowledge base.*

```
attributes:
\ INPUT ATTRIBUTES
A: sgl
      (A1,
      A2,
      A3,
      A4)
{question: "What is the value of A?"}.

B: mlt
       (B1,
       B2,
       B3,
       B4)
{question: "What is the value of B?"}.

C: mlt
      (C1,
      C2)
{question: "What is the value of C?"}.
\
\INFERRED ATTRIBUTES
\
Management: truth.
D: sgl.
      (D1,
      D2,
      D3,
      D4).
E: sgl.
      (E1,
      E2,
      E3).
%
classes:
     group:
          attributes:
        entry1:  mlt     (B1,B2,B3).
        entry2:  mlt     (B1,B2,B3).
%
rules:

Rule1:
if       A = A1
         and B = B1
then     D = D1<0.7>.
endif.

Rule2:
if       A  = A1
         and B = B1
then     D = D1<0.4>.
endif.

Rule3:
if        A = A3
then     C = C1.
endif.

Rule4:
if       C = C1
         and B = B2
then     D = D2.

Rule5:
if       C = C1
         and B = B1
then     E = E2.
endif.

Rule6:
if        A = A4
then     C  = C2.
endif.

Rule7:
if        C = C2
      and B  =  B1
then     E = E3.
endif.

Rule8:
if       D = D1 : D2
then     E = E1.
endif.

Rule9:
X: group
if     X>entry1  =  B1
then     D = D1<0.6>.
endif.

obtain E.
message "The value of E is:".
display E
message "Thank you for using KES 2.2".

stop.
%
```

Any KES 2.2 rule using classes includes a *type definition* of the class variables used in the body of the rule. For example, consider the following variable rule from the sample knowledge base:

```
Rule8:
X: group
if
        X>entry1 = B1
then  D = D1<0.6>.
```

Define the variable "X" as a member of the class "group." This rule will fire if the attribute "entry1" of the class "X" has a value of "B1."

The KES approach is both powerful and straightforward. KES 2.2's classes are more transparent than M.1's variable rules but somewhat less powerful because M.1's variables can be used to define facts with any number of levels of definition. Object–attribute–values would be three levels of definition, episode–object–attribute–values would be four. Classes, like frames in Personal Consultant Plus, can only describe objects with three levels.

KES supports both user and expert *confidence*. The number range is from −1 (FALSE) to 1 (TRUE). Moreover, KES offers three types of confidence factors. The KES manual provides guidance on selecting the certainty calculation appropriate to a particular problem.

Control is either forward or backward, but KES lacks forward chaining interrupts like M.1's WHENFOUND or Personal Consultant Plus's ACTIVEVALUES.

The overall structure of the consultation is described in the *actions*, a list of commands resembling a traditional programming language, like WHILE loops, print commands, and so on. Whenever an OBTAIN command is found in the action block, it invokes backward chaining to find a value. KES combines procedural and declarative programming, freeing the user from having to write difficult and nontransparent control rules to affect the sequence of events during the consultation.

The Developer Interface

The original KES was developed via line entry. The new version allows the user to develop off-line knowledge bases and to interact with the system via menus, windows, and a mouse. The KES 2 interfaces are not exciting, but are adequate and much improved over the earlier version.

Like VP Expert and M.1, the knowledge base is created in any external ASCII text editor and then read into the system. If errors are found in the knowledge base, KES tells the developer about the type of error and its specific location. When the knowledge base is syntactically correct, KES produces a new "compiled" version, which begins execution without the delay of reading and parsing the file.

Another handy feature of KES is the DISPLAY TREE command that shows the hierarchy of attributes in a knowledge base. The command can also be used to display all the attributes related to a chosen attribute.

You must declare all variables in the knowledge base before they can be used. While this has the advantage of preventing rules from being rendered useless from slight misspellings, it is frustrating, especially when you are trying to build a quick prototype.

See Figure 7.10 for a sample KES menu screen.

The User Interface

Consultations are started by typing KESR followed by the file name of a compiled knowledge base.

Information is entered by typing either information in response to an open-ended question or a number corresponding to a choice made from a menu of options. If the windowed version of KES is being used, questions can be answered by "pointing and clicking" on a selected menu option.

Text explanation clauses can be linked to rules or attributes. KES draws on these messages if the end user types "explain" when prompted for information. This explains why a question needs to be asked of the user. If no explanatory information can be found in the knowledge base to explain the need for a question, the system responds "No explanation available."

The new version, KES 2.2, has added an additional explanatory command, WHY? This displays the undetermined attributes that depend on the attribute

```
Knowledge Engineering System (KES), Release 2.3
Copyright (C) 1986, Software Architecture & Engineering, Inc.
Loading the knowledge base "fish1.pkb".

Welcome to the Tropical Fish Diagnosis System.

Fish appearance

        1. Small bumps on body
        2. Slow weaving motion without getting anywhere
        3. Swollen body especially on one side
        4. Tail part missing


(multiple answers allowed)
=?
```

Figure 7.10 *KES menu screen.*

whose value is being asked of the user. A further option is for the system to elaborate on its explanation, displaying entire rules relating to the question at hand.

The Systems Interface

KES can use ASCII communications files to exchange information with other programs. This file contains a list of attribute names with their values beside them. These lists can be created using the WRITE command to write attributes out to a file or READ in from a file created by an external program.

External programs can be called from KES using the EXTERNAL command. After the applications program terminates, control is returned to KES.

When you consider all the expert systems you have examined thus far, they have all been *integrated* with other software in one of three ways:

1. As an embedded, invisible component of software code written in some conventional programming language. This approach is seen in M.1 with links to Microsoft C, as well as future versions of Turbo PASCAL which will allow direct linkage with Turbo PROLOG code.
2. As part of an integrated package like GURU or the Macintosh version of Nexpert which provides a comprehensive environment with shared data and a consistent set of commands throughout.
3. As commands in the rule base to share data with other applications by reading or writing data files and making calls to other programs through DOS, the approach most systems have taken.

These three methods are illustrated in Figure 7.11.

KES takes the first approach. You can make direct calls from a C program to routines to activate a knowledge base, send or receive facts from the knowledge base, or make calls to saved files of cases. This functionality could be imitated by other tools that use the third approach, provided the application was simply sharing facts. But KES also provides C routines to initiate more sophisticated operations like pursuing a particular goal or retrieving explanatory text.

An example of this can be seen in the sample knowledge base, shown integrated in a C program.

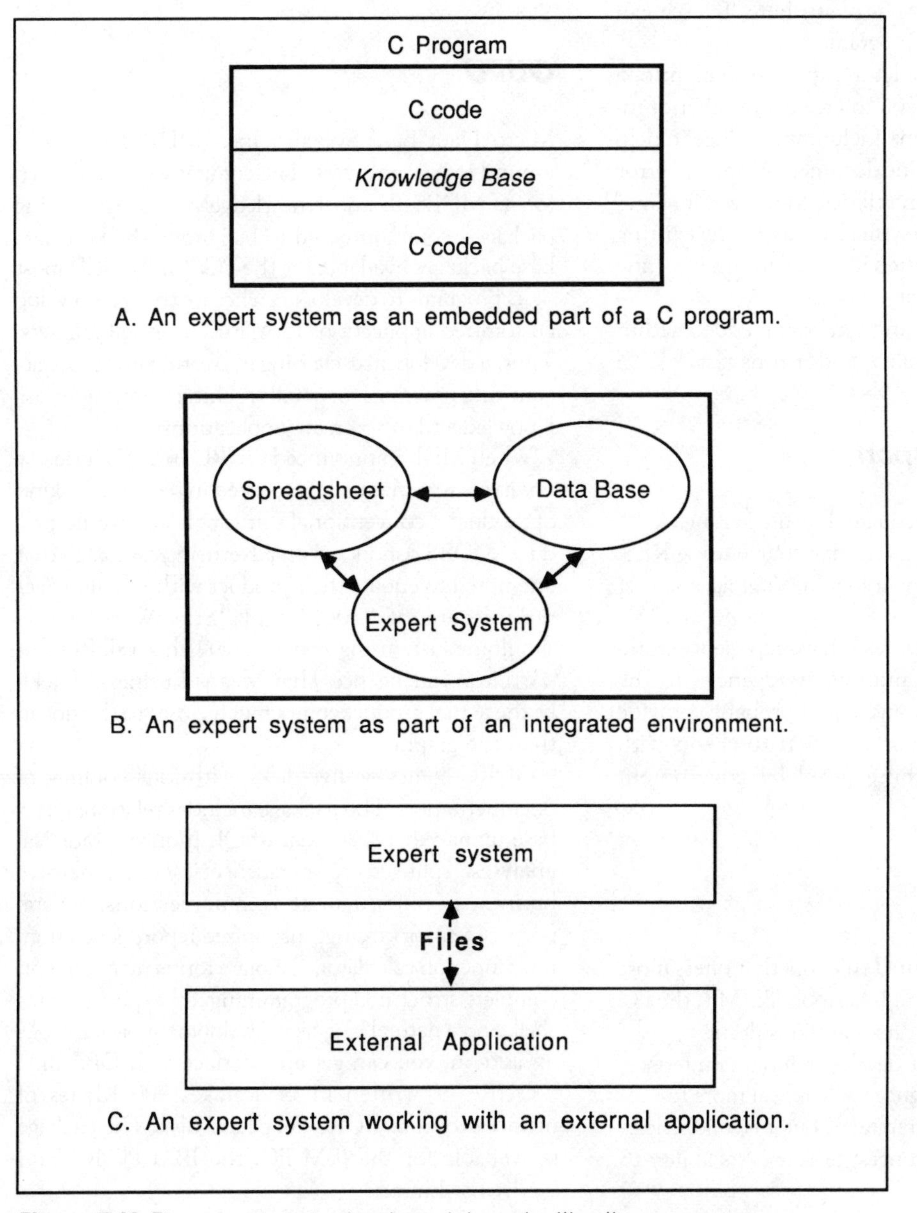

Figure 7.11 *Three ways expert systems interact with other programs.*

First, the C program displays a message with the C command PRINTF. Next, the function KES__assert__str() is called to assert the fact "A=A1" in the knowledge base. Now the function KES__obtain( ) is called to cause KES to backward chain and find a value for the attribute "E." Finally, after control is returning from the expert system, the function KES__g__str() is called to retrieve the value of attribute "E" so it can be used later in the C program.

The ability to embed an expert system into a language like C allows you to create a number of interesting PC applications including intelligent help systems, intelligent on-line documentation, and error detection and correction utilities. Moreover, it allows you to embed an expert systems utility in any existing application program written in C and to run it on any micro or mainframe that supports C.

KES 2 is written in C and can be embedded within a C program and compiled, and it runs fast.

Training and Support

The KES manual is adequate, but unexciting.

Software A&E offers a four-day course using KES. The courses are taught in Arlington, Virginia, and cost $1,200 per student.

The people at Software A&E have experience working with both civilian and military agencies in the Washington, D.C., area and could probably provide significant consultation and support to clients with problems typical of those faced by government agencies.

Summary

KES 2 provides a structured rule tool that offers most features found in other mid-size tools like M.1, the PC version of AION, and Personal Consultant.

KES 2 has an adequate developer and user interface. The structured rule language will appeal more to programmers than nonprogrammers, but it is solid. Clearly, however, KES 2's strongest feature is its ability to fit within a C program.

KES 2.2's rivals are M.1, S.1, the PC version of AION, and GURU, all tools designed to appeal to people who want to develop expert systems on PCs in conventional languages. KES 2, S.1, M.1, and AION all offer the opportunity to develop systems to incorporate in programs that can be delivered on mainframes.

GURU

Micro Data Base Systems, Inc. (MDBS) has been around for several years. The company is best known for its MDBS III and KnowledgeMan programming packages, commonly said to be among the best data base packages available for the PC. MDBS sells most of its programs to developers who use them to develop customized applications for narrow vertical markets. Thus, a developer specializing in creating inventory accounting programs for small trucking firms might use KnowledgeMan to create applications.

When MDBS announced GURU in 1985, industry observers were naturally interested in seeing what kind of product a conventional software house would produce. MDBS conducted an advertising campaign that attempted to equate their product with visual images reminiscent of "2001" and "Star Wars" while simultaneously using text to argue that GURU was "Artificial Intelligence That Means Business." Luckily, the actual product comes much closer to the slogan than the graphics.

GURU comes on five disks, with four volumes of documentation. The package includes relational data base management, standard SQL inquiry, statistical analyses, split-screen spreadsheets, comprehensive business graphics, remote communications, general purpose text processing, customized report generation, multifunction calculator, elaborate forms management, complete structured programming, an expert systems shell, and a natural language development package. (As an add-on, you can get an interface to MDBS III.)

GURU is written in C. It takes 900 Kbytes of memory to store GURU on a hard disk. The package is available for the IBM PC, the IBM PC-RT, and UNIX hardware.

Given its price and power, GURU is clearly positioned as a mid-size tool that competes with M.1, Personal Consultant, and AION. In evaluating GURU, again consider the six general characteristics.

Power and Flexibility

If you were to consider the GURU expert systems shell in isolation, you would say it was a simple rule-based system that represents facts and rules via attribute–value pairs and relies primarily on backward chaining to control its reasoning process. In fact, it's not fair to consider the GURU expert systems shell in isolation from the GURU environment, which includes many facilities that allow GURU to rival more sophisticated structured rule tools like AION and Personal Consultant.

If you were using the language of AI, you would say that facts are represented as attribute–value pairs. The GURU manual calls them *variables*. (GURU documentation was not written to be compatible with the existing AI literature, but to be familiar to those experienced with other MDBS products and with the relational data base literature.)

GURU's variables come in four types:

1. *Working variables*—general system variables that can hold numbers or strings. They are not specific to any spreadsheet or data base.
2. *Cell variables*—spreadsheet cells that begin with a pound sign followed by the address of the cell they refer to. Cell variables refer to the spreadsheet that has been brought into memory with the LOAD FILE command.
3. *Field variables*—a field of a data base file appearing in the format FILE.FIELD. The value of a field variable is taken from the current data base record being examined.
4. *Pre-defined or environment variables*—special reserved words that define the working environment and can be set by a GURU command. They control everything from screen color to the formulas used to compute certainty factors. Environment variables begin with "E." followed by four letters.

In many cases, setting an environment variable can accomplish the same thing a meta-rule would in other systems.

It is always an asset to give the user the greatest degree of control over program operation. But it is also critical if you do so that a setting take on a reasonable default value if the user chooses *not* to alter it. In some cases, the default values for GURU's environment variables are obviously atypical and will usually have to be reset. For example, the environment variable E.LSTR, denoting the maximum length of text messages, has a default value of 10 characters long, insufficient in almost all cases. This requires the developer to reset this to a reasonable value at the start of the consultation. A similar inconvenience is the requirement that every variable be initialized to "unknown" at the start of the consultation to erase values from a previous consultation. The default should be to automatically initialize all variables unless the developer specifies otherwise.

How are rules represented? Rules are represented as:

```
PRIORITY: N
COST: N
IF
        (variable) (operator) (value)
              "
              "
THEN
        (variable) = (value)
              "
COMMENT: (text)
READY: (GURU commands)
CHANGES: (variables)
REASON: (variables)
```

PRIORITY. Rules can be given a priority that tells the system what order they should be tested in (if they refer to the same variable in their conclusion). If priority is omitted, the system processes rules from top to bottom.

NEEDS. Each rule also has an optional NEEDS list that specifies the variables to seek before testing the rule. If the NEEDS list is omitted, the system seeks values for all variables referred to in the premise of the rule.

CHANGES. Similarly, every rule can have an optional CHANGES list that tells what variables the rule applies to. If the CHANGES list is left out, the system assumes the rule is relevant for only the variables listed in its conclusion.

READY. Rules also have a READY option allowing a sequence of GURU commands to be specified which are executed at the time the rule is considered. In the sample knowledge base Beta, Rule 5 uses the READY clause to issue the GURU command: "totalrev=#E10." This causes the variable "totalrev" to be given the contents of the spreadsheet cell #E10.

REASON. This is text that explains the rule in an English paragraph.

Although the knowledge in GURU is not structured in the hierarchy that a system with a context tree or objects system has, it does provide some of the same functionality. Part of the utility of frames is their ability to conveniently process many cases using the same logic. Although GURU does not use frames, it does provide an easy way to process multiple cases. Rules can refer to general data base fields and then be processed repeatedly using continued data base search commands.

The rule:

```
IF      clientfile.purchases > 10
AND     clientfile.income > 30000
THEN    select = clientfile.Iname
```

picks out the name of any client in a data base who fits the conditions of the rule premise. The logic of the rule could be repeatedly applied—once to every record in the data base.

GURU lacks means to make generalizations easily about the contents of a spreadsheet. All references to spreadsheets in rules are to specific, single cells. It would be hard to write a rule that meant "apply this logic to every cell in this range of cells."

Inference or uncertainty. Each value of a variable can be assigned a *certainty factor* from 0 (UNKNOWN) to 100 (TRUE). This resembles the representation of certainty in M.1 and Personal Consultant Plus. GURU goes a step further by offering the user a choice of 31 different formulas for controlling how these certainty factors are used by the system. You can control:

1. How the system combines CFs of components of the rule's premise into a single number which tells whether the rule will pass.
2. The relationship between the overall CF of the rule premise and the CF of the conclusion.
3. The manner in which the CFs increase as evidence accumulates toward a conclusion.

This approach gives a solution to the dilemma of certainty factors. New users or those unconcerned with perfection can ignore the settings and rely on the default CF formulas as a rough approximation of reality. As systems become complex and mathematical accuracy becomes important, the system has enough flexibility to let the user select the formulas appropriate for the problem or subproblem at hand.

The formulas can be set in two ways. System variables can be given a code that tells what formula to use in computing their certainty. The other method is to set the GURU environment variable E.CFVA, which controls the default method of certainty calculation. Some problems may demand using more than one CF formula during the consultation. This can be done several ways; for example, you can set E.CFVA in the "READY" clause of certain rules that use a different method of computing certainty.

An example of this can be seen in the sample knowledge base shown in Figure 7.12. (Figure 7.13 illustrates the flow of the knowledge base consultation.) The circled area contains two rules that use a different CF formula than the rest of the system. While all other rules take the minimum CF in the premise as its overall certainty, these two rules take an average of all the CFs of their premises.

Initial messages, questions, and other operations can be programmed in a special INITIALIZATION procedure executed before the system's goal is pursued. This procedure is written in the GURU language and can set environment variables, select data bases, or select worksheets for the consultation to utilize. In the

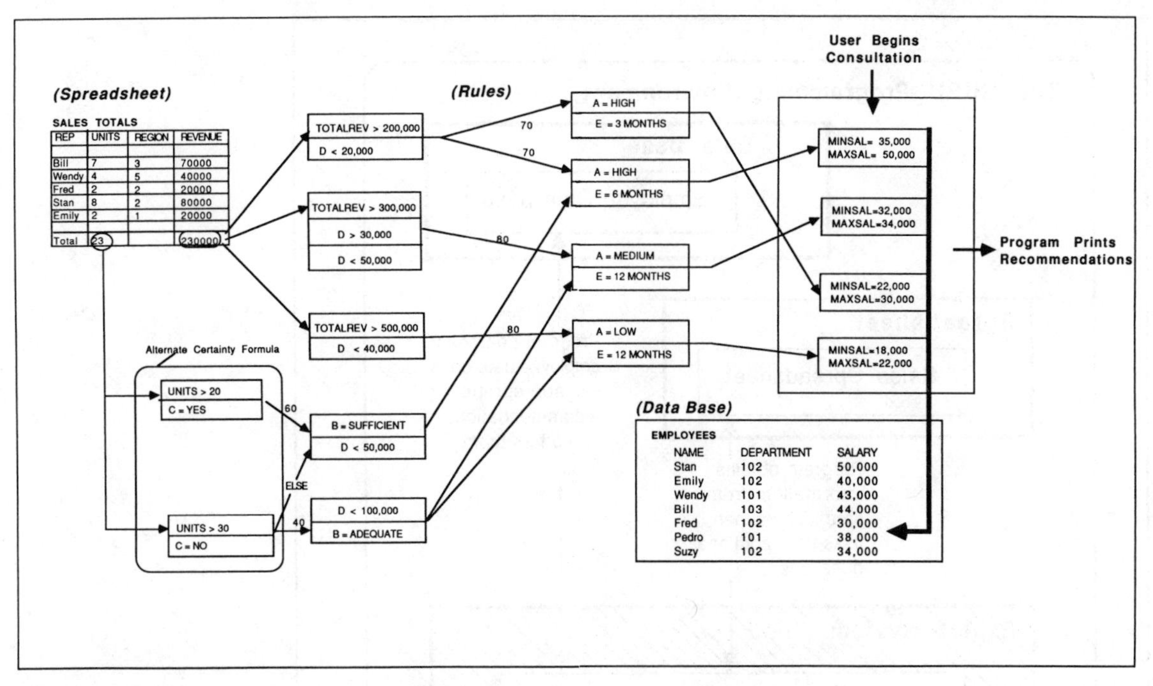

Figure 7.12 *GURU sample knowledge base.*

sample knowledge base, the INITIALIZATION procedure commands:

load sales.iss
use emps

tell the system the consultation uses information from the data base file called "emps" and from a spreadsheet file called "sales."

Similar to the INITIALIZATION procedure, a COMPLETION procedure contains GURU commands to execute after the goal has been sought. Typically this would be used to generate a report of the results of a consultation.

The knowledge base uses the COMPLETION procedure to search a data base as directed by the results of the consultation. The GURU command:

"obtain record from emps for salary >= minsal and salary <= maxsal"

searches the data base named "emps" for the employee whose salary is within a certain range. This range is specified by the variables MINSAL and MAXSAL, which have been determined by the first four rules in the consultation.

Control. Although the default mode of operation is backward chaining, GURU offers some alternate methods. The mode of control is specified at the outset of the consultation with the CONSULT command. The CONSULT TO TEST command causes the system to forward chain, testing every rule that applies to a particular variable.

The Developer Interface

Knowledge bases can be built two ways in GURU: in a menu-driven knowledge base editor or in an internal or external text editor. The menu-driven editor closely resembles that of TI's Personal Consultant Plus or AION, a hierarchy of menus and windows in which

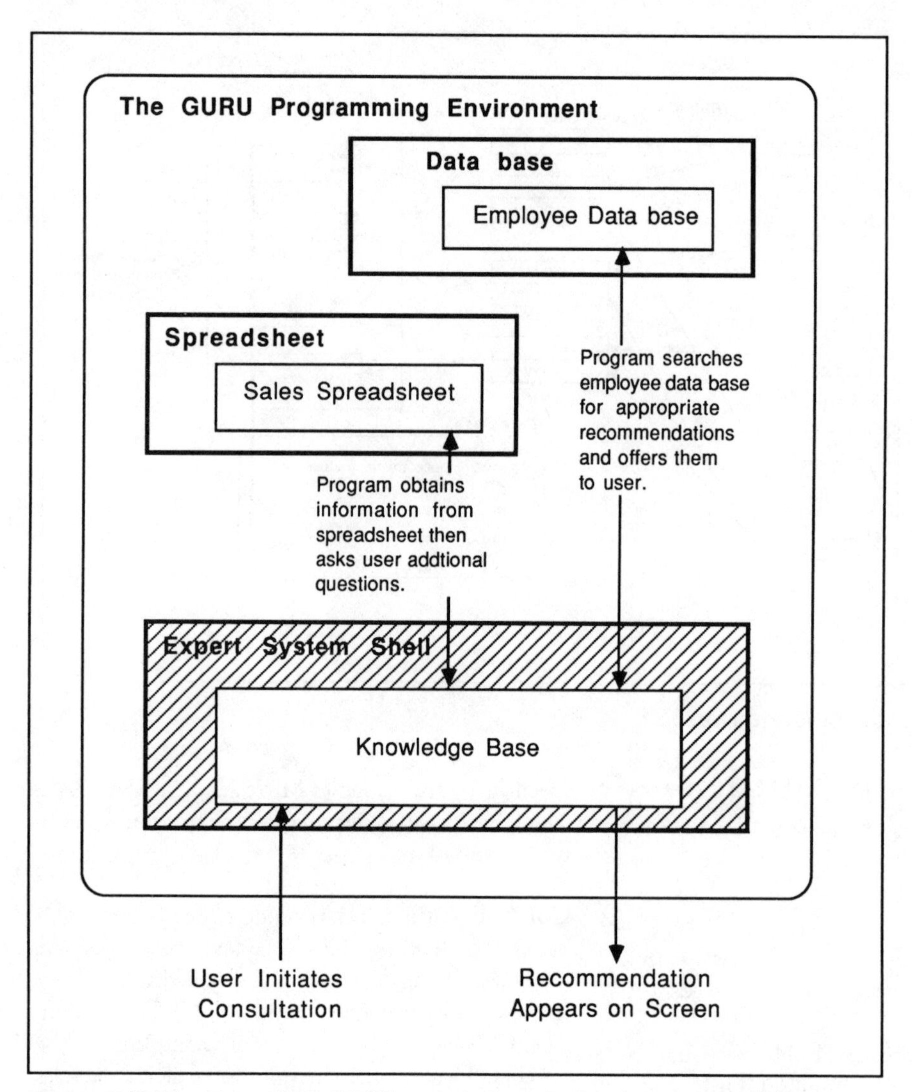

Figure 7.13 *The flow of the GURU sample knowledge base consultation.*

to enter information about rules, variables, the system's goal, and so on.

Variables used in the rules of GURU must be defined, even if the only content of the definition is the variable's name. Other optional information can be entered such as the certainty formula to use with a variable, a one-line English description of the variable, and a FIND clause telling how to get a value for the variable if one cannot be concluded by rules. (The system has no means to automatically generate a question about a variable if not found in the FIND clause).

The menu editor lacks such shortcut features as allowing you to copy names or clauses into rules from other rules.

The system records the rules that fired and what their values were when they passed. It does not, however, record all the rules that were tested or any rules that failed.

As mentioned earlier, procedures written in the GURU language can be included anywhere in the knowledge base. Although some systems allow you to write procedures in the underlying AI language of LISP or PROLOG, the GURU approach has many distinct advantages. Generally people don't write procedures because the rule language is insufficient to represent or control their knowledge. Instead, these procedures tend to have nothing to do with AI; they are conventional things like I/O, graphics, or communication with other programs. Such conventional procedures are more suited to a conventional language than an AI language. For cases where even the GURU environment is insufficient, you can make DOS calls to execute other programs and then return to GURU. Figure 7.14 illustrates a GURU menu screen.

The User Interface

A consultation can be triggered in two ways: (1) by selecting the GURU menu option to run a consultation, and (2) by issuing the GURU command CONSULT FILENAME anywhere where commands are allowed. This means one consultation can be started by another consultation. Since GURU commands can

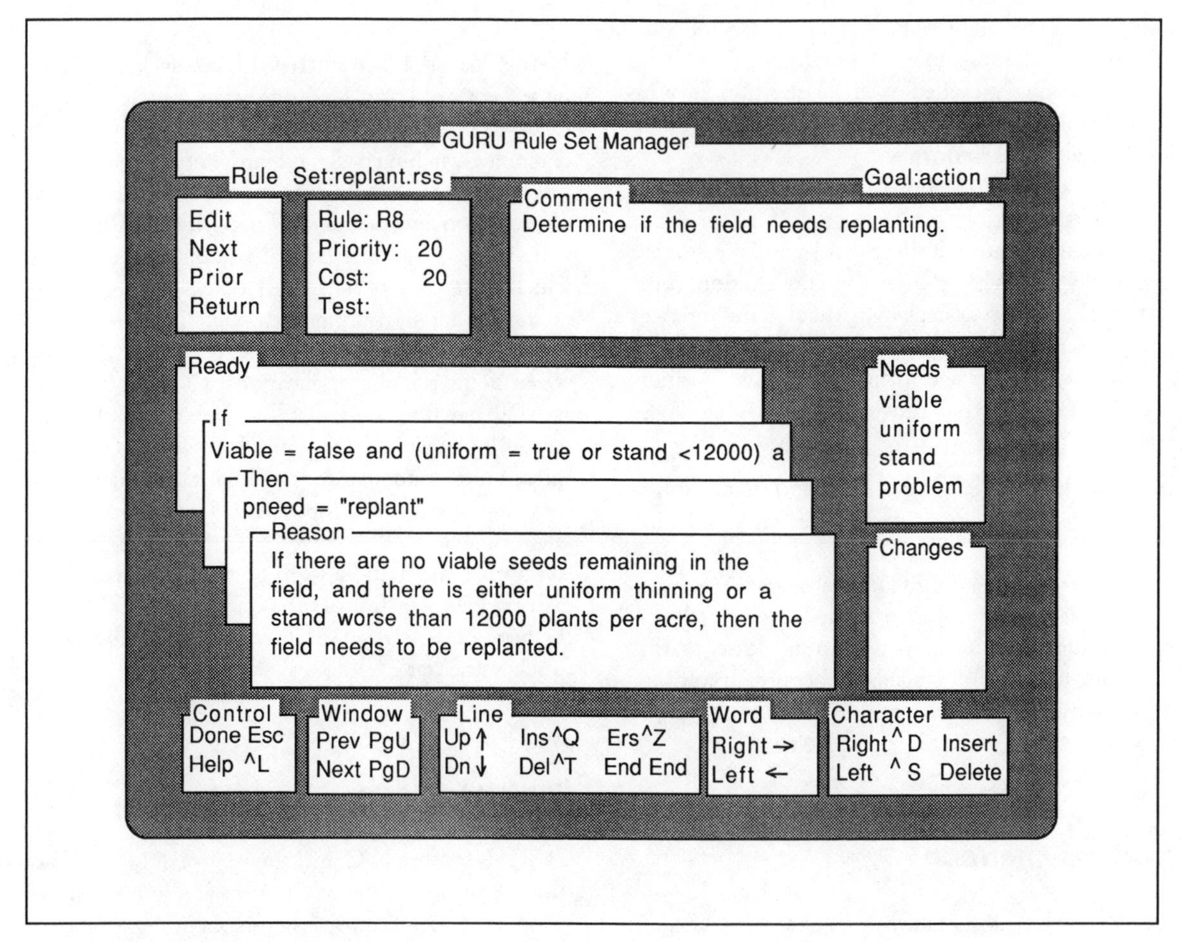

Figure 7.14 *GURU menu screen.*

also define the contents of a spreadsheet cell, a consultation can be triggered from a spreadsheet to determine the contents of that cell.

Questions posed by the system are responded to by typing on the keyboard, followed by an optional "CF N" to attach a certainty factor to a response. GURU allows input forms to be designed to highlight the areas to be filled in by the user. GURU automatically produces an underlined area for input. The size of the underlined area indicates the maximum length of input.

GURU offers menus, but they don't seem to work, and are not clearly documented.

Hitting a control key causes the system to display the current rule under consideration during a consultation. This is the extent of the explanation facilities during the consultation. You cannot ask specifically why a conclusion was reached or why a question must be asked, although you may be able to determine this by looking at the current rule.

The lack of sophistication in the on-line explanation facilities is surprising. Text translations for knowledge are given importance during the design phase, but are not easily accessible during the consultation. This defeats the purpose of explaining the system's variables and rules to the layman during the consultation.

The GURU package includes a limited business graphics program that can be called by the expert system.

Natural language. GURU comes with a natural language program useful in developing user-friendly interfaces for special purposes. Casual examination suggests that the current GURU natural language program is unusable, but perhaps a truly dedicated developer could figure out how to use it. In any case, as the technology of natural language processing improves, perhaps this component of GURU will improve.

A demo disk of GURU is available.

Systems Interface

GURU is of the most immediate value to those already familiar with KnowledgeMan, since the Expert System Shell is simply an addition. Users of programs like Lotus 1-2-3 or dBASE III would have two options: learn the full GURU environment and use it in place of their existing programs, or continue using other programs to enter information and share that data with GURU.

The first approach has advantages and disadvantages. The spreadsheet provided by GURU, considered by itself, is by no means comparable to Lotus 1-2-3 and would not be an adequate substitute for 1-2-3 for some applications. On the other hand, since the spreadsheet is an integrated part of GURU, GURU's relational data base, natural language query, graphics, and so on are also available within GURU and may be able to make up for what GURU's spreadsheet lacks.

Using Lotus 1-2-3 with GURU. If you already have a copy of Lotus 1-2-3 on disk, it can actually be executed from GURU. This provides the convenience of rapidly switching back and forth between programs. But the time to start up execution is only a small part of the inconvenience of working GURU in tandem with Lotus 1-2-3. The critical issue is the ease with which data can be switched between them. The method of datafile transfer is through .DIF files, a data interchange format standard used to transfer data between many popular applications. Having always to save DIF files from 1-2-3, then hop over to GURU, may be too inconvenient for some. However, if GURU's spreadsheet is adequate for the application, such users have the option to adopt GURU as a permanent environment.

Another way DIF files can be used is to ship your existing files over from Lotus one time and then do the rest of the work in GURU. This prevents having to rekey the data.

Runtime Speed

GURU is written in C and runs reasonably fast. The runtime version of the system runs at about the same speed, but is significantly faster in obtaining data from the data base or the spreadsheet.

Training and Support

The documentation accompanying GURU is poor. It's not integrated; each part of the GURU environment is described, but no example shows how to connect a spreadsheet to the expert systems shell, and so on. One step-by-step example could have made a huge difference. As it is, if you don't know how to build an expert system before you start reading this material, you probably won't learn from GURU's four manuals. Clyde W. Holsapple and Andrew B. Whinston's book, *Manager's Guide to Expert Systems Using GURU* (Dow Jones-Irwin, 1986, $25, available in bookstores), although biased as to how GURU fits into the whole expert systems marketplace, does provide a detailed discussion of how to use GURU to create an expert system. The book focuses on combining an expert system with a data base and provides comprehensive discussion of the problems and opportunities.

MDBS offers a three-day workshop on using GURU. The course focuses primarily on the expert systems component of GURU and, thus, may make up for the poor documentation. People who have never used KnowledgeMan and have purchased GURU might want to attend one of MDBS's data base courses as a prerequisite to the GURU course. Courses are scheduled throughout the United States.

Summary

GURU is an interesting option for those who want to develop and field a mid-size expert system that involves calls to data bases or spreadsheets. Its primary power is in its seamless integration of several different programs to form a common environment. Consequently, it would be most interesting to someone who wanted to develop an application from scratch. It would be less useful for those who already have their company records in Lotus 1-2-3 or dBASE II and simply want to develop an expert system to interface with those existing programs.

GURU lacks the ease of use and editing facilities a serious knowledge engineer would want to build a large expert system. The more heuristic knowledge you try to capture with GURU, the more frustrating it becomes. The tool is better suited for someone who wants to build a smaller mid-size system to integrate a little heuristic knowledge with some well-understood procedures and data stored on either a spreadsheet or in a relational data base.

GURU relies on its own technical vocabulary, which will seem more familiar to a conventional programmer with relational data base experience and will seem quite strange to someone coming from an AI background. Moreover, it doesn't provide a very powerful developer interface, which would quickly frustrate someone used to developing expert systems on a tool with browsers and trace facilities.

Anyone buying GURU should consider investing in the *Manager's Guide to Expert Systems Using GURU* since GURU's materials do not provide adequate help in conceptualizing how to use an expert system, how to connect it with existing programs, or how to acquire and refine expert knowledge.

GURU represents a significant effort on the part of a conventional software vendor to integrate the best of the expert systems techniques in an effective conventional programming environment that will seem straightforward to anyone familiar with relational data base programming. It's easy to imagine that some interesting systems are going to be built using this tool. All the expert system building tool vendors will necessarily need to move in this direction as they seek to develop mid-size expert system building tools for MIS programmers.

The weakness of GURU is the flip side of its strength; the developers of GURU have added an expert system to KnowledgeMan without providing the buyer with any idea of how it will be used. They have not included anything on how to select appropriate expert systems applications, how to integrate an expert system with other programs, or how to do the knowledge engineering necessary to capture the expert's knowledge in the first place. They have conceptualized the role of expert systems narrowly, as frontends for data bases and other existing programs, and have created a tool that lacks the facilities that would make it reasonable for a programmer to develop a larger expert system to embody a large amount of heuristic knowledge. Moreover, since they have relied on their own vocabulary, their documentation uses terms familiar to data base programmers but unfamiliar to those who approach programming from an expert systems perspective. Indeed, MDBS has identified an interesting niche and designed a tool that will prove very popular with programmers developing applications for that niche.

OTHER MID-SIZE RULE-BASED TOOLS

Several other mid-size structured rule tools are available. Moreover, most of the larger structured rule tools described in the next chapter offer PC-AT or workstation versions of their tools that could be classified as mid-size tools. Table 7.3 lists mid-size rule tools.

SUMMARY

Five mid-size rule-based tools have been reviewed: M.1, Nexpert, Personal Consultant Plus, KES 2, and GURU. Each is aimed at a specific audience and has advantages and disadvantages.

M.1 is unique among mid-size tools in its use of an external editor to create the knowledge base and for variable rules allowing a single rule with variables to be instantiated as a number of particular rules. It is targeted at those who want to develop expert systems that can be easily integrated into a conventional computer environment.

Nexpert introduces a powerful new inference strategy allowing you to write rules without specifying forward or backward chaining. Nexpert is targeted primarily at the research market.

Personal Consultant Plus, a significantly enhanced version of Personal Consultant, has a number of new features, including frames and demons. It is targeted

Table 7.3 *Mid-size rule-based tools.*

TOOL (Vendor)	Price of Tool	Hardware: Mini/ Mainframe	Workstation (UNIX, RISC, VMS, etc.)	LISP Machine Workstation	PC
ADS-PC (Aion)	$7K				IBM PASCAL
GURU (Micro Data Base Systems)	$6.5K		MicroVAX C		IBM C
HUMBLE (Xerox Corp.)	$400-1.5K		•		IBM-AT MAC Smalltalk
KES II (Software A & E)	$4K		• C		IBM C
M.1 (Teknowledge)	$5K				IBM C
Nexpert (Neuron Data)	$3K				Mac Assembler
Personal Consultant Easy (Texas Instruments)	$300	VAX C	MicroVax C		TI, IBM Scheme
XI Plus (Expertech)	$1,250				IBM PROLOG

• = Wide variety of hardware.

at the widest audience, including educators and researchers. It is popular with those wanting to develop small, practical, standalone applications, including intelligent job aids.

KES 2.2 is a structured rule tool whose strongest feature is its ability to fit within a C program. It is designed to appeal to those who want to develop expert systems on PCs in conventional language; consequently, it appeals more to programmers than to nonprogrammers.

GURU's primary power is its seamless integration of several different programs to form a common environment. It is targeted at people wanting to develop a system involving calls to data bases or spreadsheets and ready to start from scratch.

Depending upon your specific application, any one of these mid-size expert system building tools could be of value.

8

Large Rule-Based Tools

INTRODUCTION

This chapter discusses the larger, rule-based tools used in many companies today. Most are not significantly different from the mid-size tools discussed in Chapter 7. They are larger in the sense that they are designed and priced to be used on mini and mainframe computers, or on LISP machines and UNIX workstations. Like the mid-size tools, they enable their users to develop sophisticated mid- to large-size rule-based expert systems.

Large tools typically allow users to partition the rule base to take advantage of multiple instantiation and inheritance factors. They also generally provide confidence factors or make it possible for the system developer to encode confidence factors within the system. Large tools typically make it easy to develop complex user interfaces, although this feature has not been successfully provided by some IBM mainframe versions of these tools.

These tools do require a longer learning curve, but once users become familiar with them, they can aid in solving very complex problems (often requiring several thousand rules). Large tools have different hardware needs than their smaller counterparts. Computers required for running a large system tool range from IBM and DEC mainframes and minis to Xerox 1100s, IBM and TI PCs, and the Symbolics 3600 machine. As you may have guessed, large tools are designed for users already familiar with computers and computer programming languages.

This chapter begins by considering some problems in getting expert systems to run on mainframes and then discusses some tools currently run on mainframes. It then discusses some tools that run on DEC VAX computers.

AN OVERVIEW OF THE IBM WORLD

Much of the world's most lucrative computing is done on IBM mainframes and will continue so for a variety of reasons (principally, to avoid the unthinkable task of replacing the installed software, databases, and hardware). These computers are at the heart of many of the world's largest business organizations.

IBM Hardware

To keep the record straight, this does not refer to IBM's Personal Computers or their System 38 office mini. The machines that interest large business organizations are the descendants of the IBM 370 and are referred to collectively as 370-architecture machines. Three main classes of machines are included: the "smallish" 4300 series; the mid-range machines, including the 3080 series; and the huge 3090 series machines at the top end. (A newly announced machine, the 9370, is a very small 370-architecture machine intended mostly for interactive applications.)

Operating Systems

Three different operating systems run on the 370 mainframes.

1. DOS, not to be confused with the PC operating system of the same name, which runs on the smallish mainframes. This operating system is used by most smaller 370 users.

2. VM, IBM's main interactive operating system, used by a relatively small subset of IBM's large mainframe users.
3. MVS, the main IBM production system designed for high-speed transaction processing on IBM's largest machines.

VM and MVS are the environments where the money is. Each operating system has two conceptually distinct parts, one that deals with the hardware and resource management, and the other that manages the user interactions. (See Figure 8.1.)

The VM Operating System. VM (Virtual Machine) was developed at IBM's Cambridge Scientific Center as the interactive operating system (i.e., for office systems). It is often used to develop software applications to be delivered in an MVS environment. Thus, VM is, in fact, available on all hardware families.

The resource management side of VM is called CP (Control Program). One interface environment is CMS, which once stood for Cambridge Management System, but now means Control Management System.

The MVS Operating System. MVS (Multiple Virtual Storage) is the workhorse of the world of large-scale computing. A descendant of OS 360, MVS is *the* IBM production environment. It is designed for high-speed transaction processing on the largest mainframes.

MVS is also the name used for the resource management side of MVS.

MVS User Interactions. The MVS world is the world of batch computing, and the user interface side of any MVS operating system determines all the more advanced interactions with the machine. Besides batch mode, a few acronymed environments are very important to the economics of mainframe computing.

First is IMS (Information Management System), the original data communications manager under OS/360 (and now MVS). The importance of this system (which predated interactive computing and relational data bases) is that it is established, with a capital E. Some vendors who are bringing KE tools into the mainframe world feel their tool's ability to interface to existing IMS-based application programs (and particularly to

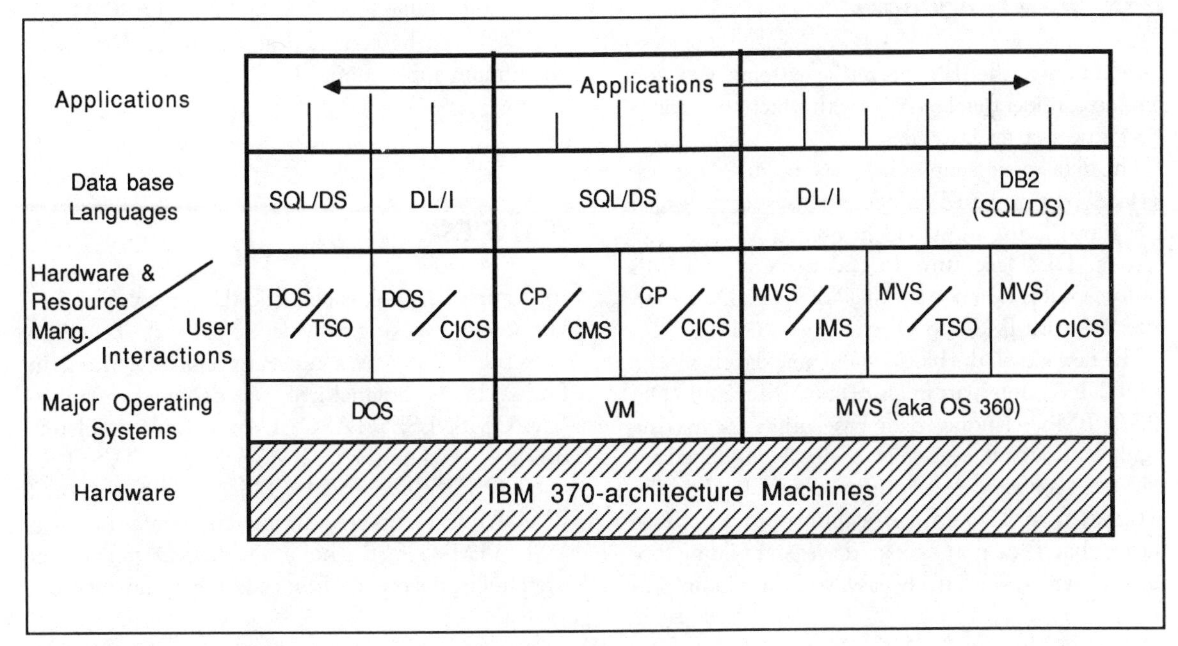

Figure 8.1 *An incomplete guide to the IBM 370 world.*

the original IMS data base language DL/I) is absolutely critical to their success.

In an effort to move toward interactive computing, a Time Sharing Option (TSO) was developed for MVS (remember, VM was designed from the beginning to be interactive). TSO is a very popular product and has an important place in the near-term transfer of AI to mainframes simply because of its conceptual similarity to the time-sharing environments that AI came from.

CICS (the Customer Information and Control System) is the MVS workhorse for applications that run a very few types of interactions an enormous number of times. CICS is a *very* important program.

CICS came into existence to allow some truly interactive transactions in computing applications in which events occur thousands of times per minute. Most important applications are on MVS/CICS, but CICS also runs on VM and DOS. In other words, it is possible to develop application software in VM's CP/CICS system (which, of course, is already interactive) and then deliver it on MVS/CICS.

Data Base Languages

In addition to the IBM operating systems, you also have to consider the data bases with which the various operating systems interface.

The data base system in IMS, the original "user interface" part of the MVS operating system, is called DL/I and is the most widely used IBM data base system. DL/I accounts for 60 percent of IBM's customers. It is so important that CICS and DOS both interface with IMS and DL/I.

The new kid on the block, mainframe-data base-wise is DB2. Its counterpart in DOS and VM is SQL/DS. DB2, IBM's relational data base utility, is making significant inroads, especially for newly developed applications software. As a "proper subset," DB2 can be accessed from TSO in a straightforward way. This means that if you port an expert system building tool to TSO, which is relatively easy, you can obtain proper access to DB2 data bases. (The problem is that most of the big-money, IBM-mainframe-based data base applications are in DL/I and that situation is not likely to change soon.)

Language Interfaces with IBM Operating Systems

IBM's data bases and operating systems are written in a proprietary IBM language similar to PL/1. In one sense, any application, including any expert systems tool, in any one of the higher level languages like C, PASCAL, or FORTRAN, could run on top of any one of the IBM operating systems. In constructing the various user interfaces (especially CICS), however, IBM incorporated some hooks that are easy to attach via COBOL. Thus, if the tool is written in COBOL or includes some COBOL, it can more effectively control the MVS resource allocation code, and thus the developer has more control over things like the screen the user interacts with. Except for interface control, however, the language the tool is written in doesn't make any difference. A tool in C, PASCAL, or COBOL can be compiled and embedded within a mainframe application.

IBM'S ESE

IBM's first KE tool, called ESE (Expert Systems Environment), was originally developed at the Palo Alto Scientific Center as a research vehicle. Written in PASCAL, the original ESE was designed to run in VM/CMS. ESE's PASCAL code was completely overhauled when the tool was ported to MVS/TSO and DOS/TSO from VM/CMS. (Some 95 percent of PASCAL segments are now interchangeable between VM and MVS. ESE is not available in DOS.) Besides overhauling the original ESE code, the documentation, code-naming conventions, and strings in other languages were all cleaned up during the port.

ESE is essentially an EMYCIN-level KE tool focusing on rules with some important added facilities like structured editors and control blocks. The development environment, ESDE, requires 6 megabytes of memory to get started with a small knowledge base.

IBM is actively using and promoting ESE, which is now a product program. ESE has the most mainframe site licenses to date. There is no PC version. Since there is no COBOL code within ESE to facilitate hooks, ESE interfaces to DBs by means of external procedure calls in PASCAL.

The "mission" within IBM that supports ESE has recently moved to Bethesda, MD, and incentives are strong to push IBM's AI products (which include LISP and PROLOG besides ESE). IBM has been known to offer ESE to customers free for six months to get their applications started.

The TSO Shortcut

What about the CICS applications that are so important in the IBM world? IBM is well aware that their customers want to do knowledge engineering for the production environments in CICS and want to access DL/I. The company is working on it, although small companies might be able to move a little faster.

In fact, most tools ported directly from VAXes or PCs to the mainframe environment will be working under the TSO environment. This is much easier to accomplish than moving it to CICS. (For one thing, neither CICS nor IMS like large blocks of code.) But because of the 370 architecture, programs running under TSO cannot offer a single interface. They can't access the user-programs interface, and they can't access DL/I without a great deal more work.

Many vendors are porting to TSO just to get a product on an IBM mainframe. This approach allows them to become familiar with the 370 architecture and to at least learn about interfacing to DB2/SQL data bases.

TEKNOWLEDGE'S S.1

In December 1986, Teknowledge announced that their large tool, S.1, was available on VM/CMS. S.1, like ESE, is essentially an EMYCIN-like tool with some important additions, including structured editors and control blocks. By electing to port to VM, Teknowledge chose the easiest port, since VM is a time-sharing environment. According to Daniel Sagalowicz, VP of New Product Development, Teknowledge also intends to port to the MVS/CICS environment since many of their customers' applications exist under IMS.

Teknowledge's S.1 offering in VM is intended for use by trained knowledge engineers engaged in developing large systems. Eventually, however, Teknowledge would like to see retrained COBOL programmers developing small knowledge bases that can be embedded within large MVS applications. Most of the coding will not involve knowledge-base development, but will involve developing code for user interfaces, for data base access, and for accessing existing applications software. Sagalowicz notes that VM (or PCs or workstations) will still be the development environment. You can't develop under MVS/CICS.

Sagalowicz offers an illuminating example. Every bank has a program that goes through each account every night and adds the credits received by 3 P.M. that day, subtracts the debits, calculates any interest, and posts the new balance. Within that gigantic program is a little procedure, now written in COBOL, of course, that decides what to do if there is not enough money in the account. Should you send a form letter, notify a branch officer to call in the morning, or close the account and call the police?

The decision about what to do depends on state and federal regulations, bank policy, and maybe even a branch officer's familiarity with a particular account, all of which can change from time to time. Thus, the banks have a knowledge problem, and the corresponding code would be a smallish knowledge system that could explain what it did and why. The small knowledge system would certainly be much easier to understand and modify than the corresponding COBOL.

OTHER EXPERT SYSTEMS ON MAINFRAMES

Software A&E's KES 2

Like Teknowledge, Software A&E has also implemented their KES 2 tool under MVS/TSO, and they are also looking at a CICS implementation to satisfy customer demand. KES 2 is written in C.

Nixdorf/LogicWare's TWAICE

LogicWare is marketing TWAICE, an EMYCIN-like tool originally developed by Nixdorf for mainframe and VAX environments. Although major extensions are planned for TWAICE, it currently runs only under TSO.

IntelliCorp's KEEconnection

Intellicorp's recently announced mainframe interface products, the IntelliScope user interface and the KEEconnection, both interface to mainframe data base programs through SQL. IntelliCorp, in effect, has elected to keep its inference engine (KEE, a large hybrid tool) on a LISP machine, but interface with mainframes by means of a package that automatically generates commands that SQL can execute. Thus, users can draw on the power of the KEE environment to quickly access data in any mainframe data bases that can be accessed via SQL and then can model and monitor that data in KEE. On the other hand, you cannot develop a knowledge base in KEE and run it inside a mainframe environment per se. (KEE is a large hybrid tool discussed in the next chapter.) KEEconnection is a utility that allows KEE to connect to a mainframe to acquire data.

AION'S AES

AION has taken a different approach. They have implemented AES (the delivery environment of their AION Development System tool) into a MVS separate address space. In effect, AES runs as an independent application in MVS. The system is available on CICS and IMS. AES and the application program are linked in a novel fashion using IBM's VTAM (Virtual Telecommunications Access Method), originally designed to link equipment or programs running on separate machines.

In addition to allowing AES the right kind of interaction with the DL/I applications, this architecture also allows the inference engine to be implemented on a separate mainframe. Most customers have less trouble justifying the cost of an additional mainframe than trying to fit yet another piece of software on their already gigantic mainframes. Eventually, the development environment, ADS, will be delivered on the mainframe in the same way as ESE.

The way AES manages the display under IMS and CICS does not involve GDDM, IBM's display manager. According to Dave Patrick of AION, GDDM is a CPU hog, and using it negatively affects customer interest. Instead, AES's implementation deals with the raw 3270 data stream and, although most of AES is written in PASCAL, the tool has COBOL hooks into the MVS resource allocation code that makes it look like a standard MVS application. In other words, where the tools implemented in TSO tend to have line entry interfaces, AION's AES controls the user interface using conventional mainframe techniques.

In addition to the mainframe implementation of AION, the company offers an implementation on a PC. The PC application is designed to facilitate delivering programs developed on the PC version of AION to any mainframe delivery environment.

SYNTELLIGENCE'S SYNTEL

Syntelligence doesn't sell a tool, but they have seriously considered fielding systems on IBM mainframes to bring their large financial applications to market on mainframes.

The Syntelligence approach involves using supplemental hardware. They use Xerox 1188/86 LISP machines for their development work. The LISP code created in the development portion of Syntelligence's proprietary tool, SYNTEL, is compiled into an intermediate code. This intermediate code is then interpreted by a distributed, but purely IBM delivery environment composed of the inference engine running on mainframes (written in PL/I) and the user interface running on 3270 ATs (written in C). The use of intermediate code means the runtime environment is complete. There are no escapes to LISP, PL/I, or COBOL from the knowledge base.

SYNTEL's inference engine runs on MVS as a standard CICS application. Since SYNTEL has a relational data base management system within it, the tool can support both active-value and data base monitoring functions. Users have called SYNTEL "the first mainframe applications program that looks like a Macintosh." Syntelligence has recently signed a joint marketing agreement with IBM for end-user products built with SYNTEL, so you'll probably hear a lot more about this tool. Syntelligence intends to focus on applications in the financial domain and does not intend to offer its tool for sale.

CULLINET'S IMPACT

Cullinet is also developing a KE environment for the mainframe. Their new product, IMPACT, is being ported from a VAX implementation written in COBOL, into a CICS application that can be called by other programs.

SO WHAT CAN I BUY RIGHT NOW?

Mainframe software economics and the entrenched nature of critically important mainframe applications are only beginning to be addressed. At the moment, ADS, ESE, KES 2, S.1, and TWAICE are the only tools available on an IBM mainframe, and AION's ADS has taken a strong early lead.

TOOLS ON DEC VAX MACHINES

In addition to the tools just discussed, some other large-rule tools run on DEC VAX machines including Envisage, OPS83, and VAX OPS5.

Envisage

Envisage is the second generation of a PROLOG-derived tool originally called Sage. It was developed by Systems Designers, an English company that recently opened offices in the United States (Systems Designers Software Inc.). The earlier version of this tool has been used to develop several mid-size expert systems being used in England.

A PROLOG-based tool like OPS5, Envisage is more appropriate for experienced programmers. Instead of entering rules, you primarily enter logical assertions. Envisage has the feel of PROLOG, but it clearly has many additional features including demons, a feature that allows you to suspend one line of questioning temporarily and re-answer a set of questions and compare results (simulation), as well as fuzzy logic and Bayesian probabilities.

Although Systems Designers is British-based, they seem to have made a real commitment to offering their products and services in the United States. If a company is interested in developing an expert system in a logic-based tool that has a track record, Envisage is worth investigating.

OPS83

OPS83 is a second-generation version of the original OPS5 that incorporates an imperative sublanguage that resembles C and a new compiler technology that makes it run substantially faster than the LISP-based version of OPS5. The tool is being offered by Production Systems Technologies, a small new company located close to Carnegie-Mellon University. No systems have been implemented in OPS5 yet, but

Carnegie-Mellon University is currently developing a large military application in the tool. OPS83 runs on a VAX under VMS and on AT&T3B machines and several workstations under UNIX.

VAX OPS5

OPS5 was originally developed by C. L. Forgy at Carnegie-Mellon and used by John McDermott when he developed the initial version of XCON (R1). OPS5 has also been used by IBM for developing YES/MVS (Yorktown Expert System for MVS operators), an expert system that exerts real-time interactive control of an MVS operating system, and ACE (Automated Cable Expertise), the expert system developed by Bell Labs to identify trouble spots in telephone networks and recommend appropriate repairs. In essence, OPS5 and EMYCIN are the two most important "original" expert system building tools. EMYCIN puts more emphasis on ease of use and on capturing uncertain knowledge. And EMYCIN is a backward chaining system. OPS5 is much less friendly, it is more like an environment than a tool, and it uses forward chaining. While EMYCIN has generated a whole second generation of easy-to-use, backward chaining rule-based tools, OPS5 has been favored by programmers for complex tasks and has built up a very impressive list of large, successful applications.

When the DEC AI group got ready to implement XCON, they recoded OPS5, which was originally written in LISP, in BLISS, a language that makes DEC's VAX OPS5 the fastest commercial version currently available. In addition to XCON, which has some 4,500 rules and has been used to configure over 90,000 VAX systems, DEC's AI group has developed and fielded several other expert systems, including XSEL, XSITE, PTRANS, NTC, and INET. Much of the experience that DEC has acquired in the process has gone into improving OPS5, and you could easily argue that VAX OPS5 has the best track record of any commercial tool. Keep in mind that this tool is better used by experienced programmers. The AI group at DEC, which now numbers over 100, has developed an impressive array of training and support services.

In addition to the large-rule tools discussed, several tools like Teknowledge's M.1 and Software A&E's KES 2 have been rewritten in C and can be run on a DEC VAX or any other hardware that supports C compilers. In addition, some small tool vendors like Exsys and Level Five Research have versions of their tools for the VAX.

Also several rule-based tools are written in LISP or PROLOG and run on DEC VAXes or other mini or mainframe machines. Control Data, for example, sells a LISP-based version of KES that runs on a CYBER.

ART, KEE, and Knowledge Craft, discussed in Chapter 9, are all available in LISP on VAX hardware.

Nexpert Object

An object-oriented version of Neuron Data's Nexpert has recently been developed for the VAX, and DEC seems eager to promote its use. Nexpert Object has the same wonderful interface features that the original Nexpert has and seems like it might be an important entry into the emerging mid-size hybrid tool category.

OTHER TOOLS

Other mainframe tools are available in Europe, but are not readily available in the United States.

No large, hybrid expert system building tools commercially available for mini or mainframe computers run in conventional languages, although Inference Corporation has announced that ART will soon be available in C. The startup companies that have developed the most innovative and user-friendly tools have developed those tools on mini or mainframe computers in LISP or PROLOG and, more recently, have concentrated on LISP machine or workstation versions of their tools. The large, powerful tools available on mini or mainframes run in LISP environments and hence cannot be easily integrated into traditional computer systems, although IBM's recent announcement of an IBM Common LISP should allow several tool vendors to get into mainframes in short order.

Table 8.1 *Large rule-based tools.*

TOOL (Vendor)	Price of Tool	Hardware: Mini/ Mainframe	Hardware: Workstation (UNIX, RISC, VMS, etc.)	Hardware: LISP Machine Workstation	Hardware: PC
ADS-MVS (Aion)	$25K-60K	IBM/VS PASCAL			
ENVISAGE (Systems Designers Software)	$8.6-21K	VAX PASCAL	MicroVAX PASCAL		
ES Environment/VM & /MVS (IBM)	$60K	IBM PASCAL			
IMPACT (Cullinet)	$30-90K	IBM, VAX COBOL			
KES/VS (Control Data)	$11-71K	Cyber LISP			
Knowledge Workbench (Silogic, Inc.)	$1.5-12K		SUN, MicroVax C		
OPS5e (Verac, Inc.)	$3K			Symbolics LISP	
OPS83 (Production Systems Technologies)	$1.9-20K	VAX C	MicroVAX Apollo, Sun C		
PRL 3 (Level Five Research)	$9.6-28K	VAX PASCAL			
S.1 (Teknowledge)	$25-60K	IBM/VM, VAX,C	• C		IBM-AT C
TWAICE (Nexdorf)	$12.9-48.9K	IBM/VM VAX,Cyber PROLOG	MicroVAX, Tectronics, PROLOG		IBM PROLOG
VAX OPS5 (DEC)	$7.5K	VAX Bliss	MicroVAX Bliss		

• = Wide variety of hardware.

THE VERY NEAR FUTURE

The expert system building tools discussed in this chapter represent the initial effort to make expert systems technologies available in conventional mini and mainframe computer environments. Better tools are available in LISP, and more cost-effective tools are available on AT and Macintosh machines.

Expect in the near future to see the introduction of more powerful expert system building tools written in conventional languages that will run on existing mini and mainframe systems. In the meantime, if you want to get started in a conventional language-based tool and do not mind paying a lot for a first-generation tool, the tools described in this chapter can get you going.

SUMMARY

The tools focused on in this chapter, with the exception of Syntelligence's SYNTEL, which is not for sale, are large structured rule tools designed to be integrated into traditional computer environments. In all cases, power and flexibility have been sacrificed to obtain compatibility.

Table 8.1 summarizes basic information about each of the larger rule-based tools.

9

Hybrid Tools

INTRODUCTION

This chapter introduces and discusses hybrid tools. The hybrids are tools lacking the narrow focus typical of large, structured rule-based tools. They use frames, objects, semantic networks, and a rich variety of inheritance techniques in a programming environment that allows for the structures and relationships typical of more complex expert knowledge.

In other words, the designers of hybrid tools did not develop these tools to build a specific type of knowledge system. Instead, these tools can be used to build other tools that, in turn, will be used by other developers to build other expert systems. Presently, many hybrid tools should be considered research tools rather than practical tools that can be used to rapidly prototype a knowledge system. Hybrids are *not* the ideal tool for a company beginning to develop its first system. But hybrid tools are undoubtedly the tools of the future. As more and more companies become involved in knowledge engineering and gain practical working experience developing expert systems, hybrid tools will be the overwhelming choice for developing large, complex knowledge systems.

In the past two years three commercial expert system building tools have emerged as the top-of-the-line options for research groups wanting to explore the development of their own large expert systems. Some individuals in the expert systems industry assert that these three software packages should not be called tools, but should be referred to as *tool kits* or *knowledge engineering environments*, because they offer a variety of ways to approach a given problem. While these tools are called *hybrid* here, it is certainly agreed they are considerably more complex and offer many more options than the large, rule-based tools of narrower scope.

When you start to work with hybrid tools, you must first decide which techniques and strategies to employ to maximize the tool's effectiveness. Early decisions must be made so you can be assured a hybrid tool is really suited for your application. Once you have made these decisions, the hybrid tool can be used to create a narrower tool to build your knowledge system. As a result, you have a lot of flexibility in system design when you select a hybrid. However, the price you pay for this flexibility is considerable. You need to know a lot about knowledge engineering and symbolic programming just to use a hybrid tool effectively. This fact alone makes it much easier to make poor decisions or mistakes early on that will result in wasted time and ineffective systems. So be forewarned; hybrid tools are much more like a true programming environment than a tool. They use knowledge in different ways and can manipulate their knowledge bases to solve problems. It is their programming environment that makes these hybrids so versatile.

OBJECT-ORIENTED PROGRAMMING CONCEPTS

Just about all hybrid tools offer the developer some kind of objects and inheritance. An object (or unit, schema, or frame) is like a record. It has a name and contains information about the thing named. Figure 9.1 illustrates a typical object.

Notice that the object has a name and a number of slots. Each slot, in turn, is made up of facits. One facit contains an attribute while another contains the values, fact, rule, procedure, or pointers associated with the attribute. Still other facits can contain meta-

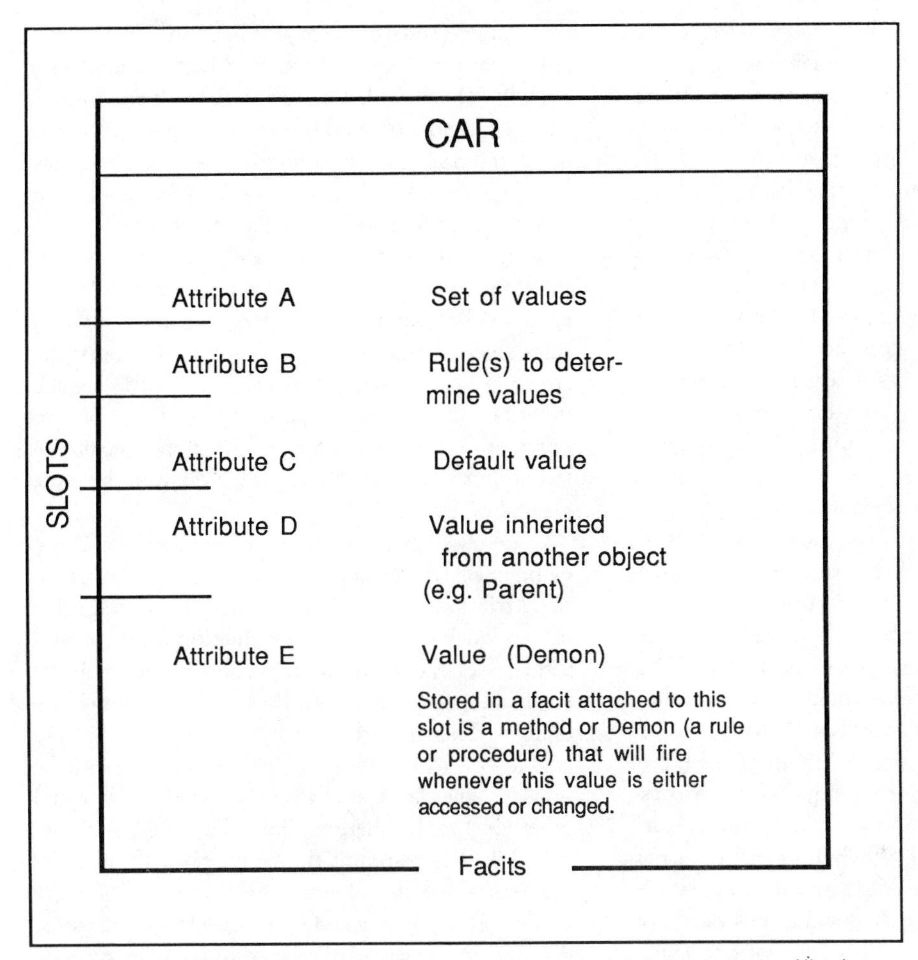

Figure 9.1 *An object (or frame or schema) with several slots and some of the types of information that may be stored there.*

information about the information in the slot. For example, you could place a rule (demon) in a facit that would automatically fire whenever the value of the slot is altered. The use of demons that wait for values to change and then spring into action is often referred to as action-oriented programming or active values.

In the following discussions, objects, units, schema, and frames are used as synonyms. Some knowledge engineers prefer to distinguish frames from objects. Frames are usually implemented in LISP, while objects can be used in any language. Objects were initially used in Smalltalk, which is coded in assembly language. Frame-based systems tend to have much more complex inheritance patterns, which they acquire from LISP than do object-oriented systems implemented using conventional languages.

Some developers find it easier to use objects, frames, and schema as synonyms, and to treat the unique types of inheritance relationships allowed by a particular tool or system as a separate issue. At least conceptually, the great advantage of an object-oriented style of programming is that it lets you quickly describe a subject-matter domain without having to focus on actual procedures. By using this method, you can describe the subsystems of an automobile, its parts, and the connections among the parts (e.g., circuits, flow of gas) without ever considering how they work, how they change in the course of time, or even how to diagnose failures.

This descriptive picture of a domain is usually the key to understanding the domain in enough detail to consider all procedurally oriented matters. In short, you have to identify the attributes before you can combine them into rules. And the more complex the subject matter domain is, the more necessary this underlying structure becomes. It is an absolute necessity to successfully develop a model or situation that will allow a system to "reason" about a domain.

It would be erroneous to assume that to develop an object-oriented description of a domain you would start by naming each object existing in the domain and then relate that object to other independently created objects. In fact, object-oriented languages assume that root or class objects underlie more specific objects. A specific object may inherit information from other more specific or even more generic objects contained in the domain knowledge base. Consider, for example, that you were to create a generic object "car." You could then "take copies" or instantiate an object called a "Saab" and another called a "BMW," with each inheriting many characteristics of cars in general, but with each still possessing some unique characteristics. Likewise, you could make a "copy" of the Saab to represent "Paul's Saab." Therefore, while a generic car has a slot for the body-paint color (with no particular color assigned), Saabs have that slot and provide about 12 possible values (specific colors) for that slot. Paul's Saab inherits that slot from the "generic Saab" object, but still possesses a single value for the slot, being the color white.

Look at Figure 9.2. In this illustration a class object describes a generic object "car," another describes a generic Saab, and a third describes Paul's Saab. A generic object also describes "personal property." Since Paul's Saab is Paul's personal property, it inherits some information from the generic object, "personal property." Incidentally, the important concept of *data abstraction* is illustrated by these "generic" objects. They are abstract pictures of relationships that exist in the concrete instances expert systems reason about.

Examine Figure 9.2 again. It illustrates five objects and some relationships that can exist among them. In this example, three of the objects have an overall hierarchical pattern: a car, a Saab, and Paul's Saab. Paul's Saab IS A Saab, which in turn IS A car. If you assume a simple, rigidly defined hierarchical inheritance pattern, then Saab inherits everything specified about cars and Paul's Saab inherits everything known about Saabs. This process is known as *inheritance*.

In this particular example, Paul's Saab also inherits information which is specified about Personal Property. So Paul's Saab has several slots with attributes and rules all concerning personal property that don't occur in either Saab or Car. In this sense, Paul's Saab inherits information from, and is an instance of, two different objects (or contexts). The more specific object almost always inherits information from the more general object.

Of course, inheriting information often would not be practical. For example, assume a car has a slot for the attribute "taillights" and a single associated value of two. Saab inherits this information from car and then passes it, in turn, to Paul's Saab. However, as the result of a recent accident, Paul's Saab has only one taillight. Therefore, the system needs a mechanism to enable you to specify that certain objects can have unique values associated with slots where they would otherwise simply inherit a value from more generic objects. Likewise, assuming the system normally assumes that more specific objects were examples of more generic objects, you would want a mechanism to assure that if a system wanted to provide an example of a Saab and intended to infer something about taillights based on that example, the system would know to avoid using Paul's Saab as an example.

Not all relationships between objects simply reflect hierarchical or subset information. But sometimes the ability to establish relationships among objects that are more complex or specific than these common patterns is a necessity. You may need to create objects and establish causal relationships like "leads-to" or "manufactures," or procedural relations, like "is-used-to-repair." This is a true attribute of hybrid tools.

To really complicate matters, assume you want to construct a system to contain a "picture" (or viewpoint) of the objects and relationships among car, Saab, and Paul's Saab at one point in time (when Paul's Saab was

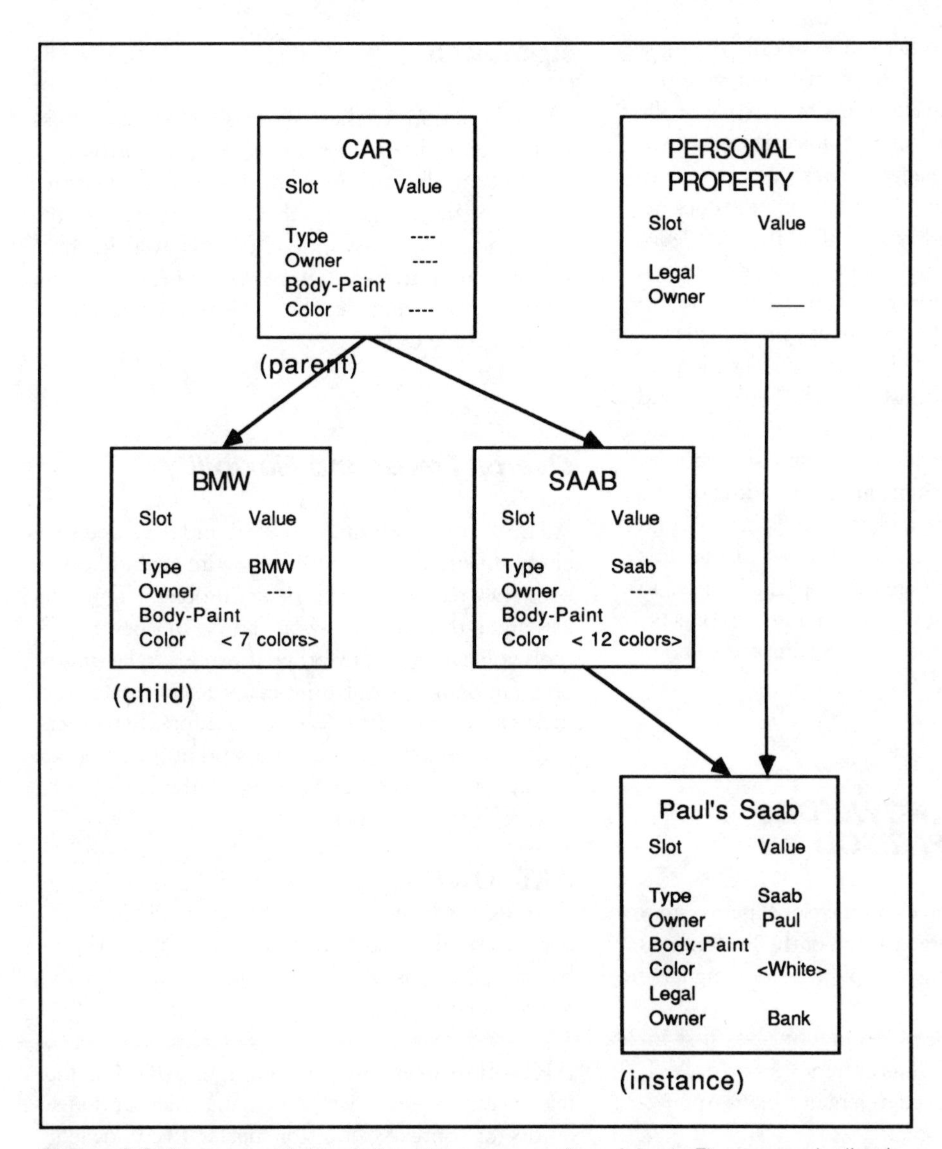

Figure 9.2 *Some possible relationships among five objects. The arrows indicate that lower objects inherit information (categories, default values) from parent objects.*

new and had two lights). Also assume the system could then create different "pictures" at a subsequent point in time (when Paul's Saab no longer had both lights).

A system like this maintains one set of objects that describe each different point in time that it can "picture." If the knowledge system has a method to note that Paul's Saab had been in an accident, thus changing its inheritance pattern in subsequent "pictures" (to reflect the fact that Paul's Saab no longer inherited "two" from Saab as the correct value of "taillights"), then you would say the system is capable of dynamic inheritance.

Some hybrid tools enforce a set of inheritance conventions with few, if any, exceptions. The less flexible tools limit the types of inheritances to only the most conventional types like IS A or set-subset patterns. Some tools even let a developer easily turn off specific relationships (known as defaults) for certain slots or objects or to create knowledge systems where their consultations might result in inheritance relationships being changed. And still other tools allow the knowledge engineer complete freedom to define what relationships exist. This lets the developer concentrate on developing without having to worry about any undesirable implications. Giving knowledge engineers freedom of choices in defining relationships is the kernel behind hybrid tool theory.

Large hybrid tools provide a wide variety of choices. Some do better than others, and, depending on the nature of your particular problem or subject, you'll find hybrid tools are more or less helpful to create generic objects and then instantiate more specific objects to describe a domain. Now, with programming concepts of hybrids described, it is time to compare some of these unique tools.

ART, KEE, AND KNOWLEDGE CRAFT: A COMPARISON

In the last two years, three commercial expert system building tools have emerged as top-of-the-line options for R&D groups wanting to explore developing large expert systems.

ART, sold by Inference Corporation, was first introduced in March 1985. The current version of ART, Version 2.0, was introduced in January 1986. Approximately 350 have been sold.

KEE, introduced in August 1983, is sold by IntelliCorp. The current version of KEE is Version 3.0, introduced in August 1985. Approximately 600 copies of KEE have been sold.

Knowledge Craft, a product of the Carnegie Group, was first introduced in April 1985. The current version is 3.0. (A new version, 3.1, combines Knowledge Craft and a natural language package, Language Craft.) Approximately 130 copies of Knowledge Craft have now been installed.

Approach

The descriptions of these systems are based on talks with vendors, literature reviews, and demonstrations. In addition, the authors studied reviews of the three tools done by corporations that sought to evaluate the tools and interviewed individuals involved in those studies. The authors also talked with researchers from a number of companies that have purchased one or more of these tools.

Overall Power and Flexibility

All three tools are written in LISP, and developers are always free to drop into LISP to write any additional code they require for a particular problem. Thus you can argue that anything you can do in one of these tools you can do in any other, if you just take time to program some special utilities. True, but each tool makes it much harder to do certain things than others. This text discusses only features and utilities that are documented and are compatible with the overall architecture of the particular tool.

ART—Overview. In essence, ART is a forward chaining rule-based system derived from OPS5. A great deal has been added to this essential framework, but basically, if you use ART, you approach problems from a rule-based perspective.

ART—Representing knowledge. ART has four major components: facts, schemata, rules, and viewpoints (or contexts). You store declarative knowledge as facts, schemata, or contexts; you encode procedural knowledge in rules.

The primary way to conceptualize knowledge in ART is to think in terms of facts and rules. Schemata, in ART, serve primarily as "macro" forms in which to express facts. That is, you can use schemata to create object-relationship semantic nets conceptually, but procedurally, ART compiles it all into facts and rules. One effective feature of ART's schemata system is that it allows you to define relations between schemata, which allows you to transverse a path through the data base in any direction.

ART supports two types of rules: state-based rules that are, in effect, if–then rules, and logical rules that take the form: while–then, and thus establish facts as long as other conditions are true. All rules can be assigned salience to prioritize their firing. ART's rules permit LISP calls from either an if clause or a then clause.

Since knowledge is kept primarily in rules, as the size of the knowledge base increases, maintenance becomes more difficult than it would be in a frame-based system.

ART—Inheritance. To implement hierarchies of relationships, you must create a substantial rule set. The inheritance relationships you can use are predetermined in ART. This is necessary to allow ART to precompile the knowledge base into working memory before inferencing can begin, which, in turn, allows ART to obtain its impressive runtime performance. Still, the result is that ART does not provide truly dynamic inheritance on slot values in schemata.

ART—Alternative worlds or viewpoints. ART's viewpoints provide an effective form of hypothetical reasoning. Each viewpoint is a separate scenario. In this manner, the system can simultaneously consider several scenarios, dropping them as they become inadequate. ART can reason about a viewpoint in the same way it can reason about facts. ART's viewpoints can be especially useful when reasoning about events in time.

ART—Truth maintenance. ART provides a useful logical dependency facility. If the if clause of a rule is satisfied (and a logical dependency clause has been associated with that clause), the system keeps track of any subsequent inferencing that follows from that clause. If subsequently the clause becomes invalidated, any assumptions made on the basis of that clause are automatically retracted.

ART—Inference and control. ART provides full forward and backward chaining capabilities. The primary control mechanism in ART is a version of the blackboard architecture.

KEE—Overview. In essence, KEE is an object-oriented programming system derived from Units, an expert system building tool originally developed at Stanford University. Though much has been added, when you use KEE, you initially approach a problem by identifying the objects in the problem domain. KEE takes full advantage of its origins in INTERLISP and object-oriented programming to provide elaborate windows, icons, and displays of objects and their relationships.

KEE—Representing knowledge. The primary knowledge representation paradigm in KEE is the unit (or schema or frame). When using KEE, you begin by conceptualizing a problem in terms of objects and the relationships among them. KEE provides a graphic overview of the objects and their relationships as they are developed or modified. You can easily begin to analyze a subject matter domain without having to consider rules or procedures. For problems that involve a large descriptive or structural component, this is an important advance over rule-based approaches.

Rules in KEE are subordinate objects attached to the slots of higher level objects. Demons can also be attached to slots in KEE. They are, in effect, rules that respond whenever the slot value is accessed or changed.

KEE has multiple rule classes that restrict the search space for rule firings. The rule class for execution can be chosen dynamically. Multiple knowledge bases can be accessed in KEE, so knowledge can be passed from one knowledge base to another.

The KEE rule editor is very slow when the rules become more complex; thus, more sophisticated customers tend to rely more on LISP for the control and program actions than on the rule language.

KEE—Inheritance. KEE provides an inheritance system with system-defined relationships like "member" and "subclass." You cannot modify the inheritance system, a significant disadvantage since several types of relationships cannot be successfully conceptualized in terms of member/subclass relations. You can specify restrictions on slot values, but with only a limited number of developer-set flags. You cannot write LISP methods to handle exceptions (e.g., to query the user for specific information). This slot restriction mechanism poses real problems when you are trying to develop systems in which constraint propagation plays a large role (e.g., systems to handle design and configuration problems).

KEE can support only changing facts. It cannot support changing relationships; that is, if a relationship exists in one context, it must exist in all. Thus, in KEE, all dynamic information must be stored as slot values rather than as explicit relationships.

Sustained use of object-oriented programming, including methods and message passing, allows developers to quickly create a highly modularized system.

KEE—Alternative worlds or contexts. KEE can support only a very limited form of data changes in contexts and cannot support changes to system relations in contexts at all.

KEE—Truth maintenance. KEE does not support truth maintenance.

KEE—Inference and control. KEE supports full forward and backward chaining. However, KEE's PROLOG lacks "cut" and "fail" and "cannot prune"; consequently, developers cannot limit search efficiently.

Knowledge Craft—Overview. Knowledge Craft is based on a semantic net approach derived from SRL, a schema or frame-based paradigm originally developed at Carnegie-Mellon University. More important, however, it is a collection of several more or less independent paradigms.

Knowledge Craft—Representing knowledge. Knowledge Craft has three basic language components: OPS5, PROLOG, and CRL. The basic knowledge representation paradigm in Knowledge Craft is the CRL schemata network. Each schema can have any number of associated slots.

Knowledge Craft makes extensive use of the meta-information associated with the slots in a schema to allow the developer to provide default values, demons, cardinality restrictions, and range and domain restrictions. Using the demon facit, for example, the developer can attach demons that frequently initiate the processing of significant events. In Knowledge Craft, the demon facit is, itself, a schema with slots for the types of slot access that will trigger the demon, as well as when and what action the demon will take. Thus, demons become a fundamental part of the representation. In addition to the meta-facits automatically associated with each slot, developers can add additional facits when needed.

Knowledge Craft provides object-oriented programming techniques to permit data abstraction, object specialization, and the passing of information via messages.

Knowledge Craft—Inheritance. In Knowledge Craft, inheritance is specified at the relation level. This means you can specify which slots and values can be included and which can be excluded in any particular relationship at the time the relationship is established. Thus, as you establish a relationship, you can specify hierarchies of relations, the transivity of relations, and the semantics of the relations, including the inclusion and exclusion of slots and values during inheritance (which slots/values can be inherited), the mapping of slots/values during inheritance (slot names or values can change), and the elaboration of slots (one slot can become many when inherited). Thus, while the other tools tend to force you to use hierarchical relationships (e.g., IS A), Knowledge Craft supports relationships like "sometimes-leads-to" and "has-repair." Knowledge Craft also allows you to specify a search path to reduce search.

Knowledge Craft—Alternative worlds or contexts. Knowledge Craft provides a context mechanism that allows for different versions of the knowledge base. This is used to model and test alternative situations. Both facts and relations are represented in schemata. Contexts can be created and schemata placed in them. These schemata can be completely new or modified from older schemata. Thus, Knowledge Craft provides the option to arbitrarily change any part of the knowledge base in any context. In other words, Knowledge Craft allows the creation of alternate worlds by duplicating schema with hypothetical information while retaining the original copy.

Knowledge Craft—Truth maintenance. Knowledge Craft lacks truth maintenance.

Knowledge Craft—Inference and control. Knowledge Craft provides forward chaining primarily through OPS5 and backward chaining via PROLOG. An agenda-control mechanism allows you to control multiple knowledge sources.

The Knowledge Engineering Interface

All three tools provide some utilities for developing menus and windows, creating graphics, and controlling how end users will interact with the system.

To use ART, the knowledge engineer must typically use either the ZMACS editor or the ART Studio, which provides utilities that can be used to browse the knowledge base, examine facts and rules, and so on. In addition, an ART Imagery Synthesis Tool lets the developer create windows, menus, icons, and the like.

KEE clearly offers the best knowledge engineering interface. The developer can easily browse through the objects and their relationships and develop graphic icons from a large collection. It is easy to use KEE's "active images" utility to associate icons with demons associated with slot values and, hence, assure that the image on the screen echoes a change in the slot value. Using KEE, it is easy to rapidly prototype a system and maintain it.

Using KEE, the developer can break forward or backward chaining to assert or retract facts during a run. KEE also provides many ways to call LISP functions. Unfortunately, many calls are undocumented with no advanced manuals to provide help. Also a number of "switches" change the way the rules execute, but these are hard to discover.

The KEE rule display editor is very slow when the rules become complex. Many knowledge engineers use the ZMACS editor once they are familiar with KEE.

To develop a system in Knowledge Craft, the knowledge engineer can use either the Knowledge Craft workbench or the ZMACS editor. The components of the tool are not well integrated, so the developer has difficulty getting started and must program some routine connections to develop a prototype. In addition, Knowledge Craft uses some reasonably old technology, like its PALM network editor and its schema editor that is not as easy to use as those provided in ART and KEE. In effect, Knowledge Craft requires more thought before you can get started, though its powerful environment may provide an adequate payback for more sophisticated developers once they have made this initial investment and wish to extend or deepen their system.

Carnegie Group claims that Version 3.1 substantially improves both the integration of their tool and the knowledge engineering interface.

The knowledge engineering interface for the three tools is summarized in Figures 9.3, 9.4, and 9.5.

The User (or Runtime) Interface

All three systems allow you to tailor the user interface in any way. None of the systems provides a preformatted interface that can be used by default, like the simpler systems, but most users of these tools will probably prefer to develop their own interface. Of the three, KEE makes it easy to develop a user interface, ART is helpful, and Knowledge Craft provides only limited help.

KEE makes it very easy to use graphics and images associated with active values. All the vendors apparently assume developers either will want to allow the user to access the underlying knowledge base or will be willing to program to create a runtime version of the system.

Rules in both ART and KEE are written in a natural language format that facilitates developing an English-language explanation facility. Carnegie Group sells a special tool, Language Craft, to develop a more sophisticated natural language interface.

Systems Interface

ART was written in ZetaLISP and is currently Common LISP compatible. ART is available on Symbolics,

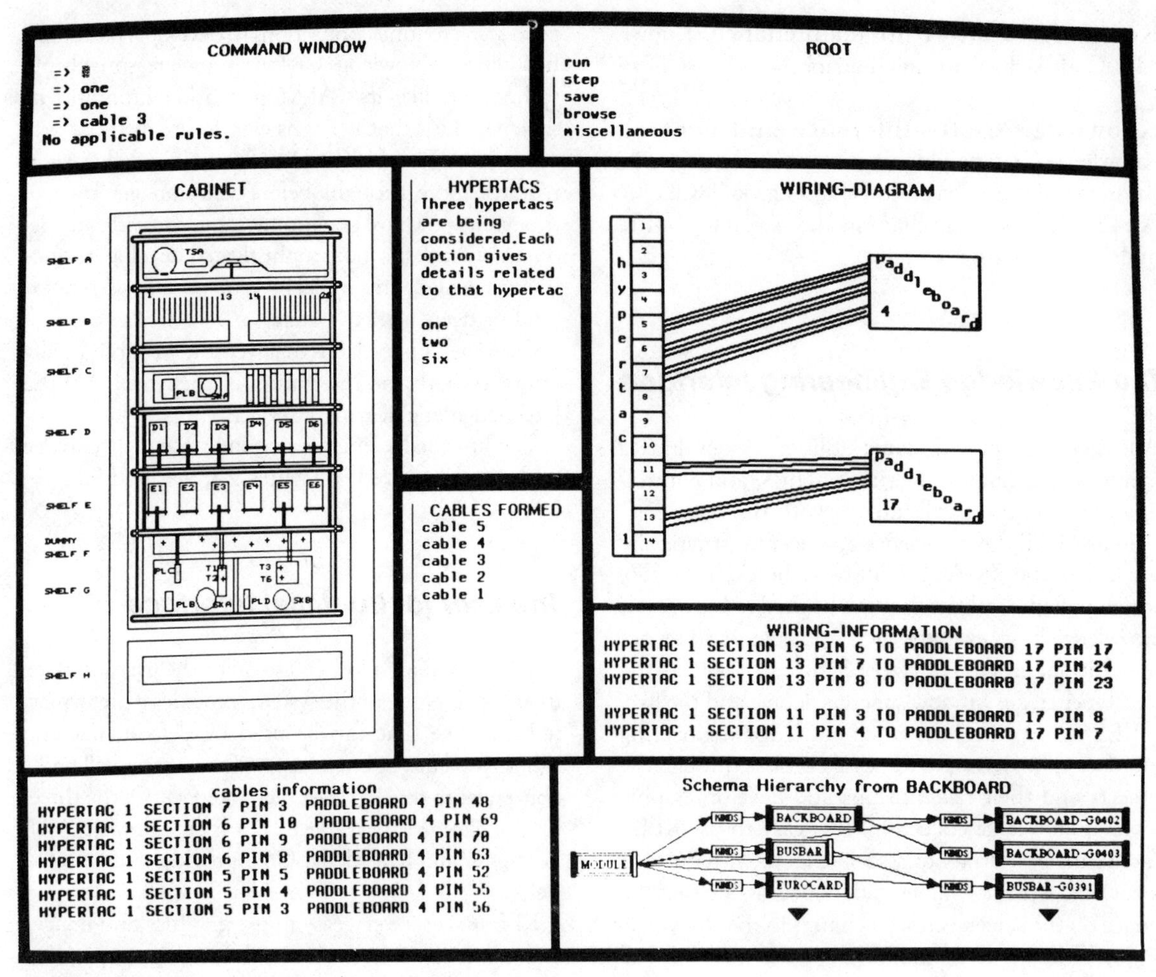

Figure 9.3 *Screen showing an ART application.*

LMI, TI's Explorer, DEC VAX, and DEC MicroVAX. ART is also available on the IBM PC-RT and a C version is available on a Sun.

KEE was written in INTERLISP-D and is currently Common LISP compatible. KEE is available on Symbolics, LMI, Xerox 1100, TI's Explorer, Apollo, Sun, DEC VAX, and DEC MicroVAX. KEE is also available on the IBM PC-RT.

KEE provides customers with the option of using either PC or Macintosh terminals connected to a larger system as delivery terminals.

Knowledge Craft is written in Common LISP. It is available on Symbolics, TI's Explorer, DEC VAX, and DEC MicroVAX. The interface between the tool and the hardware, despite considerable effort, is still rather awkward. Knowledge Craft is also available on the HP AI workstation and on the IBM PC-RT.

ART and Knowledge Craft allow developers to access other languages like C and PASCAL that are supported on the hardware they are operating on.

Runtime Speed

Of the three tools, ART typically runs faster, though not as fast as an application written in a conventional language. ART achieves this speed by reducing its knowledge base to a sequence of facts and then compiling them, using the Rete algorithm developed at Carnegie-Mellon.

Both KEE and Knowledge Craft can take quite a bit of time to run, especially if they need to process a large number of rules.

Training and Support

All three vendors offer training courses and consulting support to help customers with specific applications.

Of the three, Inference Corporation offers the best documentation. It's not that it is just comprehensive; it is skillfully written, flows smoothly, and uses excellent examples. IntelliCorp and Carnegie Group each offer adequate, but less comprehensive, documentation written with less style.

Each vendor will work with a company to determine if their tool is appropriate for a particular problem. In some cases they will provide a tool for a test period.

Choosing Among the Three Tools

To choose among the three tools, you should consider three things: (1) the nature of the problem, (2) the features offered by the tool, and (3) the skill and experience of your knowledge engineers. More than any

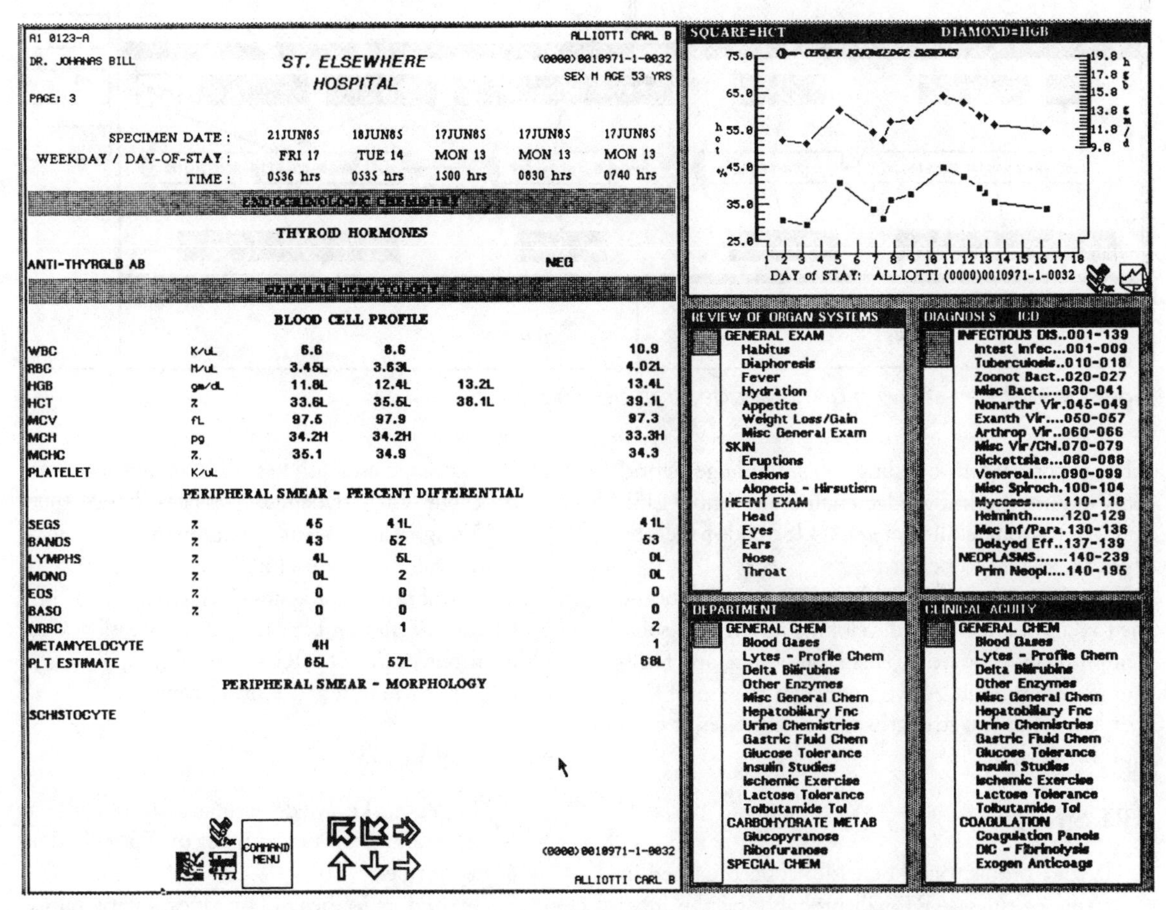

Figure 9.4 *Screen showing a KEE-based application developed by Cerner Corporation.*

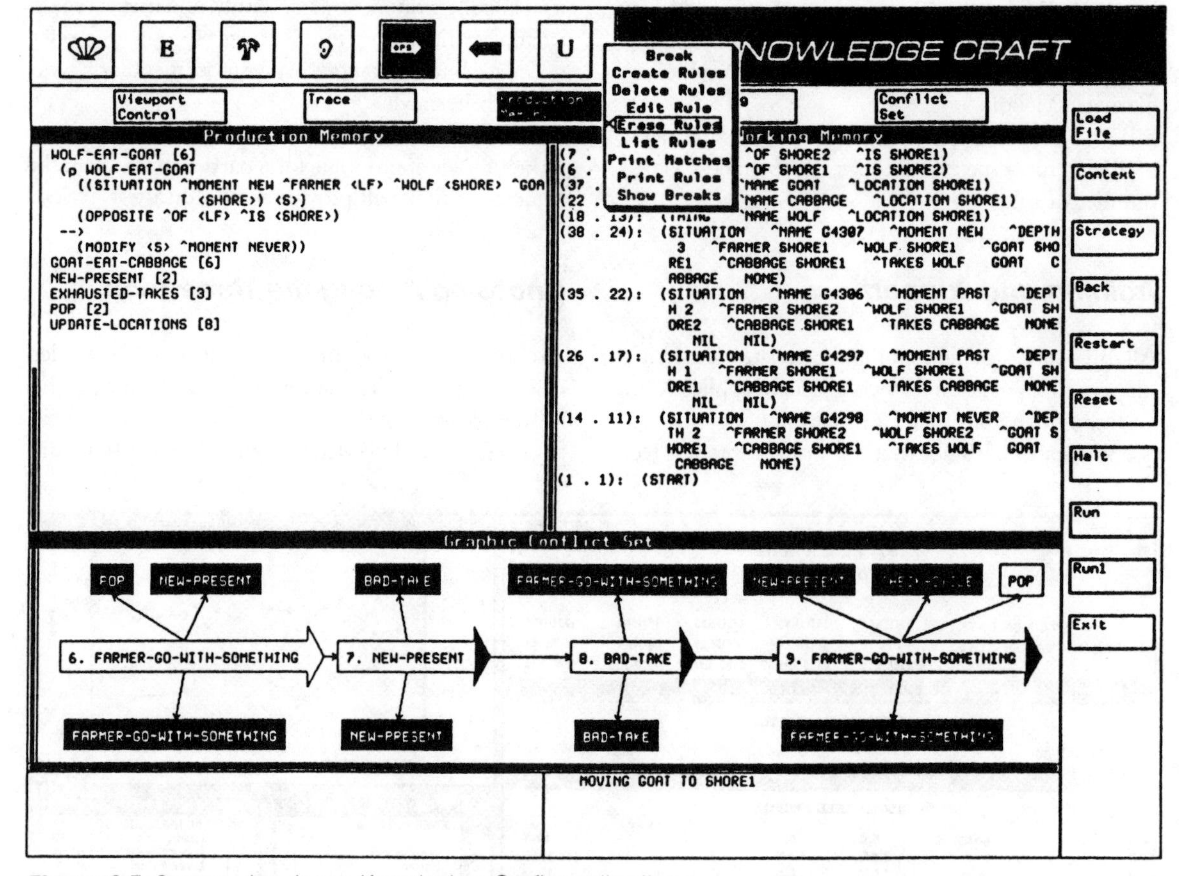

Figure 9.5 Screen showing a Knowledge Craft application.

other expert system building tools, the large hybrid tools require the knowledge engineer to know LISP and to have some skill in creating LISP code to get the resulting system to perform.

If you have a specific problem, you want to choose the tool to best facilitate developing a system to solve that problem, allow you to field the system, and facilitate maintaining it. As you consider your problem, keep the following strengths and weaknesses of each tool in mind.

ART Strengths:

- If your problem can be easily conceptualized in terms of rules, ART will probably be the most natural tool to use.
- If you need to establish logical dependencies to update your system dynamically as facts change, then ART's approach to truth maintenance and viewpoints will be very useful.
- If you will need to program special LISP functions, it's convenient that LISP functions are easily called from both sides of ART's rules.
- ART has the fastest execution time.

ART Weaknesses:

- ART keeps its knowledge primarily in rules. This is convenient if the task can be conceptualized in terms of rules.
- Since ART relies heavily on rules, maintenance can become a significant problem as the number

of rules increase, especially since all the hierarchical structure in ART is also stored as rules. Significant maintenance problems begin when systems have over 2,000 rules.

- ART does not provide the best knowledge engineering interface and lacks good graphic editing facilities.

KEE Strengths:

- KEE has the best knowledge engineering environment with superior graphic editing facilities, a large collection of icons, and good menus.
- Active values, including demons, methods, and active images, support data-directed reasoning and allow the system to recognize and monitor changing conditions.
- Object-oriented programming, including methods and message passing, allows convenient modularization of the expert system. In addition, KEE's multiple rule bases make it easy for the developer to partition the rule base efficiently.
- The availability of KEE connection and Intelli-Scope provide KEE with the best access to mainframe data bases.

KEE Weaknesses:

- KEE lacks a context mechanism and hence cannot easily represent multiple hypothetical situations.
- KEE has system-defined inheritance and will not allow you to tailor inheritance for special situations.
- The backward chaining approach used in KEE is incomplete. It lacks "cut" and "fail," which makes it difficult to perform complicated reasoning using the rule interpreter.
- KEE limits the developer's access to a limited subset of LISP.
- KEE lacks an agenda mechanism; thus, the developer cannot assert efficient control over the system's operation.

Knowledge Craft Strengths:

- Knowledge Craft's schema representation language is probably the most powerful of the three tools. It offers such features as dynamic inheritance, meta-information, demon facilities, developer-defined relations, user-defined dependency relationships, and user-defined inheritance search patterns.
- The context mechanism lets you create systems that entertain multiple hypotheses.
- The agenda mechanism lets you tailor how the system processes a knowledge base.
- Object-oriented programming permits the conceptualization of problems in terms of objects, relationships, and messages.
- The implementation of PROLOG has full resolution and includes "cut" and "fail."
- The senior staff at Carnegie Group has considerable experience in researching the design of large systems for factory scheduling and planning problems.

Knowledge Craft Weaknesses:

- The integration of the various components is poor.
- The knowledge engineering interface is poor.
- The interface between the tool and hardware is poor.

If your AI group is new and you want to purchase one large hybrid tool to develop several initial prototype systems, you face a difficult choice. Each tool has significant strengths and weaknesses, and each is clearly superior for some uses and not others. The overall capabilities of each tool are in Table 9.1.

KEE has a noteworthy developer interface and allows you to develop prototypes more rapidly than the other two tools, but will frustrate you when you try more complex tasks, especially if those tasks have significant procedural elements or you are concerned with runtime speed. KEE is clearly the best selling hybrid tool, and IntelliCorp seems destined to dominate the high end of the hybrid tool market in the next few years.

Knowledge Craft is probably the most powerful and flexible of the three tools, but it has a poor integration and a poor developer interface which make it hard to learn to use.

ART struck a nice balance between power and flex-

Table 9.1 *A subjective rating of commercially available large hybrid expert system building tools (circa Spring 1987).*

1 = Poor
3 = Acceptable
5 = Excellent

	ART	KEE	Know. Craft
Power & Flexibility	4	4.5	5
Developer Interface	4	5	3
User Interface	5	5	4
Systems Interface	4	5	3
Training/Support	5	4.5	4.5

ibility, the various interfaces, and runtime speed. ART's current popularity, however, may suggest that many developers are tackling projects that are more procedural than declarative and that ART's rule-based approach seems more natural.

All three vendors are working on new versions to incorporate new features. Several new versions of each tool will undoubtedly be released during the life of this book.

SMALLER HYBRID TOOLS

Recently, two additional hybrid tools, GOLDWORKS and Nexpert Object, have been introduced. These newer, smaller tools run on PC-ATs or larger machines.

The recent introduction of these two tools promises to redefine the market for hybrid tools by making most techniques currently available on only the larger hybrid tools accessible to PC-AT and 386 users at a fraction of the cost of the current large hybrid tools.

GOLDWORKS

Gold Hill Computer's new tool, GOLDWORKS, is a hybrid tool offering most features found in ART, KEE, or Knowledge Craft, including rules, frames, contexts. and the various sophisticated LISP-based editing features that serious knowledge engineers expect. Unlike its competitors that cost over $50,000 and run only on machines that cost about the same, GOLDWORKS runs on an IBM PC-AT and is priced at about one-seventh that price.

GOLDWORKS is designed for use at three different levels. At the highest level, "the developer interface," the knowledge engineer interacts with menu-driven interfaces to develop end-user systems. At the intermediate level, the knowledge engineer can develop a knowledge base without using the menus, while at the lower level, the knowledge engineer has access to the GCLISP 286/386 DEVELOPER package that the higher-level package is written in and thus can modify the system in any way desired.

GOLDWORKS provides a framelike knowledge representation network, integrated forward and backward chaining, and certainty factors. It supports object-oriented rule-based, action-oriented programming. GOLDWORKS also provides a graphics module, interface building facilities, power screen generation, and various browsers as well as explanation facilities, hooks to standard PC packages, and mouse support.

In addition, GOLDWORKS includes an on-line help system that provides sophisticated user assistance by developing a model of the user and tailoring help messages. For example, GOLDWORKS maintains a history of the user's help queries which provides easy reference to information previously examined. The tool is also context sensitive, providing meaningful messages about the current data and situation. These facilities, combined with an on-line tutorial, should provide new knowledge engineers with one of the easiest ways to learn and systematically upgrade their ability to handle the most complex problems.

Gold Hill used its knowledge of the Intel chip to provide considerable programming power at a very respectable speed. For example, GOLDWORKS addresses up to 15 megabytes of memory, compared to other MS-DOS tools which are limited to 640K.

GOLDWORKS' open architecture provides a flexible framework for tackling a wide variety of problems. Corporate users can integrate C functions into GOLDWORKS systems. In addition, GOLDWORKS provides access to data stored in dBASE II and III and Lotus 1-2-3.

Gold Hill Computers established its reputation by offering the best version of Common LISP available on the PC. It guaranteed its success by packaging that product with a superior on-line tutorial that has made it a favorite with schools and individuals trying to learn LISP quickly and efficiently. Gold Hill's strength is getting LISP to work on Intel chips. GOLDWORKS represents a very logical step for Gold Hill. They have developed a large hybrid tool and used their knowledge of the Intel architecture to get that system to run on an AT. They have also developed a tutorial to teach developers to use that tool to develop large applications, hoping to capture the high end of the emerging MIS market for mid- to large-size expert systems development in the same way they captured the PC LISP market a few years ago. They just may be able to do it.

Table 9.2 *Mid-size and large hybrid tools.*

	TOOL (Vendor)	Price of Tool	Hardware			
			Mini/ Mainframe	Workstation (UNIX, RISC, VMS, etc.)	LISP Machine Workstation	PC
LARGE HYBRID TOOLS	ART (Inference Corp)	$29-80K		Sun, Apollo LISP, C	• LISP	
	KEE (IntelliCorp)	$55K	VAX LISP	Sun, Apollo LISP	• LISP	
	Knowledge Craft (Carnegie Group)	$35-50K		Sun, Apollo MicroVAX LISP	• LISP	
	LOOPS (Xerox)	$300			Xerox 1100 Machines LISP	
MID-SIZE HYBRID TOOLS	Goldworks (Gold Hill Computer)	$7.5K				IBM-AT LISP
	Personal Consultant Plus (Texas Instruments)	$2,950	VAX C	MicroVAX C	Explorer LISP	TI, IBM Scheme
	Nexpert Object (Neuron Data)	$5-8K	VAX C			IBM-AT C
	Intelligence/Compiler (Intelligencware)	$990				IBM PASCAL

SUMMARY

When you decide to invest in the powerful capabilities of a large hybrid tool, remember three things:

1. The nature of the problem.
2. The features offered by the tool.
3. The skill and expertise of your knowledge engineer(s).

More than any other expert system building tools, these large hybrid tools require a knowledge engineer/developer to possess a thorough understanding of LISP and to have some skill in creating LISP code. This will enable you to make and configure the system best suited for your needs. See Table 9.2 for a summary of the mid-size and large hybrid tools.

Obviously, if you have a specific problem that does not require the variety of knowledge engineering paradigms provided by hybrids, you should probably consider investing in a large rule-based tool or a mid-size tool. These tools cost considerably less and are generally easier to learn to use. Conversely, if you have a problem that is very complex, hybrids may be the only tool capable of handling the task. Organizations that have developed large systems involving real-time process control or reasoning about time have consistently reported that they have found they soon advance beyond the capabilities of mid- to large-size tools.

Today, however, if you already have a specific problem in mind, one that is complex, then you will want to invest in a hybrid that will best develop a system to solve the problem and one that can grow as your needs (and problems) change. If you decide to get a hybrid tool right away, and many companies already have, be sure the vendor can and will provide high-quality training, documentation, and consulting support. The learning curve for these tools is very steep; you will not want to try to negotiate the climb without help.

Even though some difficulties are associated with using hybrids tools, their inherent power and flexibility provide tremendous problem-solving capabilities not found in any rule-based system building tools. Hybrids are usually selected by researchers to build very large expert systems, and, if you have an appropriate problem and a knowledgable staff, they can allow your company to quickly construct knowledge systems that can help solve some of your most complex, difficult problems.

SECTION THREE

DEVELOPING EXPERT SYSTEMS

By this point you should have a clear idea of what types of expert systems are in use commercially and the advantages and disadvantages of each. This section will help you join the ranks of those using expert systems to increase productivity. You'll be given an overview of expert systems development, including what a knowledge engineer does and the seven phases in expert systems development (Chapter 10). You'll then be taken through each of the seven steps in a more detailed presentation. Phase 1, frontend analysis, and Phase 2, task analysis, are presented first (Chapter 11). This is followed by the next three phases, prototype development, developing a complete expert system, and field testing (Chapter 12). The section ends with the final two phases, implementation and maintenance of the system (Chapter 13).

10

An Overview of Expert Systems Development

INTRODUCTION

This chapter discusses the overall process of developing an expert system. It begins by briefly reviewing the general types of expert systems currently being developed. Next it considers human skills necessary to develop various types of expert systems, and finally it describes the general approach to expert systems development that will be expanded in the subsequent three chapters.

The commercial demand for detailed information on developing expert systems is great. Unfortunately, it is difficult to provide such information. As new companies undertake expert systems efforts, they try new approaches. Many are successful and open new options for expert systems development. Because of the exploding interest in expert systems and the lack of previous commercial experience with such systems, it is too early to say what will and will not work.

Most expert systems books provide suggestions derived from the experiences of those who developed the first large expert systems in university laboratories. Those experiences are becoming increasingly irrelevant to commercial practice as companies attempt to develop new types of expert systems using new tools. Moreover, most current development efforts are focused on smaller problems than the original efforts. They intend to use existing data from data bases in new ways and assume the resulting systems will be fielded on conventional hardware.

No well-defined procedure for developing an expert system exists. Realistically, at this point, all that can be offered are some do's, don'ts, and heuristics.

At least three general types of expert systems are being developed, as illustrated in Figure 10.1.

Small procedural systems. The simplest systems are procedural, that is, knowledge about how to accomplish some process or make some decision is encoded as either examples or rules and entered into a small to mid-size expert system building tool. Any programmer who examined such a system would quickly say the program could have been easily accomplished with any conventional programming language. The driving force behind developing these small knowledge systems is the ease with which they can be developed. Most small procedural systems have been developed by a nonprogrammer who was both the expert and the developer.

For example, during a course on expert systems, in the space of two afternoon labs, one participant realized he could quickly solve a recurring problem by using an expert system. This individual worked in a dental lab and was constantly called on to tell customers when their dental work could be picked up. He had no difficulty doing this, but his two assistants always seemed at a loss to do so without checking with him. No heuristics were involved in the analysis; it involved simply determining what day the work was put in and its exact nature. With these two pieces of information, he could provide a pickup date. Since he was going to be developing a small expert system

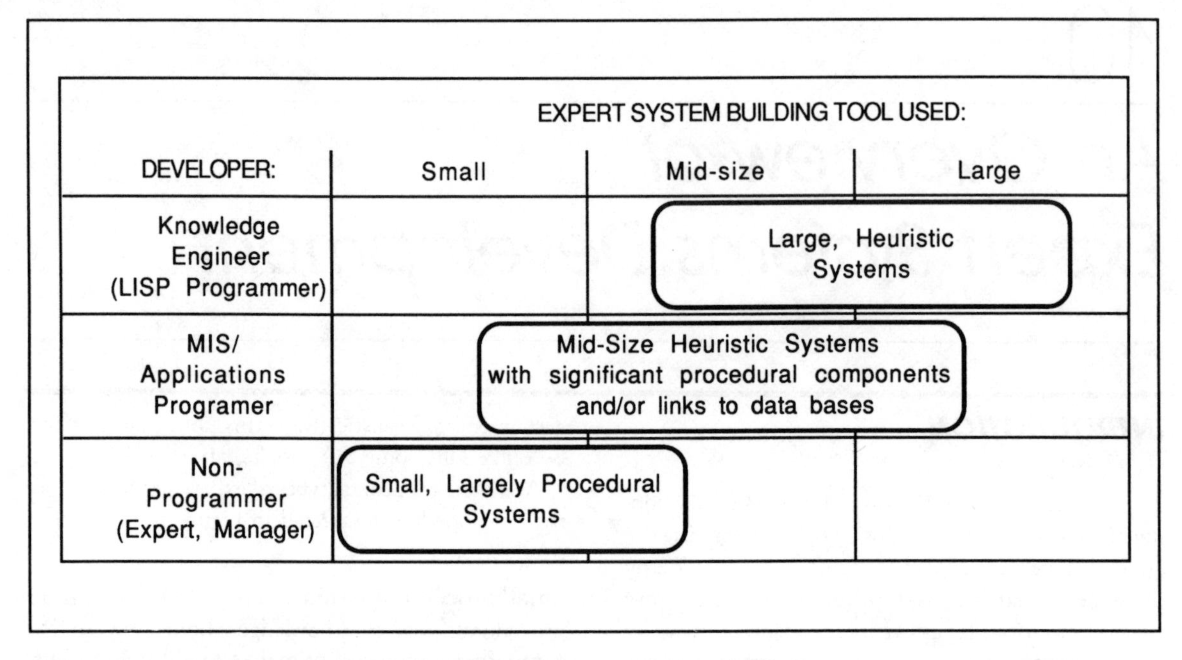

Figure 10.1 *Three different types of expert systems development efforts.*

anyway, this individual put all the relevant information into his system and was confident by the end of the lab that he had a system he could run on his dental lab computer that would allow the other technicians to determine pickup dates for customers. Use of a small expert system building tool offered the dental technician two advantages. First, no programming was required. He only had to enter the specific rules about the dental situation he already understood and he had his application. Second, whenever he wanted to change the knowledge in the system, he could quickly edit his rules and have a modified system ready to give advice within a few hours.

Many small systems like the one just described are currently used in business. In some cases the systems have many hundreds of rules. Some have thousands of rules. Since they are typically built on small tools that do not allow the developers to create variable rules or data base rules, the developer creates many rules. A different tool would let the developer create one rule to use a lookup table. Hence, the number of rules in a system must not be used to judge the power or sophistication of a system. The point is that such systems can be developed by nonprogrammers after only a little instruction in using a tool.

Most of the heuristics provided in subsequent chapters to help you select problems, establish development plans, and create knowledge bases are largely irrelevant for such simple tasks. This is not to suggest that such tasks are less valuable than developing larger systems, but simply to suggest that the range of projects that fall under the term expert systems development is wide and varied and that the suggestions will be most useful to those who are concerned with mid-size projects rather than those attempting very large or very small projects.

Mid-size, mostly procedural systems. Most expert systems currently fielded and most under development fall into the mid-size system category. Most have been developed by people familiar with conventional programming who have just learned about developing expert systems. Since most of the people who have bought expert system building tools are conventional computer programmers who became interested in expert systems to see if they could improve their current applications, it makes sense that most mid-size systems combine expert systems techniques with large amounts of conventional code. Indeed, most mid-size systems combine a little heuristic knowledge with a lot of procedural knowledge. Many are frontends for existing data bases or are embedded within existing application programs.

Most companies already have application programs that accomplish valuable tasks but remain underused because the people for whom the program was created are unable to define a particular situation for the program. By attaching an expert system to the program, an applications programmer can create a frontend that asks the user appropriate questions and then directs the underlying application program to solve the problem. Hence, a small expert systems development effort can provide a large payoff by rendering an important existing program more useful. By the same token, an expert system can serve as the frontend for a data base. Users answer questions that describe the situation they are dealing with, and the system determines the data the users need and creates the data base query commands to get that data for the users.

To date, most mid-size systems have been developed on PCs, workstations, or VAX hardware, but with the availability of structured rule tools on IBM mainframes, a rapidly increasing number of mid-size systems are being developed to enhance existing mainframe applications or to facilitate the maintenance of mainframe applications.

Mid-size to large systems with significant amounts of heuristic knowledge. The original expert systems developed in universities generally define this type of system. In this case, you want to develop a system to perform a job or part of it that an existing human expert performs. A conversation with the expert convinces you it would not be easy to develop a procedural description of the expert's job. The expert isn't very clear about what he or she knows; so much of the expert's knowledge comes down to two sets of very specific heuristics (e.g., If this. . . , and that . . ., and it's not . . ., and it's after . . ., then . . .). To develop an expert system in such circumstances, the developer must work with the expert to identify the facts, rules, and heuristics used.

It can't all be done at once, or even very logically. The developer (i.e., the knowledge engineer) must ask questions, work through cases with the expert, and develop some initial rules. These rules are placed in a knowledge base, and the resulting system is tried on some cases. The expert works with the developer to see where the system fails and determine what additional rules should be added to improve the system.

Developing an expert system that captures a large amount of heuristic knowledge is a time-consuming process in which the developer actually helps the expert verbalize what he or she knows. Since the knowledge may be inconsistent, at different levels of abstraction, and fuzzy, developing such a system is very different from the task faced by the nonprogrammer who simply wants to enter a set of procedural rules to accomplish some well-understood task.

When you are engaged in developing a large system to include a large number of heuristic rules, you are engaged in a discovery process. You enter a few rules and then check to see what the system does. Depending on how the system handles a specific case, you enter additional rules to improve the system's performance. Thus, a large system is built by successive approximations. It is a learning process that depends on repeated trials and revisions, since neither the expert nor the knowledge engineer knows exactly what knowledge is required when they begin development.

The ensuing discussion here and in subsequent chapters on expert systems development focuses primarily on developing systems that contain heuristic knowledge and on those aspects of development that involve obtaining, refining, and encoding the heuristic knowledge. No discussion is provided on converting well-analyzed information into if–then rules, or on the problems of developing connections between expert systems and conventional programs and data bases. Although these are important subjects, they are well treated in many books on conventional programming and in the manuals and courses offered by the vendors of specific expert system building tools.

KNOWLEDGE ENGINEERING

Any discussion of developing an expert system must include the knowledge engineering process and a description of the skills of the individuals who do knowledge engineering. There are, in fact, many different development processes and many different sorts of people engaged in developing expert systems (see Figure 10.2).

When Dr. Edward Feigenbaum and the researchers at Stanford University were developing the first expert systems, they coined the term *knowledge engineering* to describe the process one goes through to develop a large expert system containing a significant number of heuristics. They also started using the term *knowledge engineer* to describe the person who actually developed such systems.

At the time they coined these terms, of course, they conceptualized an expert system as a large application like MYCIN, a system that contains some 3,500 rules and took about 50 person-years to develop. MYCIN, of course, was developed from scratch, in LISP, since the first tools were yet to be developed. Moreover, they assumed that expert systems would be developed in situations where the only way to obtain information from an expert was by means of interviews, and many successive approximations of the system, each with additional rules, and numerous trials with cases to determine the effect of each additional set of rules. In other words, they intended knowledge engineering to refer to a complex, sophisticated process that could be done only by LISP programmers thoroughly grounded in knowledge representation and search strategies developed as a result of their recent research in artificial intelligence. They did not intend to suggest that a knowledge engineer knew much about conventional programming or had any special skills in packaging a program to facilitate its use in a business environment. They were not against including such things, but they were simply irrelevant in their research environment.

Since 1983 however, the number of people developing expert systems (or knowledge systems) has greatly expanded. By using expert system building tools and limiting the size of the system, nonprogrammers can develop small systems. Moreover, conventional programmers have developed most of the currently fielded expert systems.

Most fielded mid-size systems include hooks between the rules in the expert system and data stored in a data base or spreadsheet program. The programming

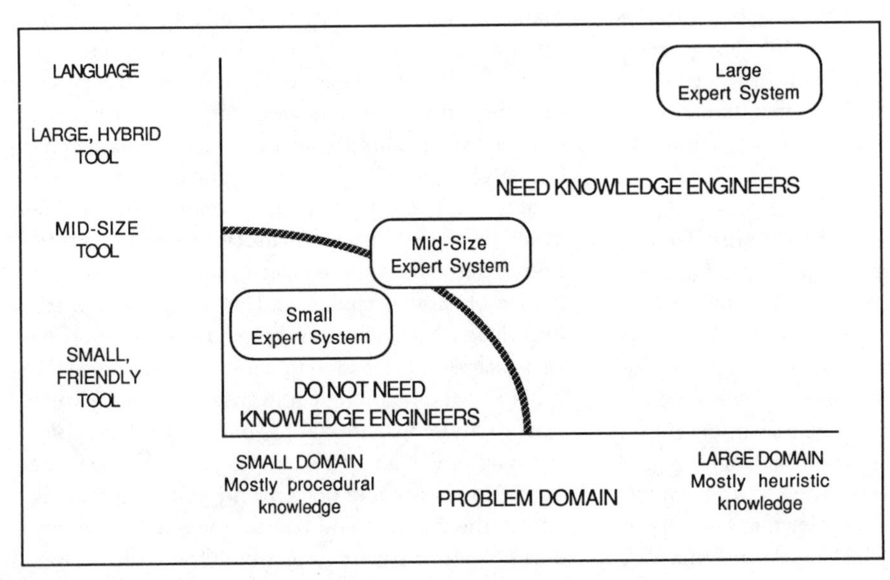

Figure 10.2 *The need for knowledge engineers.*

necessary to make these systems useful may not have been considered part of knowledge engineering a few years ago, but it is a necessary part of most successful commercial expert systems projects.

As tool vendors like Teknowledge and Software A&E have recoded their tools into conventional languages, like C, they have created a situation in which many knowledge engineers must also be C programmers if they are to develop effective systems. Moreover, the development of expert systems tools and applications that run on mainframe computers has led to the creation of mixed teams of knowledge engineers and conventional MIS/application programmers who can develop and field systems fully integrated into a large mainframe computing environment.

The current use of the term *knowledge engineer* usually suggests that knowledge engineers are like conventional programmers except that they program expert systems. This is only partially true. Many knowledge engineering activities are identical to conventional programming tasks, but others are radically different. Before looking into specific activities, consider a very broad description of the task of the knowledge engineer in commercial environments: *A knowledge engineer works with a human expert to identify and refine the knowledge needed to solve a particular type of problem. The ability to obtain the knowledge from a human expert during repeated interviews and then work with the human expert to study jointly how the system handles cases and determine how to improve the system is the essence of the knowledge engineer's job.*

The knowledge engineer is part student, part teacher, part consultant, part model builder, and part programmer. If knowledge engineers do their jobs right, human experts are led through what could be a painful, confusing process in a reasonably efficient, pleasant manner. Along the way, the human experts learn about how an expert system works and what is required to maintain the knowledge base they are creating after the system is fielded. Most routine tasks involving entering rules, developing hooks to data bases, and even running cases can be delegated to others, but the unique and central part of any large expert systems building project is the interaction between the knowledge engineer and the human expert.

Since most expert systems are built with tools, knowledge engineers are limited in the ways they can formalize the human experts' knowledge (e.g., knowledge engineers must decide if rules or an object-oriented approach will be a more effective way for experts to express what they know). Hence, knowledge engineers must teach human experts to express their knowledge in a formalism like if–then rules. Equally important, if context trees are to be developed, knowledge engineers must decide what rules belong together, what sets of rules inherit conclusions from other sets of rules, and so on. In other words, knowledge engineers must help experts develop models of their knowledge.

THE TASKS OF A KNOWLEDGE ENGINEER

One popular way to describe the knowledge engineering task is in terms of three subtasks (see Figure 10.3):

- Knowledge acquisition.
- Knowledge modeling.
- Knowledge encoding.

Knowledge acquisition. Knowledge acquisition includes all activities involved in obtaining information from experts. It includes interviewing experts and working with them to formalize terms and eliminate vagueness and inconsistencies. It also includes studying cases with the experts and slowly adding new knowledge to the system. Unlike conventional programming, developers of expert systems do not simply analyze a problem, get the user to sign-off, and then go away. Rather, they work with experts throughout the entire development process, constantly acquiring new knowledge and integrating it into the growing system.

Knowledge modeling. Knowledge modeling is the process by which knowledge engineers organize the information they acquire from the experts. This process is hardly necessary when developing an inductive or a simple rule-based system. It becomes important, however, when knowledge engineers are using a struc-

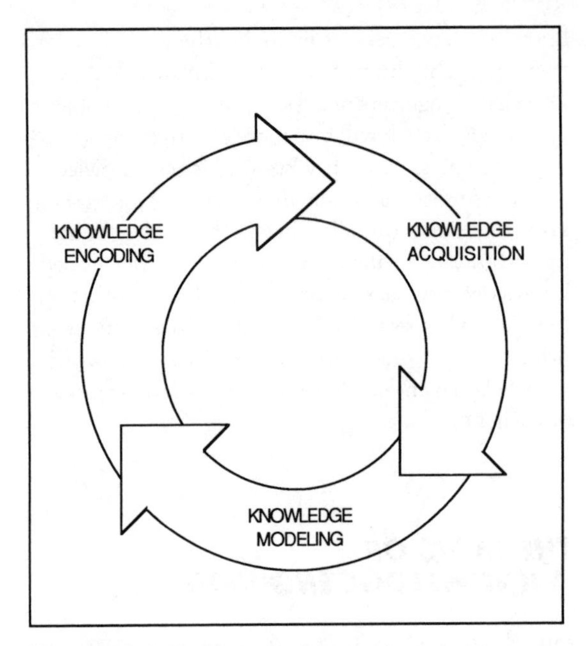

Figure 10.3 *The knowledge engineering process.*

tured rule tool and must develop a context tree. Knowledge modeling becomes the key to system development when working with a large hybrid tool. Experts provide the knowledge engineers with facts, rules, and objects, but the experts do not normally have a system for subdividing their knowledge into efficient subsets. They may have terms for some vague subsets—and it is at this point that inter-expert disagreements can get so confusing. But the experts have probably not developed those vague terms into an internally consistent "domain model." Indeed, experts probably use terms they think are of equal weight or salience that, upon closer examination, lie at very different levels in a conceptual hierarchy. Moreover, experts certainly do not think about inheriting information from one set of rules or objects to another. Knowledge engineers must address all these issues. Developing a concept tree or an object network requires a very thorough understanding of how each term relates to every other term and which terms inherit information from which others. Experts can provide the information necessary for knowledge engineers to begin to understand these issues, but, ultimately, knowledge engineers must develop a domain theory and test that theory by encoding rules, running cases, and seeing what happens.

Knowledge encoding. Knowledge encoding is the process of actually entering facts, rules, objects, and relationship information into an expert system. Developing an expert system *in a language* involves programming in LISP, PROLOG, Smalltalk, or some conventional language. Developing a system *using a tool* involves specifying the knowledge in the syntax of that tool. If you are using a small rule-based tool, this can be an easy task. As you enter more knowledge and then run cases to test the system, this task starts to involve editing facilities. Moreover, if you require hooks to other programs or to data stored in other systems, this task can quickly become a significant programming task.

If you are using a large rule-based tool or a hybrid tool, this task is always complex and tedious and requires considerable programming skill. When teams of knowledge engineers are used, a team leader usually performs most of the knowledge acquisition and knowledge modeling task and delegates the knowledge encoding to a junior knowledge engineer.

In addition to entering knowledge and developing links to other programs and data, someone may need to write a procedural program the expert system can call and execute. Further, most mid- to large-size expert systems require the developer to create a user interface, which can involve considerable work and programming skill. (In several hybrid expert systems, 30 to 40 percent of the code is used to create and control the user interface.) Most specialized tasks can be grouped under knowledge encoding and are also good tasks to delegate if the project is large.

Expert systems development companies differ on how they group and separate these activities. Some knowledge engineers are hired to perform all three tasks; others are hired to perform only one task. In most cases, everyone working on a large project is called a knowledge engineer.

An interesting aspect of this division of activities is the creation of a job slot for noncomputer professionals. The extraction of knowledge from experts need not require any computer skills, as long as the interviewer knows about the formalisms into which the knowledge must ultimately be encoded. Some companies are reputed to steer away from computer professionals when they fill this job slot. Considering that knowledge extraction can require many hours of interaction between experts and knowledge engineers, and considering that experts (by virtue of their role) are allowed considerable idiosyncrasies and eccentricities, many companies are looking for bright, analytic, social science and humanities majors for this job. Most companies, however, insist that this function be combined with programming activities.

It is safe to say that the growth of expert systems technology has spotlighted the task of knowledge extraction. The reason is simple: expert systems provide the opportunity to incorporate hundreds or thousands of times more knowledge than any conventional system could possibly capture. This occurs because knowledge engineers extract and code only the knowledge instructions; the control instructions are preprogrammed in the inference engine. You might assume knowledge engineering has achieved its mystique because of conventional programmers' failure in prolonged interactions with domain experts. Thus, it is this specific activity, the prolonged interaction with human experts, that separates knowledge engineers from the more general class of computer programmer.

Conventional Programming versus Knowledge Engineering

A subtler difference between people who make good conventional programmers but are inappropriate for knowledge engineering focuses attention on the process by which the different types of systems are developed (see Figures 10.4 and 10.5).

Conventional systems are developed sequentially. A programmer meets with an end user (or human expert in many cases) and works with that person to develop

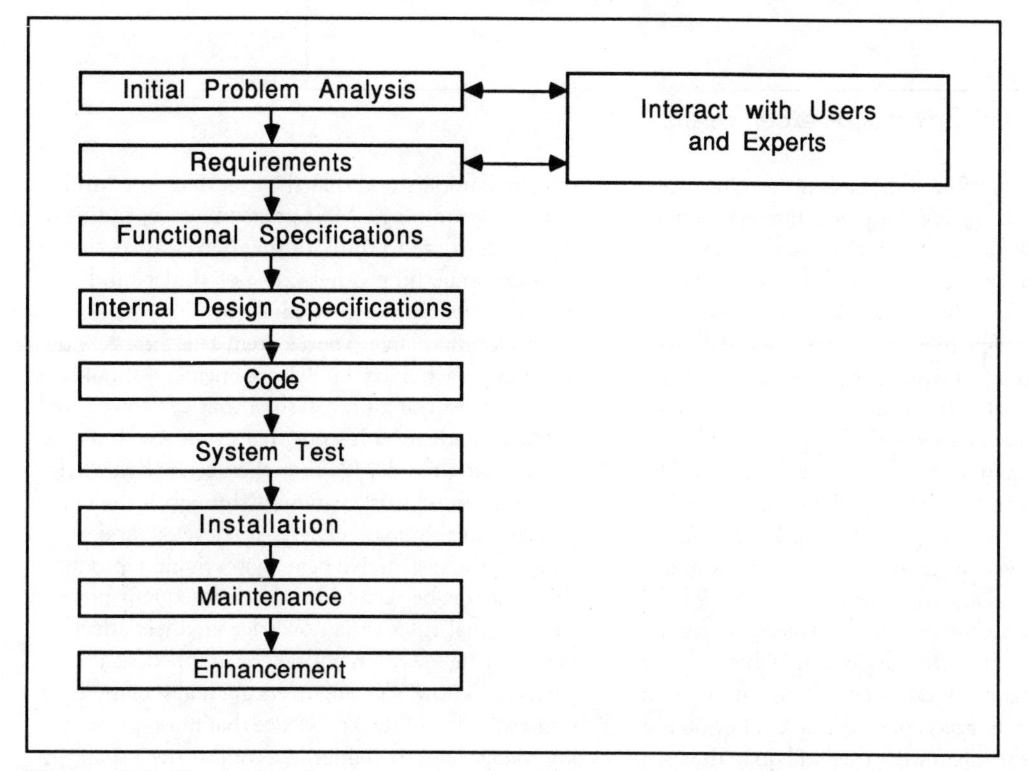

Figure 10.4 *Conventional program development versus knowledge engineering.*

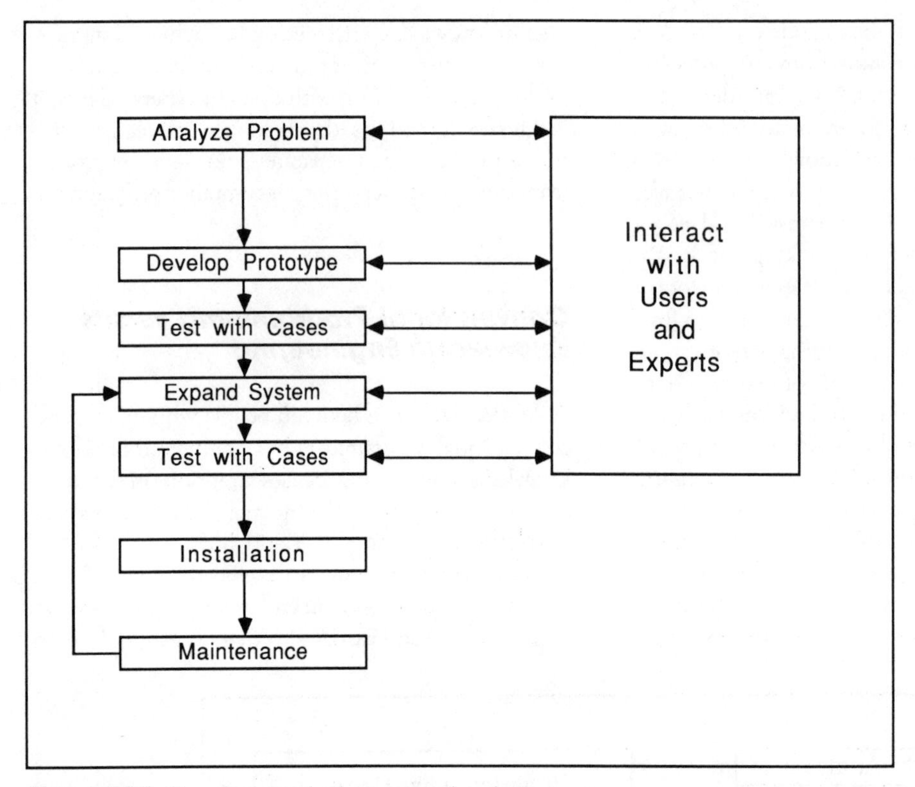

Figure 10.5 *Development of an expert system.*

a functional description of the task the program is to accomplish. At the end of this phase, the programmer assumes he or she understands the task sufficiently so that a system designed to accomplish the functional specifications will satisfy the user. The user is asked not to change anything while the programmer writes the code. In the process of writing the code, the programmer develops an algorithm that combines the knowledge gained from the user with the specific computer instructions required to execute the program. The resulting code is entirely incomprehensible to the user, who must either accept the result or ask for changes.

Programmers who are accustomed to working in this manner tend to assume that a problem can be defined once and for all during the initial analysis. Moreover, they assume that once they understand what the user expects the program to do, they will be left alone to develop the code to accomplish the task. They do not expect to have to explain what they will do to the user, since it is understood that the user does not "understand programming." Most programmers operating in this mode come to think of themselves as specialists who do something others do not understand and should probably not be told about.

Developing a large expert system calls for a very different approach. First, knowledge engineers should expect to be working on a system that cannot be well defined in advance. It's not that experts will not explain what they do, it's that they can't. Knowledge engineers must work patiently through a discovery process with human experts to develop and then enhance the system. No neat phases result in products that will not be reconsidered in subsequent phases. The original rules the knowledge engineers develop may later be rewritten entirely or dropped, as the experts and knowledge engineers gradually refine their understanding of the knowledge that must go into the knowledge base. A change in a context tree usually involves rewriting lots of rules, and context trees keep changing as the engineers gradually understand how the subparts of a problem must actually interact. In other words, knowledge engineers must be much more flexible and tentative in approaching a project, more circular than linear in their approach to problem solving.

Equally important, knowledge engineers must be able to teach human experts about the technology. An effective expert system usually requires a human expert who knows enough about the knowledge in the knowledge base to suggest how the system can be updated and improved. This will happen only if the expert actively participates in the development process. There is no room in knowledge engineering for a programmer who refuses to give the "secrets" of the technology away to the user.

So Who Makes a Good Knowledge Engineer?

As already noted, some consulting companies prefer to hire psychology and sociology majors and train them to be knowledge engineers. They argue that the personal interaction skills involved in obtaining information from experts are the key to the job and that it's easier to teach programming to a bright psychology major than to teach interviewing skills to conventional programmers. Others argue that knowledge engineers need to start with some programming skills and that data base modeling skills and simulation programming skills provide a good background for knowledge modeling. Several companies are dividing the task into parts and creating teams to develop expert systems. One team member focuses on knowledge acquisition; another formalizes the knowledge and develops the domain model; others enter code, run cases, and debug the knowledge base; while still others develop hooks to other programs and data bases or create user interfaces. Most companies developing expert systems for mainframes consider the team approach vital.

If the term *knowledge engineer* refers to someone who combines all the skills and has the ability to develop a large expert system—the meaning of the term intended by those who coined it—then you are talking about rare individuals, not most of those currently developing and fielding mid-size commercial expert systems. If, on the other hand, you use the term to refer to anyone engaged in developing expert systems, you'll include a strange mix of people with a wide variety of qualifications. Most people who have developed and fielded an expert system, including some very small knowledge systems, call themselves knowledge engineers. It's confusing, but it probably accurately represents what's going on in this rapidly expanding field. There probably are as many types of knowledge engineers as there are market segments. This text uses the term *knowledge engineer* to refer to people engaged primarily in knowledge acquisition or in knowledge modeling, as well as many people engaged in the more conventional tasks necessary to field the systems.

THE SEVEN PHASES OF EXPERT SYSTEMS DEVELOPMENT

If you take a broader view and consider the entire process involved in developing and fielding an expert system, you encounter many activities only somewhat related to knowledge engineering and many other activities very familiar to conventional programmers and managers of any large undertaking.

Figure 10.6 illustrates a broad overview of the entire expert systems development and implementation process, synthesized from interviews with many people who have fielded commercial applications. The division into seven phases applies to mid-size or large efforts. The phases of a smaller effort tend to blur together.

The seven phases described in Figure 10.6 constitute a systematic way to approach developing an expert system. In reality, phases tend to get mixed together. The larger the system, and hence the greater the amount of money involved in development, the more systematic you should be. The seven phases are described in general terms. The specifics of each phase are discussed in subsequent chapters.

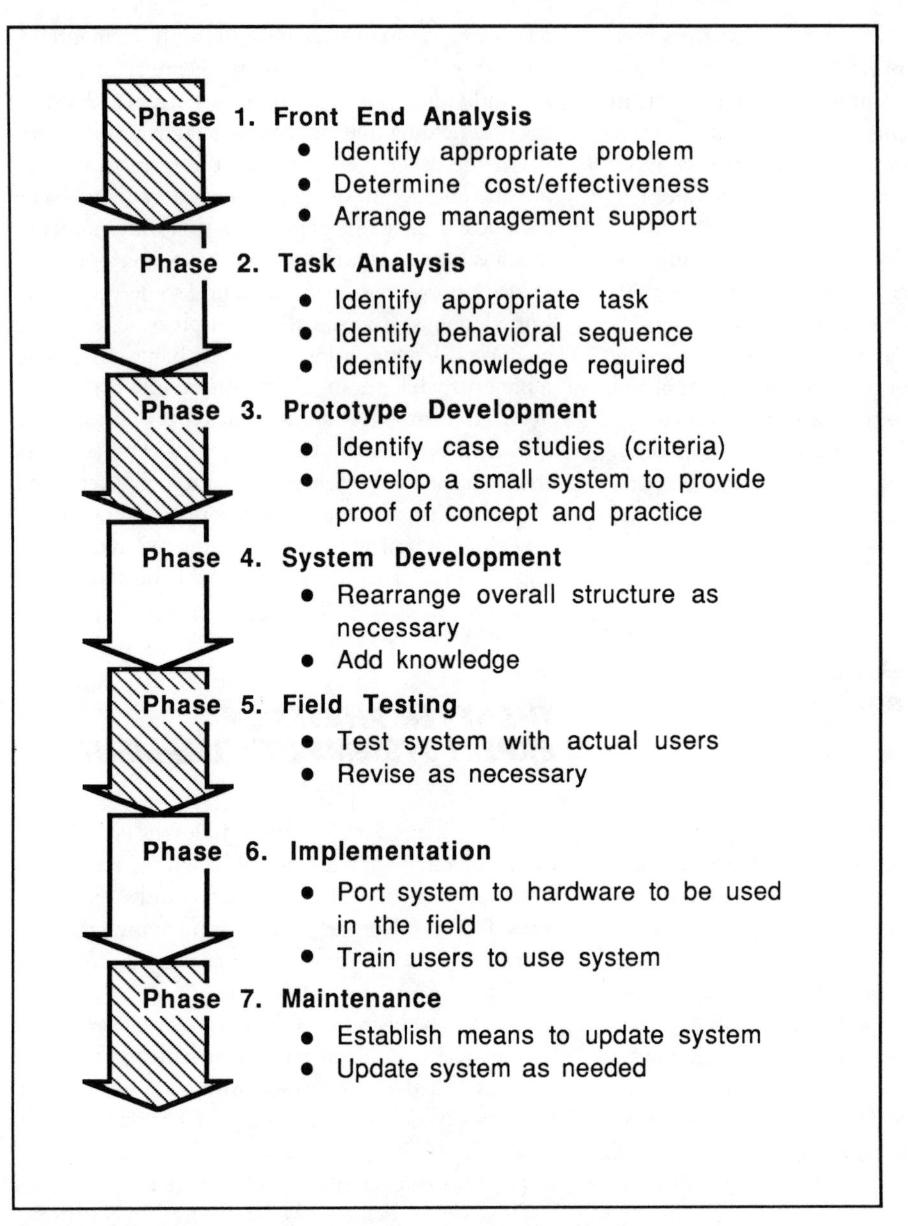

Figure 10.6 *Seven steps in expert systems development.*

Phase 1. Front end analysis. In the initial phase you select the appropriate problem or problems the system will work on. Front end analysis involves all the questions you should ask before beginning an expert systems project in the first place. If the project is large, this phase may require senior management to develop a corporate strategy to guide various middle managers in their expert systems development efforts.

As each individual project is considered, the project team must determine if an expert system is appropriate to the task, if it would be cost-effective, what hardware and software will be required, what personnel will be employed on the project, and so on. A project manager should plan to do what good managers of large projects do, including identifying corporate sponsors for the project, arranging briefings to manage expectations, and undertaking all other routine tasks required for the success of any large, costly software development project.

At this stage it is imperative to identify clearly the goals and criteria of the system. In other words, you need a clear statement of what the expert system is supposed to do. This will provide the information to use as a benchmark of comparison for the eventual development of the prototype system.

The tasks in this phase are usually performed by managers and project team leaders. Knowledge engineers sometimes do these tasks, and some even do them well, but these tasks require skills learned in a corporate environment and not taught in most computer science departments. Several expert systems projects have failed as a result of a decision to assign a knowledge engineer with little previous management experience to manage a large project.

Phase 2. Task analysis. In the second phase you study how the target task is currently performed, meet with human experts, and develop criteria to determine if the resulting system is successful. In other words, you set benchmarks against which to evaluate the system once it is up and running. You study how the new system would best fit into the environment and the exact nature and quantity of knowledge you'll hope to capture in the expert system. The work for this stage is performed by managers and project personnel with assistance and guidance provided by the knowledge engineer.

Phase 3. Prototype development. In the third phase you develop a small version of the expert system to demonstrate the overall feasibility of the proposed system. You establish concepts representing knowledge by describing the key concepts of the problem domain, interrelationships in the problem domain, and the flow of information needed to describe the problem-solving process (i.e., forward or backward chaining). Additionally, this stage offers the opportunity to make decisions resulting in appropriate software and hardware chosen for the target application. Also, the formats used for knowledge representation are selected (semantic networks, production rules, or predicate calculus techniques). To perform this task, you map the key problem concept of the system, any subproblems, and required information flow for the knowledge base isolated into a representation given various knowledge engineering tools and shells.

Information gathering strategy is finalized in this phase and is coordinated to comply with the software and hardware requirements of the system. Data input methods can be either manual or through electronic data transfer (e.g., input from an external program). Also of importance is identifying the major constraints to the selected target problem (if any) and to developing the system itself—cost or time considerations. This phase is generally performed by a knowledge engineer or other personnel familiar with the development processes.

In addition to gathering specifications and design information for constructing the prototype, the knowledge engineer starts to identify and document the reasoning processes of the human expert. These reasoning processes are the true heart of the expert system since they furnish the human thought needed to solve problems.

Finally, once a prototype is up and running in an abbreviated form, it becomes the model of the planned complete expert system. Normally at this stage adjustments are made to the performance and capabilities of the proposed system. In short, this phase lets you experiment with a scaled-down version of the expert system and examine some problems you might encounter when the full-scale development is undertaken.

Phase 4. System development. The great majority of knowledge is added to the system in the system development phase. Information is added in bulk after conferences with human experts, the user interface is tailored, and the system's working performance is monitored and compared to the established benchmarks.

During this phase the rules that embody the human experts' knowledge are refined by combining and reorganizing the knowledge contained in the knowledge base. Not only is the knowledge base dramatically expanded, but the user interface is carefully designed. These interfaces include the actual user interface and the frontend interface. The frontend interface concerns the input, modification, and maintenance capabilities of the system itself. It's how you will get information into the system. The user interface concerns the methods the end user needs to interact with the system. These usually include some type of menu-driven control featuring help screens. This phase is generally completed by the knowledge engineer.

Phase 5. Field testing. You must test the system in the user environment, again comparing its operation against established benchmarks, and modify and polish the system until it performs as you desire.

An expert system is tested and retested in many different ways and for many different problems. Testing must address the user interfaces and problem areas. The reasoning techniques and data structures are finely tuned so knowledge is best represented. The assignments and combinations of the certainty factors are also analyzed and changed if needed. The initial testing of the expert system should be performed using the feasibility study benchmarks.

The first step is to check all obvious errors that occur. From this point, the prototype is checked against the human expert to evaluate performance. Here, any shortcomings in the knowledge base become very evident. The most common method for performing this task is to give problems to the human expert and to the expert system and then compare results. The expert system, under ideal circumstances, should agree with the human expert at least 80 to 90 percent for every problem checked.

Any major modifications are performed during this phase. In a way, the prototype development, system development, and testing processes start all over whenever modifications are made to the system. The importance of this process cannot be overestimated, especially when developing a large expert system. One change can have numerous domino effects that may not be identifiable without further testing. The developing–testing loop continues until the expert system performs as expected, meeting the benchmarks. The knowledge engineer performs most of the predefined tasks and functions.

Phase 6. Implementation. The next phase in expert systems development is actually to field the system in a real-world user environment. This may involve porting the system to different hardware, and it certainly should include training users and helping them accept the system. This is an important phase since user acceptance can dictate success or failure. Indeed, this stage can be almost as difficult as the system development phase. The difficulties are organizational and psychological rather then technical. During this phase you see the payoff of all the briefings, demonstrations, and organizational politics the project manager engaged in while the knowledge engineer worked at extracting and encoding the expert's knowledge.

Integration should not be taken lightly. Many books discuss integrating computers and humans. If you are unsure how to handle this area, consult these books or hire a consultant to help you ease into the transition. Remember, an expert system—no matter how good it may be—is virtually useless if people won't use it. So your implementation plans should be well organized and offer full training, support, and documentation. This phase requires the efforts of management, project team personnel, and the knowledge engineer.

Phase 7. Maintenance. Maintenance, the final phase, is never complete; it continues as long as you use the system. The system must be continually revised and updated as necessary, against benchmarks that dictate new applications or performance improvement.

SUMMARY

The refinements to an expert system are never really complete since the systems continue to evolve as new information becomes available for problem resolution. Actually maintaining the system includes all the processes that were involved in developing and testing the system in the first place. However, maintenance also includes expanding or upgrading the software or hardware the system uses, including adding new information into the knowledge base and making any changes needed to reflect modifications to the system's reasoning processes. Again, the knowledge engineer usually performs or delegates these tasks.

11

Phases 1 and 2: Front End Analysis and Task Analysis

INTRODUCTION

This chapter focuses on the first two phases in developing an expert system: front end analysis and task analysis. During these phases you determine if an expert system is appropriate to a task, and if so, how the new system would best fit into your organization, where it would be employed, and the quantity and type of information you need to develop the system from an initial idea to a finished application.

PHASE 1. FRONT END ANALYSIS

During front end analysis you decide what types of expert systems your group or company will seek to build. Within those constraints, you will identify the problems the expert system will work on, find someone to contribute expertise, identify a tentative approach to the problem, and analyze the cost and benefits of the proposed system. This initial stage is called a *front end analysis* because it is concerned with all the things you do before you actually decide to develop an expert system.

Several activities should precede the decision to develop a system, including:

- Deciding on an expert systems development strategy.
- Identifying a problem domain and a specific task.
- Finding a person to contribute expertise.
- Analyzing the costs and benefits of the effort to be sure it is worth doing.

Deciding on an Expert Systems Development Strategy

Some companies have reviewed AI and expert systems technology at the highest levels and made a rational decision to develop a capacity in expert systems. In these cases, the company has usually investigated various approaches to expert systems development in a research setting and then identified or established an operational group responsible for subsequent expert systems development efforts. In other cases, individual managers or departments have decided they should develop an expert system for some specific need and commenced the undertaking without much consideration of how others in the company may view this new technology. As the technology develops and more people get involved, most large companies will want to develop a coordinated approach to expert systems development efforts to avoid having different groups repeat mistakes or buy incompatible hardware and software.

Figure 11.1 illustrates some expert systems development strategies currently being explored. Names of companies are identified with various strategies to provide concrete examples. In fact, dozens of companies are exploring each strategy and the companies identified in Figure 11.1 with particular strategies may also be exploring alternative strategies.

Figure 11.1 considers the possibilities resulting from two decisions: (1) what kind of expert systems tool to use, and (2) what kind of hardware is needed to develop and field the system. Several considerations go into each choice.

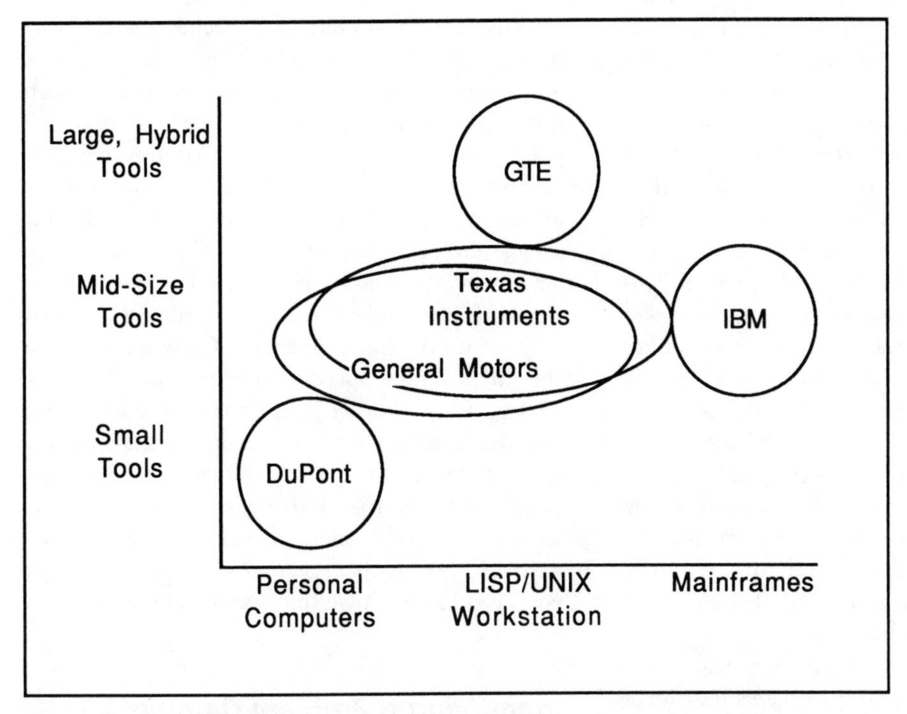

Figure 11.1 *Some well-known, early corporate strategies.*

When choosing the tool to use, you are making two important decisions: (1) who will develop the systems, and (2) what size problems can you solve with the system. If you want to solve large problems, you implicitly decide to spend lots of money and take some significant risks. You also commit yourself to finding qualified knowledge engineers (also expensive) or hiring a consulting firm to help develop your system.

If you want to get lots of managers and technical people involved in developing knowledge systems, then you will probably choose a small tool and develop a small to mid-size system. Your entry costs and risks will be much smaller, and you can engage many managers and technicians who are nonprogrammers in developing a small expert system. In effect, you can quickly explore many different ways small expert systems can be used.

As a practical compromise, most companies elect to use mid-size tools and work on some small and many mid-size problems. This strategy assumes that existing programming personnel will bear responsibility for most expert systems developed. Given the costs and skills of the people involved, most companies elect to tackle mid-size problems that offer a significant payback. In most cases, these efforts involve using expert systems in conjunction with existing data bases and applications to increase efficiency, use, or productivity.

A separate consideration, not entirely independent of your choice of a tool, involves selecting the hardware the systems will be developed or fielded on. If a company decides to develop lots of small systems, typically they choose to use personal computers, since those are what most managers and technical people have and will use when they develop and field their systems.

If a company decides to develop mid-size to large systems, they will want to use either large personal computers (e.g., PC-ATs equipped with extra memory) or workstations like the Sun and MicroVAX. Such hardware is increasingly available in locations where a company would find it cost-effective to field a mid-size system. Companies using expert systems in manufacturing or engineering operations frequently elect this option.

If a company decides to develop a very large expert system or undertakes developing a complex expert system in a domain that is not well understood, they will probably elect to use a LISP machine. This probably means they will have to port the application to a workstation or a mainframe when they are ready to field it. If the project is complex enough, the power and flexibility offered by the LISP machines justifies the costs and difficulties involved in developing a system on one piece of hardware and fielding it on another. This strategy has been widely adopted by computer companies wanting to develop considerable technical depth in expert systems development and by those high-tech companies that do work for the military and aerospace concerns and, thus, routinely work on very large, difficult applications that ultimately are fielded on specialized hardware.

Most companies have not designed a strategy for expert systems development. In many cases individual managers within the company make isolated decisions, usually selecting PC- or workstation-based tools. If a company's senior management relies on its data processing and MIS executives to develop policy on computer-related matters, the company MIS people are probably waiting for expert systems tools that run on their existing mainframe computers so any applications will communicate easily with their existing applications and data bases. In most cases, the MIS people want a tool like AION that runs on both mainframes and PCs so initial development can begin on a PC and then be transferred to a mainframe for completion and delivery. Since the most powerful commercial tools (i.e., the large hybrid tools) do not yet run in conventional languages, this strategy implicitly means the company will develop mid-size systems. Since most companies that want their expert systems to run on mainframes also want to integrate the systems with existing conventional applications, this strategy makes sense. Moreover, as hybrid tools begin to appear on mainframes, the possibilities of this option will expand.

Every large company has many opportunities to use expert systems. If you work for a company that has already adopted a clear strategy, has developed arrangements with consultants and vendors, and has acquired specific hardware and software, you should look at specific domains and tasks easily compatible with those commitments. If your company lacks an overall policy, you can either develop a strategy for your department or group or simply select a specific problem and begin. If you choose the latter course and select a large problem, you will necessarily spend a large amount of money and may not be able to use the hardware, software, and experience you gain on your first project on subsequent problems. Consequently, you should probably spend some time developing a strategy. On the other hand, if you have a problem already costing your organization a considerable amount of money, and you want to solve that problem and are not concerned with any subsequent use of the technology in other areas of your organization, then it makes sense simply to get the hardware and software you need to best solve that specific problem.

Identifying a Problem Domain and a Specific Task

Choosing the right problem is perhaps the most critical part of the entire development effort. Since the technology is still new and quite limited in the type of problems and applications it can effectively address, exercise great care in choosing problems. As time passes and technology improves, and you gain experience with expert systems capabilities, you will identify many different problems you can solve with the technology. However, if you're working on your first project, exercise considerable caution, since numerous pitfalls await the overambitious.

Figure 11.2 presents a checklist to use to assure you cover the major considerations in choosing a potential application. Consider each item on the checklist in turn.

Describing the Overall Objective of a Project

The first box on the checklist asks about the overall objective of the project. It is important to be clear

Checklist. Selecting Problems

Overall Objective of Project

- R&D/Proof of concept
- Specific benefit to organization

Problem/Opportunity

- How is the problem currently being solved?
- What opportunity is being missed?
- What is the problem or missed opportunity costing the company?
- Which of the following will the system do?
  - ☐ Capture and distribute knowledge
  - ☐ Preserve knowledge
  - ☐ Integrate the knowledge of several people
  - ☐ Faster decisions
  - ☐ Better decisions
  - ☐ Consistent decisions
  - ☐ Bookkeeping efficiencies
  - ☐ Better approach to software development
  - ☐ Better approach to updating and maintaining
  - ☐ Reduced training costs
  - ☐ Reduced labor costs

Is the Problem/Opportunity Well and Narrowly Defined?

- Is there expertise? Would an expert be available for 3 - 6 months?
- Is there documentation?
- How long does the task currently take?
- What does a good solution look like?
- How consistent are the current solutions?

Developing a System

- Do you have/need knowledge engineers? Describe their experience.
- Do you have consulting relationships with a KE company?
- How would the system be developed? On what hardware?
- On what software?
- Who would manage the project?
- What kind of budget constraints do you have?
- Do you have schedule constraints? A completion date?
- Who is sponsoring the effort?
- Do you have the support of senior management?

Fielding a System

- Who are the users? Do they currently use computers?
- How would the system be fielded? On what hardware?
- On what software?
- Would the system be integrated with existing software? How? (Describe the existing hardware and software.)

Figure 11.2 *Checklist 1. Selecting Problems.*

about the purpose of your effort. If you are conducting a research effort to determine if expert systems techniques could be useful, then say so. If you have a specific problem you expect to solve with the technology, plan on undertaking a much more rigorous cost/benefit effort to justify your choice of a specific task.

In the past few years most companies have been exploring new technologies and have not required their projects to justify themselves. In effect, the companies wanted to learn about the technology and choose an interesting project without requiring the project to justify itself in terms of its results. This has allowed companies to learn about the new technology without placing the person initiating the project under normal payback considerations. In some cases this has resulted in systems that do make their companies money, but in most cases it has been a learning experience resulting in a demonstration system. In most cases the developers learned from the experience and selected a second project that was fielded and is saving the company money.

If you are going to do R&D, be clear about it to avoid undertaking a project that will be regarded as a failure, rather than as a good first approximation. On the other hand, if you want to solve a specific problem, exercise all the care anyone else exercises when analyzing a new project. Some relevant cost/benefit considerations are discussed later in this chapter.

Identifying a Problem/Opportunity

The most important thing to remember about commercial expert systems when beginning to look for a potential application is that *expert systems do not create knowledge, and they do not learn on the job. They simply store and play back knowledge that some human expert has already developed. If no one knows how to analyze and solve the problem now, an expert system will not improve the situation.*

Research efforts are under way to develop expert systems to reason from deep models and learn as they gain experience, but this is strictly research. Many problems must be solved before these capabilities are available commercially. When you begin to look for a potential application, look for a problem that can already be solved by humans. Your challenge is to automate the process and make the problem-solving skills of one human available to many others via a computer.

Thus, your first step in identifying good potential applications is to look for bottlenecks that result either because too few people perform some critical task or because other people must stop what they are doing and find someone else to help them with a particular step in the work.

In general, small systems are developed to provide information about how to analyze problems that some people can analyze quickly while others consistently need assistance. The example provided in Chapter 10 of the dental technician who routinely predicted when the dental lab could deliver a product, but was constantly called to help the other dental technicians do the same task, is a typical example of the type of problem small expert systems are good at.

Other good examples are small systems to help clerical people analyze telephone requests or classify documents, and systems that help maintenance people analyze and correct routine problems with machinery. Still other good examples are systems that analyze customer needs and recommend which of several products will best satisfy their requirements or systems that troubleshoot customer problems and recommend simple corrections.

When you ask how the problem currently is being solved, you usually find people are going to someone or are looking in manuals. A small knowledge system makes the expertise of the best person currently analyzing the problem available to the other people who deal with the same problem. In actuality, the "best person" is your human expert.

In a similar way, large expert systems are typically developed to "clone" a specific human expert critical to the organization. At the high end, the expert is usually well known and respected, and everyone admits things would go more smoothly if that one individual could be several places at once. Or the individual may be ready to move on to another job or retire, and everyone involved is concerned about how some vital analysis and decision-making task will be accomplished when that individual is no longer available. In other words, at the high end, the question: "How is the problem currently being solved?" almost always comes down to: "We get Bill Smith to help with that. He's the only one who really understands that particular problem."

With mid-size systems, the analysis is often a bit more complex. In many cases, mid-size systems are developed to "clone" specific human experts in the same way the large and small systems are. In that case the same criteria just discussed apply.

In other cases, however, the systems are developed to improve processes. That is, you want everyone performing a task to do the task better. There may be no one expert, but at each step in the process some people do that step a little better than others. Or you may routinely convene a committee to discuss a problem and reach a group decision, avoiding errors that might result if any one individual made the decision. Analyzing a complex procedural situation and picking the best place to insert the expert system is more complex. This will be explored in the discussion of task analysis. Suffice to say you must state exactly how the task or procedure is currently being accomplished and identify errors or inefficiencies to minimize by making the knowledge of some existing individual or group available to the people who routinely perform the task.

In some cases, you will develop a system to capture opportunities currently missed by most people who perform some task. In other words, when Karen helps a customer select a hi-fi system, she typically makes a much larger sale than the other salespeople because she asks a few more questions and helps the customer conceptualize a better (or at least more complex, and therefore more expensive) hi-fi package than the other salespeople. Or Karen may be the best salesperson simply because she ends up prescribing a system the customers are always satisfied with, while 20 percent of the systems prescribed by the other salespeople result in returned items or complaints. In these cases you can expect to obtain additional business or avoid problems by enabling the other people to perform as your best performer does.

To justify developing the expert system, you must identify some costs associated with the performance or nonperformance of some task. It costs money for people to run around looking for the only person in the company who can answer some routine question. If this happens often enough, the cost of each delay adds up. It also costs the company in terms of the time individuals spend answering routine questions when they could be doing some more valuable job. Likewise, if your human expert can be only one place at a time, costs are associated each time one problem is placed on hold until your expert can get to it.

At the high end, projects placed on hold can quickly cost a lot of money. It also costs money every time someone sets up a job in a way that creates more scrap or takes longer than it would if your best person had done the setup. Similarly, it costs money when you incur losses for loans your typical loan officer makes that your best loan officers never even consider funding. And it costs money if your best performer routinely makes more money for the company than the average performer. Every large organization has numerous examples of inefficient, ineffective performance. With a little effort, you should easily identify such problems when you look for potential expert systems applications.

The lower portion of the problem/opportunity box on the checklist lists some ways expert systems can be used to improve how tasks are performed. As you examine the various tasks you might tackle, check off the benefits and make some guesstimates about the savings or the additional money to be earned by providing those benefits. After you have considered five or ten different tasks, you will probably see a pattern that provides your organization with the maximum payoff for the investment you estimate an expert systems effort will cost.

Is the Problem/Opportunity Well and Narrowly Defined?

Once you have identified two or three candidate projects, apply the criteria listed in the third box of the checklist.

If you have done your work well up to this point,

you will not consider any project involving problems no one currently knows how to solve. You should still ask yourself a number of questions about the quality of expertise you will depend on to develop a system. Will the person with the expertise be available to help develop the system? Is the expert cooperative or resistant to your efforts to learn how he or she analyzes and solves problems? With the best of intentions, some very valuable experts may be unable to help you simply because they are too busy handling their jobs, which are too critical to the company to be ignored while the experts consult with a knowledge engineer. If possible, you want the best of the available experts. In the long run this avoids problems with the "better" experts rejecting the expert system because it was developed by a junior person. Hence, try to avoid taking on a problem in which you are asked to work with a junior expert because the senior experts are too busy solving critical problems.

If you are working on a small system, the expert may very well be the person you want to develop the system. In that case, be sure the expert is willing to take on such a task. In most cases experts will be eager to develop a system to relieve them of having to spend lots of time answering routine questions, but they may be unfamiliar with computers and seek to avoid getting into a task they feel they might fail at.

If you are looking for your first project, be it large or small, choose the simplest and narrowest task that seems worthwhile. It is almost always better to develop a trivial system that succeeds than to undertake a larger system that fails. One thing developing an expert system does is demonstrate how much knowledge is brought to bear on even the simplest tasks. A task you imagine can be automated with 10 good rules typically takes 100. The reason some people are better at seemingly trivial tasks is that they do have more knowledge than their fellow workers. Assume even a simpler task will turn out to require identifying and formalizing much more knowledge than you imagine when you first examine the task.

One simple criterion is to ask how long it takes the best performer to perform the task. If your expert takes a few seconds to a few minutes, he or she is probably using enough knowledge to make a small system. If your expert takes twenty minutes, you probably want to consider a mid-size system. If your expert takes several hours, you should consider developing a large system, and you should try to divide the task into parts and go after only one part when you develop your first system. As a strong general heuristic: You cannot tackle too small a task when you begin to develop your first system. The smallest task you can imagine undertaking will prove much larger than you think.

A narrow task refers to a specialized task as opposed to one involving the integration of several different types of knowledge. Ideally, your expert should have a specialized vocabulary used to talk about the task. Experts should be able to name the parts or items that they examine when they analyze the problem. If your experts are good because they are good general troubleshooters with lots of common sense, avoid that task and look for a more precisely defined, more narrowly limited task. As with size, you can't choose a too narrowly defined problem when you undertake your first system.

Finally, since all expert systems that capture heuristics are developed by testing the system against cases the human expert has previously solved, select a problem for which case data already exist. In the best case, when you interview a potential expert, the expert should show you files, or approved applications, or troubleshooting reports that document previous work. In effect, those documents become your success criteria; that is, your system will be useful if it can solve those documented cases in the same way the human expert did.

Obviously, you should see a consistent pattern in the solutions, which is another way of saying your expert should be consistent in the way problems are solved. If the expert says she routinely solves one class of problem without difficulty but is never sure about the solutions she proposes in a different situation, obviously you want to develop an expert system to capture the knowledge used on the well-understood situations.

As a good generalization, most top-flight experts routinely solve 80 percent of their problems without difficulty. The other 20 percent of their problems are "cutting edge" problems; when they work on those problems they are, in fact, developing new expertise.

You want to develop expert systems to capture the expert's routine knowledge and avoid trying to capture knowledge the expert has not completely refined. (There are some significant exceptions to this generalization at the high end, when the solution to the problem is so valuable to the company you are willing to develop an expert system to help the experts improve their skills, but such an effort should be considered an R&D effort, not a typical commercial expert systems development effort.)

Developing a System

The checklist suggests a number of questions you should ask about the nature of the expert systems development effort you will undertake. If your management has already adopted a strategy and prescribed use of certain tools or hardware, then these questions may be simple to answer. On the other hand, if you are approaching your first development effort in a less structured manner and have identified several possible applications, ranging from small to large, you need to consider the benefits of each possible project and weigh them against the costs you will incur by selecting a particular project.

If you decide to undertake a small project using a PC-based tool and decide that the expert can develop the system, then you do not face significant costs or organizational problems. On the other hand, if you decide to tackle a major project, you will probably need to hire knowledge engineers and acquire expensive hardware and software. In most cases, you select your software vendor in part for the training and follow-up consulting they can provide. Since your staff will be new, you need access to some experienced advice.

You also need to think about who will manage the project, especially if it will be highly visible and employ several people. As already noted, knowledge engineers are not necessarily managers. As a rule, have an experienced company manager assigned to run the project. Similarly, if it is a major undertaking, think about sponsorship and senior management support. An experienced company manager will know how to support you, but a knowledge engineer fresh from graduate school will not even know what you are talking about. (The first time a crisis occurs and someone proposes your expert should drop the expert systems project and focus on troubleshooting, you will find out what support the expert systems project has, but you should have a good idea of how this will be decided beforehand.)

The more important a delivery date is, the more important it is to focus on a narrowly defined project. A successful small project can always be scaled up; that's one major advantage of expert systems technique. But a large project that doesn't get done on time may give your entire expert systems effort a bad name.

Obviously you must reach some appropriate balance between solving problems to prove the use of the technology without committing the company to excessive hardware, software, and personnel expenses. Many companies handle this problem by developing their first expert systems in a research environment to avoid the constraints operational departments are likely to impose. Most companies just beginning to develop expert systems and entrusting the task to line managers and technicians are beginning with mid-size problems and using mid-size hardware and software. They avoid the small problems simply because the immediate payback isn't enough to pay for the investment, and they avoid the large problems because the costs and risks are much greater.

Mid-size problems tackled by conventional programmers interested in using expert systems techniques to improve reasonably well-understood existing situations present an opportunity for most companies to get into expert systems with good chances of a successful, cost-effective first project.

Fielding a System

Under no circumstances should you consider developing a commercial expert system without a very clear idea of who will use the resulting system and how they will access it.

If you are developing a small system, the end users need to have access to PCs and be willing and able to use a PC when faced with the task the system is supposed to help them perform.

If you are developing a large system on a LISP machine, you need to plan to port the resulting system over to conventional hardware or justify putting expensive LISP machines in each location using the system. Companies working on aerospace projects may be able to develop systems on LISP machines and then field them on LISP chips embedded in hardware, but in most commercial settings many problems are associated with fielding large systems that must interact with data bases or programs normally residing on a mainframe.

In the mid-range, predictable hardware advances (e.g., the availability of 80386-based personal computers) should eliminate most hardware problems associated with fielding mid-size systems, but several personnel issues must still be considered. If your system is designed to help maintenance people maintain a machine, you will not face too many problems. If you are developing a system to help bank officers make loans, however, you need a clear idea of how those managers will access the system. If you are developing your system on a PC and expect to field it on a mainframe, you could face serious interface problems. Likewise, as soon as you consider assisting any important group of managers or technicians like bank officers or insurance underwriters, be sure you have a plan to explain the whole project to the people affected. If they perceive your expert system as a way to replace them by allowing the company to hire less experienced people to do their jobs, you will face great resistance.

Most companies are developing expert systems to support existing managers by allowing them to make more decisions, faster, with more consistency. They are not seeking to replace people. Some companies, however, are developing expert systems that will, in fact, allow less experienced people to perform more complex jobs—one of the best ways to improve productivity in some industries. Successful companies take great pains to assure that the company benefits from the effort rather than suffers from personnel problems that end up costing more than the system could possibly save them. In any case, these serious issues must always be faced when you consider a project that raises the specter of job automation. The wise project planner picks early projects to either minimize such problems or develops a plan early on to minimize disruptions that may result from such personnel-related issues.

Analyzing the Costs and Benefits

If considering a small expert system, you can normally skip cost/benefit analysis. If a simple problem obviously yields to an expert systems solution, the cost to develop the system will be small enough that it is cheaper to see what happens than to spend time and money trying to prove the system is worth building. If you are considering a mid- to large-size system that will probably be used by several people once it is developed, however, then consider the costs and benefits before buying the hardware and software and assigning personnel to what will probably be a three- to eighteen-month task.

The analysis that follows is very similar to the cost benefit analysis you would perform if you were considering developing a conventional software application.

The initial costs to develop the system include:

- The price of the hardware.
- The price of the software.
- The salary of the knowledge engineer(s).
- The salary of the human expert(s).
- Normal operating overhead.
- Miscellaneous costs (travel, fielding, transition costs).

Notice that the costs include the expert's time as well as that of the knowledge engineers. If the problem is a major one (definitely not recommended for your first developing endeavor), both the knowledge engineer and the expert can be expected to spend at least a year on the development effort. Additional costs might also include acquiring specific software and hardware (e.g., using a Symbolics 3600 computer for a specific LISP application).

In addition to the costs associated with developing a system, other costs are associated with fielding the system, including the time of conventional programmers to revise other programs or data bases the system needs to access and to develop communications protocols. Costs may also be associated with making copies of the expert systems tool you need to run the knowledge base developed and hardware costs associated with making the system available to end users.

Figure 11.3 provides a worksheet to estimate some events that occur during a project. You need to estimate how long each event will take and how much time each key project person will spend during that phase. Once you have some ideas of your labor costs, you can complete the worksheet illustrated in Figure 11.4 and estimate the other costs you will incur in developing and fielding your system.

Existing problems become problems for development only when they are used with an expert system that can yield a payback. Since you are in search of problem resolution abilities as well as cost savings and

Project Schedule Worksheet

Front End Analysis................................

Analysis & Design.................................
- Task analysis
- Knowledge acquisition
- Prototype development

System Development.............................
- Knowledge base extension & revision
- User interface development

Delivery...
- Field testing
- Integration into user environment
- Training and support

Figure 11.3 *Project schedule worksheet.*

Project Personnel & Budget Worksheet

Design & Development

Labor
- Manager
- Expert
- Knowledge engineer

Overhead on labor

Software
- Language or tool
- Associated training

Hardware

Delivery

Labor
- Manager
- Expert
- Knowledge engineer
- Programmer

Overhead on labor

Software
- Runtime fees
- Existing system modifications

Hardware

Training

Figure 11.4 *Project personnel & budget worksheet.*

benefits, you want to determine the size of the budget or investment required to develop an expert system. You also want to know the payback period.

Return on Investment

To calculate the estimated costs and payback period, examine the following figures for Return on Investment (ROI). Define payback as: $R = C/I$, where R is the annual rate of return determined by dividing the annualized cash benefit, C, by the amount of the total investment or budget, I.

Consider the following example. Suppose the problem you are contemplating concerns using an expert system to perform insurance application evaluation training. The expert system will train new clerks to evaluate insurance applications, freeing the senior clerk to perform other duties in lieu of training the clerks. Training new clerks is performed every Tuesday for eight hours, four times a month. Suppose the senior clerk is paid $9.00 per hour to perform the training. So the cost of training performed by the senior clerk for one year is:

($9.00 × 8 hours) × 4 days per month = $288.00 per month
$288.00 × 12 months per year = $3,456.00 per year

Because the senior clerk's knowledge of processing insurance applications is a necessity, this cost cannot be avoided. Conversely, if this training could be accomplished using an expert system, the senior clerk could perform other more important tasks. New clerks could learn to evaluate insurance applications by the information provided by the knowledge base. Therefore, the $3,456.00 annual cash benefit constitutes the value of C in the equation:

$R = 3{,}456/I$

Now, suppose you must spend the following amounts to create the insurance application evaluation data base:

$ 2,000	Software
$10,000	System development
$ 3,000	Hardware
$15,000	Total investment

The payback equation now becomes:

$R = 3{,}456/15{,}000$
$R = .2304$ or 23.04%

Each year the expert system is used to train new clerks, you receive a payback of 23.04 percent of the initial investment. You can use the following equation where Y is the number of years to complete the payback:

$Y = 100/R$

You can easily find the number of years required to recoup the entire investment by substituting the value known for R:

$Y = 100/23.04$
$Y = 4.3$ years

Now, assume you are using these formulas to calculate the budget needed to develop the expert system whose required payback period is known. Simply calculate in reverse order and solve for the unknowns. For this, use a different example.

Say you have decided not to invest in developing an expert system if it will not pay back within five years. You start by substituting 5 for Y and solving for R:

$5 = 100/R$
Multiplying by R: $5R = 100$
Dividing by 5: $R = 100/5 = 20$

This shows the return on investment must be 20 percent per year for a five-year payback. Now, returning to the initial formula, $R = C/I$, substitute .20 for R:

$.20 = C/I$
multiplying by 5(I): $5(I) \times .20 = 5(I) \times C/I$
$I = 5C$

You can see the original investment may be five times the calculated annualized cash benefit. This establishes a budget for expert systems development. This simple procedure for calculating payback is not without shortcomings. Questions may arise; for example, "If you invested the money in a customary vehicle, at the end of five years would you gain more than the original investment? How could you compensate for a gain of this type?" In response, you may rationally figure the benefits you see will also increase over the five-year period due to the tendency for business costs and salaries to rise accordingly.

Many different methods are much more precise in measuring return on investment; however, it is safe to say that if the payback period is five years or less, discounted cash-flow and present value calculations will probably produce similar results. It all depends on how your organization figures ROI. Payback is used here to present a simple example. This step is important, however, since most executives, especially those controlling the organization's pursestrings, think in terms of opportunities for improvement and the consequent benefits as they directly relate to the budget.

***Table 11.1** Resources required to develop an expert system.*

RESOURCES	SIZE OF SYSTEM Small	 Mid-Size	 Large
Rules	50-500	500-1,500	Over 1,500 or Objects
Tools available?	Yes	Yes	Maybe
Person-years to develop	1/4	1/2 - 2	3-5
Project cost	$25-50,000	$300,000	$2-5 million

Costs include design, development, knowledge engineers, computing and overhead. Company expert, travel, fielding, etc. are excluded.

Balanced against costs are the benefits you acquire from using the knowledge system. These benefits may include reduced costs, increased productivity, enhanced products or services, or even the development of new products and services. The relative costs and benefits of any particular system determine how long it takes the system to pay back the development expense. Most companies that develop large expert systems are selecting reasonably costly projects that feature very large benefits and, consequently, have very short payback times. It is expected that a trend toward less expensive projects with slightly longer payback times will occur as development tools are refined and become less expensive.

Table 11.1 provides some rough estimates of the resources different size projects should require.

Preparing a Specific Development Plan

After completing the front end analysis, you should be convinced of the following:

- A specific task can be performed by an expert system.
- It can be built using existing techniques or tools.
- An appropriate expert is available.
- The proposed performance criteria are reasonable.
- The cost and payback time are acceptable.

Only if all the aforementioned criteria are positive should the project move toward development. If they are, then the knowledge engineer is ready to prepare a specific plan to guide the development effort. The checklists and worksheets in this chapter should guide you in preparing your plan. The plan is simply a development proposal that outlines all major items in the development project. The proposal is really no different than proposals formulated for conventional system development projects.

The proposal should include the rationale of the system and specify the steps to be taken during the development process, the costs involved, and the results to be expected. In essence, it outlines, step-by-step, the procedures that will take the expert system from the initial concept to a working reality. Information in your development plan should include:

- The hardware, software, or building tool likely to be used.
- The input specifications of the system. This includes the knowledge required as well as how this knowledge will be entered into the system.
- The processing specifications—how the expert system will process the information (rules, backward or forward chaining, etc.).
- Decision criteria—how confidence factors are used, edit checks for knowledge verification, and so on.
- Output specifications—what the engineering and end user interfaces will be.
- Personnel to be involved with the project, including length of commitment.
- Areas of the organization to be affected by the system.
- Training and support issues.
- System implementation issues.
- Total costs of the system, including ROI factors.
- Project development schedule.
- Benefits to the organization.

This listing is by no means comprehensive. Your organization may have specific criteria that must be included in any computer development proposal. Naturally, your proposal should definitely include these criteria. Other information you might address is outlined in the following paragraphs. This information has been derived from actual development efforts conducted by companies in the United States.

Potential physical implementation problems. This depends on the software you plan to use. For example, with the Texas Instruments Personal Consultant Plus, you are using a LISP-based tool and will certainly have problems should you try to interface the system with a large mainframe system. All the problems of integrating expert systems to other systems are very real. At this point, your success depends on what type of software you use and the problems typically associated with the software.

Potential personnel problems. Depending on the type of system you are planning on build, as noted, some individuals will see the expert system as a personal threat to their position and employment. Most expert systems built and in use today have *not* done this. In fact, just the opposite is true; they have expanded what people (and the company) can do. Generally, once the system is built the individuals feeling most threatened often maintain it and add to its knowledge base.

Interdepartmental impacts. Most human experts operate between departments in companies (people are generally skilled at this). Building an expert system requires the same tasks. So you need assurances that upper management understands and accepts this. For example, in a company where a system is being built by the R&D group (with much management support), problems may crop up when the system is actually fielded to an external operations group (where management support may be less strong). The operations group will likely address problems the R&D group failed to consider. At this point senior management is usually called in to solve the dilemma. This is why upper management support for the overall project is critical.

Long-term benefits. Obviously, if you are going to tell someone about all the problems that may arise during the development effort, you should have some good news to include or the idea to build an expert system will be just that: an idea. Texas Instruments has perhaps been the most receptive company to realize the long-term benefits of building and using expert systems. Most companies, however, do not have such strong beliefs in AI and expert systems. This is an area where five- and ten-year plans on using the system (the benefits the company will realize by that time) can be most convincing to persuade management to invest in building a system. The long-term benefits are there; use them.

Major pitfalls to avoid. Choosing the wrong problem for the expert system can cause problems. This can occur when management dictates the problem to be solved—of a planning and not diagnostic nature—without considering (or knowing) the capabilities of the system. Choosing a problem that is too big poses a serious liability to the success of your venture. A good rule-of-thumb is to pick the applied problem, cut it in half, then cut it in half again. This way you are likely to wind up with a problem of a size that can be attacked (and solved) by the system. Since you have the opportunity to start small and then build up, use this to your advantage.

For example, after selecting a problem and listening to its attributes, you should be able to return a week later with a 10-rule system and ask if this is what they had in mind to solve the problem. If the answer is yes, continue to build from there. If it is no, rework the entire process until the simple rule system is acceptable. This methodology prevents missing the target problem by going overboard too soon. Pick the problems to work on with this in mind. Keep the problem small so you can show results quickly.

Another problem is insufficient management commitment. If someone in your organization announces that you should be using this "hot technology," but without thinking of its ramifications, problems may arise six months later when the system is ready to be fielded and management has not informed that area of the new change. Management must encourage and support the development of an expert system across all departments and lines that will be affected by the system. Failure to do this will surely doom even the most worthwhile project.

Underestimating the cost of the system and the difficulty in building it are two other concerns. These areas are more relevant to large systems and are tied into all the problems outlined previously. Picking the wrong problem or one that is too large causes cost overruns and development difficulties.

Establishing Benchmarks for Comparison

This process is very similar to preparing the development plan; in fact, the information you develop for benchmarks could be included in your development proposal. Mostly though, use benchmarks to monitor system performance expectations over a period of time. Some suggested benchmarks may include the following:

1. Lower Costs
   a. Reduction in clerical operations.
   b. Savings in space required for personnel, desks, and files.
   c. Reduction in duplication of efforts.
   d. Reduction in duplication of operations.
   e. Detection of problems before they become costly.
   f. Reduction in routine, redundant efforts.
   g. Reduction in paperwork.
   h. Combination of like functions in several departments.
2. Faster Reaction
   a. Improved ability to react to changing external conditions.
   b. Larger reservoir of information.
   c. Closer monitoring of information.
   d. Assessing impact of problems.
   e. Faster turnaround time in decision making.
   f. Ability to compare alternative courses of actions.
3. Improved Accuracy
   a. Mechanization of operations, permitting more checks and less error possibilities.
   b. Sharing of information between departments.
   c. Ability to raise confidence factors in decisions.
   d. Integrity of information used in decision-making processes.
4. Improved Information for Management
   a. Higher quality of information through feasibility to employ management science techniques.
   b. Capability to use management-by-exception principle to a greater extent.
   c. Capability of developing simulation models for forecasting and decision making.
   d. Improved performance factors derived from improved decision making.

Choosing the right initial application and the right software for the task are keys to success. Identifying the right human expert to work with and knowing how you will field the system once it is done go a long way toward guaranteeing a successful project. Not weighing each issue before beginning a mid- to large-size project simply invites disaster. Expert systems techniques are very useful, and, in fact, a vast number of problems in every organization are just waiting to be solved by this technology. But the power and simplicity of the approach has led many people to select overly ambitious initial projects that quickly get out of hand. Time spent on front end analysis is usually very well spent.

PHASE 2. TASK ANALYSIS

Once you have selected a problem domain, a task, and an expert, you have to decide exactly how to define the task the expert system will perform. If you are developing a small system, you may simply ignore this phase and develop a system to capture all the knowledge needed to perform some small analytic task. But when you consider a mid- to large-size problem, you need to put a lot more effort into scoping the exact task the system will be designed to perform. Ideally, you have done some of this during the front end analysis phase, but realistically, you usually choose the task for more general reasons and determine the exact nature of the task only when you begin to work with your expert. Another way of saying this is that the front end analysis may be done by a manager, but the task analysis is usually done by the knowledge engineer who is about to begin developing the system. Task analysis is a detailed look at exactly what the expert does, with an eye to defining the precise portion of the task that will be useful to encode in an expert system.

Task analysis begins with a detailed look at how the task is currently performed. Figure 11.5 provides a simple model of a task. Something initiates the performance of the task: perhaps someone approaches the expert and asks for help, perhaps a machine provides a signal, perhaps the expert scans printouts looking for a pattern that indicates a problem. And something results from performing the task that signals the task has been completed. The expert tells someone what to do, or adjusts an instrument so it works correctly, or hands in a report recommending a loan be granted.

One discrimination you should make at this point is whether the task is a *signal processing task* or a *dialogue task*. In many cases the expert receives materials or data to be analyzed and proceeds to analyze the material and then make recommendations. In essence, the expert reviews the input data looking for patterns that suggest what could have caused the problem. Expert systems designed to handle signal-processing tasks are normally forward chaining. They begin with the data and then apply rules until they reach a recommendation.

On the other hand, some experts ask questions and gather data throughout the analysis process. The act of questioning determines what additional data is needed. Expert systems designed to model this type of expert performance are typically backward chaining systems.

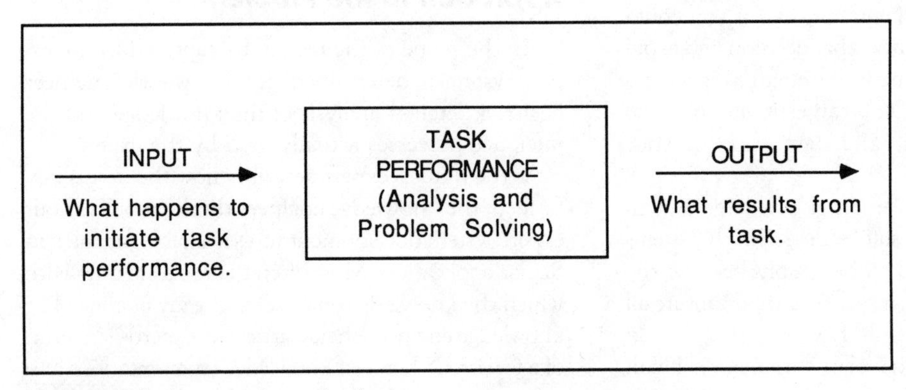

Figure 11.5 An overview of a task.

Once you are clear about the beginning and end of the task, explore the process itself. Simple tasks may involve asking a few questions and then making a recommendation. More complex tasks typically involve several steps. Sometimes the steps are sequential, but they frequently form a network or hierarchy where answers to some questions determine that other types of questions must be asked. Experts often mix questions with procedural activities they use to investigate hypotheses.

As a generalization, try to subdivide an expert's performance into as many steps or parts as possible. Then determine which steps or parts are hard and which are easy. If you are developing a system to help a group of people perform in the same way the best performer does, be very careful to determine exactly which parts of the task the best performer does better than the average performer. Do not assume that because you want to improve the performance of loan officers you must build a system to capture *all* the knowledge the best loan officer uses. A comparison of the best and the average loan officers may reveal that they all perform equally well at all but a very few specific steps or parts of the task. In this case, you can develop an expert system to capture just the knowledge necessary to perform the specific steps and ignore the knowledge that the best and the average performers possess in common.

When trying to improve an existing application program, you do not want to rewrite the entire program. Instead, determine the specific points at which the current program requires human assistance to help it decide what to do next. Then consider if you could build an expert system to make that decision and avoid requiring human involvement. If human assistance is required in several places, you can estimate the costs of developing each system and then prioritize your efforts.

The main point is: never develop a large system when a smaller system will suffice. Several early systems are larger than they need to be simply because the designers assumed an expert system should capture all an expert's knowledge, and they set off to do so without thinking about the relative value or difficulty involved in such an indiscriminate approach. Large systems are harder to build, harder to maintain, and much harder to field, since they can be more threatening to the people currently performing the job. A mid-size system that clearly assists a performer and makes no pretensions of replacing the performer is much easier and less expensive to develop and field.

Another way to think about the tasks to include is to remember that it is usually relatively easy to capture 80 percent of an expert's knowledge and very hard to capture the last 20 percent. Moreover, you can frequently capture 80 percent of the expert's knowledge in 20 percent of the time it would take you to capture all the expert's knowledge. Many companies have developed equipment maintenance or troubleshooting systems designed to cover only about 80 percent of the cases. The goal is not to eliminate the expert troubleshooter, but simply to relieve that person from dealing with the majority of routine problems that other people can troubleshoot using an expert system. If you resist the temptation to try to capture all the expert's knowledge, the resulting system will probably be a mid-size system that is easy to develop and field on a PC rather than a much larger project requiring a LISP machine and a much longer development effort.

The discipline required to resist tackling a larger task, just because it's there, and focusing on a subtask will pay handsome rewards in terms of successful early projects that are actually fielded.

Identifying a Tentative Approach to the Problem

Once the scope of the task to be captured in the expert system is determined, the knowledge engineer begins a detailed analysis of the knowledge and the inference processes actually used by the expert.

As the human expert describes how the task is performed, the knowledge engineer thinks about various expert system development tools available for the particular application. Most often the tools are ones with which the knowledge engineer is already familiar. The knowledge engineer characterizes the expertise in terms of a few broad kinds of knowledge representations and inference strategies already seen when developing other systems. In this way, the knowledge engineer starts to develop a model of the expert's knowledge and that, in turn, suggests what particular techniques are required to successfully capture the knowledge and duplicate the expert's reasoning processes.

The current knowledge representation techniques have proved effective in capturing any of the following types of knowledge: procedural knowledge, diagnostic knowledge, monitoring knowledge, scheduling knowledge, and planning knowledge.

Procedural knowledge. Actual procedures play an important role in planning the system. Procedures involve doings things in some order and deciding at some point what to do next. Procedures that remain intact over time can be attacked using conventional programming languages. Conversely, procedures that change frequently would be better accommodated using the modularity provided by a tool.

A problem that is fairly straight procedurally is already close to being algorithmic; thus, an expert system could be built using a conventional programming language like FORTRAN or PASCAL. However, if you decide to forego the programming route and use the sophisticated capabilities provided by a tool, the person building the system will not need to know programming languages and techniques. Choosing a tool is often a fast way to develop a system to help somebody perform a procedure or solve a problem.

An example of this would be using a tool to build a system to assist and give decision-making advice to a clerk. You already know what procedures the clerk performs, so you set up a small system using a few rules to assist the clerk in making decisions. Thus, for example, systems have been developed to provide clerical personnel with assistance in determining available vacation days. A system like this can be put together using a conventional programming language, but it will take considerably longer and be more expensive. The true qualifier here is, how much will the knowledge change over time?

Diagnostic knowledge. Most expert systems being built are diagnostic systems, not procedural systems. Diagnostics refers to the fact that the knowledge needed to run the system is generally limited and is assembled by observation and fact gathering. For example, a doctor would ask questions about the patient, examine lab results, make assumptions that the malady is one of a few particular diseases that correspond to the symptoms, and then prescribe the appropriate drugs to treat the disease. The idea is that you know in advance what your goals are; you know the end at which you are going to arrive, so you can select among the goals by examining elements in the surrounding environment.

Monitoring knowledge. Many monitoring systems are really just diagnostic systems that run over and over. An example of monitoring is a small expert system that analyzes a patient's condition using sensor data and simple rules. The system takes the data in, runs the system, and then tells you the patient is all right; cycling continuously. As fast as it completes an analysis, it redoes it again.

Configuration and design knowledge. Several expert systems have been built that configure or design hardware. Configuration involves examining an initial set of requirements or constraints and then determining what additional items are required and how they all fit together.

Scheduling and planning knowledge. The type of expert systems that have been operating outside of research and development environments have tended to be systems that schedule activities on shop floors, schedule the processes in chemical plants, and perform different types of strategic planning tasks. With planning and scheduling systems, you work with large numbers of knowledge variables and need good ways to represent the complex relationships existing between the variables.

As a general rule, small to mid-size rule systems are good for procedures, diagnostics, and monitoring tasks. For very simple procedures, some mid-size systems are probably too complex.

Configuration problems often call for either rule-oriented or object-oriented approaches, while planning and scheduling problems almost always call for object-oriented or semantic net representations typically found only in the hybrid, LISP-based tools.

For your first system, if you want an easy success, try a diagnostic task. A lot of literature is written about these systems that can be of great benefit to you.

Knowledge Collection

Once a knowledge engineer has a clear idea of the dimensions of knowledge used to develop the system and has identified the structure of the problem and the information needed to solve the problem, it is time to begin collecting the knowledge. This stage of development is often difficult and typically requires the most time and effort.

The knowledge engineer follows three basic steps to obtain knowledge from human experts. First, the knowledge engineer becomes familiar with the specifics of the problem. This can include becoming familiar with any particular jargon or terminology associated with the problem. It also includes becoming familiar with the procedures the expert uses to solve the problem manually.

Second, the knowledge engineer interviews the human expert, discussing the problem, the expert's job functions, the expert's problem-solving techniques, and any sources of additional information about the problem. Many knowledge engineers take extensive notes or use tape recorders to keep track of all the information they gather during their interviews.

Third, the knowledge engineer observes the human expert on the job. This allows the knowledge engineer to collect additional information that may be inadvertently omitted during the interview. It also points out any discrepancies that may result during the interviews and enables the knowledge engineer to gather information to eliminate missing information.

Once the knowledge engineer feels comfortable with the amount of information collected and understands the problem and its environment, it is time to begin developing the prototype of the system.

SUMMARY

Several activities are undertaken before making a decision to develop an expert system. These fall into the general areas of front end analysis and task analysis. *Front end analysis* includes deciding on an expert systems development strategy, identifying a problem domain and a specific task, describing the overall objective of the project, identifying a problem/opportunity, and being certain the problem/opportunity is well and narrowly defined. You also consider what size system to use, how to field it, and what costs and benefits are involved. Often you may want to analyze the return on investment. Once these steps are completed, you prepare a specific development plan, including potential physical implementation problems and personnel problems, interdepartmental impacts, and long-term benefits. Pitfalls to avoid include: (1) choosing the wrong problem, (2) choosing a problem that is too large, (3) having insufficient management commitment, (4) underestimating the cost of the system, and (5) underestimating the difficulty in building it. Finally, you establish benchmarks for determining if you have succeeded.

The second phase, *task analysis*, is critical to building a successful system. Task analysis is a detailed look at exactly what the expert does to define the precise portion of the task to encode into an expert system. Do not attempt to isolate *all* the steps. Concentrate on the 80 percent or so that the expert is confident of. This can include procedural knowledge, diagnostic knowledge, monitoring knowledge, configuration, scheduling, or planning.

12

Phases 3, 4, and 5: Prototype Development, System Development, and Field Testing

INTRODUCTION

This chapter describes some heuristics to consider when you begin developing an expert system. The comments are most relevant for those developing mid-size systems.

The idea of beginning by developing a prototype derives from larger development efforts. The prototype was originally conceptualized as a fairly complete small version of a portion of the large system, developed to prove the full-scale development effort was justified. When developing a small to mid-size system, you often develop a prototype simply to have a system to show users to acquaint them with what a full-size system will look like and to get their feedback on the overall interface you are proposing.

A prototype is developed by entering some knowledge, testing it with case studies, and then entering more knowledge. A full system is developed by doing more of the same. Hopefully, by the time you develop the prototype, you understand the overall task well enough that you can determine the final structure of the context tree if you are developing a structured rule system, but in many cases even the basic structures need to be revised as the system is developed further. Hence, the distinction between prototype and final system is really rather arbitrary. By the same token, field testing is nominally done after the system is complete, but, in fact, larger systems are never complete, and field testing is often just the point at which you let users begin to test the system under field conditions. In most cases field testing leads to another round of revisions and additions.

The tasks outlined in this chapter assume you have already successfully completed the first two phases, the front end and task analysis.

The procedures described here are derived from small and mid-size system development efforts using commercially developed building tools. The procedures are only a limited subset of the procedures a knowledge engineer working in LISP on a hybrid tool such as ART, KEE, or Knowledge Craft would employ.

PHASE 3. PROTOTYPE DEVELOPMENT

The actual development of an expert system begins in earnest when the knowledge engineer and the human expert work together to create the prototype system, a small working version of an expert system designed to test assumptions about how to encode the facts, relationships, and inference strategies of the expert. The activity also gives the knowledge engineer the opportunity to engage the expert actively in system development, and, as a result, to gain the expert's commitment to expend considerable effort required for full-scale system development (Phase 4).

Developing the prototype system includes the following tasks:

- Learning about the domain and the task.
- Specifying performance criteria.
- Developing an initial implementation.
- Testing the implementation with case studies.
- Developing a detailed design for a complete expert system.

Learning More about the Domain and the Task

This stage begins with the knowledge engineer making an intensive effort to learn as much as possible about the problem domain and the tasks required of the human expert. In a sense, this is just an extension of task analysis.

Usually, the knowledge engineer reviews documents and reads books to become familiar with the problem domain before serious discussions and interviews with the expert begin. When the knowledge engineer feels confident with a grasp of the problem domain, a dialogue is initiated with the human expert. This helps define the task further. At the same time the knowledge engineer teaches the expert to formulate the inherent knowledge in terms of heuristics and to elucidate any inference strategies.

The knowledge engineer generally asks the expert to identify four or five typical cases previously solved. The expert assembles all the documentation associated with these cases and furnishes it to the knowledge engineer for analysis. At this time the expert and knowledge engineer discuss the cases, and the knowledge engineer listens while the expert describes the approach used for each case. This dialogue provides a step-by-step protocol that can be used to develop a solution to each particular problem case.

The knowledge engineer asks the expert to think out loud and to explain the reasoning processes behind each decision. In addition, the knowledge engineer may ask the expert to justify the reasoning used. Whenever possible, the reasoning processes the expert employs are formulated into rules-of-thumb. This helps the knowledge engineer clarify the expert's analytic activity and also teaches the expert how to formulate knowledge into if–then rules. Examining the expert's problem-solving procedure and the heuristics helps the knowledge engineer to identify facts and relationships particularly important to the expert's reasoning.

While learning about the expert's problem-solving strategies and heuristics, the knowledge engineer also considers similar situations where like heuristics and strategies were used to develop other systems. The knowledge engineer asks questions to classify the knowledge structures and the inference strategies into one of several broad categories well recognized by knowledge engineers.

Among the questions knowledge engineers ask are the following:

- Is knowledge sparse and insufficient or plentiful and redundant?
- Is there uncertainty attached to the facts and rules?
- Does interpretation depend on the event occurring over time?
- How is task information acquired or elicited?
- What classes or questions need to be asked to obtain the knowledge?
- Are facts reliable, accurate, and precise (hard)? Or are facts unreliable, inaccurate, or imprecise (soft)?
- Is knowledge consistent and complete for the problems to be solved?

Specifying Performance Criteria

Formulating specific performance criteria focuses the knowledge engineer's attention on the precise nature of the initial conditions and the final output the system is expected to produce. In the process of determining exactly what the expert does, the knowledge engineer begins to refine the performance criteria by which the prototype system is to be judged.

The performance criteria should be outlined in unequivocal terms. Perhaps the system is expected to reach the same conclusions the expert reached on five specific cases. Or perhaps the system is expected to reach the same conclusions as five experts on five as yet unspecified cases, under the typical conditions the experts experience. Whatever the criteria, it must be specified so a test can be conducted to prove the knowledge engineer has successfully completed the knowledge acquisition activities.

Developing an Initial Implementation

After selecting the building tool to use for system development, the knowledge engineer starts developing the prototype as soon as the first case study is reasonably well understood and clear. The following discussions assume you are the knowledge engineer.

In developing a small expert system, the prototype and development stages follow a three-step process. First, enter "fast and dirty" rules to capture the knowledge to include in the system. Then, make any changes in the rules to get the consultation to ask questions in the proper order. And, finally, go back and polish the entire knowledge base and add additional information so the final user interface looks and acts exactly as you want it to. In short, the three steps are:

1. Declarative Knowledge Acquisition (capture basic information and enter into the system).
2. Procedural Arrangement (rearrange clauses and rule order and add confidence factors, etc., to get the overall consultation to run smoothly and effectively).
3. Interface Development (reword rules, add text of questions, displays, and special text entries, and test and revise with the end users to assure that the systems works as designed).

This sequence is not sacred. It doesn't make sense in some cases, and it certainly doesn't apply to non-dialogue systems or systems being developed without using a conventional rule-based chaining tool. However, when this approach does apply, the actual system development is an iterative process where you constantly shift back and forth among the steps. Typically, this three-step process is worked through three times, as illustrated in Figure 12.1.

	Step 1 Declarative	Step 2 Procedural	Step 3 Interface
Phase 3-a Initial Prototype	5-10 rules	Get sequence correct	GET INTERFACE CORRECT
Phase 3-b Complete Prototype	**20-50 rules**	GET SEQUENCE CORRECT	Minimal effort
Phase 4 System Development	**150-500 correct rules**	Get sequence correct	Get interface correct

Figure 12.1 *Emphasis during different steps and phases.*

Phase 3a. The initial prototype. As you can see, Phase 3 is divided into two distinct activities, 3a and 3b. During 3a, creating the initial prototype involves developing a very small prototype to provide managers, experts, or users with an example of the application you are proposing to develop. In some instances this is a vital step to convince management, the expert(s), or others, who may be still unsure or not totally committed that the project will work and is feasible.

To develop this mini-prototype, the knowledge engineer assembles a working version of the system that consists of five to ten rules. The knowledge embedded in the rules need not be very accurate or detailed. These rules typically serve simply to show how the system might ask questions and divide the task into two or three parts. It is important here to make sure you get the correct procedural flow. So, if the system will ask for initial information, this should be indicated, if only in an abbreviated form. Moreover, the sequence of questions should flow naturally.

The greatest emphasis during this first trial run is to fine-tune the user interface. If necessary, bend the wording of the rules to assure that the actual text displayed makes sense to those who look at the mini-system. If your tool allows display screens and explanations that can be attached to attributes, by all means develop them! One primary reason for limiting this first system to about five rules is to be certain you have the time needed to work out a pleasant, effective user interface. To assure this, ask a naive outsider to work through the mini-system several times to identify any bugs. Do this before showing the system to sponsors or management.

Phase 3b. Complete prototype. Once you have successfully completed the initial prototype and it works as designed, and after management gives approval to continue, it is time to develop the prototype system in earnest. During this stage, focus on two goals.

First, capture a significant block of knowledge as a sample. If you must choose, go after two deep branches rather than trying to cover the breadth of your knowledge domain. It is important that your sample knowledge block be deep enough to let you thoroughly test the prototype against selected problems such as those the completed system will be required to solve, so you can discover any inadequacies in your knowledge base structure. Be sure to arrange the broader base of knowledge in your final version in the most effective way.

Second, once you feel you have a good sample of the knowledge, play with the control aspects of your system. This ensures that the procedural aspects of the system flow smoothly. Don't worry about the user interface during this stage. Continue to refine the working mini-system until you are satisfied its performance matches your design.

Testing the Implementation with Case Studies

With the prototype built, you need to test it on a variety of case studies. These tests serve two purposes. They let you determine whether the formalisms used in representing the expert's knowledge are adequate to the tasks posed by the cases. They also enable the expert to see how an expert system uses the information being provided. By taking an active part in the testing, the expert usually becomes more committed to the knowledge acquisition processes. This is particularly critical, because in the next phase of development the expert is asked to interact with the system to fine tune its performance.

Developing a Detailed Design for a Complete Expert System

When the prototype is functioning to your satisfaction, you and the expert are in a good position to assess what will be involved in developing a full-scale system. If the original choice of objects and attributes is awkward, it must be modified. Estimates can be made about the total number of heuristic rules needed to create a complete expert system. Performance criteria can be stated with greater precision. All this information, along with a plan, schedule, and budget, is added to the original system development plans. Thus, the updated plans provide a road map for developing the complete system.

PHASE 4. SYSTEM DEVELOPMENT

Once the prototype is complete and everyone involved with the project is satisfied it can perform as desired, and the design for the complete system will result in an expert system that meets the specified performance criteria, you and the expert are ready to begin expanding the prototype into a complete system. If you did a good job developing the prototype, you now have a fairly firm idea of the type of problems you might encounter when you develop the complete system.

Developing the complete system includes the following activities:

- Implementing the core structure of the complete system.
- Expanding the knowledge base.
- Tailoring the user interface.
- Monitoring the system's performance.

Implementing the Core Structure of the Complete System

An adage popular among knowledge engineers is that it is usually best to throw away the prototype. You will probably want to start creating the knowledge base from scratch. Rules that made sense during the early development may, in retrospect, seem unnecessarily restrictive at this stage of development. Anyway, knowledge engineering tools support rapid prototyping with a minimal investment of time. Therefore, at this stage you can rethink the basic design of the knowledge base. Don't worry about this; it is very common. However, don't go overboard and abandon a particular tool here, in rethinking the basic system design. Instead, expect that the exact list of objects and attributes included in the system will probably change. Hierarchical relationships may need to be rearranged. The exact way inference is handled in the heuristics may be modified as you and the expert realize how the expert's knowledge and problem-solving strategies can be best represented.

Also, any serious problems encountered during prototype development can indicate that a different building tool should be applied to the project. If so, you need to repeat the prototype processes. Under most circumstances, however, the prototype succeeds, but the initial representation of the rules and facts may need some alterations.

During this stage you will go through the three steps outlined in the prototyping process one after another. First you enter as much of the task as possible. Then you polish the procedural sequence, and, finally, you put the user interface in order. If you have to skimp on any tasks at this point, you should probably spend a little less time on the user interface since the next phase involves user testing, and that will force you to focus on cleaning up any problems that might remain in the user interface.

When you begin the third round of development, think about how the final system will operate when complete. Rearrange and experiment with the rules in the prototype system until the knowledge is arranged in a form that supports a smooth consultation. Then reformat and re-enter the knowledge contained in the prototype system. After you accomplish this task, add additional rules to complete the declarative specification of the system.

The reconceptualization of a system usually involves identifying attributes that can be grouped to form new rules. In structured rule-based systems that support objects or contexts, this often involves adding or changing the objects. Either way, all the rules written during the prototype phase are usually heavily edited or re-entered. This occurs primarily because of what was learned in Phase 3b, when you tried to polish the procedural flow of your initial knowledge. You will normally discover that the declarative knowledge is correct, but that a different rule format will make it easier to control the procedural flow.

Consider a simple example. You are working with a committee to develop a Restaurant Selection Guide for an upcoming convention. At your first meeting you discuss the features convention attendees want to consider when selecting a place to eat. You develop a "rule template" to capture all the initial information. One rule looks like this:

IF	The establishment you want advice about IS A restaurant
AND	You would prefer a restaurant that IS A 5-minute walk
AND	The food served IS Seafood
AND	The atmosphere you desire IS Pleasant but crowded
AND	The comfort level IS Businesslike
AND	The view you desire IS Not important
AND	The clients ARE Mostly business people and tourists
AND	The price of a typical entree IS $8 to $18
AND	Standard credit cards ARE Accepted
AND	Reservations ARE Not accepted
AND	The number in your party IS Eight or less
Then	A restaurant to consider IS Scott's
AND	DISPLAY Scott's

This information could just as well have been conceptualized as a matrix, with the criteria along the vertical axis and a list of restaurants along the horizontal axis. In fact, after developing the "template," you might develop a worksheet that local chapter members could use to rate restaurants. You might also develop four rules and put them into a small tool to demonstrate how the final system might look.

Since there were only four rules in the system and since the committee didn't really think about it, the initial system impressed them. If you consider the problem a little longer, however, you can see that if the final system is made up of rules like this, it will not be very useful. The effect of having all the information in one rule is that you can make an all-or-none decision out of it. In other words, if you liked everything about Scott's and Scott's had a spectacular view besides, you would not want to eliminate Scott's from consideration.

Using the previous simple rule system, different results may occur depending on the tool used. Some will identify the price range, the number in the party, and the type of food—the true all-or-none aspects of the decision. Others will consider things like view or atmosphere and add or subtract confidence to specific recommendations. In other words, the rule captures the basic information but doesn't facilitate the correct consultation flow. Figure 12.2 illustrates how you might group attributes and add "screening" rules to facilitate a better consultation.

By the same token, after working with the prototype, you may decide to incorporate a conventional data base into your system, or you may decide you need to use some sort of control cycling or limited forward chaining. In most cases you can avoid worrying about these things during the prototype phase and simply "fake it" using rules and backward chaining. However, once the number of rules starts to become large, you need to deal with these matters.

Expanding the Knowledge Base

The main work of the third phase is adding a large number of additional heuristics. These heuristics typically increase the depth of the system by providing more rules for handling subtler aspects of particular cases. At the same time, you and the expert may decide to increase the breadth of the system by incorporating rules that handle additional subproblems or additional aspects of the expert's tasks.

Tailoring the User Interface

Once the basic structure of the system is established, you need to complete the development and refinement of the user interface. This is the interface the end user will use to interact with the system. Considerable attention is given to introducing phrases and explanations to make it easy for end users to follow the logic of the system. The system should make it easy and natural for a user to inquire about any details that may need clarification. Graphic representations may be particularly helpful. Likewise, displays that allow users to follow the system's reasoning processes may be a key to selling the system to the users. Friendliness is a virtue. Use it when you build your system.

Monitoring the System's Performance

A good tool provides a knowledge engineering interface that allows the expert to run different types of cases so you can test the system's reasoning processes. This interface enables the expert to walk through a case and ask why particular rules were fired or not fired. This helps the expert identify those points in which additional, specific knowledge is needed to allow the system to reach the appropriate conclusion. By this point in the development process, most experts have learned enough about rule entry that they can enter more rules into the system themselves with little, if any, assistance needed from the knowledge engineer. Thus, this is the beginning of the process during which the knowledge engineer begins to transfer the ownership and control of the system to the expert to polish, elaborate, and ultimately maintain without support from the knowledge engineer.

PHASE 5. FIELD TESTING

One appealing feature of an expert system is that its knowledge base is built incrementally. Because of this, the knowledge base itself doesn't need a formal test phase. In many expert systems, at no point can you say a system is complete, since the information in the

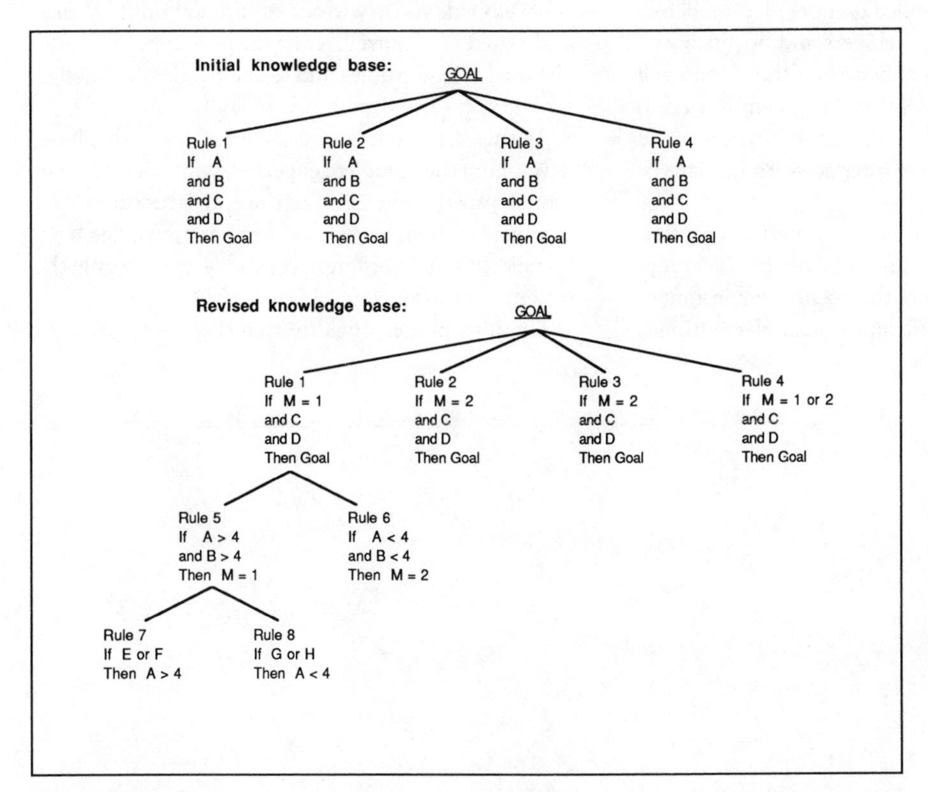

Figure 12.2 *An initial or prototype knowledge base and a revised knowledge base.*

knowledge base is subject to change from outside influences. In judging an expert system the question is not: "Does it meet specifications?" The important question is: "Is the system useful in its present form?" And: "How much more useful can the system become?"

When dealing with small systems there might be no difference between field testing and implementation. For instance, if the system were to be used by only one person in one office, you would have to implement the system to test it. When multiple users are involved, however, it is important to determine that the system actually fits into the work environment so that it is used as intended. For this a limited field test is necessary.

The major purpose of field testing is to determine user acceptance. The knowledge base has already been tested by the experts and the knowledge engineers, the input/output component has already been tested using subjects from the intended user population. Before field testing begins, the developers and buyers of the systems should be reasonably certain the system will deliver the promised benefits if the system is used in the workplace as intended. This is true whether the expert system is intended to interface with humans or with other machines.

There are many reasons why an expert system that produces perfectly good results may not be used properly by employees. Many of the possible environmental and motivational difficulties of implementing a system should have been addressed in the front end analysis phase. Field testing, however, is the only way to be sure your analysis, design, and development efforts have been successful.

SUMMARY

After front end analysis and task analysis are complete, you are ready for the third phase, developing a prototype. This is a small working version of the expert system designed to test your assumptions about encoding the facts, relationships, and inferences strategies of the expert. In this phase you become more specific about the domain and task and you specify performance criteria. Next you develop an initial implementation, the actual prototype. Once the initial prototype is developed, you try it out on a representative user and, based on that trial, refine the prototype. Next you test it with case studies and develop a detailed design for the complete expert system.

At this point you are ready for the fourth phase, developing the complete expert system. This involves four steps: (1) implementing the core structure of the complete system, (2) expanding the knowledge base, (3) tailoring the user interface, and (4) monitoring the system's performance.

The fifth phase is field testing the system.

13

Phases 6 and 7: Implementation and Maintenance

INTRODUCTION

This chapter considers some events that occur after the system is fully developed and tested. First you must actually implement the system, making final connections to existing systems and placing the system on the hardware it will actually be used on. At the same time, you must arrange for ongoing maintenance to remove any bugs in the knowledge base and to keep it up-to-date as knowledge about the task changes.

PHASE 6. IMPLEMENTATION

This phase in the expert systems development process involves installing the completed system in the work environment and training the users and individuals responsible for maintaining the system.

Implementation includes all the procedures necessary to make a new expert system work with the people and the existing systems within an organization. This does not, however, mean making any changes in the expert system itself. If, after the expert system is put to use, it is determined that major modifications to the system are needed, then you have to go back to the prototyping or development phases to make such changes. Don't make major modifications to your system without repeating the steps in the prototype or development stages. You will almost surely wind up wasting a lot of time and effort. Such changes invariably involve a knowledge engineer or someone else able to change the code or structure of the system. *Implementation* refers to developing the linkages between the expert system and the environment in which it operates. This phase is very important since the first-time users are able to evaluate the system and its performance capabilities. Keep in mind that people are naturally resistant to change, and any kind of automation of tasks always has its detractors. As the adage states, "First impressions are lasting."

Implementing an expert system is generally undertaken by the expert and systems personnel associated with the soon-to-be users of the system. Activities that occur during this phase include:

- Arranging the technology transfer.
- Interfacing the system with other data bases, instruments, or other hardware to enhance the speed or friendliness of the system.

Arranging for Technology Transfer

When the expert system is ready, the knowledge engineer must be certain the experts, users, and systems personnel know how to use and maintain the system. Once the knowledge engineer has accomplished this transfer of information and the associated technological know-how, the knowledge engineer usually withdraws from the project, leaving the system in the hands of the users.

Every organization environment offers a different challenge to those responsible for preparing company personnel to accept and use the new system. Experience to date suggests the experts within the company are most often quick to accept and use the system once they become convinced that they can obtain good advice and assistance from it. Convincing experts of the system's usefulness involves having each company expert present cases to the system and then see how the system performs. A critical aspect of acceptance is positioning the system as an aid to free the experts from onerous tasks rather than as a way to replace them.

Convincing nonexpert personnel to accept the system involves all the problems and challenges normally associated with introducing of any new technology to the organization. Here, success is totally dependent on careful planning, a lot of communication, thorough training, appropriate opportunities for all affected individuals to talk about the change, and support once the system is in place.

Without proper training, it will take longer to achieve maximum efficiency using the new system. Training can be either self-paced or more formalized as classes. Whichever method you use, take extra steps to ensure that all system personnel receive complete and thorough training and that they have a good grasp of the overall system operation. Some companies actually use the expert system to conduct training. In this manner, the system becomes the teacher, and the users the students. Of course, this means you must create a modified system that will "teach" in the long run; however, if you will be training a large number of users, the extra cost and effort will pay off. The system will get more use this way.

Interfacing the System with Other Data Bases, Instruments, or Other Hardware

Additional goals in the implementation phase involve interfacing the expert system with any existing data bases and other company systems. An expert system may need to acquire information from instruments or other hardware that will provide input to the system. Still other goals may include enhancing any time-dependent factors in the system to make the system run more quickly or more efficiently, thus enhancing the physical characteristics of the hardware if the system is to run in an unusual environment.

PUFF, the small pulmonary diagnosis system used at the Pacific Medical Center in San Francisco, is a good example of a system that has been well integrated into its working environment. After PUFF was completed and everyone was satisfied it performed as it should, the system was recoded from LISP to BASIC. Once PUFF was recoded, it was transferred to a Digital PDP-11 computer already being used at the hospital. This computer, in turn, was connected to the pulmonary measurement instrument. How does all this technology work? It is really very simple. A patient breathes into a pulmonary machine, the information from the pulmonary machine is fed directly into the PDP-11, and then PUFF processes the raw data and prints out a recommendation for the physician. The physician is not required to interact with PUFF at all. The system is fully integrated into its working environment; it is simply an intelligent extension of the pulmonary machine the doctors have been using for years.

Another system that has been integrated into its environment is General Electric's CATS-1 expert system used for diagnosing diesel locomotive malfunctions. This system was originally developed in LISP and then translated into FORTH so it could be run more efficiently in various locomotive shops. When using the system, a repairperson can interact with the system to determine a probable cause of a diesel malfunction. The system is integrated with a video disk and a video terminal to give the repairperson a visual explanation about any particular checks necessary to rectify a problem. In addition, if the operator is not sure how to fix a particular problem, the system locates the necessary training materials that were previously developed and loaded into the system and displays these materials on the terminal's screen. Thus, the repairperson can use the expert system to diagnose a problem, to verify the exact test procedure to use, to obtain a video display that explains how to make a test, or to obtain instructions related to the problem being diagnosed.

PHASE 7. MAINTENANCE OF THE SYSTEM

When a system is translated into a language such as BASIC to facilitate speed and portability, the system flexibility is often sacrificed. This is acceptable if the system has captured all the knowledge in the problem domain and if the knowledge is not going to change in the foreseeable future. If, however, an expert system has been designed precisely because the problem domain is changing, the system may remain in its development environment to allow for ongoing maintenance activities.

A good example of an expert system implemented in this manner is XCON, the expert system Digital Equipment Corporation uses to configure new VAX computers. A key problem DEC faced was the continuing changes necessitated by new equipment releases, new specifications, and so on. DEC has a staff of about 10 people who continually work to update XCON as changes occur in the parts or patterns used in VAX configurations. Each configuration produced by XCON is checked by one of the human experts who used to do the configuration task. In a very small number of cases (about 2 percent), they spot configurations that the human monitors decide to review in more depth. About half of these reviews result in minor changes in XCON's knowledge base. The highly modularized nature of rule-based systems makes the continual modification of XCON feasible and assures DEC that XCON's recommendations are always up to date.

SUMMARY

Implementing and maintaining an expert system are the last and continuing phases in developing an expert system. They are every bit as important as the preliminary stages. It is during these phases you realize the benefits all the other phases have worked to achieve. If due consideration of the human issues that affect acceptance of the system have been ignored, a lot of work may have been wasted. Likewise, unless an adequate maintenance program is established, the value of the system will deteriorate as the knowledge it contains becomes dated.

Less has been said about implementation and maintenance simply because the field is new and has limited data on the problems of implementing and maintaining mid- to large-size systems in operational settings.

SECTION FOUR

CURRENT EXPERT SYSTEMS APPLICATIONS

In this section you'll be introduced to criteria you might use in selecting an expert system, including size, the types of tasks performed, and several other criteria (Chapter 14). This is followed by an extensive catalog of commercial applications organized by field, e.g., management, financial, marketing, and the like (Chapter 15). The book ends with a brief look at expert systems and the future, and offers ideas on how you might acquire more knowledge and begin to experiment (Chapter 16).

14

An Overview of Current Applications

INTRODUCTION

The following chapter presents examples of expert systems applications. Various criteria are available for deciding what types of applications should be included in such a list.

One prevalent view is that to be called an expert system an application must (1) employ AI programming techniques, and (2) aim at emulating the performance of a human expert. The emphasis here is on the difficulty of the task, with the reasoning that systems performing nonexpert tasks don't deserve to be called expert. This academic or research perspective is entirely appropriate to those operating on the frontiers of computer science.

An opposing view concentrates on the practical uses of these new AI techniques. If AI helps solve a pressing business problem, the business person doesn't much care if the system deserves to be called expert. This book tends to adopt the second view. One exciting area for expert systems is nonprogrammer programming. Using small tools, managers with no conventional programming experience can create simple computer programs to help their staffs perform some tasks. Even if the tasks involve no real expertise, even if the programs could have been more elegantly written using conventional techniques, mid-size knowledge systems are also being used by corporate MIS and data processing personnel to solve many maintenance problems. Such systems should be considered as significant expert systems applications, even though such applications would not receive any attention from academic and research circles.

Another consideration in selecting applications for the catalog in Chapter 15 is how real the application is, that is, what stage of development the application has reached.

The catalog includes only systems that are being used or are ready to be used. A benefit of this approach is that systems on the list are the most real ones available. Be assured the list demonstrates what AI *can* do, not what it *might* do. There is a drawback to this approach, however. The literature is rich with stories of magnificent failures, brilliant ideas as yet untested, systems that would have worked "if only," and systems that "will be available," in most cases "soon." Undoubtedly, in some nonsuccess stories lie the seeds of major future successes. It is beyond the reach of this book, however, to discover those seeds.

One function of this book *is* to introduce the field of expert systems to people who want to know if expert systems might be useful in their workplaces. In this sense, a list of applications is something like a résumé submitted by a job applicant. Few successful applicants submit résumés detailing their failures. Most people have failures in their careers, and a minimally wise employer knows this. Our résumés accentuate the positive not to fool potential bosses, but to communicate clearly what it is we actually can do well. It is in this spirit that the list of fielded applications has been constructed.

The catalog is not complete. The research technique

employed aimed at gathering many examples of many different types of applications. The inclusion or exclusion of any particular application should not be seen as a reflection on the application or the tool vendor.

The list omits military applications, which represent a large part of the AI market. Not only does the required secrecy make reporting difficult, if not illegal, but the funding and performance environments of military applications is so far removed from a profit- or efficiency-driven environment that few business people should look to the military for cues on how to develop expert systems. We assume that major AI breakthroughs of significant civilian benefit will issue from the military's heavy involvement, but we do not attempt to identify or describe the military projects that will lead to major innovations.

Each application in the catalog demonstrates how a particular problem has been solved by an expert system. More importantly, the success of one expert systems application demonstrates that other problems having the same specifications can also be solved. Even if the domains are entirely unrelated, a particular expert systems building approach should be able to solve all problems meeting the same specifications.

THE APPLICATIONS CHART

To help you determine if your business problems meet the same specifications as those of existing applications, an Applications Specifications Chart is provided in Table 14.1 (see pages 208–215). The vertical axis lists the applications in the catalog. The horizontal axis contains the variables found in existing applications. The dots indicate which variables pertain to each expert systems application.

Unfortunately, this chart can be only suggestive of other possible applications. It has captured many important variables to consider when matching a problem to an expert systems development strategy. There are certainly others. Also not included are variables concerning the organizational environment in which the development effort is to take place. It can be a bitter lesson for conscientious technicians to learn that variables arising from the business environment often outweigh purely technical considerations.

Choosing the right tool for a particular problem, which is only one step in a total development effort, is itself an area of considerable expertise, suggesting a potential expert systems application. Why not a "Tool Advisor"? An expert system that takes information about a possible application and recommends the best tool to use seems like an obvious idea for AI developers. Indeed, it is.

At the time of this writing no such expert system has been revealed. A number of companies, consulting firms, and hardware vendors are actively working on this problem, but don't expect to see such a system in the near future. Such a system has yet to appear because (1) the market is too dynamic, and (2) no generally recognized experts have emerged.

Size

The size of a system, usually measured by the number of rules in the knowledge base, is a major determining factor in choosing development and runtime hardware and software, and, obviously, development costs. Rules are a very poor metric. To begin with, the larger systems rely more on objects than on rules. Besides, if a system supports variable rules or contexts, one rule can replace dozens of rules in a simple rule-based tool. Still, for all the problems associated with rules, they are the easiest metric to use. Generally, the categories are:

Small	Up to 500 rules.
Mid-Size	From 500 rules to 1500 rules.
Large	More than 1500 rules, a large number of objects, or a large semantic net.

Many systems are fielded knowing the knowledge base will grow. Frequently the initial knowledge base after shakedown in the real world is used as a paradigm in creating new knowledge bases to be added as fast as the knowledge engineers crank them out.

Task Paradigm

The types of tasks performed by expert systems tend to cluster according to the problem-solving approach.

Diagnostic. A diagnostic system starts with an existing problem with known recommendations you can choose from based on specific observations data. The systems endeavor to recommend the best remedy for the problem. This category includes medical diagnosis, mechanical problem diagnosis, crop disease diagnosis, and the diagnosis of wrong answers on students' homework.

Monitoring. A monitoring system keeps track of performance over time, whether of humans, machinery, or weather. The system compares this performance data to a model of expected performance. Discrepancies are identified and remedies recommended. In some equipment monitoring systems, the output consists of direct adjustments to operating controls.

Configuring. A configuring task is one in which a finite number of components are arranged in one of millions of possible combinations to meet specific needs. An architect's job is essentially one of configuring. There is a finite number of types of building materials an architect could possibly use. For each new building architects design, they choose some of the possible building materials and configure them in an original way to meet the developer's needs. Configuring tasks are data driven, implying a forward chaining control strategy, rather than goal driven, implying backward chaining control. Obviously, the number of possible architectural designs (goals) is infinite, and a system cannot examine an infinite number of goals.

Planning. Planning tasks are similar to scheduling tasks except that the variables or objects are unknown from task to task.

Scheduling. The purpose of scheduling tasks is to coordinate the capabilities of independent elements within an operating organization to increase efficiency. One measure of efficiency is machine and worker downtime; the less time spent not working, the greater the efficiency.

This is an easy measure for a factory that produces only one product. The situation is more complicated when the same machinery is used on different products. An efficient schedule for people and equipment must change in response to changes in the volume of new orders, changes in products, and changes in the competitive environment. The ideal scheduling expert system would constantly monitor performance and fine-tune the schedule as needed.

Scheduling applications tend to emphasize the relationships among objects and, thus, tend to demand object-based or structured rule knowledge bases.

Development Software

This column of Table 14.1 tells the kind of software used to develop a system. For the specific software used, consult the application description in Chapter 15.

Knowledge Representation

This column tells how the knowledge base is constructed. Inductive tools represent knowledge as matrices. Rule-based tools use rules; structured rule-based tools separate knowledge in hierarchically arranged multiple knowledge bases; and object-based or frame-based tools represent knowledge as mini kb's that can interrelate in any way desired.

Function of System

This column indicates how the system interrelates with other computer systems in the workplace. Standalone systems produce usable output by themselves. Front-end expert systems are attached to conventional

Table 14.1 *An analysis of some fielded expert systems.*

APPLICATIONS		AGRICULTURE					COMPUTER				
	VARIABLES / EXPERT SYSTEM	AQUAREF	PEANUT/PEST	PURDUE GRAIN MKT. ADVISOR	WHEAT COUNSELOR	PLANTING	XCON	CABLING CONFIGURATION	CONAD	CSF ADVISOR	DASD ADVISOR
1. OVERALL SIZE	Small	●	●			●					
	Mid-size				●					●	●
	Large			●			●	●	●		
2. TASK PARADIGM	Diagnostic	●	●		●	●					●
	Monitoring										●
	Configuring						●	●	●		
	Planning			●						●	
	Scheduling										
3. DEVELOPMENT SOFTWARE	Language										
	Environment						●				
	Tool (Shell)	●	●	●	●	●		●	●	●	●
4. KNOWLEDGE REPRESENTATION	Inductive	●									
	Rule-Based		●	●	●		●			●	●
	Frame/Object-Based					●		●	●		
5. FUNCTION OF SYSTEM	Standalone	●	●	●	●	●	●	●	●	●	●
	Front-end	●									
	Enhanced Conv. Sys.										
6. SOURCE OF INPUT	Signal Processing										●
	Dialogue	●	●	●	●	●	●	●	●	●	●
7. DELIVERY HARDWARE	Personal Computer	●	●	●	●	●					●
	UNIX/VAX Workstation						●				
	LISP Workstation							●			
	Mainframe								●	●	●
8. COMMERCIAL STATUS	For sale			●							●
	For internal use	●	●			●	●	●			
	Packaged				●				●	●	
9. DEVELOPER	Non-programmer	●	●								
	Internal MIS/Appl.										
	Internal Know. Eng.			●	●	●	●	●	●	●	●
	Outside Consult (KE)						●	●	●		

COMPUTER															EQUIPMENT		
DIA 8100	DRAGON	ESPm	INTELLIGENT PERIPHERAL	INTELL. SOFT-WARE CONFIG.	MASK	OCEAN	PERMAID	PRESS	REQUIREMENTS ANALYST	SITE LAYOUT ADVISOR	SNAP	SYSCON	TIMM TUNER	TITAN	ACE	CATS (DELTA)	COMPASS
●					●				●		●						
			●	●				●					●	●	●	●	
	●	●				●	●			●		●					●
●			●		●		●	●	●		●		●	●	●	●	●
		●													●		
	●			●		●				●		●					
				●						●					●	●	
						●		●				●			●		
●	●	●	●		●		●	●	●		●	●	●	●			●
					●								●	●			
●		●		●				●	●		●	●			●	●	
	●		●			●	●			●							●
●	●		●	●	●	●		●	●	●	●	●	●	●	●	●	
		●					●										●
		●					●										●
●	●		●	●	●	●		●	●	●	●	●	●	●	●	●	
●					●				●		●			●		●	
		●	●			●		●					●				
	●						●			●		●					●
				●													
●									●				●		●		
	●	●	●	●	●	●	●	●			●	●		●		●	●
															●		
	●	●	●	●		●				●		●	●	●	●	●	●
●					●	●	●	●	●		●					●	

Table 14.1 *Continued.*

APPLICATIONS		EQUIPMENT									
	VARIABLES / EXPERT SYSTEM	IDEA	BDS	CORROSION EXPERT	GEMS TTA	HOIST DIAGNOSER	HOTLINE HELPER	IMP	MENTOR	PAGE 1	PUMP PRO
1. OVERALL SIZE	Small					●					
	Mid-size	●	●	●			●	●	●		●
	Large				●					●	
2. TASK PARADIGM	Diagnostic	●	●	●	●	●	●	●	●	●	●
	Monitoring				●						
	Configuring										
	Planning										
	Scheduling										
3. DEVELOPMENT SOFTWARE	Language			●					●	●	●
	Environment										
	Tool (Shell)	●	●		●	●	●	●			●
4. KNOWLEDGE REPRESENTATION	Inductive										
	Rule-Based	●	●	●	●	●	●	●	●		●
	Frame/Object-Based		●							●	
5. FUNCTION OF SYSTEM	Standalone	●	●	●		●	●	●			●
	Front-end										
	Enhanced Conv. Sys.				●				●	●	
6. SOURCE OF INPUT	Signal Processing				●						
	Dialogue	●	●	●		●	●	●	●	●	●
7. DELIVERY HARDWARE	Personal Computer	●				●	●	●	●		●
	UNIX/VAX Workstation				●						
	LISP Workstation			●						●	
	Mainframe		●								
8. COMMERCIAL STATUS	For sale	●									
	For internal use		●	●	●	●	●	●	●		
	Packaged									●	●
9. DEVELOPER	Non-programmer										
	Internal MIS/Appl.				●						
	Internal Know. Eng.	●	●	●			●		●	●	●
	Outside Consult (KE)			●		●		●			

EQUIPMENT					FINANCIAL												
ROTATING EQUIP. DIAGNOSTIC	TEST DIAGNOSTIC ASST.	TOGA	TROUBLESHOOT-ING AID FOR F6502	TURBOMAT	MANAGEMENT ADVISOR	LENDING ADVISOR	PLANPOWER	UNDERWRITING ADVISOR	AUTHORIZER'S ASST.	EXMARINE	EXPERTAX	CORPORATE FINANCIAL ADV	FOREIGN EX-CHANGE ADV SYS	INGOT	PORTFOLIO MGMT ADVISOR	SALES TAX ADVISOR	TAX
●			●													●	●
		●		●								●	●				
	●				●	●	●	●	●	●	●			●	●		
●	●	●	●	●		●			●	●		●	●			●	●
					●	●	●				●			●	●		
					●		●										
●	●	●	●	●		●			●	●	●	●	●	●	●	●	●
		●		●												●	●
●			●							●		●					
	●				●	●		●	●		●	●	●	●	●		
●			●	●	●	●	●	●	●	●	●	●	●	●	●	●	●
	●	●															
	●	●															
●			●		●	●	●	●	●	●	●	●	●	●	●	●	●
●		●		●				●			●					●	●
			●	●	●									●			
					●		●		●	●		●	●				
	●					●		●						●			
					●	●	●	●				●	●	●	●	●	
		●	●	●					●	●							
●	●										●						
			●														
●		●	●	●	●	●	●	●		●	●	●	●			●	
	●	●		●					●					●	●		

Table 14.1 *Continued.*

APPLICATIONS		MANAGEMENT				MANUFACTURING					
	VARIABLES / EXPERT SYSTEM	COCOMO 1	CAPITAL EXPERT SYSTEMS	PERFORMANCE MENTOR	WELDER QUALIF TEST SELEC SYS	COOKER ADVISOR	ASH MIXER	BRUSH DESIGNER	COMPONENT IMPACT ANAL SYS	CRYSTAL ADVISOR	DISPATCHER
1. OVERALL SIZE	Small	●	●	●	●	●	●				
	Mid-size							●	●	●	
	Large										●
2. TASK PARADIGM	Diagnostic			●	●	●	●		●		
	Monitoring									●	
	Configuring							●			
	Planning	●	●								
	Scheduling										●
3. DEVELOPMENT SOFTWARE	Language		●						●		●
	Environment										
	Tool (Shell)	●	●	●	●	●	●	●		●	
4. KNOWLEDGE REPRESENTATION	Inductive										
	Rule-Based	●	●	●	●	●	●	●	●	●	●
	Frame/Object-Based										
5. FUNCTION OF SYSTEM	Standalone	●	●	●	●	●	●	●		●	
	Front-end										
	Enhanced Conv. Sys.								●		●
6. SOURCE OF INPUT	Signal Processing								●		●
	Dialogue	●	●	●	●	●	●	●		●	●
7. DELIVERY HARDWARE	Personal Computer	●	●	●	●	●	●			●	
	UNIX/VAX Workstation										●
	LISP Workstation							●			
	Mainframe										●
8. COMMERCIAL STATUS	For sale	●		●							
	For internal use		●		●	●	●	●		●	●
	Packaged										
9. DEVELOPER	Non-programmer	●					●				
	Internal MIS/Appl.										
	Internal Know. Eng.				●			●		●	●
	Outside Consult (KE)					●		●	●		

MANUFACTURING								MISC		OFFICE AUTOMATION							OIL
DUSTPRO	EXPERT EXECUTIVE	EXPERT PROBE	FAIS	OLEOPHILIC ADVISOR	UNIT COMMITMENT ADVISOR	WELD SCHEDULER	WELD SELECTOR	CAN AM TREATY	PTE ANALYST	LETTER CREDIT ADVISOR	BUSINESS CLASSIFIER	CLASS	CV FILTER	DATA CLASSIFIER	DATA PROTECTION ACT ADV	WATER PERMIT REVIEW SYSTEM	DRILLING ADVISOR
●										●	●	●	●	●	●		
	●		●	●	●		●	●	●							●	
		●				●											●
●	●						●	●	●	●	●	●	●	●	●	●	●
		●															
				●													
								●									
			●		●	●											
	●																
●		●	●	●	●	●	●	●	●	●	●	●	●	●	●	●	●
●	●		●	●	●		●	●	●	●	●	●	●	●	●	●	●
		●				●											
●	●	●	●	●	●	●	●	●	●	●	●	●		●	●	●	●
●	●	●	●	●	●	●	●	●	●	●	●	●	●	●	●	●	●
●			●	●			●	●	●	●	●	●	●	●	●	●	
	●	●			●	●											●
●							●		●	●			●				
	●	●	●	●		●					●	●		●	●	●	●
					●			●	●								
●											●						
		●		●	●		●	●	●			●		●		●	●
	●	●	●	●		●				●			●		●		●

Table 14.1 *Continued.*

APPLICATIONS		OIL					SCIENCE				
	VARIABLES / EXPERT SYSTEM	CEMENTING EXP SYS	DIPMETER ADVISOR	MUDMAN	SOURCE ROCK ADVISOR	WAVES	DRUG INTERACTION	GENESIS	MICROPROCESSOR ELECTROPHORESIS	DIAGNOSTICS	HELP
1. OVERALL SIZE	Small						●		●	●	
	Mid-size	●		●	●	●					
	Large		●					●			●
2. TASK PARADIGM	Diagnostic	●	●	●	●		●	●	●	●	●
	Monitoring										●
	Configuring										
	Planning					●					
	Scheduling										
3. DEVELOPMENT SOFTWARE	Language										
	Environment			●							●
	Tool (Shell)	●	●		●	●	●	●	●	●	●
4. KNOWLEDGE REPRESENTATION	Inductive										
	Rule-Based	●	●	●	●	●	●		●	●	
	Frame/Object-Based							●			●
5. FUNCTION OF SYSTEM	Standalone	●	●	●	●	●	●	●	●	●	●
	Front-end										
	Enhanced Conv. Sys.										
6. SOURCE OF INPUT	Signal Processing		●			●			●		●
	Dialogue	●	●	●	●		●	●		●	●
7. DELIVERY HARDWARE	Personal Computer	●					●			●	●
	UNIX/VAX Workstation			●				●			
	LISP Workstation		●		●	●		●			
	Mainframe							●			●
8. COMMERCIAL STATUS	For sale		●				●	●		●	●
	For internal use	●	●	●	●	●					
	Packaged								●		
9. DEVELOPER	Non-programmer						●			●	
	Internal MIS/Appl.										
	Internal Know. Eng.	●	●		●			●			●
	Outside Consult (KE)			●		●			●		

SCIENCE										TRAIN-ING		TRANSPORTATION					
HP4760AI ELECTRO-CARDIOGRAPH	IPECAC	MACSYMA	METALS ANALYST	MICRO GENIE	ONCOCIN	POWERCHART	PULMONARY CONSULTANT	SPIN PRO	TQMSTUNE	LISP-ITS	CBT ANALYST	SEATS	AALPS	CHART AND MAP EXPERT SYSTEM	HAZARDOUS CHEMICAL ADV	NAVEX	SAFETY OF LIFE AT SEA
●	●		●					●			●				●		
				●			●			●			●	●			●
		●			●				●			●				●	
●			●	●		●	●		●	●	●			●	●		
																●	
													●				●
					●			●									
												●					
●	●	●			●		●			●	●		●				
				●				●									
	●		●			●			●			●		●	●	●	●
															●		
●	●		●	●	●		●	●		●	●			●			●
	●				●	●			●			●	●			●	
	●	●	●	●	●			●	●	●	●		●	●	●	●	●
							●										
●												●					
●							●		●	●		●				●	
	●	●	●	●	●		●	●			●		●	●	●		●
	●		●	●		●		●			●			●	●		●
		●				●				●			●				
		●			●	●			●	●		●				●	
		●															
		●		●				●		●	●			●	●		
			●		●				●			●	●			●	●
●							●										
								●									
●	●	●	●		●	●	●	●	●	●	●	●		●	●		●
				●			●					●	●			●	

systems at the point where input and user commands are processed. Enhanced conventional systems contain imbedded expert systems that improve the functioning of the conventional system.

Source of Input

This column refers to the way in which functioning expert systems receive data they then process. Two general modes of input are dialogue and signals. In dialogue systems a human tells the computer the facts to consider. Sometimes the information is given all at once; in other cases the human enters information in response to questions in a back-and-forth dialogue. Signal processing systems, in essence, receive their input data from other machines. For example, a dialogue system might ask a repairperson about the temperature of a malfunctioning machine, whereas a signal-processing system would have a sensor attached to the particular machine to constantly track its temperature.

The same categories hold true for the mode of output. An expert system can produce recommendations in the form of printouts, which the user then executes, if desired. Or a system could produce output in the form of signals to other machines.

Delivery Hardware

This column indicates the type of hardware a system uses in the workplace, as opposed to the hardware used in development.

An asterisk in this column indicates that the program resides on hardware at the vendor's premises.

Commercial Status

This column indicates if and how a system might be available. Buying an expert system listed "for sale" could be as simple as a visit to your corner software emporium. On the other hand, a large system could take months to tailor and install. Even more significantly, many large systems imply serious reorganization of user groups. The cost, both monetary and emotional, of reorganization to accommodate a large system is a serious consideration in such a purchase. A large system that performs even better than the experts could easily fail if the necessary reorganization is impossible or too costly.

Often large systems are sold in a package that includes on-site consulting by the vendor to make sure the system gets up and running. This is *not* what is meant by "packaged with other items." This refers to goods and services that include expert systems. An accountant, for instance, might develop an expert system to help with estate planning. He uses this system for clients requiring such advice, but doesn't sell it to other accountants or the general public. Another entry in this category would be a system that is imbedded in a piece of machinery.

Developer

This column indicates who built the system. Many systems are developed by combinations of these categories, indicated by multiple bullets.

15

A Catalog of Commercial Applications

MANAGEMENT APPLICATIONS

In one sense most computer programs, including expert systems, are management applications. A major management responsibility is to modify the work environment to produce greater efficiency; installing computer programs is one of many methods.

In this catalog, this category has been reduced by putting many applications into other domains. PlanPower, for instance, which aids managers in financial decision making, has been placed under financial applications though it could just as well go here. What is here are applications that try to capture generic management decision-making skills.

In general, the goals of management applications are increased accuracy and completeness, as opposed to work force reduction or similar efficiencies. At the upper end these systems have to be seen as "peer counselors" discussing problems with managers rather than processing input and dictating a solution. As in medicine, business demands that important decisions be made by humans; responsibility can't be passed to a machine. Machines that provide intelligent suggestions can help the human managers who must ultimately make the decisions.

In a dialogue system, expert users should gain at least a general feeling for how their input affects the program's output. Thus, the input data can be massaged until the output is satisfactory. This shouldn't be seen as an attempt to defeat the system. Massaging or reconfiguring the input is exactly what a manager is supposed to do, and a good expert system should support this process.

Smaller management applications provide assistance at the supervisory level. A major demand in this area is for systems that help supervisors evaluate the performance of their subordinates. Often technicians are promoted to supervisory positions, not because of demonstrated supervisory skills, but because of superior technical skills. Development of supervisory skills, such as time management or interpersonal communications, within this population has been a major concern of the performance improvement community.

Cocomo 1

Date: 1985.

Domain. Scheduling and person-loading of software development projects.

Description: Cocomo 1 is a small system that helps engineers and managers schedule and person-load software development projects. It was developed with Insight 2, a small, rule-based, backward chaining tool.

The Cocomo 1 system software consists of Insight 2, CocomoA, CocomoB, CocomoC, and CocomoD. The four Cocomo knowledge bases are derived from the Cocomo software cost models developed by Barry

W. Boehm at TRW. Cocomo 1 uses Insight 2's ability to access dBASE II and is supported by subroutines written in Turbo PASCAL.

Planners can use the system in any one or all four different ways:

- To determine which knowledge base is appropriate for the costing analysis at hand (CocomoA).
- To reduce the effort associated with converting inherited code to the new product (CocomoB).
- To predict the effort and schedule needed to implement a total product (CocomoC or CocomoD).
- To predict the effort and schedule needed to implement single modules or elements that are to make up an entire software product (CocomoC or CocomoD).

As a result of a typical interactive session, Cocomo 1 produces schedule report forms with predictions of:

- The effects of modifying inherited code.
- Various development and maintenance effort multipliers.
- The maintenance in person-months required during program development.
- Programmer productivity in lines of code per month.
- The total person-months and development time by the project phases of planning and requirements, product design, programming, integration, and testing.
- The cost of program development.
- The cost of maintenance by completed project.
- Optimal distribution of personnel.

Performance/Benefits: Cocomo 1 has been used to estimate the software development costs on software-intensive development projects for the Federal Aviation Administration at the Jet Propulsion Laboratory. Cocomo 1 is not expected to outperform human experts. It is expected to increase the consistency with which the Cocomo model is applied and makes it possible for those not trained in Cocomo cost modeling to use the model to develop reasonable estimates and schedules.

Hardware required: PC/AT/XT or true compatible with 512K memory.

Development: Cocomo 1 was developed by Phil Chapman at the CIT Jet Propulsion Laboratory.

Commercial status: Cocomo 1 is currently sold by Level Five Research, the software company that developed and sells the Insight tools. The price at presstime is $485, which includes documentation and user support.

Contact:

Cornelius Willis
Level Five Research, Inc.
503 Fifth Avenue
Indialantic, FL 32903
(305) 729-9046

Additional Management Applications

CAPITAL EXPERT SYSTEMS

DEV. SOFTWARE	Personal Consultant Plus
DOMAIN	Helps prepare proposals for purchase of capital equipment.
CONTACT	Texas Instruments Incorporated P.O. Box 2909—M/S 2244 Austin, TX 78759 (512) 250-6785

PERFORMANCE MENTOR

DEV. SOFTWARE	Exsys
DOMAIN	Guides managers in shaping the performance of subordinates.
CONTACT	Garrett T. Browning AI Mentor Inc. 1000 Elwell Court, Suite 205 Palo Alto, CA 94303-4306 (415) 969-4500

WELDER QUALIFICATION TEST SELECTION SYSTEM

DEV. SOFTWARE	Exsys
DOMAIN	Helps managers select from many possible tests those needed for a particular job.
CONTACT	Gavin Finn Stone and Webster Engineering 245/10 Summer Street Boston, MA 02107 (617) 589-1567

FINANCIAL APPLICATIONS

Financial expertise has been a major target of expert systems developers because the market is huge at both ends. At the low end, nearly everyone has an active interest in maximizing their financial positions. People find themselves making important financial decisions without the benefit of helpful advice. The expertise is either unavailable, too expensive, or too difficult to access.

For example, millions of people a year go into new car showrooms thinking they will obtain a better deal if they negotiate with the salesperson. Poor lambs! The salesperson negotiates more deals in a month than most people negotiate in a lifetime. An expert system that captures a dealer's expertise would sell like hotcakes. Such an expert system would analyze a dealer's offer and respond with a counteroffer, proceeding until a deal is struck.

The upper end of the financial applications market is large, not because of a high number of potential clients—there are only so many major financial institutions—but because the stakes are so high. An expert system that could nudge a particular balance sheet amount two or three percentage points in the right direction might add millions of dollars to a large institution's net profit.

The fact that small changes in large amounts produce large amounts shows that an expert system needn't duplicate the performance of an expert to be successful. In many circumstances almost any improvement has a high payoff. In these cases, an expert system can't be criticized for only partially closing the gap between expert and average performers.

The Management Advisor

Date: 1986.

Domain: Assists corporate managers with business planning. Palladian Software.

Updates: Provided by vendor as part of the annual support package.

Description: Palladian's product is structured internally as a hybrid. The different types of knowledge included in the system are each handled in a manner that best suits the character of the knowledge itself. The system includes rule-based, object-oriented, constraint propagation, and semantic net techniques all modified into a basic underlying shell.

The program includes a random correction internal spreadsheet, data base, and graphic capabilities. The current version of the Management Advisor requires the user to enter project forecasts directly. The next release of the product will allow loading information from PC-based spreadsheets.

The user interface has some Macintosh-like elements such as pull-down menus and graphics that can be manipulated using a mouse. Basically, a session with this system involves a sequence that consists of building a base case, evaluating it, running what if tests on it, modifying it, and producing reports about it for review and decision making.

A session with the Management Advisor is an interactive, iterative process that enables users to see the financial impacts of each element of a management proposal and make adjustments accordingly. The system offers three windows of communication with the user: the control panel, the dialogue window, and the spreadsheet/graphics window. Base-case data is entered partly in response to questions and partly by filling in cells on a spreadsheet. Evaluation (which can involve rating and describing the sensitivity of proposed case variables; calculating the impact of any case scenario on such factors as internal rate of return, return on investment, net present value, and so on; coincidental calculation of impact on cash and book value; or determining the impacts of competition) can involve the dialogue, spreadsheet, and graphics windows (the graphics window illustrates spreadsheet information in a variety of chart formats). Testing can be done backward or forward. Moving a line with the mouse on a graphics window changes all corresponding spreadsheet information to reflect the graphic change. Likewise, if data in a cell of a spreadsheet are changed, all graphics and dialogue reflects the change.

A "road map" shows you where you are and where you can be at any point in the session. This is handy since a session typically involves so much iterative jumping around. When the base cases have been refined as much as possible, a series of reports can be created by the system for presentation and decision-making purposes. The user can choose just which information is important for presentation given the interests of the decision makers, but corporate executives may want to consider more information than they traditionally have, since this system makes so much so available.

Users of Management Advisor can modify the system to automatically reflect their own operating assumptions and management policies. This can be accomplished at various levels in the knowledge base, depending on the access provided by the user's password. All changed or modified assumptions are marked so they can be audited by management. In a multiprocessor configuration linked to a common file server, much of this information can be kept current on the file server for use at every workstation. In addition to the tailoring assumptions process for customizing the knowledge base, individual users can affect the outcome of a particular session by overriding some of the red-flag conflicts the system points out. These overrides tell the system not to worry about the overridden factor in its considerations. All such overrides are marked for later reference.

Hardware required:

Symbolics 3600 series
TI Explorer
Apollo DN3000

Development: The Management Advisor was developed from scratch in LISP on a Symbolics machine, and the commercial version runs on the LISP machines available from Symbolics and Texas Instruments.

Commercial status: This program is for sale for $15,000. For this, one receives:

- Software for one standalone workstation.
- Support: 15 percent of purchase price annually for support, enhancements, and updates.

Contact:

Palladian Software, Inc.
Four Cambridge Center
Cambridge, MA 02142
(617) 661-7171

Lending Advisor

Date: 1987.

Domain: Assists credit managers in analyzing commercial loan applications and structuring appropriate loan packages.

Description: Lending Advisor is a large, multi-user, generic expert system that evaluates commercial loan applications, defines the level of potential risk associated with loans, and helps structure loans accordingly. In addition, this system reviews existing loans, evaluating the borrowers' current financial condition to red-flag potential problems and suggest remedial action. The Lending Advisor is intended for use by credit managers when reviewing or managing commercial loans for middle-market companies ($5 million to $100 million annual sales).

Lending Advisor is aimed at high-end banks and lending institutions that employ large numbers of credit officers working in dispersed locations. The system is designed to allow such institutions to apply consistent management policy to loan decisions and to improve tracking of loan decision-making at the level of the credit officer.

The Lending Advisor package includes installation, training, and custom programming support. Each installation requires custom enhancement of the knowledge base to reflect the unique policies and operating assumptions of the company, as well as custom interface programming to create hooks between the program and the company's existing data base.

Lending Advisor has a polished user interface. Case information is entered on a sequence of "dynamic forms." The system automatically skips forms that ask for information with no bearing on the case at hand and leads the user through the relevant forms by highlighting the blanks in order of their importance. The system works with whatever case information the user is able to provide, even if incomplete. Red-flag alerts are required whenever unacceptable case conditions (inconsistent data or high risk) are entered into the case file. Users can ask for evaluations of the case at any point or in any context. Evaluations are expressed with graphic "assessment meters" which also indicate the degree of certainty with which the evaluation is made (based partly on the amount of relevant case data supplied). An evaluation tells the user what the problem is if any risk is determined, and the user can then respond by overriding the system's concern.

Users can inquire at any time about the sequence of reasoning that led to any particular conclusion (an audit trail) and can review summary reports that list all red-flag alerts and overridden alerts. These features can be of particular value to management when reviewing the activities of credit officers.

Development: Development of Lending Advisor began in 1984. The first prototype was created on a Xerox D series machine using Syntelligence's own LISP-based tool called Syntel, an enhanced version of KAS, the tool developed by the Syntelligence team at SRI when they developed Prospector.

The program was developed with the help of Wells Fargo Bark and First Wachovia Bank of Winston-Salem. Three senior lending and credit officers from each bank dedicated several days a month to review and advise on the details of the system. In addition to the two major development partners, Syntelligence has established relationships with about 12 other banks that acted as advisors on the project in exchange for the opportunity to learn more about the technology.

Hardware required: IBM mainframe (30/40 series) connected to 3260 PC terminals.

Commercial status: The system is for sale; and starts at about $450,000 and can go up to $1.5 million.

Contact:

Syntelligence
1000 Hamlin Court
P.O. Box 3620
Sunnyvale, CA 94088
(408) 745-6666

Underwriting Advisor

Date: 1987.

Domain: Evaluates risk in insurance applications to determine pricing. For use by field underwriters in commercial property, workers' compensation, inland marine, general liability, and commercial auto insurance.

Description: Underwriting Advisor is a large multi-user, generic expert system. Underwriting Advisor evaluates commercial insurance applications, defining the types and levels of risk involved in insuring the applicant and allowing underwriters to make fully informed evaluation and pricing decisions for each risk. In addition, each application can be stored for periodic review as conditions change. Underwriting Advisor is intended for use by field underwriters.

Syntelligence is aiming Underwriting Advisor at insurance companies that collect at least $100 million in annual premiums and that have IBM 30/40 mainframe systems. These companies are likely to have large numbers of underwriters located throughout the country or the world. It is designed to provide consistent application of management policy and corporate knowledge to the field-level decisions directly tied to the financial health of the company.

Underwriting Advisor is packaged with installation, training, and custom programming support. Syntelligence assumes most customers will already have the required hardware, and the customer will go directly to the hardware vendor for any hardware enhancements it may wish. Each installation involves enhancement of the knowledge base to include corporate knowledge (company proprietary expertise and standards) and custom interface programming to create hooks to the user's data base.

Development: Development of Underwriting Advisor took place with three development partners: American International Group, Inc., the Saint Paul Companies, Inc., and Fireman's Fund Insurance Companies. Each partner is contributing money as well as time to the effort and currently is testing a LISP version of the product on Xerox D machines. Underwriting Advisor is also being recorded in PL/1 and C for IBM mainframes with an XA/CISC environment. This will allow underwriters to access the system using terminals.

The program includes internal data base capabilities, and each running system will have an individually programmed interface to outside data bases. Underwriting Advisor has multiple knowledge bases, one for each line of insurance. A system can contain any or all of the line-specific knowledge base modules.

In this system knowledge is represented as a semantic net, with thousands of nodes and tens of thousands of relationships between nodes.

Hardware required: IBM mainframe (30/40 series) connected to 3260 PC terminals.

Commercial status: For sale; depending on options selected, the price ranges from $850,000 to $1.5 million.

Contact:

Syntelligence
1000 Hamlin Court
P.O. Box 3620
Sunnyvale, CA 94088
(408) 745-6666

PlanPower

Date: 1986.

Domain: Helps financial institutions analyze personal needs of clients to offer investment or other financial advice.

Description: PlanPower is a generic expert system for personal financial planning, intended for financial planners who are developing personal financial plans for upscale clients.

Applied Expert Systems (Apex) intends to sell the product to financial institutions that are creating or expanding their capabilities in response to the ongoing deregulation of the financial industry.

PlanPower is packaged as a complete turnkey system, which includes Apex's proprietary software spreadsheet. Word processing capabilities are part of this software package.

PlanPower is written in LISP and is basically an object-oriented system. About 200 objects that include stocks, bonds, insurance, real estate holdings, employment criteria, and descriptions of family members are known to the system. Some 125 of the objects are actual financial objects, and nearly 2,000 attributes are associated with the objects.

The product has a Macintosh-like user interface and mouse. Case information is given to the system via a series of data entry screens (rather than in response to questions). The system user is warned when contradictory or questionable case information is given. Users themselves may interrupt a session at any point to request observations and recommendations, to ask what if questions, or to learn the likely results of any specific change in a case scenario. The user may also override any specific concern expressed by the system.

While the knowledge base itself cannot be modified by the user, the outcome of sessions can be influenced by customizing the 100 or so control parameters that are a part of the system and by giving override or other directions during the course of a case-building session with the system. PlanPower produces test reports that describe and discuss a financial plan for each case. These reports can be influenced by modifying test output templates and by using the word processing capability of the system once the reports are produced. PlanPower expresses degrees of certainty about the results of specific recommendations and ranks alternative recommendations.

The knowledge base is proprietary and is updated by Apex to reflect changes in laws, programs, and experience. These updates are part of a support package that includes training, a technical hotline, and Apex Advisory Services, Inc., which makes financial professionals available to PlanPower users to supplement the advice generated by the system.

While PlanPower responds to changes in the financial environment, it does not do so through hooks to outside data bases. These changes and experience are reflected in the knowledge base updates provided periodically. Hooks to outside data bases are being considered as enhancements.

Hardware required: All hardware is included in the purchase price.

Commercial status: For sale. $50,000. Includes:

- Hardware: Workstation with a Xerox 1186 AI computer (including high-performance processor, high-resolution monitor, hard disk, and co-processor that runs software designed for IBM PC or XT). Hewlett Packard LaserJet printer.
- Software includes data base, spreadsheet, and word processing capabilities.
- Training.
- Support: Technical hotline; software and knowledge base updates, access to financial counseling consultants. One year of support service is included in the package. After one year, the support package is offered at $9,500 per year.

Contact:

Applied Expert Systems, Inc. (Apex)
5 Cambridge Center
Cambridge, MA 02142
(617) 492-7322

Additional Financial Applications

AUTHORIZER'S ASST.

DEV. SOFTWARE	ART
DOMAIN	Helps American Express credit card authorizers decide exceptional cases.
CONTACT	Anne Hamlin Inference Corporation 5300 W. Century Blvd. Los Angeles, CA 90045 (213) 417-7997

EXMARINE

DEV. SOFTWARE	FFAST/ART/GOLDWORKS
DOMAIN	Analyzes risk for marine insurance applicants and suggests appropriate premium.
CONTACT	Coopers & Lybrand 1251 Avenue of the Americas New York, NY 10020 (212) 536-2954

EXPERTAX

DEV. SOFTWARE	Golden Common LISP
DOMAIN	Assists in corporate tax planning.
CONTACT	Mark Maletz Coopers & Lybrand 1251 Avenue of the Americas New York, NY 10020 (212) 536-2954

CORPORATE FINANCIAL ADVISOR

DEV. SOFTWARE	LISP
DOMAIN	Aids in corporate financial planning.
CONTACT	Athena Group 575 Madison Avenue Suite 1006 New York, NY 10022 (212) 605-0224

FOREIGN EXCHANGE ADV SYS

DEV. SOFTWARE	ART
DOMAIN	Advises foreign currency investors on trading decisions.
CONTACT	Anne Hamlin Inference Corporation 5300 W. Century Blvd. Los Angeles, CA 90045 (213) 417-7997

INGOT

DEV. SOFTWARE	FORTRAN
DOMAIN	Assists in financial forecasting.
CONTACT	Pansophic Systems, Inc. INGOT Division 1550 Northwest Highway, Suite 208 Park Ridge, IL 60068 (312) 390-7711

PORTFOLIO MANAGEMENT ADVISOR

DEV. SOFTWARE	ART
DOMAIN	Assists investment analysts in portfolio planning.
CONTACT	Anne Hamlin Inference Corporation 5300 W. Century Blvd. Los Angeles, CA 90045 (213) 417-7997

SALES TAX ADVISOR

DEV. SOFTWARE	1st-Class
DOMAIN	Advises on the sales tax status of financial transactions in California for advertising agencies, commercial artists, and designers.
CONTACT	Don Wayne AD/PR Software Information Services, Inc. 2955 Parrin Court Concord, CA 94518 (415) 671-0990

TAX

DEV. SOFTWARE	1st-Class
DOMAIN	Classifies outcomes of tax court cases between IRS and individuals claiming deductions for a home office.
CONTACT	Ronald Copeland Cowan Research Professor Northeastern University College of Business Administration Boston, MA 02115 (617) 437-4647

OFFICE AUTOMATION APPLICATIONS

In the past five to ten years, office automation has been at the forefront of many efforts to increase productivity. The initial focus was on acquiring hardware and then on acquiring user-friendly software and training employees to use the new systems. Currently the emphasis is on getting the existing systems to operate together in networks. As this current challenge is met, however, new problems will emerge involving communicating specialized knowledge about specific office problems.

These problems will require neither new hardware nor conventional training; most companies will soon have much of the hardware they need, and these problems will defy conventional training solutions. You are faced with a much larger task than training people to use office automation products. You must decentralize the knowledge that currently resides with senior operations and staff specialists. Having made a commitment to office automation, you should now commit yourself to automating knowledge dissemination. In effect, you must automate the process that makes the policies, procedures, and decision-making skills of key employees available to other employees.

The two basic approaches to providing knowledge to employees are (1) ask employees to memorize it, or (2) provide job aids containing the knowledge. Most computer systems can be thought of as job aids. Small expert systems (intelligent job aids) will rapidly change the way knowledge is provided to employees. Small expert system building tools will allow skilled decision-makers to record and communicate their knowledge to provide practical assistance to new employees.

Letter of Credit Advisor

Date: 1986.

Domain: Analysis of letters of credit.

Description: Letter of Credit Advisor is a small rule-based expert system developed by Helix (UK) and Bank of America, London, to assist clerical personnel in preparing and paying letters of credit.

A letter of credit (l/c) is a financial instrument used in the import/export business. The exporter (seller) doesn't want to ship goods overseas without some guarantee of payment. The importer (buyer) doesn't want to pay for the goods until convinced the goods will arrive. Letters of credit take care of this problem.

Importers have their banks execute a l/c with the exporter as beneficiary and send the letter to the exporter to assure the exporter there is money in the importer's bank account to pay for the shipment and that the money will be paid promptly as soon as certain conditions are met.

Some conditions are standard, but others are negotiated between exporter and importer and change from deal to deal. These conditions include the place of delivery, criteria for completed delivery, method of documentation, and so forth.

Once an l/c has been drawn and the goods shipped, there are two steps in paying it. The exporter must submit documentation to the importer's bank to prove that all the conditions have been satisfied.

Then, office personnel at the importer's bank must examine the exporter's documentation to make sure that, in fact, all conditions have been met before authorizing payment.

Like many high-volume paper processing jobs, the level of expertise varies widely among clerical staff. Likewise, the difficulty of examining l/c documentation for payment can vary significantly from one case to another. Three solutions to this problem are:

- Develop an expert system to perform at the level of the top experts.
- Train all staff to the level of the top experts.
- Distribute work according to skill level—the easy l/c's to the beginners and the difficult l/c's to the top experts.

The first two choices are not economically feasible. A top-expert cloning system would take too much time and money, as would extensive training. The exact dollar loss due to deficiencies in the current hand-processing methods was hard to assess. Presumably there was a lot of hassle involved in troubleshooting errors resulting from inexperience, not to mention customer dissatisfaction.

The third choice offered at least some relief without large up-front development costs. Bank of America also saw a potential market for such a system among exporters and other banks.

Letter of Credit Advisor is a filtering system designed to separate easy from complex l/c's. It contains approximately 260 rules aimed at detecting discrepancies in documentation. It runs as a dialogue system.

In response to questions on the screen, the clerk enters information about the l/c and associated documents. The system checks for discrepancies. If none are found, payment is approved. If discrepancies are found, the system prints a message identifying the discrepancy and recommending further action. According to policy the clerk either follows the system's recommendation or passes the l/c to an expert. The result desired is that the expert addresses difficult or potentially difficult l/c's before they turn into customer problems.

The system, designed to be conservative, is expected to reject some l/c's that, in fact, have no discrepancies. This was thought preferrable to less stringent controls that might let some l/c's with discrepancies be paid.

The benefits of this system include a steeper learning curve and higher productivity for beginners and a refocus of expertise on preventing rather than solving problems.

Letter of Credit Advisor was developed by Bank of America in London and the British company Helix using the Helix tool, known as Expert Edge in the United States. The system runs on an IBM PC or compatible with 640K RAM and is available for purchase. The price for the first copy is UK £5,750 plus VAT with maintenance offered at 12 percent per year.

It is expected that purchasers of this system will want to customize it to include their own terminology and processing requirements. Helix offers consulting services to aid in such customizing efforts. Letter of Credit Advisor illustrates a trend in generic commercial applications. Rather than trying to capture all the expertise in a given domain, the developers go for the core knowledge that is unlikely to differ from user to user, and then builds user-friendly facilities for modifying the knowledge base with user-specific rules.

Commercial status: For sale.

Contact:

Helix Expert Systems
St. Bartholomew House
92 Fleet Street
London, EC4Y 1DH
01-583-9391

Additional Office Automation Applications

BUSINESS CLASSIFIER

DEV. SOFTWARE	Exsys
DOMAIN	Classifies incoming business at a worker's compensation office.
CONTACT	L. Johnson Creighton Companies Inc. #3 Parkway Center, Suite 1111 Pittsburgh, PA 15220 (412) 793-7410

CLASS

DEV. SOFTWARE	Exsys
DOMAIN	Helps Department of Energy staff assign security classification to documents.
CONTACT	Exsys/Dustin Huntington P.O. Box 75148 Contract Station 14 Albuquerque, NM 87194 (505) 836-6676

CV FILTER

DEV. SOFTWARE	Expert Edge
DOMAIN	Helps the user decide whether an applicant should be interviewed.
CONTACT	David Imberg Helix Expert Systems Limited St. Bartholomew House 92 Fleet Street London, EC4Y IDH 01-583-9391

DATA CLASSIFIER

DEV. SOFTWARE	Exsys
DOMAIN	Helps users classify the value of their data.
CONTACT	Exsys Corporation P.O. Box 75148 Contract Station 14 Albuquerque, NM 87194 (505) 836-6676

DATA PROTECTION ACT ADVISOR

DEV. SOFTWARE	Expert Edge
DOMAIN	Guides managers through various steps required for copyright registration under a new Act.
CONTACT	Helix Expert Systems Limited St. Bartholomew House 92 Fleet Street London, EC Y 1DH 01-583-9391

WATER PERMIT REVIEW SYSTEM

DEV. SOFTWARE	KES
DOMAIN	Speeds processing of waste water disposal permit applications at United States Environmental Protection Agency.
CONTACT	Software A&E 1600 Wilson Boulevard, Suite 500 Arlington, VA 22209-2403 (703) 276-7910

MANUFACTURING APPLICATIONS

One vision of the future includes totally automated factories. Such factories would use robots (each controlled by its own expert system) for the physical tasks and expert systems to monitor and adjust production procedures. Monitoring and adjusting the relationships between people and machines to keep a factory working at maximum efficiency requires considerable expertise. Many other types of expert systems are used in the manufacturing process and are listed below, but planning and scheduling the operation of a factory are the tasks at the heart of this application.

Considerable effort has gone into factory planning and scheduling applications with some partial successes. As with the other domains, the failure, so far, to mechanize the highest level of expertise in no way diminishes the value of the considerable contributions expert systems have already made in the manufacturing domain.

An interesting aspect of this domain is the common perception that even the best experts don't squeeze maximum efficiency out of the factories they control. Current development projects aim at doubling a factory's capacity.

Cooker Advisor

Date: 1986.

Domain: Analyzes causes of malfunctions in large cookers that sterilize canned soup before it leaves the factory. Recommends appropriate maintenance actions.

Benefits: Reduces demand for troubleshooting by the company's one resident expert, who is nearing retirement age. Eliminates the need to train the expert's replacement in the intricacies of equipment that will gradually be replaced.

Description: Campbell Soup maintains numerous plants around the world that prepare and package canned soup. An important step in the canning process is to sterilize the soup after it has been sealed in the can. The machines that perform this sterilization process are called cookers. While the general functioning of all the cookers is the same, minor differences between cookers exist based on manufacturer, model, year of purchase, and so forth.

Campbell has one employee with extensive

knowledge of all the cookers currently in operation. Maintenance engineers in the various plants turn to this person when they encounter an unusual operating problem with their cookers. Sometimes the expert can solve the problem by talking over the phone; other times he must travel to the plant. The fact that this sole expert was nearing retirement age spurred Campbell's management to seek an alternative to the costly effort of training a replacement. Campbell hired the data systems group at Texas Instruments to develop an expert system to capture as much of the expert's knowledge as possible.

The developers used Texas Instruments' Personal Consultant, which employs backward chaining and if-then rules, to create Cooker Advisor. Cooker Advisor is distributed to the various plant sites on diskettes. Consultations take place on IBM PCs.

In a consultation, the maintenance person enters data describing the problem condition of the cooker. Cooker Advisor comes back either with a request for more information or with recommendations for specific action. The expert estimates that Cooker Advisor successfully handles 95 percent or more of the problem calls he used to receive.

Hardware required: IBM PC or equivalent.

Development: Cooker Advisor was developed on a Texas Instruments Professional Computer with 768K and a 10M hard disk.

The following account of the development of this system is supplied by Texas Instruments.

Development of Campbell's first expert system took about six months from initial contact with the human expert to field testing. On November 5, 1984, the Campbell cooker expert met with TI knowledge engineers for the first time. The expert was understandably skeptical, but completely cooperative. The first four days were devoted to teaching the TI people about the normal operation of the cookers, so they could discuss malfunctions intelligently.

On December 10, TI returned to Campbell with a first-draft system that used 32 rules. TI's development philosophy is to get a prototype system up and running as quickly as possible for early evaluation by the clients. It has proven to be the best strategy for eliciting further knowledge. Few people are able to create, but most are generous with constructive criticism.

Based on the wealth of additional knowledge gathered during a three-day review of the prototype with Campbell management, TI enlarged the system to 66 rules and presented it to Campbell on January 22, 1985. This time the review produced no great changes. Rather, some terms were refined and some detailed steps were added to certain diagnostic procedures.

At this point the system was demonstrated to potential users—a shift supervisor at Campbell's Camden plant and several operations and maintenance people at the Napoleon, Ohio, plant. Their consensus was that the system would be useful. During this trip, Campbell also decided to expand the expert system to cover both start-up and shutdown procedures.

On February 12, TI presented the next refinement of the system to Campbell. It had now grown to 85 rules, plus 12 start-up and shutdown procedures. After a few minor flaws were corrected, Campbell declared the first phase of the system ready. A second phase, to cover a different type of cooker, was added after the initial effort.

On March 19, an expert system covering hydrostatic cookers, their start-up and shutdown, as well as rotary cookers, was presented. It had now grown to 125 rules. On this visit, the system was demonstrated to a wider circle of Campbell's management, and consensus was that Campbell's first expert system was nearly ready for field testing. The next month was spent refining the rotary cooker rules and including rules covering a different type of cooker used at only one plant.

At this writing, the expert system contains 151 rules plus start-up and shutdown procedures, and the system has been distributed to the plants.

According to the developers, the following important lessons were either learned or reaffirmed during this development effort:

- It's more important to put together a prototype fast than to make it complete.
- The knowledge engineer must be prepared to ac-

cept frequent correction, and the expert must be willing to give it.

- The expert must be fully cooperative, even if skeptical.
- Strong management commitment is absolutely essential. An expert's time is in short supply, and the project must have a high enough priority to assure adequate access to the expert.
- Early demonstration to potential users is important. Without their feedback about perceived deficiencies and without their support, even a well-conceived system can end up in a closet collecting dust.

Commercial status: Not for sale.

Contact:

Texas Instruments Incorporated
P.O. Box 2909—M/S 2244
Austin, TX 78759

Additional Manufacturing Applications

ASH MIXER

DEV. SOFTWARE Exsys
DOMAIN Analyzes process halts in mixing radioactive ash with concrete for burial.
CONTACT Paul D. Soper
E.I. DuPont
Savannah River Lab, Building 676-4T
Aiken, SC 29808
(803) 450-6211

BRUSH DESIGNER

DEV. SOFTWARE S.1
DOMAIN Helps DELCO engineers design brushes for electric motors.
CONTACT Teknowledge
1850 Embarcadero Road
Palo Alto, CA 94303
(415) 424-0500

COMPONENT IMPACT ANALYSIS SYSTEM

DEV. SOFTWARE C, Quintus PROLOG
DOMAIN Advises operators on proper settings for valves and switches in nuclear reactors.
CONTACT Quintus Computer Systems
1310 Villa Street
Mountain View, CA 94041
(415) 965-7700

CRYSTAL ADVISOR

DEV. SOFTWARE KES.PS
DOMAIN Helps reduce operator skill and attention requirements while it helps reduce processing pitfalls.
CONTACT Doc Ardrey
Ardrey Inc.
100 Menlo Park, Suite 314
Edison, NJ 08837
(201) 549-1300

DISPATCHER

DEV. SOFTWARE VAX OPS5
DOMAIN Selects, transports, and delivers parts for assembly while maintaining inventory records.
CONTACT Digital Equipment
77 Reed Road
Hudson, MA 01749
(617) 568-4000

DUSTPRO

DEV. SOFTWARE Insight 2+
DOMAIN Advises coal mine operators on dust control and ventilation techniques.

CONTACT	Fred Kissell Bureau of Mines Bruceton Research Center Box 18070 Pittsburgh, PA 15236 (412) 892-6679

EXPERT EXECUTIVE

DEV. SOFTWARE	Franz LISP
DOMAIN	Integrates technology code for aerospace vehicle designers' use.
CONTACT	Kathryn M. Chalfan 1141 Harbor Bay Parkway Alameda, CA 94501 (415) 769-5656

EXPERT PROBE

DEV. SOFTWARE	KEE
DOMAIN	Allows factory workers to do quality control tasks formerly done by skilled technicians.
CONTACT	UNISYS (Sperry Computer Systems Division, DPG) 8001 Metro Drive St. Paul, MN 55420 (612) 851-3000

FAIS

DEV. SOFTWARE	M.1
DOMAIN	Helps a foreman create optimum schedules.
CONTACT	Teknowledge 1850 Embarcadero Road Palo Alto, CA 94303 (415) 424-0500

OLEOPHILIC ADVISOR

DEV. SOFTWARE	M.1
DOMAIN	Assists lithography R&D groups in choosing new materials.
CONTACT	Teknowledge 1850 Embarcadero Road Palo Alto, CA 94303 (415) 424-0500

UNIT COMMITMENT ADVISOR

DEV. SOFTWARE	MAIDS
DOMAIN	Helps a system dispatcher schedule power-generating units.
CONTACT	Gavin Finn Stone and Webster Engineering 245/10 Summer Street Boston, MA 02107 (617) 589-1567

WELD SCHEDULER

DEV. SOFTWARE	KEE
DOMAIN	Helps Babcock welding engineers choose proper weld procedures.
CONTACT	IntelliCorp 1975 El Camino Real West Mountain View, CA 94040 (415) 965-5500

WELD SELECTOR

DEV. SOFTWARE	Personal Consultant Plus
DOMAIN	Helps welding engineers choose proper weld electrodes.
CONTACT	Dr. Jerald E. Jones American Welding Institute New Topside Road Rt. 4, Box 90 Louisville, TN 37777 (615) 970-2150

EQUIPMENT MAINTENANCE APPLICATIONS

In fielded expert systems applications three categories clearly have greater emphasis than the others: equipment maintenance, manufacturing, and computer-related applications. The computer domain is the birthplace of expert systems, so you'd expect to find many applications there. Heavy attention on manufacturing and maintenance may only reflect the importance of these activities in our economy. It probably also shows that expertise in these areas is easier to capture in usable form than expertise from, for instance, professional domains such as law and management.

Efforts to maintain equipment can take two forms: troubleshooting and preventive maintenance. Both types of expert systems have been built. Equipment maintenance applications tend to stand alone because the knowledge and data in any system is specific to the equipment.

Equipment troubleshooting is a classic diagnosis/prescription task for which EMYCIN-based tools are usually appropriate. The usual input mode is dialogue with a technician whose job is to fix an equipment malfunction after it occurs. The expert system asks questions about the status of the equipment, and the technician enters her answers. The system continues to ask questions, in a back-chaining strategy to fulfill conditions necessary to reach a goal, in this case a recommended repair strategy.

Preventive maintenance aims at stopping problems before they start. Two strategies are employed: scheduled service and trouble prediction. Expert systems have been developed that focus on trouble prediction. The performance of major machinery is usually monitored and recorded in some way (e.g., written service records, electrosensors, production records). Preventive maintenance experts study this data and try to predict the most imminent and costly breakdowns. Based on the recommendations of these experts, special servicing is allocated.

ACE (Automated Cable Expertise)

Date: 1985.

Description: ACE is a signal processing system that analyzes phone company repair data and identifies areas for preventive maintenance and further repair. ACE regularly examines two data bases: the Cable Repair Administrative System (CRAS) and the Trouble Repair Evaluation and Administration Tool (TREAT). These data bases contain information on telephone equipment repair activities.

This application was chosen for the following reasons:

- Limited supply of expert cable analyzers.
- Extensive knowledge required with limited formal training available.
- Discouragingly large amount of data to analyze.
- Competing needs for expert's time.

ACE delivers five different reports:

- **Found Trouble Analysis.** This program searches the CRAS data base for equipment associated with a large number of customer trouble reports. It diagnoses the nature of the trouble, its location, and its probable cause. This program is run every night.
- **Trouble Report Improvement Methodology.** This program analyzes fixed, not-fixed, and not-found troubles. It identifies and analyzes hundred-pair cable complements getting the most trouble reports over the past 60 days. The program provides a full diagnosis. It is run every night.
- **Troubles in Tracked Complements.** This program monitors user-selected complements for trouble reports. It is used to track jobs in progress and jobs recently completed.
- **PLUS 3.** This program analyzes each customer who has reported three or more troubles in the past 30 days and separates cable problems from individual customer problems. This program is run once a week.
- **Pair Transposition Analysis.** This program is also run once a week. It looks for addresses where two or more specific types of repair procedures have been performed in the last 60 days, to give advance warning of bad section problems.

Hardware required: AT&T 3B2/300, 3B2/310, and 3B2/400, under UNIX.

Commercial status: For sale. As of June 1987, 35 systems are installed and are running in five different Bell Operating Companies. Additional systems are on order.

Contact: For purchase information contact the AT&T Network Systems representative serving your company.

Fran Henig
AT&T Bell Labs
184 Liberty Corner Road
Warren, NJ 07060-0908
(201) 580-5310

COMPASS (Central Office Maintenance Printout Analysis and Suggestion System)

Date: 1986.

Domain: Assists telephone switch maintenance personnel by analyzing operating data and recommending appropriate maintenance actions.

Description: Telephone switching systems regularly put out status and maintenance data to convey information about their day-to-day operating conditions. These data are collected at monitoring stations where they are printed out. These printouts are often voluminous. The printouts are then analyzed by experts to determine what maintenance actions are indicated. The analysis of the data and prescription for appropriate action require a highly trained individual. COMPASS was built to replace the human expert in this process.

Field tests have shown that COMPASS equals or exceeds in accuracy the output of human experts. It has been field tested for over a year with excellent results and is presently being put into production use in the GTE Telephone Companies.

COMPASS is one of the largest expert systems developed. COMPASS alone takes about 5 megabytes, and the COMPASS system (including KEE and INTERLISP D) takes about 10 megabytes. The system's knowledge document is about 200 pages of concise English.

COMPASS uses multiple AI paradigms: rules, frames and inheritance, object-oriented programming, and LISP code. It was developed using KEE. Most important concepts are represented as KEE frames or KEE rules. Much of the procedural control is accomplished through object-oriented message passing.

COMPASS is also one of the first expert systems developed to be maintained by a group other than the developers. The system developers gave important consideration to maintainability in their development.

Meeting the goal of producing an expert system that performs at or above the level of human experts has been a major benefit. COMPASS significantly improves customer service while increasing staff productivity.

Development: COMPASS is the result of a pilot expert system effort by GTE Laboratories. Its purposes were to develop an expert system to solve a significant problem for the corporation, to create a paradigm for expert systems development, and to demonstrate that an expert system can perform significant diagnosis/prescription tasks at a level of accuracy and completeness above current standards. The development process followed by the researchers has been well documented, and their recommendations are extremely useful.

Following is an account of the development of COMPASS along with comments by the developers regarding what they learned about the various steps.

Problem selection: Researchers put considerable effort into selecting an appropriate problem for which to develop their pilot system. They assembled a list of over 50 criteria for selecting an appropriate problem domain. After the decision was made to select an application related to GTE telephone company facilities, researchers visited 10 operating locations and talked to over 50 managers and experts. Of those possible applications identified (more than 30), the switch analysis application best met the criteria established.

The task of switch problem analysis requires considerable judgment and expertise acquired over many years. Levels of experience varied among maintenance personnel, with the less knowledgeable consulting with their seniors when tough problems arose. Time required to analyze a particular printout varied among maintenance personnel. Some expertise regarding older equipment was being lost as senior analysts moved to other jobs.

The researchers chose a particular type of switch, the No. 2 EAX, as their first target because it was stable, widely used, and due to be in service longer than the projected development time.

Development tool selection: Researchers considered 17 development systems ranging from university research environments to fully developed commercial packages. They were considered on the basis of cost, maintenance, facilities, support, type, and host system.

Four systems were considered in detail. Considerations important to GTE researchers in choosing a system were:

- The hardware needed for development.
- Current level of staff expertise in AI.
- Project staffing required.
- Funds available.
- Milestones.

Researchers report two primary reasons for selecting KEE: KEE provides various knowledge representation paradigms, including rules, frames and inheritance, object-oriented programming and programming directly in LISP; and, being a commercial tool, it had good documentation and support.

System design: COMPASS performs the steps of diagnosis and prescription in the same order as a human expert would perform them. There are five phases in COMPASS processing. They are:

- **Input.** Data that would have been provided to an expert as a printout is put into COMPASS via data communications over telephone lines. COMPASS formats this data into knowledge structures.
- **Identify.** Problem messages are clustered into sets, each associated with a particular switch problem. Rules are applied to reduce the great number of all possible clusters to a manageable list of clusters with a high probability of identifying a particular problem. These clusters are passed to the next phase.
- **Analyze.** Expert rules are applied to the selected clusters to determine a set of possible switch faults, any one of which could have caused all the error messages in the cluster. Each fault is assigned a likelihood. For each cluster, COMPASS identifies one to five possible faults.
- **Suggest.** For each possible fault, one to three suggestions for action are made. Suggestions are then prioritized based on considerations such as likelihood of success, ease of performing the action, and potential risks.
- **Output.** The system prints out a list of suggested actions to be taken that day. Detailed instructions are provided for extraordinary or difficult actions. COMPASS also puts out a copy of its input data in the same form as it had been delivered to the expert. The system can display explanations of its reasoning in developing the clusters and their associated suggestions. The system provides graphic representations of rules and fact relationships.

GTE researchers cite the following points as major insights resulting from their pilot development effort:

1. Maintain the involvement of one expert or group of experts from problem identification to product design and to the release of the product.
2. Encourage informal communication at all levels.
3. Choose the right domain. For a first corporate application, the task should be of modest complexity, neither too simple nor too difficult. It is important that it solves a problem which has value, but is not on a critical path. An early demonstration of capability should be planned, however limited.
4. Identify real users who will participate in the project. Development should be user-driven or user-encouraged.

5. Plan for the system to be integrated into the existing method of operations. Do not plan to change the existing method of operations to fit the expert system.
6. Promote technology awareness early in the process at all levels of the organization.
7. Do not attempt to perform a cost-benefit analysis prematurely of the development of the system. Develop a first version of a system and, based upon field trial or market demonstration, begin quantifying economic impact.
8. Get an impartial technical consultant to participate in regular design reviews. A critical review, at least in the early stages, is vital.
9. Think of technology transfer in the early phases of the project. Practice participative design with the project design group.
10. Avoid unrealistic expectations by all concerned.

Hardware required: Xerox 1108 LISP Machine. A Common LISP version is also tested.

Commercial status: Being put into production use by GTE Telephone Companies.

Contact:

Shri K. Goyal
GTE Laboratories
40 Sylvan Road
Waltham, MA 02254
(617) 466-2940

IDEA (IS4000 Diagnostic Expert Advisor)

Date: 1986.

Description: IDEA assists telephone technicians in diagnosing problems with the Infotron IS4000 Local Area Network, a complex switching device. In a typical consultation, which lasts under five minutes, the technician chooses items from menus that best describe the problem situation being encountered. Based on early answers, the system asks further questions until it has enough information to make a recommendation for action.

IDEA was developed in an experimental Pacific Bell PC product called *MetaShell*, a higher level environment that enables Exsys to operate from control block patterns, similar to the new IBM ESE's Focus Control Blocks. MetaShell controls the interactions between 19 Exsys subdomain modules. These individual knowledge bases are reusable in the design of other diagnostic systems servicing similar hardware domains.

Other IDEA features include:

- On-line product manual.
- Two blackboards.
- Information sharing between knowledge bases.
- Dynamic goal strategy list.
- Unlimited rule capacity due to modular design.
- Comprehensive plain-English audit trail.
- User access to blackboard and last past session log.

Development: IDEA and MetaShell were developed in-house by Pacific Bell's Expert Systems Projects Group. The effort required six months and 1.5 person-years.

Hardware required: PC-XT or compatible; occupies 500K.

Commercial status: IDEA is available for sale from Pacific Bell. Contact Paul Chew (415) 823-3192.

Contact:

John Girard
Expert Systems Project Group
Pacific Bell
2600 Camino Ramon, Room 2E850K
San Ramon, CA 94583
(415) 823-1961

DELTA (Diesel-Electric Locomotive Troubleshooting Aid), also known as CATS-1 (Computer Aided Troubleshooting System-1)

Date: 1984.

Domain: Assists diesel locomotive maintenance personnel to diagnose maintenance needs and prescribe appropriate maintenance action.

Description: DELTA or CATS-1 are used interchangeably to describe an expert system developed by the General Electric Company in Schenectady, New York. The system is designed to help railroad maintenance personnel maintain GE's diesel-electric locomotives.

Prior to the development of DELTA/CATS-1, GE employed two methods to solve problems the railroads had with some diesel-electronic locomotives. Either they would fly a maintenance expert to the location of the engine to help with the problems, or they would transport the faulty locomotive to a maintenance yard where an expert was available. The expert used in most cases was David Smith, Senior Field Service Engineer. He has been with General Electric for over 40 years and is the acknowledged expert on the field maintenance of diesel-electric locomotives.

The DELTA system employed the hybrid forward/backward chaining inference strategy. This strategy, together with troubleshooting rules, is used to isolate faults and to generate inquiries. In addition, a help system that uses a forward chainer together with a rule-based engine taxonomy responds to user requests for information such as the location and identification of individual locomotive components, replacement parts classification, and description of repair procedures. When maintenance people first sit down at a CATS-1 terminal, they are presented with a menu of possible fault areas. After the user selects a particular fault area, the system proceeds with a detailed series of questions. For example:

"Is the fuel filter clogged?"
"Are you able to raise fuel pressure to 40 PSI?"
"If engine-set-idle and fuel-pressure-below-normal and fuel-pressure-O.K., Then fuel-system is faulty."

The basic expert system has been interfaced with a device that allows the system to print out diagrams and a videodisk player that allows the system to display diagrams to show where particular components are located on the locomotive. Moreover, if requested, the system can display training film sequences to show the user exactly how to make a particular repair. Thus, the expert system helps the maintenance person figure out what the problem is and, if necessary, switches over to the video system to show how to make the checks or measurements to generate information DELTA needs to make a diagnosis. Then, once the problem is isolated, DELTA, if requested, actually shows the step-by-step procedure for fixing the problem. It is interesting to note that the expert system is, in effect, serving as an interface for a large number of training films. The system simply helps the maintenance person figure out what the problem is, then provides the training film if desired. The expert system was originally developed in LISP, but was then converted to FORTH, a portable language easily adaptable to any microprocessor. According to GE, the FORTH implementation has proved to be easily transportable and maintains a fast execution speed.

Development: The project to develop DELTA/CATS-1 was initiated in 1981 with the clear intention of capturing David Smith's knowledge in a system that would allow GE to deliver that knowledge to less expert personnel at the various railroad yards around the country. General Electric set up a team of knowledge engineers located in a General Electric Research and Development Center in Schenectady. The DELTA team members include Pierro Bonissione, Bruce Bernstein, Lowell Bauer, and Howard Johnson. This team, managed by Frank Lynch and working with the maintenance expert David Smith, developed a laboratory prototype by 1982 and began it in 1983. The number of rules added at each phase in the development of the DELTA system provides an interesting metric of the overall effort (see Table 15.1).

Table 15.1 *Rules added to DELTA during each phase of the project.*

Number of Rules	Year	Project Phase
45	1981	Feasibility Demonstration
350	1982	Laboratory Prototype
530	1983	Field Prototype (Handles 50% of problems)
1200	1984	Production Prototype (Handles 80% of problems)

Hardware required: PDP-11/23, 10M Winchester hard disk, industrial microcomputer BT100 terminal, Selanar graphics board, Sony laser videodisk player, and color monitor.

Commercial status: For internal use only.

Contact:

General Electric Company
Research and Development Center
P.O. Box 8
Schenectady, NY 12301
(518) 385-2211

Additional Equipment Maintenance Applications

BDS

DEV. SOFTWARE LES
DOMAIN Troubleshoots large signal switching network, base band distribution system.
CONTACT Lockheed Palo Alto Research Center
3251 Hanover Street
Palo Alto, CA 94304
(415) 354-5260

CORROSION EXPERT

DEV. SOFTWARE TI Scheme
DOMAIN Assists in design of steam generators by recommending rust-resistant alloy combinations.
CONTACT: Dr. Neil Pessal
Westinghouse Research and Development Center
1310 Behulia Road
Pittsburgh, PA 15235
(412) 256-1000

GEMS TTA

DEV. SOFTWARE OPS83, C, UNIX
DOMAIN Diagnoses faults on telephone trunks.

CONTACT Paul H. Callahan
AT&T Bell Laboratories, Room 1B225
480 Red Hill Road
Middletown, NJ 07748
(201) 615-5199

HOIST DIAGNOSER

DEV. SOFTWARE Insight
DOMAIN Diagnoses faults on hoist equipment.
CONTACT Steve Oxman
Oxman Knowledge Organization
P.O. Box 6674
Annapolis, MD 21401
(301) 956-6956

HOTLINE HELPER

DEV. SOFTWARE Personal Consultant Plus
DOMAIN Helps hot line workers give advice to caller with TI Printer malfunctions.
CONTACT Texas Instruments Incorporated
P.O. Box 2909—M/S 2244
Austin, TX 78759

IMP

DEV. SOFTWARE Personal Consultant
DOMAIN Troubleshoots Epitaxial reactor machinery.
CONTACT Texas Instruments Incorporated
P.O. Box 2909—M/S 2244
Austin, TX 78759

MENTOR

DEV. SOFTWARE LISP
DOMAIN Diagnoses preventive maintenance needs for large central air conditioning systems.
CONTACT George D. Hadden
Honeywell MN 65-2100
3660 Technology Drive
Minneapolis, MN 55418
(612) 782-7769

PAGE 1

DEV. SOFTWARE INTERLISP D Xerox LOOPS
DOMAIN Troubleshoots nonimpact page printing systems.
CONTACT Chuck Strandberg
Honeywell Information System
1000 Boone Avenue North
Golden Valley, MN 55427
(612) 541-6578

PUMP PRO

DEV. SOFTWARE Basic, MAIDS
DOMAIN Diagnoses problems in centrifugal pumps.
CONTACT Gavin Finn
Stone and Webster Engineering
245/10 Summer Street
Boston, MA 02107
(617) 589-1567

ROTATING EQUIPMENT DIAGNOSTIC

DEV. SOFTWARE Exsys
DOMAIN Diagnoses unusual vibrations in rotating equipment.
CONTACT Gavin Finn
Stone and Webster Engineering
245/10 Summer Street
Boston, MA 02107
(617) 589-1567

TEST DIAGNOSTIC ASST

DEV. SOFTWARE ART
DOMAIN Analog/digital circuit diagnosis.

CONTACT	Anne Hamlin Inference Corporation 5300 W. Century Blvd. Los Angeles, CA 90045 (213) 417-7997

TOGA

DEV. SOFTWARE	RuleMaster
DOMAIN	Analyzes insulation oil to diagnose faults in large utility transformers.
CONTACT	Charles Riese Radian Corporation 8501 MoPac Boulevard P.O. Box 9948 Austin, TX 78766-0948 (512) 454-4797

TURBOMAT

DEV. SOFTWARE	RuleMaster
DOMAIN	Diagnoses vibration problems in large turbomachinery.
CONTACT	Radian Corporation 8501 MoPac Boulevard P.O. Box 9948 Austin, TX 78766-0948 (512) 454-4797

COMPUTER APPLICATIONS

That the domain of computer-related expertise has been a frequent target of expert systems developers should be no more surprising than the fact that many Hollywood movies concern themselves with the Hollywood movie industry. Unfortunately, success stories of computer-related applications don't carry the same impact with the layperson as those concerning successful applications in noncomputer domains. Many computer-related applications have been developed by companies that sell both hardware and software, but frequently these systems are for internal use only.

A success story in expert systems usually credits at least two people: the knowledge engineer and the domain expert. When these two roles are played by the same person or the same company, the success story seems less dramatic. On the other hand, the efforts made in this domain have yielded many interesting successful expert systems. Problems addressed by these systems appear in other domains, and if only for the volume of attention, many breakthroughs have been in this context.

XCON, originally called R1

Date: Ongoing.

Domain: Accepts orders for large computer installations and determines the exact specifications and layout of the hardware needed to meet the order within the customers' constraints.

Benefits: XCON has allowed Digital Equipment Corporation to reduce the size of its technical editor staff and has allowed the remaining editors to focus their attention on the exceptional tasks that the system can't handle.

Description: XCON is an expert system that routinely configures Digital Equipment Corporation's (DEC) VAX-11/780 computer systems. XCON's input is a customer's order, and its output is a set of diagrams displaying the spatial relationships among the components on an order. These diagrams are used by the technicians who physically assemble the system.

Digital does not market preconfigured systems; instead, it offers a customer a wide selection of components to choose from. In 1979, for example, some 420 components were associated with a VAX-11/780. In effect, most systems DEC sells are one-of-a-kind systems.

Development: Digital had made several unsuccessful efforts to develop a conventional computer program that would configure a VAX-11/780. The major problem was not so much that the knowledge was ill-structured but rather that it kept changing so rapidly. In the fall of 1978 the company began a discussion with John McDermott of the Computer Science Department of Carnegie-Mellon University about the possibility of developing a knowledge-based system that would solve the configuration problem. During the next two years McDermott and a number of colleagues from both CMU and DEC developed and implemented XCON.

The first stage in the development of XCON involved creating a general design and then building a prototype system to demonstrate the effectiveness of a knowledge system approach to DEC's configuration problem. Many DEC managers were skeptical about the possibility of developing a knowledge-based system that could solve their problem. Luckily, John McDermott and Carnegie-Mellon University were able to support the development of a prototype with academic funding. It was also convenient that OPS4 (the precursor to the OPS5 system building tool described in Chapter 8) was already in existence and well understood by the Carnegie-Mellon staff. Dr. McDermott determined that DEC's configuration problem was the type of problem that could be appropriately modeled with OPS4.

McDermott began the project by meeting with DEC configuration experts to discuss the procedures they followed when they configured a VAX-11/780. After satisfying himself that he had a good overview of the task, Dr. McDermott took two DEC configuration manuals and retired to Carnegie-Mellon University to study them in great detail. Using this input, he developed a prototype system in about three person-months. The prototype had approximately 250 rules. When it was demonstrated in April 1979, it was able to satisfy all the basic configuration problems it was given. The people involved in the project were satisfied, and it was decided to proceed to the next phase. DEC was willing to fund the development of a larger version of the system.

McDermott notes in passing that they almost decided to focus their initial effort on developing a prototype of a PDP-11 configuration system rather than focusing on the VAX-11-780. Their actual choice was extremely fortuitous since the PDP-11 is a much larger system with many more components. Moreover, the constraints that apply to a configuration of a VAX-11 are much less ambiguous than those that apply to the PDP-11 system. In retrospect, conservation paid off since the VAX-11 task was the perfect size. McDermott suggests that if the PDP-11 system had been chosen instead, the project would probably have been slightly beyond the capability of the OPS4 system, and the whole effort might have resulted in a failure.

Between May and September 1979, Dr. McDermott and his colleagues expanded their initial prototype system from 250 rules to 750 rules. At the same time a component data base being developed by DEC personnel was expanded from the initial 200 components to cover all 420 components that could be involved in a VAX-11-780 configuration. The expert system consulted this data base whenever it needed a description of a VAX component.

McDermott describes how they developed the system from 250 to 750 rules. It was a classic case of how extensions can be driven by case studies. In fact, an expert was sat down, and a case was given to the computer which resulted in configuration recommendations. The expert was then asked to evaluate the recommendations and suggest why it was inappropriate. As the expert and the knowledge engineer talked over the particular configuration, rules were directly or indirectly generated to assure that in the future that particular configuration would be correct and also to assure that similar configurations would be correct. The goal for Stage 2 was a system that would correctly configure 75 percent of the orders it was given, and that would be designed so that it could easily be extended to accommodate additional cases. This goal was achieved in September 1979. The original XCON was developed in just under one person-year.

The third stage was validating XCON. This was accomplished in October and November 1979. During these two months, XCON configured the 50 most recent orders received. Each configuration it produced was then evaluated by a group of six experts. Some errors resulted from inadequate descriptions of the components in the data base. These were forwarded to the

DEC programmers to correct. Twelve of the mistakes resulted from errors in the knowledge base, and these were forwarded to McDermott. Significantly, ten of these mistakes involved problems with specifications at a level of detail *below* that which human experts normally configure systems. In effect, by attempting to provide detail that human experts didn't normally provide, XCON designers had made some minor errors. After these problems were corrected, DEC was satisfied with the validation test and implemented the system throughout the company.

Stage 4 was in a five-month hiatus during which DEC began to plan how to actually fit XCON into its organizational structure. Two functions were important. The first was how the system was to be controlled and monitored. It was determined that the technical editor who had previously been supervisor for all the editors checking orders would now become, in effect, supervisor for XCON, and that XCON's configuration orders would be given to this person, who then approved them and sent them out. The second problem involved determining how XCON was to be maintained and extended. To accomplish this, DEC established an internal team of knowledge engineers assigned the task of maintaining XCON on a day-by-day basis and developing extensions to it.

While Digital was working through the problems of developing an organizational structure to maintain XCON, the Carnegie-Mellon team reconfigured OPS4 into the system building tool now known as OPS5. Because of new efficiencies achieved in the OPS5 design, the total number of rules used by the system was reduced from 750 to something under 500. Moreover, in re-implementing XCON on OPS5, McDermott realized that the task was not so much a generate-and-test task, as originally supposed, but was, in fact, a matching task that required only a little backtracking. This reconceptualization of the task allowed the designers to change the way the rules were written and reduce the total number of rules.

Stage 5 occurred between June and December 1980. During this period the organizational changes that Digital had decided on were implemented. A problem report form was developed to assure that all errors resulting from the use of XCON were reported, investigated, and corrected. During this period 32 percent of the orders had problems that required action. This failure rate bothered some people at DEC. Since the computer had done so well on standard problems they were unprepared for the fact that the system would have additional problems when it tried to deal with the more specialized cases.

During this same period DEC and Carnegie-Mellon each added some features to the system that would allow customers to set specific constraints on the space in which the hardware was to be installed. Certain components were dictated or avoided on the basis of the customer's constraints. This and other additions had not been anticipated at all in the initial design, yet they were added to the XCON system without any significant change in either the architecture of the system or the existing rules. In other words, modifying XCON was largely a matter of adding rules to systematically expand the system's capabilities.

During this same period OPS5 was reimplemented in BLISS, a variation on LISP designed to be compiled into very efficient code. The average time it took for order configuration at the beginning of the implementation phase had been approximately 15 cpu minutes. Changing OPS5 to make it a BLISS-based system reduced the average order configuration time to its current 1.5 cpu minutes.

The final stage in developing and implementing XCON began in June 1981, when the system was put into place in all manufacturing facilities of DEC. It has been in use and maintained since then. The group within DEC is now fully responsible for the system and has provided additional rules to improve its function and operation and its effectiveness in configuring more difficult cases. At the same time they have continued to update the data base that describes the components of a VAX-11-780 and have continued to be satisfied with the system. They have started to extend the system in two different ways. They are working to extend it at XCON so it can configure PDP-11s.

At the same time DEC launched a new effort to develop a frontend for XCON to help salespeople in the field. XSEL takes the customer's original specifications and suggests what additional components are needed to satisfy the customer's needs. This allows a salesperson to more accurately configure and price the customer's initial order. After XSEL, the salesperson, and the customer have agreed on the overall order, XSEL passes the order to XCON, and it actually configures the order.

By using XCON, DEC has considerably reduced the population of technical editors employed in configuration. The editors that continue to work on configuration problems now focus almost entirely on the various specialized problems that XCON still cannot solve. Thus, the human experts have become more expert in very specialized problems. And as the human experts learn new heuristics for solving the more specialized problems, the resident knowledge engineers working at DEC incorporate the new rules into XCON, making it more effective.

The development of XCON and XSEL illustrates a number of themes that run through the development of all recent expert systems. First, it was not developed from scratch, but, rather, was developed by means of an expert system building tool, OPS4/5. This tool allowed the developers to build the initial prototype of 250 rules in three person-months and to develop the entire first version of the system with some 750 rules in a little under one person-year. Throughout the entire development and implementation period, however, components of the system and tasks the system was expected to do were continually changing; thus, additional rules were constantly required. Even today, the system continues to be modified and improved.

This development process also illustrates the concept of exploratory programming. The initial system was developed rapidly. It was then expanded and tested while it was being used on the job. Several changes were made without having to start over. And even today the system continues to be improved and maintained by adding rules.

One unique feature of XCON is that, unlike most other recent expert systems, it does not use probabilities or certainty factors. A component is either included or omitted.

The success of the XCON has fostered the creation of a very enthusiastic AI group at DEC that is seeking to develop knowledge systems for a number of additional applications. It has already encouraged several other computer companies to develop computer configuration systems.

Hardware required: DEC-VAX, requires 1.5 cpu minutes per case/run.

Commercial status: None.

Contact:

Jeffry R. Gibson
Digital Equipment Corp.
200 Baker Avenue (CFO 1-1/M 18)
Concord, MA 01742
(617) 493-2775

Additional Computer Applications

CABLING CONFIGURATION

DEV. SOFTWARE	ART
DOMAIN	Helps configure computer cables.
CONTACT	Anne Hamlin Inference Corporation 5300 W. Century Blvd. Los Angeles, CA 90045 (213) 417-7997

CONAD

DEV. SOFTWARE	TWAICE
DOMAIN	Helps configure large computer hardware orders.
CONTACT	Logicware, Inc. 6915 Airport Road, Suite 200 Mississagua, Ontario L4Z-1 (416) 672-0300

CSF ADVISOR

DEV. SOFTWARE	ES Environment/VM
DOMAIN	Guides development of cost estimates for moving DPS equipment.

CONTACT Dick Ten Dyke
IBM
AI Products and Technology
1000 Westchester Avenue
White Plains, NY 10604
(914) 696-4435

INTELLIGENT PERIPHERAL TROUBLESHOOTER

DEV. SOFTWARE LISP
DOMAIN Helps diagnose computer peripherals.
CONTACT Hewlett Packard
Artificial Intelligence Program
3404 East Harmony Road
Fort Collins, CO 80525
(303) 226-3800

INTELLIGENT SOFTWARE CONFIGURATOR

DEV. SOFTWARE LISP and LOOPS
DOMAIN Helps configure software for DPS 6 computers.
CONTACT Barbara Braden
Honeywell Information System/CSD
151 Needham Street
Newton, MA 02161
(617) 552-6000

MASK

DEV. SOFTWARE 1st-Class
DOMAIN Assists helpline personnel diagnose user problems for a complex software program.
CONTACT John Andersen
General Partner
NORCOM
P.O. Box 020897
Juneau, AK 99802
(907) 780-6464

OCEAN

DEV. SOFTWARE LISP-based object-oriented environment.
DOMAIN Checks orders and configures NCR computers.
CONTACT James A. King
NCR Corp.
Advanced Software Technologies
WHQ5E
1700 South Patterson Boulevard
Dayton, OH 45479
(513) 445-1090

DASD ADVISOR

DEV. SOFTWARE AION
DOMAIN Identifies problem DASD devices and workloads, describing problem and recommending solutions in plain English.
CONTACT Dennis White, Director of Marketing
Boole & Babbage, Inc.
510 Oakmead Parkway
Sunnyvale, CA 94086
(408) 735-9550

DIA 8100

DEV. SOFTWARE M.1
DOMAIN Diagnoses faults and recommends corrective measure on IBM 8100.
CONTACT Teknowledge
1850 Embarcadero Road
Palo Alto, CA 94303
(415) 424-0500

DRAGON

DEV. SOFTWARE Envisage
DOMAIN Configures ICL's Series 39 computers.

CONTACT Systems Designers Software
444 Washington Street, Suite 407
Woburn, MA 01801
(617) 935-8009

ESPm

DEV. SOFTWARE S.1
DOMAIN Analyzes computer maintenance logs to identify future faults.
CONTACT Gerald L. Matthews
NCR Corp.
Advanced Software Technologies
WHQ5E
1700 South Patterson Boulevard
Dayton, OH 45479
(513) 445-6054

PERMAID

DEV. SOFTWARE LOOPS
DOMAIN Diagnosis and predictive maintenance of large disk drives.
CONTACT David Rolston
Honeywell
P.O. Box 8000, m/s 710
Phoenix, AZ 85066
(602) 862-6925

PRESS

DEV. SOFTWARE OPS5 and MacLISP
DOMAIN Debugs operating system software.
CONTACT David Rolston
Honeywell
P.O. Box 8000, m/s 710
Phoenix, AZ 85066
(602) 862-6925

REQUIREMENTS ANALYST

DEV. SOFTWARE Lotus 1-2-3
DOMAIN Helps accountants choose appropriate accounting software.
CONTACT Computer Training Services
5900 Tudor Lane
Rockville, MD 20852
(301) 468-4800

SITE LAYOUT ADVISOR

DEV. SOFTWARE UTILISP (Tokyo Univ)
DOMAIN Configures machine-room floor for computers and peripherals.
CONTACT Hitachi Research Inst.
6, Kanda-surugadai 4 Chome
Chiyoda-ku, Tokyo 101 Japan
(03) 258-1111

SNAP

DEV. SOFTWARE Personal Consultant
DOMAIN Helps retail shoppers assess their computer needs.
CONTACT Texas Instruments Incorporated
P.O. Box 2902—M/S 2244
Austin, TX 78759

SYSCON

DEV. SOFTWARE OPS5, MacLISP
DOMAIN Configures DPS 90 mainframes.
CONTACT David Rolston
Honeywell
P.O. Box 8000, m/s 710
Phoenix, AZ 85066
(602) 862-6925

TIMM TUNER

DEV. SOFTWARE	TIMM
DOMAIN	Assists system operator in tuning a VAX/VMS operation system.
CONTACT	General Research Corporation Software Sales and Marketing 7655 Old Springhouse Road McLean, VA 22102 (703) 893-5915

TITAN

DEV. SOFTWARE	C, UNIX, RuleMaster
DOMAIN	Helps train and aid technicians servicing the Texas Instruments 990 Minicomputer.
CONTACT	Steve Pardue Radian Corporation 8501 MoPac Boulevard P.O. Box 9948 Austin, TX 78766-0948 (512) 454-4797

OIL AND GEOLOGY APPLICATIONS

The economic conditions prevailing as this book goes to press have dampened the enthusiasm of developers of oil-related expert systems. Conditions at the beginning of the decade had made the oil industry a natural development partner of early AI vendors. As a result of the drop in oil prices, AI conferences contain presentations on applications, especially in oil drilling, that have performed successfully and will probably be used again "if we ever do any more drilling."

An intriguing area within this domain is computer-assisted prospecting for minerals. One famous research project at Stanford, called Prospector, attempted to do just that. The system had at least one trial in which it was able to identify an already known deposit. It is probably a sign of the economic times that many researchers involved in Prospector are now building large applications for the banking and insurance industries.

Drilling Advisor

Date: 1984.

Description: Drilling Advisor is a prototype knowledge system developed for the French oil company Societe Nationale Elf-Aquitaine (ELF) by Teknowledge Inc. The system is designed to assist oil rig supervisors in resolving and subsequently avoiding problem situations. The oil rig supervisor is completely familiar with the technology, equipment, and procedures involved in the drilling process, but occasionally requires assistance when special problems occur. Normally, an expert is flown to the rig site when such problems occur. Since it is not unusual for drilling-related expenses to exceed $100,000 per day for shutdowns related to special problems that last for several weeks until an expert can be brought to the site, the savings an on-rig knowledge system could effect are considerable.

Drilling Advisor has been implemented on two different systems. It can be run on either a DEC 20 or a Xerox Dolphin.

At the same time that the Teknowledge staff was developing the prototype Drilling Advisor, members of the Elf Aquitaine team who were to continue the development of Drilling Advisor and to implement it were being trained at Teknowledge.

Currently the knowledge base of Drilling Advisor consists of some 250 rules. Approximately 175 of those rules are used in diagnosis; the other 75 are used in prescribing the treatment. The results to date are very encouraging. The system has successfully handled a number of difficult cases not included in the original set used during its development. Current plans call for extending the capabilities of Drilling Advisor and for integrating it into the actual drilling environment.

Development: Teknowledge and Elf agreed to develop a prototype system designed to solve one specific problem—down-hole sticking—which occurs when the rotary and vertical motion of the drill is completely impeded.

Drilling Advisor was developed with a tool called KS 300, an EMYCIN-like tool. Thus, Drilling Advisor is a backward chaining, production rule system, like MYCIN, that takes full advantage of MYCIN, and MYCIN's friendly user interface and knowledge acquisition facilities.

By using KS 300, Teknowledge was able to develop the initial problem assessment and design in a little under three months. It was able to develop a prototype of the drilling advisor sticking system in a little under nine months.

Contact:

Teknowledge
1850 Embarcadero Road
Palo Alto, CA 94303
(415) 424-0500

Additional Oil and Geology Applications

CEMENTING EXP SYS

DEV. SOFTWARE M.1
DOMAIN Advises on "cementing" process in oil drilling.
CONTACT Teknowledge
1850 Embarcadero Road
Palo Alto, CA 94303
(415) 424-0500

DIPMETER ADVISOR

DEV. SOFTWARE STROBE/IMPULSE
DOMAIN Analyzes data from oil well logging instrument.
CONTACT Schlumberger-Doll Research
Old Quarry Road
Ridgefield, CT 06877-4108
(203) 431-5000

MUDMAN

DEV. SOFTWARE OPS5
DOMAIN Diagnoses problems with "mud" used in oil well drilling and recommends new compositions.
CONTACT Gary Kahn
Carnegie-Mellon University CS Dept.
Pittsburgh, PA 15213
(412) 268-3832

SOURCE ROCK ADVISOR

DEV. SOFTWARE M.1
DOMAIN Evaluates oil potential of rock.
CONTACT Teknowledge
1850 Embarcadero Road
Palo Alto, CA 94303
(415) 424-0500

WAVES

DEV. SOFTWARE KS300
DOMAIN Aids in developing data-processing control strategies for seismic survey data.
CONTACT Teknowledge
1850 Embarcadero Road
Palo Alto, CA 94303
(415) 424-0500

TRANSPORTATION APPLICATIONS

An interesting feature of the transportation industry is its heavy reliance on planning and scheduling expertise. Given the same rolling stock (or flying or floating stock) and the same access to routes, competition between transportation companies comes down to two factors: marketing expertise and planning and scheduling expertise.

Transportation planning and scheduling lends itself

to object-oriented programming. A company's fleet consists of individual vehicles, each with its own operating constraints. While additions and subtractions are occasional, a fleet is relatively stable, as are the company's established routes. While additions or subtractions of destinations are strategically important, far more attention is paid to maximizing the profitability of the current fleet serving current routes.

Scheduling departures and maintenance involves manipulating the relationships between certain objects, namely vehicles, destinations, and service facilities. While the objects persist through time, relationships between objects change daily or hourly. Scheduling expertise is called every time a severe weather condition closes an airport. Aside from responding to emergencies, schedulers and planners are expected to initiate changes in the relationships between objects to improve profits. Whether the adoption of expert systems will improve passenger safety and convenience is an open question. At least in the future it will not be a conventional system but a sophisticated expert system that is blamed for sending your luggage to Bangkok instead of Indianapolis.

Seats

Date: 1986.

Domain: Assists pricing analysts in adjusting the number of discount seats available on airline routes.

Description: Airline Seat Advisor was developed by programmers at IntelliCorp in a joint effort with Sperry and Northwest Orient Airline. Northwest Orient worked with the programmers as domain experts.

The purpose of this system is to increase the productivity of the airline company's "yield management departments." These departments work round-the-clock determining the number of discount seats to be offered on each particular flight. Enough discounted seats must be made available to remain competitive with other carriers, but no more than necessary.

The Airline Seat Advisor monitors bookings as they are taken for all flights. Combining this data with approximately 30 other parameters, the computer, when appropriate, recommends an increase or decrease in the number of discounts on individual flights.

Prior to development of this expert system, the pricing managers were able to examine and manipulate data on only a few selected routes. SEATS should allow the airline to examine all its major routes.

Potential benefits can be dramatic. As one developer said, "If Northwest Airline can upgrade one passenger from discount to full fare per flight on only 25 percent of its routes, it would realize additional profits of approximately $10 million."

Contact:

Ray Carhart
IntelliCorp
1975 El Camino Real West
Mountain View, CA 94040
(415) 965-5502

Additional Transportation Applications

AALPS

DEV. SOFTWARE	PASCAL, Assembly, Quintus PROLOG
DOMAIN	Configures aircargo ship loads.
CONTACT	Quintus Computer System 2345 Yale Street Palo Alto, CA 94306 (415) 494-3612

CHART AND MAP EXPERT SYSTEM

DEV. SOFTWARE	Exsys, PASCAL
DOMAIN	Helps maritime chart-readers identify important map and chart features.
CONTACT	Dustin Huntington Exsys Corporation P.O. Box 75148 Contract Station 14 Albuquerque, NM 87194 (505) 836-6676

HAZARDOUS CHEMICAL ADVISOR

DEV. SOFTWARE 1st-Class
DOMAIN Advises how to handle, label, and ship hazardous chemicals.
CONTACT Sam Shepherd
Air Products and Chemicals
P.O. Box 538
Allentown, PA 18105
(215) 481-8226

NAVEX

DEV. SOFTWARE ART
DOMAIN Monitors controls on space shuttle flights.
CONTACT Anne Hamlin
Inference Corporation
5300 W. Century Blvd.
Los Angeles, CA 90045
(213) 417-7997

SAFETY OF LIFE AT SEA

DEV. SOFTWARE KES
DOMAIN Helps government inspectors inspect for proper communications equipment on vessels in Canadian waters.
CONTACT Ricki Kliest
Software A&E
1600 Wilson Boulevard, Suite 500
Arlington, VA 22209-2403
(703) 276-7910

AGRICULTURE APPLICATIONS

Expert systems applications in agriculture have two main user groups: producers and traders. Commodities traders, like the players in other markets, would like to predict rises and falls in prices of agricultural products. Agricultural producers have this same need to predict the prices of various products to determine what and how much to plant. Additionally, the farmer needs to know how to troubleshoot a crop once it's in the ground and must decide when to harvest it.

Expert systems that assist farmers in producing crops differ from systems designed to help the commodities trader. The difference lies in the type of expertise they try to capture.

Agricultural science has identifiable, agreed-upon experts in its various subdomains. For instance, a professor generally considered the nation's leading authority on raising milo might be happy to share his expertise with a knowledge engineer, and an expert system could be developed to provide valuable advice to milo producers.

The domain of commodities trading is not nearly so well defined. Who are the experts in this field? The traders who make the most money? This seems logical. But traders are successful in the market presumably because they know something other traders don't. What incentive does that trader have to share that expertise with other traders? Even if this cutting edge expertise *were* shared, the net effect would be to reduce the competitive advantage provided by the expertise. This is in sharp contrast to a research setting in which scientists, if they are to make money from, or even be recognized for, their expertise do so by sharing it.

Wheat Counselor

Date: 1984.

Domain: Wheat Counselor serves two functions. It serves as a buying guide for farmers shopping for agrochemicals and as a sales aid for chemical manufacturers' salespeople.

Description: With Wheat Counselor, Imperial Chemicals offers agricultural expertise as a sales feature for farmers in the market for agro-chemicals.

"Counselor selling" seeks win-win outcomes. A salesperson who practices counselor selling seeks to work out a deal with a customer that not only creates profits, but also meets the customer's needs cost-effectively. This approach to selling is necessary when profits depend on long-term relationships with customers. For instance, a new accounts clerk might seem to generate more profit by encouraging customers to put their money in accounts that pay the lowest interest. This is not advisable in a competitive market. If your bank doesn't help the depositor earn the highest return, the bank down the street is more than willing.

Counselor selling demands that the salesperson act as a counselor to customers, helping them determine what their real needs are, and then honestly telling them what products can and can't help. The purchase, year after year, of agricultural chemicals demands the counselor selling approach. Since the performance of the chemicals is so vital to the farm's profitability, the expertise of the salesperson is an important factor when the farmer chooses a chemical dealer.

In creating Wheat Counselor, Imperial Chemicals endeavored to standardize a high level of sales expertise and to make it available to each customer, regardless of the level of expertise of the particular salesperson involved.

Wheat Counselor was developed with Savoir. It resides in a central computer and is accessed via Videotex terminals located at distributors' offices and sales rooms.

The program is run by the customers. Customers, responding to questions, enter information about their specific crop. Wheat Counselor takes this information and projects the probable crop loss if the crop were to receive no chemical treatment. The system then recommends a regimen of chemicals. Finally, the system predicts the increase in yield to be caused by the recommended chemicals. It is left to the customer to determine if the increased yield justifies the expense of purchase and application.

Contact:

Imperial Chemicals (ICI)
P.O. Box 11
The Heath
Runcorn
Cheshire WA 7 4QE
England, UK

Additional Agriculture Applications

AQUAREF

DEV. SOFTWARE 1st-Class
DOMAIN Frontend for aquaculture reference library.
CONTACT Samuel Waters, Associate Director
National Agricultural Library
Beltsville, MD 20705
(301) 344-3780

PEANUT/PEST

DEV. SOFTWARE Exsys
DOMAIN Offers irrigation advice to peanut farmers.
CONTACT James Davidson Jr.
National Peanut Research Lab./USDA
1011 Forrester Drive, SE
Dawson, GA 31742
(912) 995-4441 or 995-4481

PLANTING

DEV. SOFTWARE Exsys
DOMAIN Helps farmers identify appropriate planting equipment.
CONTACT Dustin Huntington
Exsys Corporation
P.O. Box 75148
Contract Station 14
Albuquerque, NM 87194
(505) 836-6676

PURDUE GRAIN MARKET ADVISOR

DEV. SOFTWARE Personal Consultant Plus
DOMAIN Helps farmers select the best way to market their grain.
CONTACT Dr. Larry Huggins
Purdue University
West Lafayette, IN 47907
(317) 494-1162

SCIENCE AND MEDICINE APPLICATIONS

Expert systems development in science and medicine has provided some of the grandest disappointments and sturdiest successes the technology has to offer. Genesis, a large scientific application that analyzes the structure of DNA molecules, has been running productively since 1981. On the other hand, MYCIN, a meningitis diagnosis/prescription system, the grandfather of most successfully fielded expert systems in use today, has itself never been fielded, and, given the nature of the domain, probably never will be.

Medicine was an attractive domain to researchers because it provided generally agreed-upon experts performing what most people consider to be expert tasks. The problem with MYCIN was that it aimed to replace a human expert with a computer in a life-or-death decision-making process.

Expert systems have slipped into medical practice most easily when embedded in equipment. These systems seek to add "intelligence" to conventional measuring devices. How ironic that to gain acceptance in medical practice, AI must disguise itself as mere machinery.

Drug Interaction

Developer: Evlin L. Kinney.

Description: Dr. Kinney developed Drug Interaction while at the University of Miami School of Medicine, where it was first fielded. Following is an abstract from a paper describing her system.

Drug interactions are a common cause of morbidity. But the large number of potential interactions precludes clinicians from either remembering the majority of them or from looking them up manually, on a routine basis. To assess the benefit of automated drug interaction lookup, we had six hospital-based clinicians use our expert system daily.

Our expert system is rule-based, uses the Exsys program, runs on a microcomputer, and lists each potential interaction, and the probability, when known, in the individual patient, based on the drugs taken, and a small number of host factors. Data from 100 consecutive patients were utilized.

The clinicians correctly suspected seven drug interactions, whereas the expert system noted 35 additional potential interactions, of which 20 had actually occurred. These 20 interactions included angina, CHF, marked hypokalemia, pharmacologic antagonism of two drugs, and psychosis. In 18 of the 20 cases the interactions were easily corrected once the clinicians were made aware of them. Thus our expert system enhanced the detection of drug interactions and was a valuable resource for patient care.

Commercial status: For sale.

Contact:

Dr. Evlin Kinney
1015 West 47th Street
Miami Beach, FL 33140
(305) 672-5084

Genesis (Genetic Engineering Scientific System)

Date: 1981.

Domain: Analyzes data regarding composition of DNA molecules and reports findings to research geneticists.

Description: The specific problem that Genesis deals with is analysis of a DNA molecule's structure. A DNA molecule is a long chain of four different bases: adenine, cytosine, guanine, and thymine. These four bases can be arranged in an almost infinite variety of ways. It is of critical importance to those working in molecular genetics to be able to determine the specific order of the bases in particular DNA molecules. A number of different techniques can be used to determine this molecular sequence. One common type of experiment involves labeling one end of a DNA chain with a radioactive element. Enzymes are then used to "cut" the chain by dissolving a particular base. The remaining initial piece of the chain, identified by the radioactive label, can then be measured to determine its length. By repeatedly cutting a chain with different enzymes, each eliminating a different base, you can ultimately figure out the exact sequence of bases in a particular strand of DNA. Obviously, this type of experiment can be very complex. It requires extremely careful planning so as not to waste time and money.

The resulting Genesis package currently includes seven different expert systems:

- SEQ—A nucleic acid sequence analysis, comparison, and manipulation tool.
- GEL—For the management of large-scale DNA sequencing projects.
- SIZER—For use in calculating fragment length.
- MAP—Determines restriction maps from enzymatic digests.
- PEP—For polypeptide analysis, comparison, and manipulation.
- GENED—Facilitates the simplified entry of nucleic and amino acid sequences.
- QUEST—A data base search, location, and retrieval system.

As of July 1983, over 500 scientists were using IntelliCorp's Genesis programs in their ongoing research.

When a molecular researcher wants to use the Genesis package, he or she sits down at a terminal, connects with one of the large data bases established by the National Institutes of Health, and then calls up one of these Genesis programs.

Data from those data bases or from current research can then be manipulated by one or some combination of the Genesis programs.

Recently, IntelliCorp has begun offering the Genesis package on a genetic engineering workstation called BION.

The BION workstation represents a prototype of the sort of workstations that probably will be built in a large number of areas in the next few years. The workstation allows the user quickly to draw on a number of different knowledge systems to solve a particular class of problem while working at a conveniently arranged terminal.

Development: Two different MOLGEN programs were developed at Stanford University in the late seventies. (MOLGEN stands for Molecular Genetics.) Each program was a variation on an expert system that would help a molecular geneticist design complex experiments to determine the nature of a particular DNA molecule.

The core of both MOLGEN programs was an expert system building tool called UNITS. UNITS uses a constrained natural language interface whose vocabulary is familiar to molecular biologists. The earlier MOLGEN system, developed by Mark Stefik, emphasized creating abstract plans for genetic experiments. (The modification of UNITS that resulted from Stefik's further research became Xerox's LOOPS.) The second MOLGEN program, developed by Peter Friedland, focused on determining which of several skeletal plans would be most appropriate to a user's needs. Friedland's MOLGEN program also helped users plan how to implement the details of a particular plan once it was selected. In effect, the program uses skeletal plans that have proven useful for closely related problems, thus the user can avoid reinventing general strategies. Friedland's work on MOLGEN led to the development of Genesis, a collection of commercial systems sold by IntelliCorp. (In addition, Friedland's further work on UNITS resulted in KEE, which IntelliCorp also sells.)

In 1981 some Stanford professors who had been involved in the MOLGEN project established Intelligenetics (which has since changed its name to IntelliCorp). IntelliCorp modified Friedland's original MOLGEN software to create a set of new expert systems that are useful in the commercial environment.

Commercial status: For sale. There is also a PC version called PC/GENE.

Contact:

IntelliGenetics
700 East El Camino Real
Mountain View, CA 94040
(415) 961-4666

A Microprocessor-Based Electrophoresis Interpreter

Date: 1981.

Domain: Analyzes results of serum protein electrophoresis.

Commercial status: This expert system has been reduced to a chip and added to scanning densitometers sold by Helena Laboratories.

Hardware required: Included as a component of scanning densitometers.

Description: In 1980 Sholam M. Weiss and Casimir A. Kulikosski, Computer Science Department of Rutgers University, and Robert S. Galen, Pathology Department of Columbia University, collaborated to develop an electrophoresis interpreter. This system was designed to take data from a scanning densitometer, a widely used laboratory instrument that does a serum protein electrophoresis analysis.

Development: This system was developed on Expert, a system building tool that Weiss and Kulikosski had previously used to build expert systems in medical consultation. Expert is primarily an event-driven system, rather than a goal-driven system like EMYCIN, but it uses backward chaining and production rules.

Using Expert, Weiss and Kulikosski were able to assemble an electrophoresis interpreter in six months, relying on one principal expert and several additional consultants. The initial model they developed had 10 production rules, each leading to a single conclusion. The final version has 82 production rules that lead to 38 different conclusions. Although the system is not designed to cover all possible cases that a Scanning Densitometer can encounter, it covers all common cases.

In a test, the system was given 256 cases that covered a wide range of situations. The system's analyses were considered 100 percent acceptable.

Once Weiss and Kulikosski were satisfied with the electrophoresis interpreter as it functioned in the Expert environment, they used Expert to translate the program into a microprocessor assembling language program. An instrument manufacturer then interfaced the interpretive program to an existing program for printing out instrument readings. In effect, an instrument that had previously printed out only raw data now adds a line beneath it offering an interpretive analysis. The electrophoresis interpreter has been incorporated in a medical instrument that has been sold since 1981.

To an observer, the compiled microprocessor version would look just as if it had been either coded directly in assembly language or compiled from some traditional algorithmic language. There is, however, a fundamental difference. Using Expert, the authors were able to quickly produce a prototype version of the system. They were then able to test it numerous times and rapidly expand the system until it was able to satisfy all their performance criteria. Moreover, since the initial version still exists as a knowledge system, it is easy to modify it or include additional information as new laboratory data become available or as clinical field tests indicate that changes are appropriate. A new microprocessor version could be rapidly generated from the modified Expert version.

A considerable effort would be involved if you tried to recode directly on the microprocessor, or if you tried to recode a traditional algorithmic version of the system. The elaborate testing and revision that initially went into developing the model could have been accomplished only on an expert system building tool. Moreover, the modular nature of the Expert version incorporates a wealth of data that allows researchers to see exactly how the program is making its judgments. Thus, researchers can work with the Expert version of the system to satisfy themselves regarding the logic of the system before using the embedded version.

Weiss and Kulikosski argue that by incorporating this small knowledge system directly into the instrument, they have made it much more acceptable to the medical community. Physicians and researchers already routinely accept the printouts from microprocessor-controlled medical instruments. Thus, in many cases, making an instrument more effective involves simply adding an interpretive module to an existing instrument.

Additional Science and Medicine Applications

DIAGNOSTICS

DEV. SOFTWARE Exsys
DOMAIN Assists psychiatrists in diagnosing to generate complicated psychiatric diagnosis.
CONTACT Roy Shapiro, Ph.D.
12 East 10th Street
New York, NY 10003
(212) 475-8899

HELP

DEV. SOFTWARE (Unknown)
DOMAIN Combines expert medical advice with conventional patient tracking system.
CONTACT Hommer Warner
LDS Hospital
University of Utah School of Medicine
Salt Lake, UT 84132
(801) 581-4080

HP4760AI ELECTROCARDIOGRAPH

DEV. SOFTWARE LISP
DOMAIN Aids physicians in interpreting electrocardiograph readings.
CONTACT Ray Wardell
Hewlett-Packard Co.
McMinnville Div.
1700 South Baker St.
McMinnville, OR 97128
(503) 475-5101

IPECAC

DEV. SOFTWARE IQLISP Personal Consultant
DOMAIN Diagnoses human poison cases.
CONTACT Dr. Andrew Goldfinger
Johns Hopkins Road
Laurel, MD 20707
(301) 953-5000, ext. 8292

MACSYMA

DEV. SOFTWARE LISP
DOMAIN Assists scientists, engineers, and mathematicians in solving mathematical problems.
CONTACT Symbolics Inc.
4 Cambridge Center
Cambridge, MA 02143
(617) 577-7500

METALS ANALYST

DEV. SOFTWARE Exsys
DOMAIN Identifies commercially used metals and alloys.
CONTACT Tom Anthony
Research and Development Division
General Electric Corp.
P.O. Box 8
Schenectady, NY 12301
(518) 387-5000

MICRO GENIE

DEV. SOFTWARE PASCAL and assembly
DOMAIN Analyzes long sequences of nucleic acids in RNA, DNA, and proteins.
CONTACT Beckman Instruments
1050 Page Mill Road
Palo Alto, CA 94304
(415) 857-1150

ONCOCIN

DEV. SOFTWARE LISP
DOMAIN Advises physicians on the treatment of patients receiving chemotherapy.

CONTACT	Medical Computer Science Medical School Office Building, 215 Stanford, CA 94305-5479 (415) 723-6979

POWERCHART

DEV. SOFTWARE	KEE
DOMAIN	Improves access to medical records.
CONTACT	Jack Dynis IntelliCorp 1975 El Camino Real West Mountain View, CA 94040 (415) 965-5000

PULMONARY CONSULTANT

DEV. SOFTWARE	PASCAL
DOMAIN	Interprets output of pulmonary function measuring instruments, diagnosis of lung diseases.
CONTACT	Michael Snow Medical Graphics Corp. 501 West County Road, East St. Paul, MN 55112 (800) 328-4138

SPIN PRO

DEV. SOFTWARE	Golden Common LISP
DOMAIN	Advises scientists performing ultra-centrifuge procedures.
CONTACT	Beckman Instruments 1050 Page Mill Road Palo Alto, CA 94304 (415) 857-1150

TQMSTUNE

DEV. SOFTWARE	KEE
DOMAIN	Assists in tuning triple quadripole mass spectrometers.
CONTACT	Lawrence Livermore Lab C. Kalina Wong L/793 P.O. Box 808 Livermore, CA 94550 (415) 422-1100

TRAINING APPLICATIONS

Numerous efforts have been made to apply AI technology to training problems, both in educational and real-life settings. These efforts are of two types.

The first, and simpler, application aims at assisting training developers and instructional designers in analyzing training needs and developing appropriate solutions. These are similar to other dialogue-driven, rule-based, diagnosis/prescription systems. These systems aim at helping a rather small user group, instructional designers.

Considerably more interesting is the second type of training application, called *Intelligent Computer Aided Instruction.*

Computer aided instruction (CAI) has been with us since the mid-sixties and has long been disparaged as mere "page turning" for "books on computer." A typical (nonintelligent) CAI session proceeds as follows:

- Computer presents information to the student.
- Computer asks multiple-choice questions of the student.
- Student enters multiple-choice answers.
- Computer determines next lesson based on which choice selected by student, e.g.:
  - Choice A Page 194
  - Choice B Page 219
  - Choice C Page 205
- Repeat.

The criticism of these programs as "page turners" comes about because printed instructional materials obtain the same result by simply telling the student which page to turn to, making the computer nothing but a very expensive delivery medium. There have been successful applications of CAI, especially in the area of simulation modeling, but with these exceptions, CAI hasn't lived up to expectations.

Intelligent CAI expands two aspects of these programs. First, rather than testing knowledge with multiple-choice questions, the student is asked to perform more complicated tasks that demonstrate understanding of the subject matter. Secondly, ICAI uses heuristic knowledge to analyze student performance and to *create* remedial lessons and exercises tailored to the individual student's needs at each point in the program. The goal is to make the system behave as much as possible like an expert human tutor giving one-on-one attention, helping the student perform exercises that simulate real-world tasks.

Every ICAI program seeks to capture knowledge from two domains: the domain of instructional technology and the particular subject matter addressed. It is somewhat ironic that computer science and instructional technology join forces in the area of ICAI.

A prominent trend in the field of industrial training is to replace memorization, which requires instruction, with job aids. Instruction is expensive in employee downtime. Job aids can be mass produced and allow a beginner to practice on the job and gradually memorize the most commonly performed tasks. In some industrial training settings, instruction has become a dirty word.

Even the most avid proponent of job aids against instruction will admit that training in some tasks requires instruction and off-the-job practice. Job aid proponents should be pleased to note that effective ICAI should increase rather than decrease the amount of time tied up in the instructional process.

LISP-ITS (Intelligent Tutoring System)

Date: 1984.

Domain: Computer aided instruction for students learning to program in LISP.

Description: LISP-ITS is an excellent example of intelligent computer aided instruction. It functions as an adjunct to a traditional course in LISP programming which includes lectures and homework exercises to be performed on a computer.

LISP-ITS functions like a human tutor in that it monitors the student's work, determines when the student's responses begin to stray from the ideal path, and offers guidance and additional exercises to bring the student back to the ideal path.

LISP-ITS is a mid-size, rule-based, diagnostic system. It is a signal processing system in that it continuously monitors the student's keyboard strokes, as opposed to obtaining its input by asking the student questions.

When incorrect or inappropriate responses are detected, the system diagnoses the problem and prescribes output in the form of messages on the screen, to help remedy the problem.

Descriptions of LISP-ITS knowledge base components follow.

Ideal student model: This knowledge base contains approximately 375 rules which describe the way an ideal beginning student would try to write LISP code. Note that this model tries to describe an ideal beginning student, not an expert LISP programmer. A beginning LISP student, no matter how ideal, should not respond in the same way as an accomplished expert. It is assumed the student knows only the material already covered in the course.

Bug catalog: This knowledge base contains rules that define over 1,000 mistakes and misconceptions. After a mistake has been detected by the Ideal Student Model knowledge base, the Bug Catalog is consulted to determine the probable causes of the mistake.

Tutorial method: This knowledge base contains rules that determine when to interrupt the lesson to help the student, what type of help to provide, what type of remedial practice problems to provide, and when to advance the student to new material.

User interface: Each lesson provides exercises that require the student to enter LISP code. When the student's responses diverge sufficiently from the Ideal Student Model, the system interrupts.

The top part of the screen states the system's understanding of the goal of the student's input (in this case testing a number argument's equivalence to zero). It then suggests a better method for reaching that goal.

In instances of simple coding, the system will simply suggest the next step to put the student back on track. In cases of more complex coding, the system will guide the student in creating an algorithm for solving the problem.

It is significant to note that these elements of LISP-ITS are constructed around specific homework exercises as might be found in a text. The goal of the system is limited to helping students perform the exercises successfully.

Curriculum: LISP-ITS aims to teach basic functions and techniques common to all dialects of LISP. When deviations occur, the conventions of Common LISP are followed.

LISP-ITS currently contains 11 lessons, as follows:

1. Introduction to LISP.
2. Defining LISP functions.
3. Predicates and conditionals.
4. Programming style.
5. I/O and local variables.
6. Numeric iteration and input-controlled iteration.
7. Introduction to recursion.
8. List iteration.
9. Advanced recursion.
10. Advanced iteration, do and mapcar.
11. Data structures: property lists, arrays.

According to promotional literature, LISP-ITS is currently in use in government, industry, and educational institutions, and has been in use at Carnegie-Mellon University since 1984.

Two small tests of LISP-ITS have shown it to reduce the amount of time spent on homework exercises and to increase test scores of students using it compared to students doing the same homework on their own. Interestingly, one test compared LISP-ITS to a human tutor. Students working through the same homework with a human tutor took less time and tested higher than students working with LISP-ITS, who, in turn, performed better than the students with no assistance. This failure of the system to perform as well as a human expert cannot be seen as a significant drawback since the real world provides few if any beginning LISP students with on-site tutors.

Individual tutoring is probably the richest educational environment available. Calling LISP-ITS a tutoring system is an overstatement. More appropriately it could be called a homework helper. To a beginning LISP student burning the nice midnight oil, a homework helper is better than no help at all.

Hardware requirements: LISP-ITS runs under both VMS and UNIX operating systems and is completely self-contained.

LISP-ITS can be run on single-user workstations with 2mb–3mb of memory, such as VAXstations, the Tektronix 4400 Series AI workstations, Xerox 1100 Series LISP machines, or Sun Workstations. A dedicated VAX 730 or MicroVAX 1 (or equivalent) with 3mb–4mb of memory can serve two students. A dedicated VAX 780 or Pyramid with 6mb–8mb of memory will support three to five students. A VAX 780 with less memory or with other users on the system would serve fewer students.

Development: LISP-ITS was developed by a group of researchers at Carnegie-Mellon University with backgrounds in psychology and cognitive science.

Commercial status: LISP-ITS is for sale.

Contact:

Advanced Computer Tutoring, Inc.
Suite 205
4516 Henry Street
Pittsburgh, PA 15212
(412) 621-5111

Additional Training Applications

CBT ANALYST

DEV. SOFTWARE	Turbo PASCAL
DOMAIN	Assists in designing computer-based training programs.
CONTACT	Greg Kearsley Park Row Software 1418 Park Row La Jolla, CA 92037 (619) 459-2121

OTHER APPLICATIONS

CAN AM TREATY

DEV. SOFTWARE	GURU
DOMAIN	Advises on legal aspects of international trade transactions.
CONTACT	Pierre Lessard Raymond, Chabot, and Co. 600 La Gauche Tiera West, Room 1900 Montreal, Quebec, CN H3B4L8 (514) 878-2691

PTE ANALYST

DEV. SOFTWARE	Personal Consultant Plus
DOMAIN	Assists attorneys in analyzing employee benefit transactions governed by ERISA.
CONTACT	Jill Swenson Computer Law Systems 11000 West 78th Street Eden Prairie, MN 55344 (612) 941-3801

16

What to Do Next

This final brief chapter provides some very general advice about how to prepare for the ongoing impact of expert systems on the workplace. In a nutshell, you should: (1) acquire more knowledge, (2) experiment with developing an expert system, and (3) think about the implications of the changes expert systems technologies will introduce.

ACQUIRE MORE KNOWLEDGE

The changes being ushered in by the current expert system building tools and the initial crop of expert systems applications are only the beginning of a whole new way of thinking about computers. The result of this process will be a vast increase in the use of computers in every aspect of business, industry, and government. The past has truly been just a prologue to what will happen in the remaining years of this century.

Business people who want to help create the future rather than simply wait to find out what fate has in store for their business, their operation, or their technology will necessarily want to keep up on new developments in the commercialization of artificial intelligence and the various technologies that develop out of expert systems.

This book has provided only an overview. Entire books have been written on each topic discussed here in a few paragraphs. Appendix B provides references to books and articles that contain more information on each topic.

Keep in mind that knowledge engineering is still a new field. The literature reflects its youth in two ways. First is the annoying tendency for two authors to use entirely different terms for the same concept, or, perhaps worse, for two authors to use the same word to mean entirely different things. You will have to track down terms and meanings by studying the specific examples and consulting more than one source.

The second sign of the field's youth is that many experts strongly disagree about the importance of various aspects of the technology. Thus, one article may argue that the future of large expert systems development lies on mainframes and will be programmed in tools written in conventional languages, while another, equally respected author may assure you that large expert systems will be written in LISP and run on LISP coprocessors slipped into personal computers.

This book has avoided the more academic disputes. Where good arguments exist on both sides, it has taken a middle path. As you venture into other literature, however, you will find considerable disagreement. As with all emerging technologies, you must read several different authors to gain an overall perspective of the various arguments.

Magazines and Journals

Magazines and journals are a particularly good way to keep abreast of what is happening in the field. The best of the current magazines and journals include:

AI Magazine. This is the official journal of the American Association for Artificial Intelligence—the premier academic AI association. Join the AAAI to get this.

AAAI
445 Burgess Drive
Menlo Park, CA 94025
(415) 328-3123

IEEE Expert. This is a publication of the IEEE Computer Society. Join the Computer Society and subscribe to this.

IEEE Computer Society
10662 Los Vaqueros Circle
Los Alamitos, CA 90720-2578
(714) 821-8380

AI Expert. This is a good commercial AI magazine. It is available at newsstands, and focuses primarily on language-related issues.

CL Publications Inc.
650 Fifth Street, Suite 311
San Francisco, CA 94107
(415) 957-9353

PC AI. This is a new commercial AI magazine that is focused on PCs and looks promising.

PC AI
3310 West Bell Rd.
Suite 119
Phoenix, AZ 85023
(602) 439-3253

Expert Systems: The International Journal of Knowledge Engineering. This British publication has many descriptions of systems being built in both Europe and the United States.

Learned Information Ltd.
143 Old Marlton Pike
Medford, NJ 08055

Newsletters

Newsletters are more expensive than magazines and journals, but they provide more timely information, and they are usually more willing to criticize since they do not carry advertising.

AI Trends. This newsletter keeps track of the financial side of the AI market. DM Data's market projections are frequently quoted.

DM Data Inc.
6900 East Camelback Road, Suite 1000
Scottsdale, AZ 85251

Applied Artificial Intelligence Reporter. This newsletter provides brief news items. It's a good way to keep up on announcements and contract awards.

ICS Research Institute
P.O. Box 1308-EP
Fort Lee, NJ 07024

Expert Systems Strategies. This newsletter is edited by Paul Harmon and Bill Morrissey, two authors of this book. The newsletter provides the same type of reviews and applications reports included in this book.

Cutter Information, Inc.
1100 Mass Avenue
Arlington, MA 02174

Conventions and Conferences

Yearly, dozens of conferences, workshops, and meetings are organized to provide participants with a chance to learn about what is happening in one or more areas of AI or expert systems. At the same time, many conventions nominally devoted to other professional or technical concerns (e.g., accounting meetings, banking conventions, medical conventions, laser optics meetings) will include sessions on AI and expert systems in their programs. This will continue for several years as information about AI and expert systems applications affect different groups. The best way to keep up on all these conventions and meetings is to subscribe to one of the magazines or newsletters listed above.

If a meeting you already attend has a session on AI or expert systems, you will certainly want to attend. Likewise, if a small meeting near you focuses on a special topic of interest you should consider attending.

If you want a broader overview and at the same time more technical depth, consider attending one of the two or three major conventions devoted to AI each year. Each includes exhibits of the latest hardware and software. If you are interested enough to attend one of these conventions, you should probably join the society that sponsors the convention and use both the society journal and the convention to help you keep up to date.

The AAAI Annual Convention. The annual meeting of the American Association of Artificial Intelligence is usually held in July or August. Every fourth year the AAAI meeting is held in conjunction with the IJCAI Conference.

AAAI
445 Burgess Drive
Menlo Park, CA 94025
(415) 328-3123

The IJCAI Conference. The International Joint Conference on Artificial Intelligence is a joint meeting of several different national AI groups. This conference is held every other year. Every other IJCAI conference meets in North America and that meeting is co-sponsored by AAAI. In 1989 IJCAI will co-meet with AAAI somewhere in North America. The easiest way to get information about IJCAI is to call the AAAI.

The Annual IEEE Computer Society AI Applications Conference (CAIA). This is an annual meeting, usually in February or March, which is second to AAAI in terms of the quality of the research discussed. This conference is more focused on practical applications than AAAI.

IEEE Computer Society
1730 Massachusetts Avenue, N.W.
Washington, DC 20036-1903
(202) 371-1013

Special tutorials are offered in association with each of these conventions. They are usually a relatively inexpensive yet effective way to get an overview of one of the more specialized aspects of AI or expert systems.

Seminars and Workshops

A number of seminars and workshops are offered by tool and language vendors and by a wide assortment of workshop vendors and private consultants. These workshops vary widely in quality and cost so exercise appropriate caution.

Most tool vendors discussed in earlier sections of the book offer training, and in most cases the training is a good way to learn how to use a tool. In all cases, if you want to learn to actually build an expert system, be sure the workshop you attend includes a significant number of hands-on exercises. Most small and mid-size tools are easy enough to use, but they all have their tricks. There is no substitute for creating four or five small systems with someone available to answer your questions when the manuals became obscure, as they all do at some point.

Consultants

Expert systems consultants range from large consulting companies like Arthur Andersen and Arthur D. Little, SRI International and major computer vendors like Texas Instruments and Unisys, through a wide variety of mid-size concerns to individuals. Most of the large to mid-size tool vendors also offer consulting services.

Some consultants will help you analyze potential applications and plan an expert systems development effort while others are prepared to develop expert systems for you.

In considering a consultant, you will certainly want to know about the other clients they have helped and the specific systems they have developed. Most consultants are specialized in terms of the hardware, software, and the specific domains they understand. The field is very new, so specific practical experience is at a premium and is very valuable. Lots of companies and individuals are eager to become AI/expert systems consultants and most would be happy to have you pay their expenses while they learn how.

DEVELOP A SMALL EXPERT SYSTEM

The best way to get an overview of how expert systems are developed is to develop one yourself. You can approach this task in a number of different ways. Some tool vendors offer demo disks that allow you to save from 10 to 25 rules. This makes it easy to get a feel for the tool and experiment with a very small knowledge base at the same time.

Texas Instruments offers such a disk and provides effective documentation with it for $25—an inexpensive way to learn first-hand what's really involved in developing a small knowledge system.

To explore a bit more, you will need to purchase a tool. VP Expert, for $99, is a very inexpensive way to begin.

If you have specific applications in mind, however, you may want to consider one of the other tools discussed in this book. If you decide to acquire a more expensive tool, also consider attending a workshop offered by the tool vendor. The addresses of all expert systems tool vendors are included in Appendix C.

ACQUIRE AN EXPERT SYSTEM

Good expert systems applications are just beginning to be offered for sale. If an application is being offered in your area of competence, try to arrange for a demonstration. Expert systems vendors will be appearing at most of the major technical and professional meetings in the next few years, and you should certainly see what they have to offer.

Many companies are going to repackage some existing system and call it an expert system to try to cash in on the current interest in AI and expert systems. To make matters more confusing, several conventional software vendors will, in fact, be incorporating a small expert system in their existing products. When you think about purchasing any computer system, your first concern should be what that system will do for you. It either solves problems and saves you money, or it doesn't. The underlying techniques really aren't as important as what the system does for you. If expert systems succeed, as they probably will, they will succeed because programmers can use expert systems techniques to build products that will outperform any of their competitors.

Smarter analysis, better advice, and interfaces that are much easier to use should be easy to observe and measure. The other benefits you should expect include access to the knowledge base that will let you determine just what knowledge and inferences are built into the system and the ability to quickly modify the assumptions the system uses.

DEVELOP AN IN-HOUSE KNOWLEDGE ENGINEERING GROUP

Several companies are trying to develop knowledge engineering groups. A few years ago, most large companies thought they would want to build very large expert systems and found themselves bidding for a very scarce population of knowledge engineers. If your company wants to build a knowledge engineering group that includes well-known AI research scientists and experienced knowledge engineers, you will face some very difficult problems. It will be hard to find the people you want, and it will be expensive to hire and equip them if you can find them. Moreover, since the field is still very hot, if you find top-flight people, you should anticipate that they will be getting exciting offers from other companies and from venture capitalists that may lure them away at any time.

Many people are studying AI and building expert systems at the moment, so the crunch should be much less severe in a few years. Meantime, however, most companies have decided they do not want to build large systems and, hence, do not need to hire scarce AI experts.

What most companies are interested in is developing an in-house capacity to build small to mid-size systems. They expect to develop and field the systems they build on conventional hardware (i.e., personal computers or mainframes). Most companies involved in building expert systems in the past few years have found they can find people who can create such systems within their own ranks. In many cases, conventional programmers, after learning to use one of the mid-size tools, have proved to be good knowledge engineers.

Conventional programmers are especially valuable if your expert system will be interfaced with existing programs. Programmers with experience in data base design and with simulation modeling seem to take to knowledge engineering very easily. Other companies have found that psychologists, training analysts, and anthropologists make good knowledge engineers. If your applications will involve lots of interviewing, then a background in one of the social sciences sometimes results in a good knowledge engineer. And, as the applications illustrate, numerous expert systems are being developed by technical staff people who simply develop a single knowledge system to help them deliver the services they are expected to provide.

As the number and type of applications expand in the next few years, a lack of people qualified to build systems will limit only those who are trying to build very large systems.

ANTICIPATE THE FUTURE

Whatever else you do, begin to think about how your job or other jobs in your business will be performed in the future. Expert systems work only if they contain knowledge. If a portion of your expertise lends itself to an expert systems application, think about the possibility you could help develop such a system.

Expert systems will be used in a wide variety of situations because they offer exactly the type of help many businesses need. They allow some individuals to analyze problems and make decisions and recommendations by providing those individuals with an easy way to access the expertise of others. In other words, expert systems significantly increase the productivity of the people using them.

Between now and the year 2000 there is no good reason to think the introduction of computers and expert systems will reduce overall employment. In fact, large numbers of people will be employed to build and service the computers and the expert systems. Some jobs will be replaced, while others will be created. You will want to position yourself to help facilitate the overall process rather than become inconvenienced by it. Knowing about expert systems is a good start and thinking about how to create valuable new systems to help you and your company prosper is one of the best ways to benefit and enjoy the revolutionary changes that will occur in the remaining years of this century.

appendix A

Glossary

(Note: Several of the definitions below first appeared in Harmon and King's *Expert Systems: Artificial Intelligence in Business.*)

Active Value. A special type of method that allows the user to change values in a system by simply changing a graphic image on the screen.

Agenda. An ordered list of actions. Some systems maintain or develop lists of possible actions. An agenda is used to control the reasoning during a consultation.

Algorithm. A step-by-step procedure that guarantees a correct outcome. To develop a conventional computer program, the programmer specifies the algorithm that the program will follow.

Artificial Intelligence. "A subfield of computer science concerned with the concepts and methods of symbolic inference by a computer and the symbolic representation of the knowledge to be used in making inferences. A field aimed at pursuing the possibility that a computer can be made to behave in ways that humans recognize as 'intelligent' behavior in each other." (Feigenbaum and McCorduck, 1983) Artificial intelligence is an academic discipline, like physics; it isn't a product, it is a broad research program aimed at improving what computers can do.

Attribute. A property of an object. For example, *tire* is an attribute of a car. Attributes can have various values. They have specific values in particular situations. Thus, a 1985 Saab came equipped with four Pirelli 185/65 tires.

Backtracking. The process of backing up through a sequence of inferences in order to try a different path. Planning problems typically require backtracking strategies that allow a system to try one plan after another until the system finds a path that has no unacceptable outcomes.

Backward Chaining (Back-Chaining). A control strategy that regulates the order in which inferences are drawn. In a rule-based system, backward chaining is initiated by a goal. The system attempts to determine a value for the goal. The system identifies rules that conclude a value for the goal, then backs up and attempts to determine if the if clauses of the rule are true. Thus, the attributes of the if clause of the rule become secondary goals, and the system backs up again to find rules that would determine the value of those attributes. This, in turn, leads the system to consider other rules that would confirm the if clauses. In this way the system backs into its rules. Eventually, the back-chaining sequence ends when a question is asked or a previously stored result is found.

Blackboard Architecture (HEARSAY Architecture). An expert systems design in which several independent knowledge bases each examine a common working memory, called a "blackboard." An agenda-based control system continually examines all of the possible pending actions and chooses the one to try next.

Breadth-First Search. A control strategy that examines all of the rules or objects on the same level of the hierarchy before examining any of the rules or objects on the next lower level.

Certainty. The degree of confidence one has in a fact or relationship. As used in AI, this contrasts with probability, which is the likelihood that an event will occur. There are two types of certainty: the certainty that the expert has in a relationship expressed in a particular rule or relationship, and the certainty that the user has when he or she provides information during a consultation.

Certainty Factor (Confidence Factors). A numerical weight given to a fact or relationship to indicate the confidence one has in the fact or relationship. The most common system of certainty factors are sometimes called "EMYCIN Certainty Factors" to indicate that they are calculated by the formula developed during the development of MYCIN. In general, methods for manipulating EMYCIN certainty factors are more informal than approaches to combining probabilities. Most rule-based systems use EMYCIN certainty factors rather than probabilities.

Common LISP. The standard dialect of LISP that is used in commercial AI.

Consultation Paradigm. A consultation paradigm describes a generic problem-solving scenario. Most expert system building tools are good for one or a few consultation paradigms but not for others. Most of the smaller rule-based tools are designed to facilitate rapid development of expert systems that utilize the Diagnostic paradigm.

Context Tree (Object Tree or Frame Tree). A context tree arranges rules into sets (or contexts) and determines, in a hierarchical manner, which set is used in what order. Most context tree systems have several contexts. A context tree provides the structure in a structured rule system. A static context tree describes the structure of the knowledge base when it is not being used. When the system is being used, a dynamic context tree is created. The dynamic tree may omit unnecessary static contexts or may use a single static context several times (i.e., multiple instantiation).

Context-Parameter-Value Triplets (Object–Attribute–Value Triplets, or Frame–Parameter–Value Triplets). The way that facts are described in EMYCIN. A context is an actual or conceptual entity in the domain of the consultant, e.g., a patient, an aircraft, an oil well. Parameters are properties or attributes associated with each context, e.g., age and sex of a patient or location and depth of an oil well. Each parameter (or attribute) can take on values: e.g., the parameter "sex" could take the value "male."

Control (of a knowledge system). The methods used by the inference engine to determine the order in which reasoning occurs. Backward chaining and depth-first search are both examples of control methods.

Deep Knowledge. Knowledge of basic theories, first principles, axioms, and facts about a domain. This contrasts with domain models and surface knowledge.

Default or Default Values. Computer programs often have prespecified values that they use unless they are given alternative values. These assumed values are called default values. Object-oriented systems typically have higher-level objects with default values that lower-level objects inherit.

Depth-First Search. A control strategy in which one rule or object on the highest level is examined and then the rules or objects immediately below that one are examined. Proceeding in this manner, the system searches down a single branch of a tree until it reaches the end. It then backs up to the first unsearched branch and goes down that branch, and so on. This contrasts with breadth-first search.

Diagnosis. A consultation paradigm that assumes that you know the possible outcomes or recommendations that a system can make and that you search for evidence that will confirm or deny each of the possible recommendations.

Domain. A subject matter area or problem-solving task. Finance and factory automation are very broad domains. Existing systems only provide good advice when they are used to assist users in solving problems that lie within very narrowly defined domains. Analyzing auto loans, or diagnosing what could be wrong with a particular type of robotic device are examples of narrow domains or tasks.

EMYCIN. The first expert system building tool. EMYCIN was derived from the expert system MYCIN. After the developers of MYCIN completed that system they decided that they could remove the specific medical knowledge in MYCIN (hence Empty MYCIN). The resulting shell consisted of a backward chaining inference engine, a context tree system, confidence factors, a consultation driver, and several knowledge acquisition aids. By adding new rules about some new task to this shell or tool you can produce a new expert system.

Environment. See Programming Environment.

Example-Driven System. See Induction System.

Exhaustive Search. A search strategy that systematically examines every possible path through a decision tree or network. Exhaustive search is costly or impossible for many problems. Small expert systems typically search exhaustively through all of the rules in their knowledge bases.

Experiential Knowledge. Knowledge gained from hands-on experience. This typically consists of specific facts and rules-of-thumb (surface knowledge). This is in contrast with deep knowledge of formal principles or theories.

Expert System. As originally used, it referred to a computer system that could perform at, or near, the level of a human expert. Evaluations of MYCIN place its competence at or near that of highly specialized physicians. Configuration systems like XCON (R1) probably exceed human competence. As the term is currently being used, it refers to any computer system that was developed by means of a loose collection of techniques associated with AI research. Thus, any computer system developed by means of an expert system building tool would qualify as an expert system even if the system was so narrowly constrained that it could never be said to rival a human expert. The popular press and various software entrepreneurs have already used the term "expert system" in so many ways, however, that it now defies any precise meaning.

Expertise. The skill and knowledge that some humans possess that result in performance that is far above the norm. Expertise often consists of massive amounts of factual information coupled with rules-of-thumb, simplifications, rare facts, and wise procedures all compiled in a way that allows the expert to analyze specific types of problems in an efficient manner.

Explanation. Broadly, this refers to information that is presented to justify a particular course of reasoning or action. In expert systems, explanation normally refers to a number of techniques that help a user understand what a system is doing. Many knowledge systems allow a user to ask "Why," "How," or "Explain." In each case the system responds by telling the user something about its assumptions or its inner reasoning.

Fact. Broadly, a statement whose validity is accepted. In most expert systems a fact consists of an attribute and one or more values that are associated with the attribute.

Forward Chaining. A control strategy that regulates the order in which inferences are drawn. In a rule-based system, forward chaining begins by reviewing the known facts and then firing all of the rules whose if clauses are true. The system then begins another cycle and checks to determine what additional rules might be true, given the facts where established during the first cycle, and so on. This process is repeated until the program reaches a goal or runs out of new possibilities.

Frame (or Object or Unit). A knowledge representation scheme that associates an object with a collection of features (e.g., facts, rules, defaults, active values). Each feature is stored in a slot. A frame is the set of slots related to a specific object. A frame is similar to a property list, schema, or record, as these terms are used in conventional programming.

Heuristic. A rule-of-thumb or other device or simplification that allows its user to draw conclusions without being certain. Unlike algorithms, heuristics do not guarantee correct solutions.

Heuristic Rules. Rules written to capture the heuristics an expert uses to solve a problem. The expert's original heuristics may not have taken the form of if–then rules, and one of the problems involved in building a knowledge system is converting an expert's heuristic knowledge into rules. The power of an expert system reflects the heuristic rules in the knowledge base.

Hierarchy. An ordered network of concepts or objects in which some are subordinate to others. Hierarchies normally imply that subordinate concepts or objects inherit some or all of the properties of the superordinate or parent objects, in the sense that Fords and Hondas are both cars and inherit the generic properties of Car. "Tangled hierarchies" occur when a lower level entity inherits properties from more than one higher level entity.

If–Then Rule. A rule establishes a relationship among a set of facts in an if clause and one or more facts in a then clause. Rules may be definitional (e.g., If female and married, then wife) or heuristic (e.g., If cloudy, then take umbrella).

Induction System (Example-Driven System). A knowledge system that generates a decision tree or rule from a set of examples.

Inference. The process by which new facts are derived from established facts.

Inference Engine. That portion of an expert system that contains the inference and control strategies. More broadly, the inference engine also includes various knowledge acquisition, explanation, and user interface subsystems. When an inference engine is separated from a knowledge base, it is, in effect, an expert system building tool.

Inheritance. A process by which characteristics of one object are assumed to be characteristics of another. In effect, inheritance is the inference strategy used by object-oriented systems. Thus, if we determine that a company is a bank, then we automatically assume that the company sells checking and savings accounts to customers.

Inheritance Hierarchies. When knowledge is represented in a hierarchy, the characteristics of superordinate (parent) objects are inherited by subordinate objects (children).

Instantiation. The process by which a static rule or object is used during a consultation and assigned specific values.

Interface. The link between a computer program and the outside world. A single program may have several interfaces. Expert systems typically have a developer interface, a user interface, and a systems interface through which they relate with other software and with hardware.

Job Aids (Performance Aids). Job aids are devices that individuals use when they perform tasks. Well-constructed job aids allow the performer to avoid memorization. Thus, they allow individuals to perform jobs more quickly and more accurately than they would if they had been trained in any conventional manner. Moreover, performers memorize frequently used responses while using job aids, hence they serve as structured on-the-job training. Whenever they are appropriate, job aids are the current medium of choice among instructional designers. Small knowledge systems are ideal job aids for a wide variety of tasks and will rapidly replace most of the checklists, procedures manuals, and other common job aids currently in use.

Knowledge. An integrated collection of facts and relationships which, when exercised, produces competent performance. The quantity and quality of knowledge possessed by a person or a computer can be judged by the variety of situations in which the person or program can successfully obtain results.

Knowledge Acquisition. The process of locating, collecting, and refining knowledge. This may require interviews with experts, research in a library, or introspection. The person undertaking the knowledge acquisition must convert the acquired knowledge into a form that can be used by a computer program. Knowledge is derived from current sources, especially from experts.

Knowledge Base. The portion of an expert system that consists of the facts and heuristics about a domain. The knowledge may be in the form of examples, facts, rules, or objects.

Knowledge Engineer (Knowledge Engineering). An individual whose specialty is assessing problems, acquiring knowledge, and building knowledge systems. Ordinarily this implies training in cognitive science, computer science, and artificial intelligence. It also suggests experience in the actual development of one or more expert systems.

Knowledge Representation. The method used to encode and store facts and relationships in a knowledge base. Semantic networks, facts, rules, objects, and frames are all ways to represent knowledge.

Knowledge System. A computer program that uses knowledge and inference procedures to solve difficult problems. The knowledge necessary to perform at such a level, plus the inference procedures used, can be thought of as a model of the expertise of skilled practitioners.

Language-System Spectrum. A dimension along which various software products can be placed. At one extreme are expert systems. In the middle are the narrowly defined tools that are optimized to help developers build systems to perform specific tasks. At the other extreme are general purpose languages that can be used for many different applications.

Large, Hybrid System Building Tools. A class of knowledge engineering tools that emphasize flexibility. The systems are designed for building large knowledge bases. They usually include a hybrid collection of different inference and control strategies. Most commercial hybrid tools incorporate frames and facilitate object-oriented programming.

Large, Rule-Based Expert System Building Tools. A class of knowledge engineering tools that sacrifice flexibility to facilitate the efficient development of more narrowly defined expert systems.

LISP. A programming language based on List Processing. LISP is the AI language of choice for American AI researchers.

Machine Learning. A research effort that seeks to create computer programs that can learn from experience. There are no commercial systems that can currently be said to learn from experience.

Maintenance of an Expert System. Unlike conventional computer software that is only infrequently updated, expert systems by their nature are very easy to modify. Unlike conventional systems that are "completed," most expert systems that are currently in use are constantly being improved by the addition of new rules. In most applications, the user organization will want to establish a regular routine to capture and incorporate new knowledge into the system. One can imagine that an application processing advisor system would be maintained by the senior application processing clerk. That clerk would be responsible for entering new rules whenever data or procedures changed or whenever questions arose that the current system could not answer.

Mental Models or Domain Models (of human experts). The symbolic networks and patterns of relationships that experts use when they are trying to understand a problem. Mental models often take the form of simplified analogies or metaphors that experts use when first examining a problem. Mental models can sometimes be converted into rules or context trees. They are easier to represent via object-oriented techniques, but in many cases the models that experts use still defy commercial AI techniques and are the object of considerable research in cognitive psychology.

Mid-run Explanation. The ability of a computer program to stop upon request, and explain where it currently is, what it is doing, and what it will seek to accomplish next. Expert systems tend to have features that facilitate mid-run explanation while conventional programs do not.

Monotonic Reasoning. A reasoning system based on the assumption that once a fact is determined it cannot be altered during the course of the reasoning process.

Multivalued attribute. This refers to a knowledge system that allows the designer to specify that the system will seek all possible values that could apply to a particular attribute. If one developed a system to recommend an appropriate restaurant and the system did not allow for multivalued attributes, the system would determine the first restaurant that satisfied all the criteria and recommend it. If one could specify that restaurant was a multivalued attribute, however, the system would identify every restaurant that could satisfy all of the criteria.

MYCIN. An expert system developed at Stanford University in the mid-1970s. The system is a research system designed to aid physicians in the diagnosis and treatment of meningitis and bacteremia infections. MYCIN is often spoken of as the first expert system. There were other systems that used many of the AI techniques associated with expert systems, but MYCIN was the first to combine all of the major features with the clear separation of the knowledge base and the inference engine. This separation, in turn, led to the subsequent development of the first expert system building tool, EMYCIN.

Natural Language. The branch of AI research that studies techniques that allow computer systems to accept inputs and produce outputs in a conventional language like English. At the moment, systems can be built that will accept typed input in narrowly constrained domains (e.g., data base inquiries). Several expert systems incorporate some primitive form of natural language in their user interface to facilitate rapid development of new knowledge bases.

Nonmonotonic Reasoning. Reasoning that can be revised if some values change during a session. In other words, nonmonotonic reasoning can deal with problems that involve rapid changes in values in short periods of time. If one were developing an on-line expert system that monitored the stock market and recommended stocks to purchase, one would want a system that used nonmonotonic reasoning and was thus able to continually revise its recommendations as the prices and volumes of stock changed.

Object (Context, Frame). Broadly, this refers to physical or conceptual entities that have many attributes. When a collection of attributes or rules are divided into groups, each of the groups is organized around an object. When a knowledge base is divided into objects, the knowledge base is often represented by an object tree that shows how the different objects relate to each other. When one uses object-oriented programming, each object is called a frame or schema and the attributes and values associated with it are stored in slots. An object is said to be "static" if it simply describes the generic relationship of a collection of attributes and possible values. It is said to be "dynamic" when an expert systems consultation is being run and particular values have been associated with a specific example of the object.

Object–Attribute–Value Triplets (O–A–V Triplets). One method of representing factual knowledge. This is the more general and common set of terms used to describe the relationships referred to as context–parameter–value triplets in EMYCIN.

Operating System. The computer software system that does the "housekeeping" and communication chores for the more specialized systems. Most conventional computers have standard operating systems that software is designed to utilize. Thus, for example, the IBM Personal Computer uses MS-DOS. AI languages can be used to write operating systems so that the expert system and the operating system are written in the same language. LISP workstations, like the Symbolics LISP machines and the Texas Instruments Explorer, are computers that use a LISP operating system to improve their efficiency and flexibility when running expert systems written in LISP. In a similar manner, a Macintosh uses an operating system especially designed for object-oriented programming.

Performance Aids. See Job Aids.

Probability. Various approaches to statistical inference that can be used to determine the likelihood of a particular relationship. Expert systems have generally avoided probability and used confidence factors instead. Some systems, however, use a modified version of Bayesian probability theory to calculate the likelihood of various outcomes.

Problem-Solving. Problem-solving is a process in which one starts from an initial state and proceeds to search through a problem space in order to identify the sequence of operations or actions that will lead to a desired goal. Successful problem-solving depends upon knowing the initial state, knowing what an acceptable outcome would be, and knowing the elements and operations that define the problem space. If the elements or operators are very large in number or if they are poorly defined, one is faced with a huge or unbounded problem space and exhaustive search can become impossible. Methods are domain independent strategies like "generate and test." Strong methods exploit domain knowledge to achieve greater performance. This is usually accomplished by avoiding exhaustive search in favor of exploring a few likely solutions.

Problem Space. A conceptual or formal area defined by all of the possible states that could occur as a result of interactions between the elements and operators that are considered when a particular problem is being studied.

Procedural versus Declarative. Procedures tell a system what to do (e.g., Multiply A times B and then add C). Declarations tell a system what to know (e.g., V=IR).

Programming Environment (Environment). A programming environment is about halfway between a language and a tool. A language allows the user complete flexibility. A tool constrains the user in many ways. A programming environment, like OPS5, provides a number of established routines that can facilitate the quick development of rule-based programs.

PROLOG. A symbolic or AI programming language based on Predicate Calculus. PROLOG is the most popular language for AI research outside North America.

Prototype. In expert systems development, a prototype is an initial version of an expert system that is developed to test effectiveness of the overall knowledge representation and inference strategies being employed to solve a particular problem.

Pruning. In expert systems, this refers to the process whereby one or more branches of a decision tree are "cut off" or ignored. In effect, when an expert systems consultation is under way, heuristic rules reduce the search space by determining that certain branches (or subsets of rules) can be ignored.

Reasoning. The process of drawing inferences or conclusions.

Representation. The way in which a system stores knowledge about a domain. Knowledge consists of facts and the relationships between facts. Facts, rules, objects, and networks are all formats for representing knowledge.

Robotics. The branch of AI research that is concerned with enabling computers to "see" and "manipulate" objects in their surrounding environment. AI is not concerned with robotics as such, but it is concerned with developing the techniques necessary to develop robots that can use heuristics to function in a highly flexible manner while interacting with a constantly changing environment.

Rule (If–Then Rule). A conditional statement of two parts. The first part, composed of one or more if clauses, establishes conditions that must apply if a second part, composed of one or more than clauses, is to be acted upon. The clauses of rules are usually A–V pairs or O–A–V triplets.

Rule-Based Program. A computer program that represents knowledge by means of rules.

Runtime Version or System. Knowledge system building tools allow the user to create and run various knowledge bases. Using a single tool, a user might create a dozen knowledge bases. Depending on the problem the user was facing, he or she would load an appropriate knowledge base and undertake a consultation. With such a tool the user can easily modify a knowledge base. Some companies will want to develop a specific knowledge base and then produce copies of the tool and that specific knowledge base. Under these circumstances the organization will not want the user to have to "load" the knowledge base, nor will they want the user to be able to modify the knowledge base. When an expert system building tool is modified to incorporate a specific knowledge base and to deactivate certain programming features, the resulting system is called a runtime system or a runtime version.

Search and **Search Space.** See Problem-Solving and Problem Space.

Semantic. Refers to the meaning of an expression. It is often contrasted with syntactic, which refers to the formal pattern of the expression. Computers are good at establishing that the correct syntax is being used; they have a great deal of trouble establishing the semantic content of an expression. For example, the sentence: "Mary had a little lamb" is a grammatically correct sentence; its syntax is in order. But its semantic content—its meaning—is very ambigious. As we alter the context in which the sentence occurs, the meaning will change.

Semantic Networks. A type of knowledge representation that formalizes objects and values as nodes and connects the nodes with arcs or links that indicate the relationships between the various nodes. *Nodes*, usually representing objects, concepts, or situations, are joined with *arcs* or *links* representing relational meaning.

Slot. A component of an object in a frame system. Slots can contain intrinsic features such as the object's name, attributes and values, attributes with default values, rules to determine values, pointers to related frames, and information about the frame's creator, or may represent derived attributes such as value, significance, and analogous objects.

Small Expert System Building Tools. As used in this book, small tools are tools that can run on personal computers and that lack either variable rules or any way of structuring the rules into sets (i.e., context trees). The line between small and mid-size tools is rapidly being obscured as the newer small tools add more powerful features.

Small Expert Systems. In general, small expert systems contain under 500 rules. They are designed to help individuals solve difficult analysis and decision-making tasks without aspiring to being the equivalent of any human expert. In general they are being developed by nonprogrammers and thus represent a significant extension of who is involved in software development.

Software, Levels of. A continuum that begins at the lowest level with computer assembly language and extends up through low-level languages, through high-level languages, to tools, and finally to systems that users use to actually solve problems.

Software Engineer. An individual who designs conventional computer software. This individual serves a role similar to a knowledge engineer in the development of a conventional software program.

Surface Knowledge (Experiential or heuristic knowledge). Knowledge that is acquired from experience and is used to solve practical problems. Surface knowledge usually involves specific facts and theories about a particular domain or task and a large number of rules-of-thumb.

Symbol. An arbitrary sign used to represent objects, concepts, operations, relationships, or qualities.

Symbolic versus Numeric Programming. A contrast between the two primary uses of computers. Data reduction, data base management, and word processing are examples of conventional or numerical programming. Knowledge systems depend on symbolic programming to manipulate strings of symbols with logical rather than numerical operators.

Syntactic. Refers to the formal pattern of an expression; in contrast to semantic. Computers are good at establishing that the correct syntax is being used; they have a great deal of trouble establishing the semantic content of an expression. For example, the sentence: "Mary had a little lamb" is a grammatically correct sentence; it is syntactically correct. But its semantic content—its meaning—is very ambiguous. As we alter the context in which the sentence occurs, the meaning will change.

Technology Transfer. In the context of expert systems, this is the process by which knowledge engineers turn over an expert system to a user group. Since expert systems need to be continually updated, the knowledge engineers need to train the users to maintain a system before it arrives in the user environment. In effect, some users must learn how to do some knowledge engineering.

Tools. As used in this book, tools are computer software packages that simplify the effort involved in building an expert system. Most tools contain an inference engine and various user interface and knowledge acquisition aids and lack a knowledge base. Expert system building tools tend to incorporate restrictions that make them easy to use for certain purposes and hard to impossible to use for other purposes. In acquiring a tool one must be careful to select a tool that is appropriate for the type of expert system one wishes to build. More broadly, a tool is a shell that allows the user to rapidly develop a system that contains specific data. In this sense, an electronic spreadsheet program is a tool. When the user enters financial data, he or she creates a system that will do specific financial projections just as the knowledge engineer uses a tool to create an expert system that will offer advice about a specific type of problem.

Uncertainty. In the context of expert systems, uncertainty refers to a value that cannot be determined during a consultation. Most expert systems can accommodate uncertainty. That is, they allow the user to indicate that he or she does not know the answer. In this case the system uses its other rules to try to establish the value by other means or relies on default values.

User Interface. See Interface.

Value. A quantity of quality that can be used to describe an attribute. If we are considering the attribute "color," then the possible values of color are all of the names of colors that we might use. If we are considering a particular object, we observe it and assign a specific value to the attribute by saying: That paint is colored bright red.

Windows. Conventional computer terminals use the entire screen to present information drawn from one data base. Computer terminals that can utilize window software can divide the screen into several different sections (or windows). Information drawn from different data bases can be displayed in different windows. Thus, for example, with a Macintosh computer one can have a word processing program going in one window and a graphics program going on simultaneously in a second window. Most current expert systems research is being conducted on computers that allow the user to display different views of the system activity simultaneously. Windows are an example of a technique originally developed by AI researchers that has now become a part of conventional programming technology.

Workstation (Professional Workstation, Intelligent Workstation). In this book, workstations generally refer to LISP machines or 32-bit computer systems that are used by expert systems developers, professionals (e.g., engineers), or to field expert systems. The coming generation of PCs will be 32-bit machines and thus workstations will soon be a synonym for PC.

appendix B

References and Notes

This annotated list of references is not intended to be comprehensive. Instead, we have tried to indicate the most important and most readily available sources that you should consider if you wish to learn more about the topics discussed in any chapter of this book. In most cases we have cited books, even though they tend to be less current than magazine articles, since books tend to be more readily available. Except in rare cases we have avoided journal articles and monographs because they are often difficult to obtain. All articles cited in the text are included in this list of references. In addition, we have included an occasional note regarding something in the chapter in this section.

Chapter 1. Using Expert Systems to Improve Performance

Harmon, P. (Ed.) Various issues of *Expert Systems Strategies* newsletter have published surveys from which many of these generalizations have been drawn. *Expert Systems Strategies* is published in the United States by Cutter Information Publications, 1100 Mass. Ave., Arlington, MA 02174. (617) 648-8700. (The newsletter is published in Japan by Knowledge Engineering Lab. Corp., 2-6-2 Higashi-Kanda, Chiyoda-ku, Tokyo 101 Japan. Phone (03) 865-7771.)

Harmon, P. and D. King. *Expert Systems: Artificial Intelligence in Business.* New York: John Wiley, 1985.

McCorduck, P. *Machines Who Think.* San Francisco: Freeman, 1979.

Reitman, Walter (Ed.). *Artificial Intelligence Applications for Business.* Norwood, NJ: Ablex Pub. Corp., 1984.

Winston, P.H. and K.A. Prendergast (Eds.). *The AI Business: The Commercial Uses of Artificial Intelligence,* Cambridge, MA: MIT Press, 1984.

Chapter 2. The Expert Systems Market

As in Chapter 1, most of the survey information in this chapter was originally developed and published in various issues of *Expert Systems Strategies* newsletter.

Some survey information used in this chapter was developed by Branscomb Associates, 1491 Canada Lane, Woodside, CA 94062. (415) 851-4735.

Another newsletter that consistently provides a good analysis of the economic trends in the AI market is *AI Trends*, a newsletter edited by Harvey P. Newquist III, and published by DM Data, Inc., 6900 E. Camelback Road, Suite 1000, Scottsdale, AZ 85251. (602) 945-9620.

Chapter 3. Language and Software

Abelson, Harold; Gerald Jay Sussman; et al. *Structure and Interpretation of Computer Programs.* Cambridge, MA: MIT Press, 1985.

Brownston, Lee, et al. *Programming Expert Systems in OPS5: An Introduction to Rule-Based Programming.* Reading, MA: Addison-Wesley, 1985.

Charniak, E., C.K. Riesbeck, and D.V. McDermott. *Artificial Intelligence Programming.* Hillsdale, NJ: Lawrence Erlbaum Associates, 1980.

Chorafas, Dimitris N. *Fourth and Fifth Generation Programming Languages: Volume 1: Integrated Software, Database Languages, and Expert Systems.* New York: McGraw-Hill, 1986.

Clocksin, W.F., and C.S. Mellish. *Programming in Prolog.* Berlin, West Germany: Springer-Verlag, 1981.

Cox, Brad J. *Object Oriented Programming: An Evolutionary Approach.* Reading, MA: Addison-Wesley, 1986.

Goldberg, Adele and David Robson. *Smalltalk-80: The Language and its Implementation.* Reading, MA: Addison-Wesley, 1983.

Kaehler, Ted and D. Patterson. *A Taste of Smalltalk.* New York: W.W. Norton, 1986.

LISP. The best way to learn about LISP is to buy Gold Hill Computer's Golden Common LISP software (which runs on a PC) and study the excellent tutorial that is included with their LISP package. Gold Hill Computers, 163 Harvard Street, Cambridge, MA 02139. (617) 492-2071. With the Gold Hill package, you will also get the two most important books on LISP:

Steele, G.L., Jr. *Common LISP: The Language (Reference Manual).* Billerica, MA: Digital Press, 1984.

Winston, P.H. and B.K.P. Horn. *LISP* (2nd Edition). Reading, MA: Addison-Wesley, 1984.

Stroustrup, Bjarne. *The C++ Programming Language.* Reading, MA: Addison-Wesley, 1986.

Walker, Adrian (Ed.), et al. *Knowledge Systems and Prolog: A Logical Approach to Expert Systems and Natural Language Processing.* Reading, MA: Addison-Wesley, 1987.

Chapter 4. An Overview of Expert System Building Tools

For more detail regarding the concepts underlying the various expert system building tools, see Harmon and King's *Expert Systems: Artificial Intelligence in Business.*

Chapter 5. Simple Rule-Based Tools

For more details on any of the tools discussed, contact the vendors. In most cases, the vendors offer demo disks that can help you gain familiarity with the tool in an inexpensive manner.

The addresses and phone numbers of the vendors are provided in Appendix C.

Chapter 6. Inductive Tools

The best theoretical discussions of inductive techniques occur in books on machine learning. See especially the articles by Donald Miche.

For more information on the specific tools discussed, consult the vendors listed in Appendix C.

Chapter 7. Mid-Size Rule-Based Tools

Most of the mid-size rule-based tools were derived from the work at Stanford on MYCIN and EMYCIN. The best book on that original research is:

Buchanan, Bruce G. and E.H. Shortliffe. *Rule-Based Expert Systems: The MYCIN Experiments of the Stanford Heuristic Programming Project.* Reading, MA: Addison-Wesley, 1984.

Holsapple, Clyde W. and A.B. Whinston. *Manager's Guide to Expert Systems Using Guru.* Homewood, IL: Dow Jones-Irwin, 1986.

Weiss, Sholom M. and C.A. Kulikowski. *A Practical Guide to Designing Expert Systems.* Totowa, NJ: Rowman & Allanheld, 1984.

For more information on the specific tools discussed, consult the vendors who are listed in Appendix C.

Chapter 8. Large Rule-Based Tools

For more information on the specific tools discussed, consult the vendors who are listed in Appendix C.

Chapter 9. Hybrid Tools

Kunz, J.C., T.P. Kehler, and M.D. Williams. "Applicatons Development Using a Hybrid AI Development System." *AI Magazine,* 5 (3), 1984.

For more information on the specific tools discussed in this chapter, consult the vendors who are listed in Appendix C.

Chapter 10. An Overview of Expert Systems Development

Bachant, J. and J. McDermott. "R1 Revisited: Four Years in the Trenches." *AI Magazine,* 5 (3), 1984.

Brownston, Lee, et al. *Programming Expert Systems in OPS5: An Introduction to Rule-Based Programming.* Reading, MA: Addison-Wesley, 1985.

Hayes-Roth, F., D.B. Lenat, and D.A. Waterman (Eds.). *Building Expert Systems.* Reading, MA: Addison-Wesley, 1983.

Holsapple, Clyde W. and A.B. Whinston. *Manager's Guide to Expert Systems Using Guru.* Homewood, IL: Dow Jones-Irwin, 1986.

Keller, Robert. *Expert System Technology: Development and Application.* Englewood Cliffs, NJ: Yourdon Press, 1987.

Klahr, Philip and D.A. Waterman (Eds.) *Expert Systems: Techniques, Tools, and Applications.* Reading, MA: Addison-Wesley, 1986.

Kraft, A. "XCON: An Expert Configuration System at Digital Equipment Corporation." In P.H. Winston and K.A. Prendergast (Eds.) *The AI Business: The Commercial Uses of Artificial Intelligence.* Cambridge, MA: MIT Press, 1984.

Scown, Susan J. *The Artificial Intelligence Experience: An Introduction.* Billerica, MA: Digital Press, 1985.

Waterman, Donald A. *A Guide to Expert Systems.* Reading, MA: Addison-Wesley, 1986.

Weiss, S., and C. Kulikowski. *A Practical Guide to Designing Expert Systems.* Totowa, NJ: Rowman & Allanhead, 1984.

Chapter 11. Phases 1 and 2: Front End Analysis and Task Analysis

Bailey, Robert W. *Human Performance Engineering: A Guide for System Designers.* Englewood Cliffs, NJ: Prentice-Hall, 1982.

Gilbert, Thomas F. *Human Competence: Engineering Worthy Performance.* New York: McGraw-Hill, 1978.

Zemke, Ron and T. Kramlinger. *Figuring Things Out: A Trainer's Guide to Needs and Task Analysis.* Reading, MA: Addison-Wesley, 1982.

Chapter 12. Phases 3, 4, and 5: Prototype Development, System Development, and Field Testing

Gale, William A. (Ed.) *Artificial Intelligence and Statistics.* Reading, MA: Addison-Wesley, 1986.

Hart, Anna. *Knowledge Acquisition for Expert Systems.* New York: McGraw-Hill, 1986.

Holland, John H., et al. *Induction: Processes of Inference, Learning, and Discovery.* Cambridge, MA: MIT Press, 1986.

Kowalik, J.S. (Ed.). *Coupling Symbolic and Numerical Computing in Expert Systems.* (Papers from a workshop) New York: Elsevier Science, 1986.

Methlie, Leif B. and R.H. Sprague Jr. (Eds.). *Knowledge Representation for Decision Support Systems.* (Papers from a workshop) New York: Elsevier, 1985.

Shneiderman, Ben. *Designing the User Interface: Strategies for Effective Human-Computer Interaction.* Reading, MA: Addison-Wesley, 1987.

Chapter 13. Phases 6 and 7: Implementation and Maintenance

See any of the books listed for Chapters 11 and 12. Note especially the articles on the XCON experience, since XCON is the one large system that has been in service for a long time and for which good data are available.

Chapter 14. An Overview of Current Applications

The material in this chapter and the following chapter was originally developed for the *Expert Systems Strategies* newsletter. For further information, check with the developer or owner of the system.

appendix C

Vendor List

Aion Development System/MVS & Aion Development System/PC
Aion Corp.
101 University Avenue
Palo Alto, CA 94301
(415)328-9595
Contact: Tom Halfaker

Apes
Programming Logic Systems
31 Crescent Drive
Milford, CT 06460
(203)877-7988
Contact: Roberta Hanson

Arity Expert System Development Package
Arity Corporation
30 Domino Drive
Concord, MA 01742
(617)371-1243
Contact: Meredith Bartlett

ART
Inference Corp.
5300 West Century Boulevard, Fifth Floor
Los Angeles, CA 90045
(213)417-7997
Contact: Donald Gammon

DUCK
Smart Systems Technologies
7700 Leesburg Pike
Falls Church, VA 22043
(703)448-8562
Contact: Doug Berry

ENVISAGE & SAGE
Systems Designers Software Inc.
444 Washington Street, Suite 407
Woburn, MA 01801
(617)935-8009
Contact: Bruce Holt

ES Environment/VM & ES Environment/MVS
IBM
P.O. Box 10
Princeton, NJ 08540
(201)329-7000
Contact: W.S. Redfield, Jr.

ESP Advisor
Expert Systems International
1700 Walnut Street
Philadelphia, PA 19103
(215)735-8510
Contact: Wendy Crowell

EST (Expert Systems Toolkit)
Mind Path Products
12700 Park Central Drive
Suite 1801
Dallas, TX 75251
(214)329-2142
Contact: Michael Archuletta

ExperOPS+
ExperTelligence
559 San Ysidro Road
Santa Barbara, CA 93108
(805)969-7874
Contact: Dick Messler

Expert Controller
Umecorp
700 Larkspur Landing Circle
Larkspur, CA 94939
(415)925-2000
Contact: James R. Raphel

Expert Ease & Super Expert
Softsync, Inc.
162 Madison Avenue
New York, NY 10016
(212)685-2080
Contact: Rod Campbell

Expert Edge
Helix Expert System Limited
St. Bartholomew House
92 Fleet Street
London EC4Y 1DH, U.K.
01-583 9391
Contact: David Imberg

Exsys
Exsys Inc.
P.O. Box 75157, Contract Station 14
Albuquerque, NM 87194
(505)836-6676
Contact: Dustin Huntington

EX-TRAN 7
Intelligent Terminals Ltd.
c/o Jeffrey Perrone & Assoc.
3685 17th Street
San Francisco, CA 94114
(415)431-9562
Contact: Jeffrey Perrone

1st Class
Programs in Motion
10 Sycamore Road
Wayland, MA 01778
(617)653-4422
Contact: Amy Mitzenbon

GOLDWORKS
Gold Hill Computers
163 Harvard Street
Cambridge, MA 02139
(800)242-LISP or (617)492-2071 (in MA)
Contact: Trini Semo

GURU
Micro Data Base Systems, Inc.
P.O. Box 248
Lafayette, IN 47902
(317)447-1122
Contact: John Daily

HUMBLE
Xerox Special Information Systems
250 North Halstead
P.O. Box 7018
Pasadena, CA 91109-7018
(818)351-2351
Contact: Ben E. Dody

Insight 1 & Insight 2+
Level Five Research
503 Fifth Avenue
Indialantic, FL 32903
(305)729-9046
Contact: Cornelius Willis

Intelligence/Compiler
IntelligenceWare Inc.
9800 South Sepulveda Boulevard,
Suite 730
Los Angeles, CA 90045
(213)417-8896
Contact: Kamran Parsaye

KDS 2+3
KDS Corporation
934 Hunter Road
Wilmette, IL 60091
(312)256-4201
Contact: William J. Wallace

KEE
IntelliCorp
1975 El Camino Real West
Mountain View, CA 94040-2216
(415)965-5683
Contact: Lisa Sheeran

KES and KES II
Software Architecture & Engineering
1500 Wilson Boulevard, Suite 800
Arlington, VA 22209
(703)276-7910
Contact: Ricki Kleist

KES/VS
Control Data
P.O. Box 0 HQW096
Minneapolis, MN 55440
(612)853-6137
Contact: Kim Kusnier

Knowledge Craft
Carnegie Group
650 Commerce Court
Station Square
Pittsburgh, PA 15219
(412)642-6900
Contact: Arlene Fingley

Knowledge Workbench
Silogic, Inc.
9841 Airport Boulevard, Suite 600
Los Angeles, CA 90045
(213)337-7477
Contact: Jim Boates

Knowol & Knowol+
Intelligent Machine Co.
1907 Red Oak Circle
Newport Richey, FL 33553
(813)844-3262
Contact: Jeffrey Ferris

Lisp In-Ate & Micro In-Ate
Automated Reasoning Corp.
290 West 12th Street, Suite 1-D
New York, NY 10014
(212)206-6331
Contact: Richard Cantone

LOOPS
Xerox Corp.
250 North Halstead St.
P.O. Box 7018
Pasadena, CA 91109
(818)351-2351 (Ext. 1603)
Contact: Deborah Kelfer

M.1 & S.1
Teknowledge, Inc.
1850 Embarcadero Rd.
P.O. Box 10119
Palo Alto, CA 94303
(415)327-6600
Contact: Judy Harris

MacKIT
Knowledge Systems Environments
201 South York Road
Dillsburg, PA 17019
(717)766-4496
Contact: Ed Beauregard

MicroExpert
McGraw-Hill Book Company
Professional & Reference Division
11 West 19th Street
14th Floor
New York, NY 10011
(212)337-5916
Contact: Ed Mathew

Nexpert and Nexpert Object
Neuron Data
444 High Street
Palo Alto, CA 94301
(415)321-4488
Contact: Patrick Perez

OPS5e
Verac, Inc.
9605 Scranton Road
San Diego, CA 92121
(619)457-5550
Contact: Sally Tumia

OPS83
Production Systems Technologies, Inc.
5001 Baum Boulevard
Pittsburgh, PA 15213
(412)362-3117
Contact: Diana Connan

Personal Consultant Easy & Personal Consultant Plus
Texas Instruments
12501 Research Boulevard MS 2244
P.O. Box 2909
Austin, TX 78769
(512)250-6785

PICON
Lisp Machine Inc.
6033 West Century Boulevard
Suite 900
Los Angeles, CA 90045
(617)682-0500
Contact: Rod Khanna

RuleMaster
Radian Corp.
P.O. Box 201088
Austin, TX 78720
(512)454-4797
Contact: Mike Haecker

Super Expert
Softsync, Inc.
162 Madison Ave.
New York, NY 10016
(212)685-2080
Contact: Rod Campbell

TIMM
General Research
7655 Old Springhouse Road
McLean, VA 22102
(703)893-5915
Contact: Wanda Rappaport

TOPSI
Dynamic Master Systems, Inc.
P.O. Box 566456
Atlanta, GA 30356
(404)565-0771
Contact: David Smith

TWAICE
Logicware, Inc.
(Representing Nixdorf Computer)
5915 Airport Road
Suite 200
Mississauga, Ontario L4V 1T1
Canada
(416)672-0300
Contact: Michael Anthony

VAX OPS5
Digital Equipment Corp. (DEC)
77 Reed Road (HL02-3/E09)
Hudson, MA 01749-2895
(617)568-5038
Contact: Sandy Mills

VP Expert
Paperback Software Inc.
2830 Ninth Street
Berkeley, CA 94710
(415)644-2116
Contact: Cynthia Towle

Wisdom XS
SIL, Inc.
1593 Locust Avenue
Bohemia, NY 11716
(516)589-1676
Contact: Connie Chun

XPER
Abacus Software
P.O. Box 7211
Grand Rapids, MI 48510
(616)241-5510

XSYS
California Intelligence
912 Powell Street #8
San Francisco, CA 94108
(415)391-4846
Contact: Ray Winestock

Index